ESCHATOLOGY
IN THE ANGLICAN SERMONS
OF JOHN HENRY NEWMAN

Colm McKeating

MELLEN RESEARCH UNIVERSITY PRESS
Lewiston/Lampeter

Library of Congress Cataloging-in-Publication Data

McKeating, Colm, 1940-
Eschatology in the Anglican sermons of John Henry Newman / Colm
McKeating
p.   cm.
Includes bibliographical references and index.
ISBN 0-7734-9231-3
1. Eschatology--History of doctrines--20th century. 2. Church of
England--Doctrines--History--19th century. 3. Anglican Communion-
-Doctrines--History--19th century. 4. Newman, John Henry,
1801-1890--Views on eschatology. 5. Sermons, English--History and
criticism. 6. Church of England--Sermons--History and criticism.
7. Anglican Communion--Sermons--History and criticism. I. Title.
BT819.5.M34 1993
236'.092--dc20
92-44666
CIP

Editorial inquiries

Mellen Research University Press
Lampeter, Dyfed, Wales
UNITED KINGDOM SA48 7DY

Order Fulfillment:

Edwin Mellen Press, Ltd.   The Edwin Mellen Press
Lampeter, Dyfed, Wales   Box 450
UNITED KINGDOM SA48 7DY   Lewiston, New York 14092
                                        USA

Printed in the United States of America

In remembrance of my mother
who was a source of joy and hope

"...we would not have you ignorant... concerning those who are asleep, that you may not grieve as others do who have no hope. For since we believe that Jesus died and rose again, even so, through Jesus, God will bring with him those who have fallen asleep."

1 Thess. 4, 13-14

TABLE OF CONTENTS

ACKNOWLEDGEMENTS

The pleasant duty of acknowledgement naturally comes after the event when past favours are seen with the clarity of hindsight. In completing this dissertation therefore, I am in the happy position of being able to appreciate and thank others for what they have done for me. Besides this, however, the insights of eschatology have helped me to look with gratitude on the steps of the journey long before the time of acknowledgement has come. It was this perception of support during an otherwise solitary enterprise that enabled me to sustain my hope until the end.

My first thoughts go to Monsignor Michael Sharkey under whose direction this work has reached completion. It is to him I owe my introduction to Newman, an introduction so warm and inviting that my interest has never waned. It was he who sowed the seeds of this dissertation by his lectures on the Dream of Gerontius. His combined gifts on the professional level of scholarship and on the personal level of friendship have kept the spirit of Newman alive and greatly enriched my life.

The second reader of the thesis was Fr. Gerald O'Collins, my former Dean at the Gregorian University and Professor of Fundamental Theology. I gratefully acknowledge his valuable suggestions and patient guidance in the final presentation of the study.

I record a special word of thanks to the Society of St. Columban. First, to my superiors and colleagues of the Philippine Region, for their consideration and trust in permitting me such a long study leave. Their unstinted support, despite the growing demands for personnel on mission, has eased the burden I have felt of my prolongued absence. Lubos na pasasalamat sa inyong pagkaunawa. To the Region of Britain for the hospitality and kindness I received on three extended periods of time at Solihull.

I am indebted to the priests of the Birmingham Oratory for their open acceptance and ready provision of the means of research. Particular mention must be made to Father Gregory Winterton, the

Father of the Oratory, and to Mr. Gerard Tracey, the archivist of the Newman papers. My days at the Oratory were a time of quiet solitude and freedom in a supportive atmosphere.

A similar experience and interest was shown by members of "The Work" at the Newman Centre in Via Aurelia in Rome. Despite the numerous demands on their limited accommodation, I was granted full access to the rich library resources they tend with diligent care.

The writing of the thesis was done at Corso Trieste which has been my home for several years. Studia proveniunt hilaritate has been an honoured tradition at Collegio San Colombano. To the Rector, Fr. Charles Duster, for his cheerful administration of the house and to Fr. William Halliden, the Procurator General, for his invaluable help in proof-reading and rendering the text more readable. It was with them and with my fellow Columbans that I found the strength to complete my task and be content.

The friendship of individuals at home and abroad grew in importance as the pressure of study increased. I have appreciated the kind interest of Fr. Patrick Bastable whose love for Newman was the basis of a new mutual friendship. To my friends of long-standing reliance I record with deep gratitude and affection the support of their prayers and love: to Áine, Norma, Jim and Kathleen, who were silently present throughout the course of this study.

Lastly, I extend thanks to my family who thought my ordeal would never end; to my father, who read Newman before I was born, for the interests and principles I have inherited from him; to my brother, Dermot, and Judy, my sister, Maura, her husband, John, my nieces Gráinne and Elaine for their unfailing support.

My final words of appreciation are reserved for my mother who sadly departed this life some months ago and who, I firmly believe, now enjoys the rest of the just. To her memory of faith and Christian witness, I dedicate this work.

Easter 1992

C. McKeating

PREFACE

John Henry Newman was one of the greatest theologians that England has ever produced. Both his Anglican and his Catholic works continue to be read: in fact the study of them is growing, spreading across the continents. His influence was deeply felt at the Second Vatican Council in Rome, and the significance of his major works is continually praised by theologians of every hue and denomination.

Study of Newman, though, has tended to concentrate on his finished works, the great treatises. In this monograph about Newman's eschatology in his Anglican sermons, the author takes us into the workshop of Newman's mind while he is still developing his ideas. We see not only Newman's doctrine, but we see his struggles with method and emphasis and the need for balance.

We are able to follow his own maturation. The famous line in the *Development of Christian Doctrine* "To live is to change; to be perfect is to have changed often" is as much a personal confession as a reference to the historicity of doctrine.

Anyone who has read Newman's Anglican sermons cannot but be struck by the overwhelming sense of a future judgment. We see Newman's greatness as he reflects on the majesty of God, the Moral Governor of the Universe, on our accountability, on His particular providence for each of us, on the passion, death and resurrection of His Son, Jesus Christ. However, we also see a certain relentless anxiety about salvation, an anxiety which disappeared when he became a Roman Catholic. As he wrote in his *Apologia*, "it was like coming into port after a rough sea." In Newman's early preaching, he was very much under the influence of the evangelicals. He concentrated on the passion of Christ who will bring judgment to all. Then, under the influence of the Fathers, he moved from the Atonement to the Incarnation as the central doctrine of the Church, finding the eschatological significance of Christ's first coming a necessary, merciful balance to the second. Newman knew how to explore the subjectivity of his listeners, but, without losing that sensitivity, he came more and more to emphasise the objective truth of the Gospel.

Colm McKeating's monograph is masterly. It is a thorough reading of Newman's texts, both published and unpublished. It will be a basic work of reference for many years to come. The author takes us through the main themes, showing Newman sifting, reflecting, proclaiming: he also shows us Newman struggling with the hard questions on the "dark" side of eschatology. Newman had too big a mind to ignore these hard questions, or to explain them away. McKeating writes without comment; he lets Newman speak for himself. He does not add any word of praise or reproach, until his final chapter in which he gives us a very perceptive assessment of Newman's eschatology.

There was a preoccupation with death during the Victorian era, as is evident in the statuary and inscriptions in old cemeteries. Suffering and death were commonplace then, and so was the romantic sentimentalism of the Victorians with which they consoled themselves. However, readers of this monograph will see that Newman's eschatology is characterised by realism and depth rather than romanticism.

Popular Victorian eschatology concentrated on the death of the individual and the life beyond the grave, as though someone had come back from around the corner of the future and told us what it is like, which is why individual eschatology fell into neglect in this century. Newman, on the other hand, treats both individual and collective eschatology, and he does so on perennially valid theological principles and evidence. This is what makes his work so valuable: not only are we able to compare it with other nineteenth century approaches, but it makes a major contribution to our contemporary understanding of the meaning of death, judgment and the future, the nature of Christian hope and its foundation. Although Newman's eschatology was to develop further after becoming a Roman Catholic, the main lines were worked out as an Anglican. His knowledge of the Bible and the Fathers was extraordinary and his insight into character quite brilliant. His theology, therefore, is extremely well informed and is expressed in prose of the greatest eloquence and sympathy. In bringing out Newman's Anglican eschatology so substantially, clearly, and, I would say, definitively, the author enables us to assess Newman's contribution in this area to his own time and to ours.

Michael Sharkey
Pontifical Gregorian University
Rome

LIST OF ABBREVIATIONS

The abbreviations used for Newman's works are taken from those listed in The Letters and Diaries of John Henry Newman. References are made to the uniform edition which was begun in 1868 and concluded in 1881. This edition was published by Longmans, Green and Co. and the dates in brackets are those of the uniform volumes.

Apo.	Apologia pro Vita Sua (1873)
A.W.	John Henry Newman: Autobiographical Writings, ed. Henry Tristram, 1956
Dev.	An Essay on the Development of Christian Doctrine (1878)
D.A.	Discussions and Arguments on Various Subjects (1872)
Ess. I,II	Essays Critical and Historical, two volumes (1871)
G.A.	An Essay in aid of a Grammar of Assent (1870)
Jfc.	Lectures on the Doctrine of Justification (1874)
L.D.	The Letters and Diaries of John Henry Newman, ed. C.S. Dessain et Alii, 1961
P.P.S.	Parochial and Plain Sermons (1868)
Pett.	D.E. Pett, The Published and Unpublished Anglican Sermons of John Henry Newman / Prolegomena to an Edition, unpub. diss. University of Sussex, 1974
S.D.	Sermons bearing on Subjects of the Day (1869)
Tract	Tracts for the Times I-XC, 1833-1841
U.S.	Fifteen Sermons preached before the University of Oxford (1872)
V.V.	Verses on Various Occasions (1874)

INTRODUCTION

It is an implausible proposition that George Bush should have any hand in a dissertation entitled Eschatology in the Anglican Sermons of John Henry Newman. His namesake, however, has the dubious honour of contributing to part of its title. It was an earlier George Bush who in 1843 popularized the word "eschatology" in the English-speaking world. The term had first been coined in Germany around the beginning of the nineteenth century and was then imported to England some forty years later. Whether Newman knew the word or not is uncertain; what is certain however, is that it does not appear in any of his Anglican sermons. One may well suspect that he would frown on the neologism and inquire what exactly was meant by it. Be that as it may; the first task in this introduction is to give a summary of Newman's life and outline the major influences which shaped his theology. This is then followed by a brief word on the meaning of Christian eschatology and on the scope and plan of the dissertation.

Newman's Life and Early Influences

John Henry Newman was born on 21 February 1801 and died on 11 August 1890. He was the eldest of six children of John Newman, a banker in the City of London, and Jemima Foudrinier, the daughter of a paper-maker. He began his early education in 1808 at a private boarding school at Ealing, and later entered Trinity College, Oxford as an undergraduate at the age of sixteen. On 12 April 1822 Newman was elected a fellow of Oriel, an event he described as the most memorable day of his life. This led to his taking orders in 1824, after which he became curate at St.Clement's from 1824-1826. In March 1828 he was appointed Vicar of St.Mary's, an office he held until his resignation in 1843. In the company of Archdeacon Froude and his son, Hurrell, who was Newman's closest colleague at Oriel, he left Oxford for Italy in December 1832. On his return to England on 9 July 1833, Newman joined and led what became known as the Oxford Movement, whose aim was the institutional renewal of the Church of England on Catholic principles. By the influence of his preaching and his Tracts for the

2

Times, the Movement reached a crisis in 1841 with the publication of Newman's Tract XC on the Thirty-Nine Articles. He then withdrew from Oxford to the neighbouring village of Littlemore where on 9 October 1845 he was received into the Roman Catholic Church. Newman's life as a Catholic was a relatively quiet time of pastoral activity at the Oratory in Birmingham, which he founded in 1848. It was however punctuated by periods of distress and strain. His attempt to lay the foundations of a Catholic University of Ireland, 1852-1858, was at a great personal cost and sadly ended in failure. However, his *Apologia pro Vita Sua* in 1864 had a happier outcome with the successful defence of his good name against the false accusations of Charles Kingsley. In 1879 Newman was called to Rome to receive a Cardinal's hat, an honour he regarded as conferring approval on his life's work. Eleven years later he died peacefully and was buried at Rednal with the fitting epitaph over his grave: *ex umbris et imaginibus in veritatem*.

The sources of Newman's theology, and, in particular, the influences which shaped his eschatology, have never been clearly and precisely documented. However, from Newman's own account in the *Apologia* of the history of his religious opinions, we can construct a general picture of the formative ideas in his early life. Here we find two major sources of influence, an earlier evangelical one which predominated up to 1826, and a subsequent and more lasting influence of the Fathers of the Church. As a child, Newman was nourished on the Bible, in which he learned to "take great delight". It was not however until he was fifteen, that he began to form "a definite Creed" from books given him by Walter Mayers, "all of the school of Calvin". It was Mayers, his evangelical teacher at Ealing, who shepherded him through the course of his first conversion.

Evangelicalism was a popular Protestant movement which had its origins in Church renewal in Britain around the 1730s. Though not confined to any particular religious denomination, its four main characteristics - conversionism, activism, biblicism and crucicentrism - gave it a unity and coherence.[1] Within this broad consensus there existed two distinct branches of the evangelical creed, a liberal branch of Arminian stock represented in J.Wesley's Methodism, and a strict form which adhered to the Calvinist preaching of G.Whitefield. It was the latter kind of evangelical belief which Newman was introduced to by Walter Mayers.

---

[1] Cf.D.W.Bebbington, *Evangelicalism in Modern Britain*, London, Unwin Hyman, 1989.

Of the authors mentioned in the *Apologia* as having an impact on his early life, Newman singled out Thomas Scott (1747-1821) as the one "to whom (humanly speaking) I almost owed my soul". Scott had been deeply influenced by John Newton (1725-1807) whom he succeeded as Vicar of Aston Sandford. It was through Newton that the Calvinist line extends back to G. Whitefield (1714-1770) whose close acquaintance led Newton into the ministry.[2] Thus the fervent Calvinism which Newman imbibed in his evangelical years has led scholars to denote this period of his life as his "Scott and Newton days".

The *Apologia* also mentions another Newton whose *Dissertation on the Prophecies* (1754) takes us more directly to the question of eschatology and particularly to Newman's long-standing belief in the Papal Antichrist.[3] This dissertation was a three-volume work of Thomas Newton (1704-1782) who became Bishop of Bristol. It was patterned on an equally hostile anti-Catholic study by Joseph Mede (1586-1638), whose *Clavis Apocalyptica* published posthumously in 1642, was an allegorical interpretation of Daniel and the Book of Revelation.[4] Other, more moderate influences on the interpretation of Biblical prophecy which Newman became acquainted with in Oxford, were those of John Davison (1777-1834), whose *Nature and History of Prophecy* was published in 1819, and Samuel Horsley's (1733-1806) *Dissertations on the Prophecies among the Heathen*.[5] Both of these illustrate Newman's gradual relinquishing of evangelical views of prophecy and his being won over to High Church principles. However, the list of authors which Newman consulted in the composition of his early sermons, gives

---

[2] George Whitefield's friend and patroness, the Countess of Huntingdon is the subject of an essay by Newman in 1846. In a less than appreciative book review of a recent biography of the Countess, Newman does not conceal his high regard for the evangelical renewal; though he considered it a heresy, there "never surely was a heresy so mixed up with what was good and true, with high feeling and honest exertion...". Cf. *Essays Critical and Historical*, Vol.1, London, Longmans, Green and Co., 1890, pp. 387-425.

[3] Cf.Apo. p. 7 where Newman states: "My imagination was stained by the effects of this doctrine up to the year 1843; it had been obliterated from my reason and judgment at an earlier date; but the thought remained upon me as a sort of false conscience."

[4] For an account of evangelical eschatology, cf. S.C.Orchard, *English Evangelical Eschatology, 1790-1850*, Diss. Ph.D., Cambridge University, 1968 and D.N.Hempton, 'Evangelicalism and Eschatology', *The Journal of Ecclesiastical History*, Vol.31, 1980, pp.179-194. S.Gilley has drawn attention to the influence of Newton and Mede on Newman's view of prophecy in 'Newman and prophecy, Evangelical and Catholic', *Journal of the United Reformed Church History Society*, Vol.3, 1985, pp.160-188.

[5] Both of these are referred to in footnotes to P.P.S.ii,8 and ii,21. Newman also wrote an appreciation of Davison: cf. *Essays Critical and Historical*, Vol.2, London, Longmans, Green and Co., 1888, pp. 375-420.

strong indications of his initial evangelical leanings.[6]

The second major influence in Newman's eschatology can be found in his study of the early Church Fathers. Once again, a a precise account of the nature of this influence has not yet been documented;[7] one must therefore rely on the general picture given in the *Apologia*, which can be supplemented by reference to his *Letters and Diaries* and his published work in *Tracts Theological and Ecclesiastical* and *Select Treatises of St.Athanasius*. One general observation may be made: the years following his first conversion represent the high-point of evangelical influence, which by 1822, under Whately and Hawkins, begins to go into decline. The idea of the Fathers as the authentic witness of Church doctrine rises steeply in Newman's mind to gradually replace, though not obliterate, his early views and to become the major influence of his theology.

Newman's first introduction to the Fathers was by way of Milner's *Church History*, which he read at the time of his conversion. He was so enamoured of the extracts from St.Augustine and St.Ambrose, that he observed in retrospect the contrary direction they took to his then staple diet of Scott and the two Newtons. Milner however had something in common with Scott in his simplicity and unworldliness which appealed to Newman. Newman's interest in the Fathers began seriously, however, in 1826 when he offered to write a long article on the Church of the third century. He had first requested Pusey, who had recently departed for Germany, to bring him back a set of Patristic volumes.[8] These he

---

[6] In several of the sermons up to No.43, Newman indicates on the cover page of the manuscripts the authors he has consulted, the majority of whom were non-conformist and sympathetic to evangelical ideas. The names most frequently mentioned are those of J.Trapp (1679-1747), D.Whitby (1638-1726) whose hostility to Popery was notorious, T.Scott (1747-1821), P.Doddridge (1702-1751) and S.Clarke (1684-1750) both non-conformists, G.Horne (1730-1792) who was sympathetic to Wesley, Z.Pearce (1690-1774) who helped Bishop Thomas Newton in preparing his books, C.Simeon (1759-1836), leader at Cambridge of the evangelical revival, on whose sermons Newman's early compositions are modelled. Cf. *Dictionary of National Biography*, London, Smith, Elder and Co., 1908-37; *The Oxford Dictionary of the Christian Church*, Oxford, Oxford University Press, 1985. Most of these writers were consulted for their well-known Scripture commentaries and sermons.

[7] While everyone agrees on the immense influence of the Fathers in Newman's work, the secondary literature on this point is rather sparse, and nothing can be found documenting the Patristic influence on his eschatology. Recently however an important contribution has been made by B E Daley in pulling together the many strands of Patristic eschatology. Cf. B.E.Daley, *The Hope of the Early Church*, Cambridge, Cambridge University Press, 1991. Such a handbook may enable future Newman students to track down the references to the Fathers in his theology of the last things.

[8] Cf. I.Ker, *John Henry Newman, A Biography*, Oxford, Oxford University Press, 1988, pp. 26ff.

received in the autumn of 1827 and he began to study them systematically in the Long Vacation of the following year. This period from 1826-1828 marked a crossroads in Newman's life.

Among the Fathers, the school of Alexandria held a principal attraction for Newman.[9] In his Apologia he names Clement, Origen and Athanasius as carrying him away with the breadth of their doctrine. His attention settled on the Arian controversy and its aftermath, and led to his first published book, *The Arians of the Fourth Century* in 1832. St.Athanasius, "the champion of the truth", became Newman's favorite author whose writings he continually had recourse to throughout his life.

The Meaning of Christian Eschatology

Though the term "eschatology" is now common currency in theology, it still presents some difficulty in knowing what precisely it refers to. A study of how the word has been used reveals a bewildering array of meanings.[10] From its innocuous beginnings as a technical word for the last things ($\tau\acute{a}$ $\emph{ἔσχατα}$), the term soon acquired a life of its own, which led at times to its meretricious use and to calls for its abolition. It had the singular merit however, of opening up a subject which had long become sterile.[11] The traditional treatises on the four last things had entered a cul-de-sac by their exclusive concentration on the destiny of the individual. The end of history and of the world had been strangely ignored and the biblical roots which nurtured theology had withered. With the coining of the new term, we have the moment of release from the standstill of the past, to a free flowing traffic of ideas. Theology then turned its attention to questions of collective eschatology

[9] For the influence of the Alexandrian Fathers on Newman's thought, cf. C.F.Harrold, 'Newman and the Alexandrian Platonists', *Modern Philology*, Vol.37, 1940, pp. 279-291; V.F.Blehl, 'The Patristic Humanism of John Henry Newman', *Thought*, Vol.50, 1975, pp. 266-274.

[10] Cf.J.Carmignac, *Les Dangers de l'Eschatologie*, New Testament Studies, Vol. 17, 1971, pp. 365-390.

[11] Commenting on the rebirth of eschatological thinking, Von Balthasar observes: "If Troeltsch, speaking on behalf of nineteenth- century liberalism, could say that 'the eschatological office is usually closed,' we can now say that it is working overtime." This new situation was brought about principally by the work of J.Weiss (1863-1914) and A.Schweitzer (1875- 1965), long after the period covered in this dissertation. For a concise account of the new directions in eschatology fundamental for Catholic theology, see H.Urs Von Balthasar, 'Eschatology' in J.Feiner et alii (eds.), *Theology Today*, Milwaukee, Bruce Publishing Co., 1965, pp. 222-244.

under the symbol of the Kingdom of God, in which all creation finds its ultimate fulfillment.

This change in the concept of the last things was not without its debit side. After some time it became clear that the content of eschatology was in danger of becoming shapeless and subjective. To prevent further attrition, J.Carmignac has recently proposed two definitions to reduce the multiplicity of meanings, which had led to such confusion. Eschatology, he suggested, should either denote the "ensemble of the last things, whether of the individual, or of humanity or of the world", - which was its primary meaning in the nineteenth century - or in the way favoured by the twentieth century as denoting "the dynamics of God's plan of salvation", which is close in content to the Pauline concept of $\mu \upsilon \sigma \tau \acute{\eta} \rho \iota \upsilon \nu$.[12] The two definitions however, were not to be understood as mutually exclusive, but complementary in nature, and it is in their two-fold significance that the word eschatology is used in this dissertation.[13]

From a Christian perspective, eschatology finds its origin and content in the revelation of God in Christ, which is full and definitive. In the Christ-Event we have the presence of the end. By virtue of this event, our personal history and the history of our world are directed centrifugally as towards the object of their ultimate fulfillment. Thus eschatology must not be understood in its etymological sense as "the science of the last things"; its real meaning is already contained in the unique appearance of the eschaton in the person of Christ. In Him the fullness of the Reign of God was announced and it is the unfolding of Christ's Reign, from now till the end of time, that is the subject of eschatology. When all things have attained their completion in Christ through the Spirit, He will then hand over His Kingdom to the Father so that God may be all in all.

In simpler and more immediate terms, eschatology is the reflection

---

[12] op.cit. pp. 380-1: "comme au dix-neuvième siècle, désigner l'ensemble des fins dernières, soit de l'invididu soit de l'humanité et du monde" or "la dynamique de l'économie du salut, en somme presque le contenu du terme $\mu \upsilon \sigma \tau \acute{\eta} \rho \iota \upsilon \nu$, tel qu'il est employé par S.Paul".

[13] The developments in Biblical eschatology since the beginning of this century are set out in N.Perrin, *The Kingdom of God in the Teaching of Jesus*, London, S.C.M. Press, 1963. See also R.Schnackenburg, *Christ - Present and Coming*, Philadelphia, Fortress Press, 1978. In the field of systematic theology cf. M.Kehl, *Eschatologie*, Würzburg, Echter Verlag, 1986; J.L.de la Peña, *La otra dimensión*, Santander, Sal Terrae, 1986 and J.Ratzinger, *Eschatology, Death and Eternal Life*, Washington D.C., Catholic University of America Press, 1988. For other modern studies on eschatology the reader is referred to the bibliography.

on the future of the promise made to us in Christ and kept alive by Christian hope. This is a promise of final salvation, a promise which may be forfeited by our neglect, but can never be taken away. It embraces not just our individual selves but the whole of creation reconciled by the blood of the cross. As far as the work of Christ is concerned, our redemption is complete and perfect, but as far as the fruit of salvation comes to us, it is both in our possession and not yet fulfilled. Hence there is a paradox in the history of our salvation which is expressed in the intrinsic tension of the now and the not-yet of eschatology. We are already brought into a state of grace, which is the assurance of our promised fulfillment, but the future glory of what we are to become, has not yet been revealed. Christian hope presupposes the beginning of eternal life but the attainment of its final end, which is the possession of God Himself, awaits the future appearance of Christ at the Second Coming.

From the above brief description of the nature of eschatology the following constitutive elements may be noted. The doctrine of the last things is ultimately a Christology under the aspect of our future fulfillment in Christ. Since it concerns the future, it is a theology of hope whose content is defined by the mystery of Christ. Thirdly, since salvation has already come, eschatology cannot be other than a reflection on the present state of salvation, which is by its very nature oriented towards the end. These elements point to the revealed truth in its objective sense; now we must look at its reception and interpretation in the subject of faith.

In Christ, God not only revealed Himself to man but in so doing also revealed man to himself. Hence, besides a Christology at the base of eschatology, we also have an understanding of man under the light of faith. Man's whole existence is a mystery to him; he is conscious of holding his being in time, with the past and the future entering into his present self-understanding. It is the future which is the cause of most anxiety to him, for it is outside his control and is most hidden from him. Moreover, the fulfillment of his identity is always seen in the horizon of the future, which is as yet unknown. Eschatology is a reflection on this future, both as it appears in time and at the end, as known only by faith. It is not a forecast of future events which can objectively be determined, or a study of final causes, but an inner moment of his present existence, perceived under the sign of the future. Christian existence is a life of faith and hope which opens us to the knowledge of what we are to become. However, the knowledge of our future is essentially concealed, for faith would cease to be faith if we knew by sight, and hope would no longer be hope if the future were certain and self-evident. We are therefore dealing with the futurity of the present as it grows out of man's reception of Christ's message of salvation by faith and hope[14].

Without pre-defining Newman's theology of the last things, a preliminary view of his Anglican sermons shows how closely his approach lies to the principles on which the modern understanding of eschatology is based. Newman however, cannot be regarded as a systematic theologian who sets out ex professo to present a dogmatic treatise. It is better to think of him as a priest for whom theology plays the important role of deepening our spirituality. His doctrine of the last things is thus woven into the seamless garment of a theology of Christian Life. It is this life, hidden with Christ in God, which is Newman's all-absorbing interest. Christ is the centre of all his thoughts and the experience of communion with Him the focus of all his sermons. From his reflection on this mystery he draws out the meaning of the last things for their practical import on Christian living. Newman's eschatology may be described as "existential"; it is the futurity of the present which commands his attention. It is not the addition of supplementary truths and events on which we may speculate about the future. The end, though hidden, is already operative in the life of faith and hope.

The Scope of the Dissertation

Having briefly introduced the topic of eschatology, we may now turn to the Anglican sermons which define the scope and limits of the thesis. During his Oxford period, Newman composed 604 sermons in all, which extend from 1824 to 1843. Those published under the description of "sermons" run to ten volumes. They include eight volumes of the Parochial and Plain, one volume of University Sermons and a volume of Sermons on Subjects of the Day. In addition to these, he also published a set of Advent Sermons on Antichrist as one of the Tracts for the Times, No.LXXXIII. The Lectures on Justification, on the Prophetical Office of the Church and Tract No.LXXXV, also had their origin in Newman's preaching and were numbered by him as part of one series with the sermons. These too may properly be considered as belonging to the same literary genre. It is difficult however to determine

---

[14] For an account of the principles involved in interpreting eschatological statements see K.Rahner, 'The Hermeneutics of Eschatological Assertions', *Theological Investigations*, Vol.4, London, Darton, Longman and Todd, 1966, pp. 323-346.

their precise relationship to the original lectures, since several revisions were made before publication and the manuscripts are no longer extant. This is true also of all his published sermons - with the exception of those preached before the University - none of whose original manuscripts have survived.

The published volumes of sermons and lectures represent less than half of Newman's output as a preacher. Still to be mentioned as forming an essential part of the research is a large body of unpublished sermons kept at the Birmingham Oratory. It consists of 206 complete manuscripts and 54 fragments as well as 34 abstracts of sermons which have been lost. This sermon material proved an invaluable asset in the study of Newman's eschatology. Not only could one base the study on the complete corpus of sermons, but the development of his ideas could also be traced. In particular, the manuscripts of his early sermons showed the series of courses he followed up to the end of 1831. This provided a means of determining the underlying system and trajectory on which the published volumes were based. Moreover, the unpublished material is a self-critical commentary on each stage of Newman's theology. This is evident from the multiple redactions and glosses, the editing and scoring, which fill the pages of the manuscripts. They take us into the sanctuary of his thought and bring us behind the curtain of his polished, published sermons.

The primary sources of this dissertation are clearly the sermons themselves, about 500 of which are either published or in manuscript. Besides the sermons, two other principal fonts are Newman's Tracts for the Times and his Letters and Diaries. The Tracts are intrinsically connected with the study since they were intended in Newman's own professed aim to deepen the theological content of the sermons. He composed 29 of them, several of which have a direct bearing on the theme of eschatology. The second additional source was the six volumes of Letters and Diaries, which cover the Anglican period up to the end of 1838.[15] Newman's life and work displays a singular unity and it is only at the cost of misinterpretation that one can divorce his writings from his actual life and ministry. The Letters and Diaries corroborate this view and show the influence of his personal and pastoral experience on his sermons.

---

[15] Four more volumes are planned to complete the Anglican years, 1839-1845. At present the material is arranged according to the names of correspondents, and not as in the published volumes, in chronological order. While I had the opportunity to examine them, the time at my disposal and the limits of the thesis, did not appear to merit further research.

10

The Need for the Present Study

In his survey of secondary literature on Newman's theology,[16] C.S.Dessain notes the absence of any book on Newman's eschatology. This was the state of Newman research up to 1973. Since then, nothing substantial has appeared to fill this lacuna, and later bibliographies, such as that of Griffin, only confirm the continuing neglect of studies in this area. Some work however has been done on the Dream of Gerontius, which most immediately comes to mind as an example of Newman's contribution to eschatology, with its theme of death and purgatory. Articles by Rowell and Wamsley have treated these themes, but no full-length study of the poem from a theological perspective has yet been undertaken.

Newman's eschatology, again in its individual dimension, is well summarized by Rowell in a chapter on the Tractarians, as part of his wide survey of Anglican eschatology in the nineteenth century. Another aspect of the subject is an account by Oliver of Newman's basically sympathetic though critical attitude to the phenomenon of Adventism, which stirred England during the 1820s and 30s. S.Gilley, in a pamphlet on Newman and Prophecy, has also drawn attention, somewhat melodramatically, to the latter's tendency towards a fundamentalist conception of the last things. C.S. Dessain has considered another theme in an article on the Cardinal's belief in eternal punishment. But beyond these directly related papers, there is very little and certainly no systematic or comprehensive study of Newman's eschatology. There is however an abundance of work which indirectly touches on the subject, from which an implicit view of Newman's eschatology can be inferred.

Judged against the scant attention paid to Newman's eschatology, the sermons have fared comparatively well. They were at once an object of admiration among his contemporaries and tributes poured in from all quarters praising their elegance and profound wisdom. In his weekly preaching at St. Mary's we have the embodiment of the spirit of the Oxford Movement and the quintessential Newman in a most personal and appealing way. Apart, however, from the peculiar attractiveness of his preaching, there is a still more important quality that can be attributed to the sermons. This is their role in being the medium and the seed-bed of Newman's ideas. It is scarcely an exaggeration to say that

---

[16] M.J. Svaglic & C.S. Dessain in D.J. De Laura (ed.), *Victorian Prose - a Guide to Research*, New York, Modern Language Association of America, 1973, pp. 115-184.

there is no work of Newman which does not find its ground and origin in the seminal ideas contained in them.

In spite of the paramount role which the sermons play in the whole of Newman's published work, they have been relatively neglected as an area of research. Secondary studies have tended to concentrate on themes which are more readily accessible in his other writings. Thus, with notable exceptions, the Anglican sermons have not yet been fully harvested by scholars. One basic reason for this is the nature of the sermons themselves, each of which is limited, in Newman's own stated aim, to a single definite point, thereby making attempts to systematize his theology extremely difficult. We have in the published sermons particular and discrete compositions, each complete in itself, apparently unaffected by any overall design, which might reveal a synthesis of his thought. They are the work of the accomplished artist, who has acquired such a high degree of freedom that he can lay aside artificial structures of composition. Such maturity however presupposes a process in which Newman learned to construct his theological framework and design, and this can be seen in his early courses.

For these reasons there is ample justification to undertake the present study. Both as regards the theme and the area of research, Newman's eschatology and the Anglican sermons have not received adequate attention. In contrast to the vast amount of Newman studies in other fields, this rich vein of the author has virtually gone unexplored.

The Plan of Development of the Dissertation

The thesis is a systematic presentation of Newman's eschatology based on a detailed analysis of his Anglican sermons. In a field left fallow for so long, it is a preliminary work designed to prepare the ground for future, more intensive sowing. To walk the land and make it even for the furrow, to feel the texture of the soil and distinguish loam from marsh, is the immediate goal of this study. The survey therefore tries to follow the contours of the terrain, so as to reflect as far as possible Newman's own order of ideas. In a general way, this can be done by noting how the liturgy acts as the guide and measuring-rod, particularly in his later sermons. On this liturgical pattern, the various aspects of Newman's eschatology are ordered. Each of the seasons has its own particular bearing on the subject, beginning with Advent and ending with the feast of All Saints.

The dissertation begins with a survey of Newman's Advent sermons on the theme of the Coming of Christ. Here we have a starting point which conforms both liturgically and theologically to a Christian understanding of the last things. These sermons are divided into four groups, each dealing with a particular aspect of the Advent theme. The first group is related to the Second Coming and the prelude to this event in the form of the Antichrist. Newman denounces the wickedness of his age and warns of the suddenness of the judgment to come. The second series shifts our attention to the present period of spiritual preparation, as an anticipation of our future encounter with Christ. Next we have a defence of Christian belief in the Parousia and the call to wait and watch for Christ's return. Finally there is a series of late Advent sermons written at a time of controversy. In these Newman looks for the signs of Christ's presence and thereby forges a link between eschatology and a theology of the Church.

Chapter Two, entitled the Severe Side of Eschatology, continues the theme of the Second Coming under its foremost aspect of judgment. This chapter is largely based on Newman's Lenten sermons. In line with his general view of religious experience, the encounter with Christ will be "fearful before it is ecstatic". He will judge the world before gathering the faithful into glory. The chapter begins with a look at the roots of severity and the dreadful possibility of the futility of human life. It underlines the nature of human accountability, which will finally be weighed in an eternal balance at the Last Judgment. The significance of present affliction and the relation between God's justice and mercy are also considered within the theme of judgment. A separate but related issue is the question of eternal punishment, a belief which Newman defends as revealed doctrine, while at the same time noting the perplexity and trial of faith it entails.

After the Lenten season, the liturgical theme of Eternal Life is portrayed in Newman's Resurrection and Ascension sermons. This Third Chapter brings us to the core of Christian eschatology. It first considers the present state of salvation and the principle of new life imparted by the resurrection. The revolution of a new heavens and a new earth is set in motion, and we have been brought under the ministration of the Spirit. Hence the state of grace in which we live and the state of glory to which we are destined, are in substance one and the same. By virtue then of Christ's saving work, our human condition is fundamentally one of hope and joy.

The theme of hope and joy is the central part of Chapter Three.

Hope looks forward to the future where the fullness of salvation lies, while joy celebrates its presence in the gift of Christ Himself. The paradox of Christ's absence as the condition for His spiritual presence, illustrates the mixed economy of hope and joy in the Christian life.

The final section on Eternal Life is Newman's treatment of immortality and final resurrection. It begins with the intimations of reason concerning the immortality of the soul, and is then followed by the progressive disclosure of life after death in the Old Testament. From this we take a quantum leap to the distinctive Christian belief in the resurrection of the body. Christ is the origin of our immortality and His Spirit the instrument of the resurrection of the body, the final fruit of redemption.

Up to this point the dissertation is concerned with the inner dynamic of eschatology, which is derived from the Christ-Event. Now we are to see its application and significance for the community and the individual. The community aspect is considered first, since salvation is primarily a corporate mystery in Christ as members of His Body. Chapter Four therefore deals with the Church as the sign of our final destiny in the Heavenly Jerusalem. While the first three chapters follow closely the pattern of the liturgical year, the theme of the Church extends through all the seasons. It is placed however, after the central event of the New Creation, to which it is related as mystery and sign. As a divine institution the Church represents the end-time in which the Reign of God has reached its final phase. It is also the Body of the Elect, of those who are predestined for the blessedness of heaven. Since it is a kingdom not of this world, it must suffer persecution at the hands of evil men. It is the little flock, the holy remnant which is meant not for this world but for the next. Lastly, the Church is the sacrament of the Communion of Saints. It is already in communion with the faithful departed and the saints in heaven, and this communion anticipates its final perfection.

In Chapter Five we see how the journey of the Church towards perfection is concretely enacted in the life of the individual. Each member passes through the stages of probation and purification on the way to the Heavenly City. Thus the Chapter examines Newman's theology of death, his inquiry into the nature of the Intermediate State and his conception of heaven. The anxiety of death which is experienced on the natural level as the end of all things, is transformed by faith and seen as a moment of change, not the termination of Christian life. It is the passage to a new form of existence, to a state between death and the resurrection of the body on the Last Day. Newman understands this Intermediate State as a school of contemplation mercifully designed to complete the process of sanctification, until God will be all in all. The end of the journey is the bliss of heaven where the glorified humanity of Christ dwells. The experience of isolation in death and the solitude of incompleteness in the Intermediate State gives way to a fullness in Christ, in whom the individual and the community are united. Christ is the centre of heaven and the fulfilment of the human quest for happiness. In presenting these themes of closure and culmination of the Christian life, Newman appropriately attaches them to the Feast of All Saints.

With these five chapters, the major elements of Newman's eschatology are covered in much the same way as they are presented in the liturgical calendar. However, his intention all along is not simply to impart theoretical knowledge but to inspire his hearers with motives for Christian living. Chapter Six underlines this aspect by showing how his spirituality is shaped by his theology of the last things. Once again, it is to the Liturgy he turns, not for its didactic role, but for its power to form the Christian character. Through our participation in it, we come to understand eschatology as a lived experience and not merely as a system of notional belief. Public and private prayer enable the Christian to live as though the End has come. Fasting and self-denial signify the condition of the "not yet" and are meant to enhance our consciousness of the life hereafter. The spirit of devotion in prayer and detachment in self-denial does not however tend to a rejection of the present world but is the means of promoting the greater glory of God.

The Chapter ends with the significance of the Eucharist as the eschatological meal. The sacrament is first of all the pledge and portion of eternal life. It is also the connecting link between Christ's First Coming and His Second. A third aspect is the relation of the Eucharist to the Last Judgment and its power to protect the Church from the evil day. Finally it is the food of immortality which gives a present assurance of the resurrection of the body.

The final chapter reviews the main points of the dissertation and evaluates Newman's contribution to eschatology.

CHAPTER ONE
THE COMING OF CHRIST

Introduction

An appropriate starting point for a systematic presentation of Newman's eschatology is his treatment of the Coming of Christ. The very frequency of this theme in his sermons is an illustration of the importance Newman set on it; in fact it may be argued that it represents the governing principle of his theology. It is to be found from the very earliest[1] of his Anglican sermons in 1824, and, though not confined to the liturgical season of Advent, it is there that it is most extensively treated. The Advent sermons constitute a generally well-defined genre within the total corpus of the Anglican sermons.[2] Newman himself specified the Advent courses he delivered up to 1831; thereafter, though he had given up writing courses, he maintained the practice of an Advent series of sermons up to 1842.

A study of these sermons illustrates the different aspects under which Newman treated the significance of Advent. It is considered first from the perspective of prophecy, prescinding for the moment from the question of how Newman understood the concept. Secondly, Advent denotes a period of intense spiritual preparation, and so Newman underlines the dispositions which the Coming of Christ suggests for our meditation. A third class of sermons focuses on the problem of the delay of the Parousia and the consequent dilemma Christians face in sustaining a spirit of readiness. Finally, we have in Newman's own words, the special nature of the Advent sermons preached in the aftermath of Tract xc, when controversy was closely followed by disillusionment.

The classification of these sermons attempts to follow the logical ordering of Newman's ideas on the theme. It is combined with a chronological survey of them, so as to highlight the stages of his development within the various perspectives. By this division into four

---

[1] The influence of Charles Simeon can be seen in Newman's *early course on the Parables*, many of which are interpreted with reference to the last days e.g. No. 8, 10.

[2] Of the 604 numbered sermons, 37 can safely be described as Advent sermons. Other sermons written or preached during Advent which are not directly related to the theme are not classified under this genre e.g. P.P.S.i,5; ii,2.

different groups, each dealing with a particular aspect of the Coming of Christ, it is possible to present a systematic picture of his reflections.

Advent at St. Clement's

Newman's first sermons on the Coming of Christ were given for the Sundays of Advent in 1824, while he was curate of St. Clement's. He preached both in the morning and in the afternoon on two distinct aspects of the subject. The morning conferences were devoted to the theme in the light of the fulfilment of prophecy.[3] Christ's First Coming had been foretold by the prophets and had raised the hopes of the people of Israel. There had also been a corresponding expectation on the part of the Gentiles for the advent of some powerful prince. The Coming of Christ in the flesh was the fulfilment of hope for those who sought Him. It also spelt dire consequences for those who rejected Him, which can be seen in the visitation of His wrath against Jerusalem.[4] These sermons have two practical aims: first, they provide an example of the use of prophecy and how it has been confirmed by history. Second, they are intended for the conversion of Jews and Christians alike: for the Jews that their promised restoration may be hastened, and for Christians to take note that a punishment far worse than the destruction of Jerusalem will overcome them on the last day, if they do not repent.

The afternoon series are of a very different character. The aspect now considered is that of prayer and the means of grace in our spiritual warfare against the world. Newman now turns to the Collects of the Advent Sundays as the springboard for his theme.[5] These sermons stress the radical opposition between the standard of the world and the

---

[3] The four sermons on Sunday mornings are on a single prophetic text Mal.iii.1-3. The sermons are numbered 37,39,41 and 43. No manuscript remains extant but we have abstracts for all four.

[4] The hopeful side is treated in Nos. 37 and 39 on the theme of the Coming of Christ in the flesh. Nos. 41 and 43 present the severe side symbolized in the destruction of Jerusalem.

[5] It is interesting to note how closely Newman follows the collects from the Book of Common Prayer for the themes of these Advent sermons.

standard of Christ.[6] Their aim is to exhort Christians to "come out and be separate" from the corrupt influence of the world, which can only be overcome by having recourse to the means that God has provided, viz. Scripture, the Church and the help of the Holy Spirit. The reading of Scripture is necessary to create a frame of mind in which humility, faith, simplicity, self-application and prayer for grace are instilled. Conversion to holiness of life and the grace of the Holy Spirit, are also necessary to deliver us from the evil attractions of the world. Such graces are to be obtained by attending the sacraments, and through private prayer. In this set of Advent sermons, the liturgical spirit of the Prayer Book is the leading motif.

It would be wrong to draw any premature conclusions at this stage on the direction of Newman's later sermons since we are dependent mostly on abstracts for this Advent series.[7] All that we have is a prelude and outline of the trajectory which future sermons took. Two things however should be noted: he acknowledges his dependence on Pearce and Newton for his sermons on the use of prophecy[8]; secondly, the afternoon sermons show Newman's early reverence and reliance on the Prayer Book, which was uncommon in one under the strong influence of evangelicalism.[9]

Part One
The Prophetic Perspective

Newman's first Advent sermons of 1824 considered the Coming of Christ as an event which had been predicted and later fulfilled in the

---

[6] The manuscripts for sermon No. 40 *On Reading Scripture* and for No. 42 *On Attending the Ordinances of Grace* are still extant. The other two sermons No. 38 *On The World* and No. 44 *On the Necessity of Divine Grace* are in the form of abstracts.

[7] Moreover the abstracts by their clarity and precision show signs of being written after the sermons though we cannot tell when.

[8] Newman has written at the bottom of these abstracts "Greater part from Newton and Pearce" (No. 41) and "Greater part from Newton" (No. 43).

[9] Fr.Dessain has argued that Newman's first conversion was not strictly speaking an evangelical one. Unlike evangelical conversions it was not a sudden bolt but took place over several months. Newman's early reliance on the Prayer Book lends support to the view that his conversion did not exactly fit the evangelical model.

On Newman's strict adherence to the Prayer Book from the beginning cf L.D. Vol.1 p. 82.

18

historical birth of Jesus. In these sermons he takes us back to the Jewish Church's expectation of the Messiah and to its subsequent accomplishment in history. History also ratified the consequences of Jewish rejection, which were realized in the destruction of Jerusalem. As we stand now in the Christian era of the Church, are there parallels and lessons to be learned from the prophecy of His Second Coming? From the pattern of the past do we have a paradigm of how God will act when He comes to judge the world? Thus, by transposing the situation of the Jewish Church to that of the Christian era, Newman views the prophecy of the First Coming as a type and presage of the Second.

The Advent sermons of 1830 are based on Newman's understanding and use of prophecy. Together with doctrine and precept, prophecy is one of three dimensions of Scripture.[10] It is the most difficult of the three to interpret, but its inherent ambiguity should not prevent us from pondering on its significance. Scripture in all its parts conveys truth[11] and has been intended by God to be put to good use. From a study of unfulfilled prophecy we may learn some practical lessons for today, and it is this which holds Newman's attention rather than speculation about the future.[12] The daily reading of Scripture is to acquire wisdom for our present life rather than to build theories and prognostications of what is to come. Scripture, however, throws enough light on the future to help us evaluate our present history and discern the moral implications of our times.

The titles of the Advent sermons indicate the futurist perspective under which Newman now considers the Coming of Christ. The past is the mirror of the future and so the prophecies surrounding the First Coming are a paradigm for His return. Just as He came in the flesh to a wicked generation, He will come again in a wicked age.[13] He came

---

[10] This structure of Scripture into its three constituent parts is frequently used by Newman in his Feast Day sermons. He first treats the history of the Saint, follows it with the doctrine implied and ends with the application of the moral precept.

[11] Newman's early view of Scripture is influenced by Scott, whose conviction of the Bible as the ultimate source of truth is seen in the following quotation: "When I first began to desire and seek...wisdom, I set out with the assurance that it was to be found in the Holy Scriptures and nowhere else; they alone being able to make us wise unto salvation", *The Force of Truth*, 1779, p. 75.

[12] It must however be admitted that in his early life Newman shows a proneness for and fascination with inquiry into the future Cf. S. W. Gilley, "Newman and Prophecy, Evangelical and Catholic." *Journal of the United Reformed Church History Society*, vol. 3, No. 5, 1985, pp. 160-188.

[13] No. 273 entitled *Christ will come in a wicked age - with a reference to these times*.

without fanfare and took the world unawares by the suddenness of His arrival; He will likewise come again when we least expect.[14] Moreover, though circumstances have changed from the time of His First Coming, we are still in a period of expectation, and the religious frame of mind of Christians today is similar to that of the pious Jew.[15] In 1824 Newman had treated the First Coming as an event which the prophets saw in the future. Now he looks at the Second Coming in much the same light, as a prospect in store for the Christian Church. Under this perspective he views with dismay the religious situation of his time.

> "...and now especially should we dwell on the prospect of His appearing, both because the Church reminds us of it at this season and again because the *world* reminds us of it - the evil world, not thinking indeed of God or meaning it so, but warning us by its own strange restlessness and unwonted tumult to think upon the day of Christ's coming."[16]

Judgment on a Wicked Generation

The double destruction of Jerusalem by Nabuchadnezzar and by the Romans is, in the view of Scripture, a judgment of God on the apostasy of the Jewish nation. In a temporal kingdom such as theirs was, temporal punishments were appropriate for offences committed against the King. However, with the First Coming of Christ and the new dispensation of grace, no such judgments of God are to be expected.[17]Nonetheless, though God is not judging the world in the present age, He continues to send affliction and turmoil as warnings and threats which serve as reminders of a future judgment. Thus disasters which occur from time to time mirror and anticipate the final judgment which will take place at the Second Coming of Christ.

---

[14] No. 274 entitled *Christ will come suddenly - with a reference to these times*.

[15] The third sermon of this series, No. 276 will be treated separately as it is quite distinct from the other two. It is entitled *Waiting for Christ is like Jewish waiting for his First Coming*. It is based on the principle he states in No. 110 that the religious feelings produced by revelation, as distinct from doctrine, are common to all its forms.

[16] No. 273 p. 2.

[17] Newman makes this distinction in Sermon No. 92 which he acknowledges was written while he was under the influence of Whateley.

"Former judgments on Israel are threats upon Christian
nations; and will be brought into effect again and again,
working up and hastening towards Christ's final coming to
end the world. Let us then in this season turn our thoughts
to the day of Christ when He shall come in judgment and
consider what it is which will especially provoke that
coming, and how far we at present are interested in
anticipating it."[18]

Newman notes that the wrath of God is suspended in the present
age of history, and that the prophecies of destruction await the end of
time. The judgments of the Old Testament were but partially fulfilled
and prophecies such as Zeph.iii have not yet been fully realized; not
only Jerusalem but "all the earth shall be devoured by the fire of God's
jealousy."[19] It is for this reason that we must cast our mind on the
future coming of Christ when they will be fulfilled.[20] God did not
revoke His wrath on sin, but merely suspended it in His mercy, to allow
us time to repent. We do not know the hour of His coming and must
remain content with our ignorance of the future. Nevertheless, we have
the assurance of Scripture that when He comes, it will be to judge the
world. And thus the present troubles and evils are His way of reminding
us of the coming judgment.

"What time indeed He *will* come in judgment, *we* cannot say
- no one knoweth the hour but God Himself. Yet He
Himself has joined together trouble and perplexity with the
end of the world - so that the more of distress and
commotion that exists among the nations of the earth, the
more hope there is that Christ is coming - and in all times of
fear and amazement at least we may be *reminded* of His
coming even when we see no ground for expecting it."[21]

Besides the recurring phenomena of evil throughout history, and
its continual power to remind us of the final judgment, Scripture gives
us special signs, which will be the prelude to the consummation of the
world. Evil will accumulate until a universal apostasy is formed, which

---

[18] No. 273 p. 2. This is a redaction in his later handwriting, but undated.

[19] No. 274 p. 2.

[20] ibid p.3: "I shall consider with reference to an event still future, that last fearful
visitation of the world for its wickedness is to close the history of man."

[21] No. 273 p. 2.

will immediately precede the end. It will be seen in the world's utter rejection of Christ. Then God's patience will run out, for evil will have provoked Him to act in judgment. This unbelief is the progeny of pride, and as we see the pride of nations grow, we can contemplate the imminence of coming destruction. A general infidelity will therefore be a sure sign of the approaching wrath of God.

> "And that wickedness of the world, which will bring down the fire of heaven upon it, will be of a peculiar kind, ...by peculiar I mean it will be something marked out and distinct from that mere ordinary guilt which marks the course of the world's history in all ages. We must speak cautiously as about the future. Still does it not appear, as if that unpardonable sin would be, not superstition, nor hypocrisy, nor mere immorality which in the next world will receive their full punishment, - but infidelity?"[22]

The Suddenness of Christ's Coming

A second characteristic of the Second Coming which Newman underlines, is the suddenness of God's visitation. His former judgments were carried out in this manner and the Day of Judgment will likewise occur unexpectedly, despite the warnings and signs we have been given. At present we are lulled by an apparent tranquillity on the surface of things, but such was the case when the deluge overtook the world in Noah's time, or in the days of Lot, when Sodom and Gomorrha were destroyed. Though warnings have been given, men have put their trust in human remedies to avert disaster rather than turn to God.

These signs of the final cataclysm remind us that the end of the world will come not just by God's fiat, but also by the agency of man. They manifest the extraordinary grip which evil has on man, and its power to provoke God's wrath. Unbelief may appear as something of little consequence to men who are blind; they do not understand the gravity of the offence or its significance. The sin of unbelief, however, is the root of evil, which God permits until such time as He is faced with universal rejection. Such rejection is not to be wondered at, for it is the result of the evil principle within us in our corrupt nature. Thus the Last Day will be due as much to man's calling down judgment on himself, as

---

[22] No. 273 p. 5.

22

to an act of God's transcendence.

> "I will proceed to explain how it may naturally happen - and
> to show you that *unbelief*, which is given as the reason of it,
> is not merely an unintelligible name put forward by us to
> cover our ignorance of the real cause, but a principle which
> operates daily, the character of which we shall have no
> difficulty in recognizing both in the world around us and in
> our own hearts."[23]

The Context of the Day

It is clear from these sermons of 1830 that Newman meant the
alarming situation of his day to be read in the light of the Scripture
prophecies.[24] While he cautiously avoids identifying the apocalyptic
signs with the present signs of the times, he notes the parallel between
them. The Catholic Emancipation Act[25] had just been passed and
Parliament was now engaged in reform legislation,[26] which many
perceived as meddling in the life of the Church. 1830 was also a year of
revolution on the Continent and came as a delayed aftershock of the
social and political earthquake of 1789. The Church in Newman's view
was in deep crisis and the forces of liberalism, which he regarded as the
parent of unbelief, were gathering strength. The future appeared grim to
one whose interests and energies were spent in the defence of the
Church and the stability of civil institutions. Thus, in this ferment of
change, he felt an urgent need for a fixed standard by which he could
measure the ideas and events of the times. Antiquity became his
criterion for determining religious truth, and thus he compared the
present situation to the first age of the Church.

---

[23] No. 274 p. 11-12.

[24] And not vice-versa. This is the main objection Newman has against Cooper's
Crisis: "...we cannot but think it has been from considering the events of the present day,
that he has been led antecedently to conclude that they must be predicted in Scripture;
and has thus rather brought the prophecy to the history, than made the history
subservient to the prophecy", cf. Cooper's Crisis, *Quarterly Review*, June 1825, p. 43.

[25] Passed in 1829. Newman's campaign against Robert Peel, who had been an
elected member of Parliament by Oxford University, is noteworthy. Vid. L.D., Vol.ii,
pp.124ff in which his jubilation at Peel's defeat is seen.

[26] The Great Reform Bill of 1832 was followed by a series of legislation of an
emancipatory kind. Cf L.Woodward, *The Age of Reform*, pp.75-87; 340-4; S.C.Carpenter,
Church and People 1789- 1889, pp. 49-67.

"We seem to be coming round again to the early times of the Church - Jewish hard unbelief, Gentile mockery raise their voices again as of old time - and what says the fixed oracles of God to such rage and tumult against Him?"[27]

Newman's account of the situation of the time is a scathing and relentless attack on the infidelity and pride of the nation. A new age of progress had begun, symbolized by the new means of transport and commerce in the railway. In the glow of victory after the Napoleonic wars, England quickly advanced to being the foremost power in the world. There was a spirit of optimism and ambition, and such confidence, in Newman's view, augured a forgetfulness of God and religion. He recognized that all ages have their share of evil, but he considered his own age a particularly "heinous" one. He accused the nation of apostasy, a charge which Keble later made in 1833 in his famous Assize sermon.[28] Apostasy was for him the fruit of pride; it could be seen in the complacency of the period, the supreme reliance on scientific knowledge, the so-called enlightenment of the emerging middle class, the all-sufficiency of the nation and the lack of dependency on God.[29] He apologizes for introducing politics into the pulpit but is constrained to make his congregation recognize the signs "in these unquiet times."

The Practical End of Prophecy

Newman's interest in prophecy was partly spurred on by what he perceived was a deepening crisis of faith. A search for God's plan, though dimly expressed in prophecy, was an urgent need for the times. He recognized the uncertain nature of unfulfilled prophecy, but believed that an understanding of God's Word depended largely on personal holiness.[30] Those who are really close to God indeed see below the surface of things; though the future remains clouded, they have an intuitive grasp of the ultimate meaning of life. Moreover, the prophetic texts should not be dismissed on the grounds that they are obscure and

---

[27] No. 273 p. 28.

[28] Newman considered that Keble's sermon on *National Apostasy* marked the launching of the Oxford Movement.

[29] No. 273 p. 12ff.

[30] No. 274. On pages 12-30 Newman gives his views on the use of prophecy. We also have an untitled and undated sermon, No. 261 which is a fragment on prophecy.

24

give rise to contrary opinions. The wild interpretations, which were
common at the time, cannot be used as a pretext for our neglect in
studying the sacred Word. In the prophecies Scripture "interprets and
comments on the world's history as it passes on even to its close - tells
us what to admire and what to shun and what to expect."[31] So attention
to the prophecies as yet unfulfilled can help us see more clearly their
inner significance for the present age, particularly at a time of crisis.

> "These are serious thoughts at all times - most serious at a
> time like this when there is upon our country plain marks of
> that sin, which has been the forerunner and the provocation
> of punishment in all nations - pride."[32]

Newman warns of the consequences of the liberalism of the day as
inevitably leading to widespread unbelief. The apocalyptic vision of the
future judgment at the Second Coming should inspire a salutary fear
and bring about personal conversion. He tells his congregation to look
to their own salvation and prepare for the onslaught of evil, which will
affect both the world and the Church. Though the prospect is bleak, the
true Christian will nonetheless retain a spirit of equanimity, in the
knowledge that Christ's coming is a time of hope as well as one of fear.
But it will be through suffering and persecution that Christ will gather
His elect from the wickedness of the world.

> "Considering the state of affairs without being alarmed, to be
> prepared for any judgments which sooner or later may be
> coming on us. The Church of God must not fear. But while
> she is in the world she will suffer with the world the world's
> punishment - and take it calmly."[33]

Comparison of the First and Second Coming

There is a dramatic change both in content and tone in the last of
the series of Advent sermons for 1830. This sermon[34] was in fact

---

[31] ibid.p.19; P.P.S.ii,10.

[32] ibid. p. 28.

[33] No. 273 p. 29-30.

[34] No. 276 was entitled *Waiting for Christ is like Jewish Waiting for His First
Coming*.

preached on Christmas Day, and this may account for the change from the futurist perspective of the Second Coming as the Day of Judgment, to the present realization of God's mercy in the Incarnation. But a more telling reason for the quite remarkable difference is that the extant manuscript is a fair copy written seven years later, and assigned by Newman as a "Commune for Christmas tide, or Advent, or Purification."[35]

The unfulfilled prophecy of the Second Coming is retained as the point of departure,[36] but is considered in a new framework by introducing a comparison with Christ's First Coming in the flesh. Thus the severe side of the Second Coming is now balanced by the significance of the Incarnation. Since the past is the assurance of the future, the mercy of God shown in the birth of Christ, creates a hopeful expectation for His future coming. Nevertheless, Newman notes the primary end of the Second Coming as one of judgment, while that of His First was salvation. Comparing the First and Second Coming he remarks:

"As the first coming of Christ lay in prospect before His Church, so does His second coming. The Jews looked out for His coming to save them, and we Christians look out for His coming to judge us. These two events differ of course in many important respects; they differ as much as the world's redemption differs from its judgment; and Christ's humiliation from His final triumph. And yet they are also parallel in several points of view; in their circumstances and in the duty of the faithful under them. The Jews were bound to look forward to the day of Christ in faith and love, though His coming was to try them; we are bound even more to look forward with the same feelings towards His second and last day which is still more fearful and still more joyful. Let me proceed to draw out this parallel."[37]

The prophets of the Old Testament saw in the promise of the

35 Cf. the cover page of the manuscript. The handwriting is distinctly different from 1830. Though it was first preached on Saturday afternoon of Christmas Day, it has been rewritten for the feast of the Purification in 1837. It was later preached in 1839 and 1842 for the same feast and for the 4th Sunday of Advent in 1840.

36 The prophetic text Mal.iii.2, which was used for the original sermon in 1830, is also the first reading for the Feast of the Purification in the Book of Common Prayer.

37 No. 276 pp. 3-4.

Messiah a message of comfort and hope, and this has been fulfilled in
the Christian Church. But they did not ignore the element of tribulation
and fear which would attend His coming. Each of the prophecies
combined the element of judgment with the visitation of God's mercy.
They foresaw the future rejection and the day of separation which
would occur between the faithful remnant and the nation of Israel.
"Thus thankful joy and solemn awe and fear were the mingled feelings
with which the servants of God were to regard Christ's first Advent."[38]
The Christian temper towards the Second Coming must be of a parallel
kind. His First Coming was a visitation of mercy, but it involved the
challenge of discipline. Now that Christians have experienced His
mercy, there is all the more reason for purifying themselves for the
coming judgment.

Despite the trepidation at the thought of judgment, the Second
Coming is something to be desired and contemplated in Christian hope.
We have also here a parallel between the feelings of the Jews and of the
Christian Church. In the same spirit of mingled joy and fear, Christians
are to watch out and pray that He will hasten His coming. But there is a
crucial difference between the Jewish and Christian standpoints. The
Jews could only look out in hope on an undetermined future, while
Christians have the assurance of a definite goal, which enables them to
sustain a spirit of readiness.

"They saw it but afar off; they could not live in a continual
expectation of His appearing. It is different with us; we have
reason to think that He will come with little preparation, and
that the sure and distinct signs of His coming will precede
Him by only a few years. Thus the prospect of it is a much
more practical doctrine to us than it would be to the Jews,
keeping the heart awake and warning us against giving it to
the world, and weaning us from over-earnestness even in
prosecuting religious objects."[39]

In the concluding pages of this sermon, Newman issues a
reminder that the Coming of Christ is the unique object to which all
Christians should direct their thoughts. He rejects the idea that the
moment of death[40] is the goal of our life's preparation. Scripture

---

[38] No. 276 p. 10.

[39] No. 276 p. 14.

[40] Newman's theology of death will be treated under individual eschatology in

proposes a different standard, and the end it speaks of properly refers to that of the community. However, the death of the individual resembles the coming of Christ in two respects:- it is both certain to occur, and uncertain as to when it will happen. But Christ will not come until all is ended, and it is His project, and not our own, which should be the object of our thoughts.

> "Christ will not come till all is ended, till the salvation of His elect is secured, their purification finished, their works completed, their influence on each other fully exerted and exhausted, till all are saved, not this one or that. In looking out for His coming, we are looking out for the salvation of all saints, we are looking out also for our own finished salvation."[41]

Within the Advent sermons on unfulfilled prophecy, the series for the season of 1835 have special significance. These four sermons[42] were later published in 1838 as Tract LXXXIII and republished under the title of The Patristical View of the Antichrist.[43] Newman saw the function of the Tracts to offer theological instruction and support to the published sermons, which were in their nature more pastoral and practical. As there are no original manuscripts of these sermons,[44] the views expressed in the Tract represent his mind in 1838, and so it cannot be determined how accurately they reflect his preaching in Advent 1835.[45] One important observation may be made at the outset: there is virtually no mention of the Antichrist[46] in the eight volumes of the Parochial and Plain Sermons, though the mystery of evil is always

---

Chapter 5.

[41] No. 276 p. 15. This is in contrast to the admonition he had issued in No. 273 when we are told to look out for ourselves and our own salvation .

[42] They are numbered 394, 395, 396 and 397 in Newman's list.

[43] In *Discussions and Arguments*, pp.44-108.

[44] Cf.Pett, p. 102: "It is certain that the manuscripts of published sermons were destroyed and the manuscripts of unpublished sermons were preserved." Pett notes Newman's record that the latter "burnt some papers on justification - above 600 pages", and mentions the custom, common in those days, of destroying manuscripts once they were printed, cf.op.cit.p.194.

[45] I am following Pett's sound principle on p. 200, that "the sermons within any volume must be regarded as examples of that stage in Newman's development at the date of its first edition and cannot be taken as evidence for his views when the original sermon was first preached."

[46] Vid. however P.P.S.vii,18 .

28

assumed. The nature of these sermons therefore may have seemed to Newman to be better suited to a Tract than to a volume of sermons.

The "mystery of iniquity", or the Antichrist of the last days, is presented as a summary of the teaching of the Fathers. Since unfulfilled prophecy is a difficult field of inquiry, Newman once again issues strong words of caution. An important distinction is drawn between the authority of the Fathers in matters of doctrine and their authority in questions of prophecy. In interpreting doctrine, the Fathers are the authentic witnesses of the Catholic faith, while on the subject of unfulfilled prophecy, their voice, even when unanimous, is not invested with the same moral authority. In fact, rather than bearing testimony to the universal belief of the Church, they are in the case of prophecy simply recording uncertain traditions, or expressing their own private opinions.[47] They speak for the most part as individuals, but their combined reflections can be of great importance to our interpretation of the prophecies today.

Just as in the 1830 Advent sermons, the present series entails a commentary on the contemporary situation of society and the Church. The aim therefore of studying the Fathers on the Antichrist is to reap the practical benefit of enabling us to interpret today's signs of the times.

The Time of the Antichrist

The time of the Antichrist is that brief period (which Newman seems to take literally as three and a half years),[48] in which widespread apostasy triggers the Advent of Christ. He reiterates his conviction that since we are ignorant of the time of Christ's final coming, we therefore cannot identify any particular age as the Time of the Antichrist.[49] But signs will suddenly appear when the mystery of iniquity will be fully

---

[47] Tract LXXXIII p. 2-3.

[48] Tract LXXXIII p. 4: "it appears that the time of Antichrist's tyranny will be three years and a half, which is an additional reason for believing he is not come...."

[49] Cf.Cooper's Crisis. *Quarterly Review*. loc. cit. Cooper's method of applying prophecy had brought the subject into disrepute. The main point of discussion was "how far, namely, the events of the present day may be known to be the subject of Scripture prediction. That there have been times when the interpretation of prophecy has even preceded the event is undeniable; that these are such times, is a much more hazardous position."

manifested. Though it is being held back until the End, we have at present "shadows and forebodings, earnests and operating elements of that which was one day to come in its fullness."[50] It is both now and not yet. Whatever way we may judge the historical question of the precise time of the Antichrist, we are to expect such a situation to arise, and have been told something of the nature of the age in which he will come. We are also told that the Antichrist is a person or shows the traits of personality embodying the principle of evil.[51]

> "...the coming of Christ will be immediately preceded by a very awful and unparalleled outbreak of evil, called in the text an apostasy, a falling away, in the midst of which a certain terrible man of sin and child of perdition, the special and singular enemy of Christ, or Antichrist, will appear; that this will be when revolutions prevail, and the present form of Society breaks to pieces; that at present the Spirit which he will embody and represent, is kept under by "the powers that be", but that on their dissolution, he will rise out of the bosom of them, and knit them together again in his own evil way, under his own rule to the exclusion of the Church."[52]

The special sign of widespread apostasy is the means of estimating the degree to which our present age is a prelude or approximation of the end. History itself confirms rather than contradicts the belief that a great onslaught of evil has followed upon times of public apostasy. These may be regarded as types and tokens of the final eruption of evil in the age of Antichrist. The aftermath of Antiochus, of Julian the Apostate and in more recent memory the French Revolution, are times of unbelief which led to "a confederacy of evil", and bore the inexorable mark of the Antichrist.

> "These instances give us this warning. Is not the enemy of Christ, and His Church, to arise out of a certain special falling away from God? And is there no reason to fear that some such Apostasy is gradually preparing, gathering,

---

[50] ibid.

[51] Newman postulates the presence of personal being at the heart of all reality. Evil is not simply the negation of good but a real personal principle. Furthermore, he rejects the idea of impersonal trends or forces; personality was the operating power in the world.

[52] Tract LXXXIII p. 10.

hastening on in this very day.....Surely there is at this day a confederacy of evil, marshalling its hosts from all parts of the world, organizing itself, taking its measures, enclosing the Church of Christ in a net, and preparing the way for a general apostasy from it. Whether this very apostasy is to give birth to Antichrist, or whether he is still to be delayed, we cannot know; but at any rate this apostasy, and all its tokens, and instruments, are of the Evil One and savour of death."[53]

The chief strategy of the Antichrist will be deceit and counterfeit. He will act surreptitiously under the guise of good. His insidious nature is to take us off guard and overcome us with his blandishments. These supposed benefits are under the attractive banner of progress and disguised as the values of liberty, equality and fraternity proclaimed by the French Revolution. We must beware of such enticements for the situation is already alarming and the only recourse the Christian has is complete separation from the world.

"He promises you civil liberty; he promises you equality; he promises you trade and wealth; he promises you a remission of taxes; he promises you reform...or he promises you illumination, - he offers you knowledge, science, philosophy, enlargement of mind. He scoffs at times gone by; he scoffs at every institution which reveres them."[54]

The Religion of the Antichrist

Newman now takes a closer look at the evil nature of the so-called religion of the Antichrist. Its primary characteristic will be the the denial of the Incarnation. On this basis of negation a new form of religion will be set up. It will begin its destructive path by iconoclasm and gradually work its way towards a full profession of atheism. In a clever way it will still recognize man's need for religion; it will substitute more appealing idols than those it has demolished and will thereby establish a pseudo-religion. Such an apparent contradiction between the destruction of idols and the raising up of a new form of idolatry is illustrated by the

---

[53] ibid p. 12.

[54] ibid p. 13.

French Revolution.

> "...in the capital of that powerful and celebrated nation, there took place, as we all well know, within the last fifty years, an open apostasy from Christianity; not from Christianity only, but from every kind of worship which might retain any semblance or pretence of the great truths of religion. Atheism was absolutely professed; yet in spite of this, it seems a contradiction in terms to say it, "a strange worship" was introduced ...they proceeded to decree in the public assembly of the nation, the adoration of Liberty and Equality as divinities; and they appointed festivals besides in honour of Reason, the Country, the Constitution, and the virtues." [55]

Throughout these sermons Newman clearly states that he has confined his address to the patristic teaching on unfulfilled prophecy. He has however drawn instances from history in which the power of evil was unleashed, and presented a prima facie case for appealing to the imminent advent of the Antichrist. But in no such instance were all the marks of prophecy fulfilled. He refrains from identifying any particular case of widespread apostasy with the age or religion of the Antichrist. Nevertheless, such events constitute a paradigm of the future and as such are worthy of our notice and instruction.

The whole drift of these sermons is not to defend the Fathers on whether they were right or wrong in their historical judgments, or in the fearful presentiments they had for their age. When however the true meaning of history is considered, it is not the surface of events which matters, but their underlying depth and tendency. Subsequent events rather tend to confirm the interpretations of the Fathers and throw greater light on the mystery of evil. While the ambiguity remains in identifying the present signs as those of which prophecy speaks, we can still draw moral conclusions for our practical understanding of the times. Thus Christians may see the parallel with the past and begin

> "to *understand* that we are in the place in which the early Christians were ... to realize a state of things long past away; to feel that we are in a sinful world, a world lying in wickedness; to discern our position in it, that we are

[55] ibid. p. 21.

witnesses in it, that reproach and suffering are our portion -
so that we must not "think it strange" if they come upon us,
but a kind of gracious exception if they do not -to have our
hearts awake, as if we had seen Christ and his apostles, and
seen their miracles - awake to the hope and waiting for his
second coming, looking out for it, nay desiring to see the
tokens of it; thinking often and much of the judgment to
come, dwelling on and adequately entering into the thought,
that we individually shall be judged. All these surely are acts
of true and saving faith."[56]

The City of the Antichrist

Rome was the seat of empire when the prophecies concerning the
Antichrist were foretold, and hence it was thought that the Antichrist
would rise out of the imperial city. It is for this reason, and for its
relevance to the contemporary bitter opposition to Rome, that Newman
considers not only the time but the place of the Antichrist.

The background to Newman's changing regard for Rome can be
seen in Home Thoughts Abroad,[57] and later in the Apologia.[58] He first
regarded it as the centre of an evil Empire in opposition to the growth of
the Spiritual Kingdom of Christ. Influenced by the extreme
Protestantism of Joseph Mede (1586-1638) and Thomas Newton
(1704-1782), he applied to it the image of the whore of Babylon. Later
we find him under the influence of Froude struggling with his prejudice
towards the Roman Church, and gradually learning to distinguish the
genius loci, the pagan influence of Rome, from the Church of that name.
He then formulates the history of the city in three stages, as Rome
designating the seat of paganism, followed by the Church in Rome, and
finally the pagan spirit of Rome in the Church.[59]

Newman first presents the extreme Protestant position of the
Roman Church's connection with Antichrist. He gives a qualified

---

[56] Tract No. 83 p. 27.

[57] "Home Thoughts Abroad" first appeared in the British Magazine in 1836 and
was later published under the title, "How to Accomplish it," in *Discussions and
Arguments*, pp. 1-43.

[58] Cf. Apo. pp. 52ff.

[59] L.D. Volume iv.p.32. Cf. P.Misner, *Papacy and Development: Newman and the
Primacy of the Pope*, Leiden, 1977, pp.45-49.

answer to the question whether Rome "[as commonly said and believed among us] ... having an especial share in the events which will come at the end of the world by means or after the time of Antichrist."[60] The "stain on the imagination" still exercises its influence over him and he is still prepared to grant some substance to the Protestant view. "So far it would seem to be clear, that the prophecy itself has not been fully accomplished, whatever we decide about Rome's concern in it."[61]

At this time the "Prophetical Office of the Church viewed relatively to Romanism and Popular Protestantism" had now been published.[62] He had by now rejected his anti-Roman prejudice - "what accomplishment remains [of this prophecy] has reference not to Rome, but to some other object or objects of divine vengeance."[63] Indeed Rome may be absolved from God's wrath because of the Church's presence there, and the restraining power of God's elect. History has shown how the Church in Rome has so often stayed the power of destruction and suspended God's visitation. It may be chastised but not utterly overthrown. However, it is more to the point to believe that the prophecy refers not to the city, but to the spirit of evil which Rome has traditionally symbolized. It may simply be a type "whether of some other city, or of a proud and deceiving world."[64] There is still however a spirit of cruelty and corruption which has infected the Roman Church, which is a warning to us to avoid the contamination of the "mystery of iniquity."

The Persecution of Antichrist

Public persecution of the Church has long ceased since Christianity was established throughout the Roman Empire. With 1500 years of peace since the days of Constantine, it is understandable if Christians should fail to see that persecution though "not the *necessary* lot of the Church [is] at least one of her appropriate badges." This seems to be Christ's own intimation that persecution is something the

---

[60] Tract LXXXIII, p. 39.

[61] ibid.

[62] It had been published in 1837.

[63] Tract LXXXIII p. 35.

[64] ibid p. 38.

34

Church may expect, as being in keeping with her nature. Thus the persecution which is foretold at the end, is a mirror image of the Church's first beginnings. In this note of persecution, a common characteristic may be found between Christ's First Coming and His Second.

> "He left her in persecution, and He will find her in persecution. He recognizes her as His own, - He framed, and He will claim her, - as a persecuted Church, bearing His Cross. And that awful relic of Him which He gave her, and which she is found with at the end, she cannot have lost by the way."[65]

The apocalyptic passages from Daniel,[66] the Book of Revelation and the Gospel of Matthew are the basis for believing that a general persecution of the Church will come as a sign of the end. The early Fathers distinguished this final catastrophe from the violent persecutions they themselves experienced, and did not consider their own sufferings as the fulfilment of the prophecy. This final assault upon the Church differs therefore from former persecutions and is distinguished from them in four respects. Summarizing the teaching of the Fathers on this point, Newman observes:

> "In these four respects, then, not to look for others, will the last persecution be more awful than any of the earlier ones: in its being in itself fiercer and more horrible; in its being attended by a cessation of the ordinances of grace, 'the Daily Sacrifice'; and by an open and blasphemous establishment of infidelity, or some such enormity, in the holiest recesses of the Church; lastly, in being supported by a power of working miracles. Well is it for Christians that the days are shortened! shortened for the elect's sake, lest they should be overwhelmed - shortened, as it would seem, to three years and a half."[67]

Newman reiterates his caution not to suppose that times of trial for the Church can be other than warnings and signs that one day the final

---

[65] Tract No. 83 p. 42; S.D.xviii, p. 264

[66] Newman clearly has in mind Dan 7:15-27; 8:14; 9:27; 12:7,11,12.

[67] ibid. p. 46.

persecution will arrive. He warns of the danger of falling prey to credulous and alarmist calls that the end is near. Nevertheless,"signs do occur from time to time, not to enable us to fix the day, for that is hidden, but to show us that it is coming."[68] Persecution is a reminder to the Church that the victory over evil is not yet complete, but that a future final conflict is in store. Our present distress however is an image or token of the last battle to be fought, and personal holiness is the weapon to prepare for it. The purpose of these meditations is not to instil fear or speculate on the future, but to inspire a longing for Christ's coming. On that Last Day evil will be finally overcome, and the elect will be gathered from the hands of a wicked world.

Part Two
Prepare the Way of the Lord

A second group of sermons on the Advent theme underlines the necessity of spiritual preparation for the Coming of Christ. The first indication of this aspect was given in the afternoon series of 1824 when Newman chose the Sunday Collects as his text. The perspective is taken up again in 1829 when he gave a course on Personal Religion and Private Prayer, in which two of the sermons are for Advent Sundays.[69] There are however only slight allusions in these sermons to the Coming of Christ; they were written on the general theme of prayer and do not contain any specific reference to the present theme.

The idea of Advent as a time of personal meditation on the last things has a dominant place in Newman's sermons. It is developed under several aspects which underline the note of anticipation of Christ's Second Coming. Spiritual preparation is seen as a full-scale rehearsal for the drama of the Last Day. We are like actors preparing our lines and thereby anticipating the actual production before the curtain is raised. Without such diligent preparation we will not be able to play our part before the court of heaven.

---

[68] ibid p. 49.

[69] Course xxix *On personal religion and private prayer* contained two Advent sermons, Nos.220 and 221. The theme of prayer and eschatology will be considered later in Chapter Six.

Joy and Fear at the Day of Judgment

Though Christians long for the Coming of Christ and are indeed commanded to pray for it, it is first and foremost a time of judgment. Such a prospect instils great fear and raises the question how we can pray with sincerity for something which will be dreadful in its implications. Newman reminds us to

"...think of all this, and you will not deny that the thought of standing before Christ is enough to make us tremble. And yet His presence is held out to us by Himself as the greatest of all goods; all Christians are bound to pray for it, to pray for its hastening; to pray that we may speedily look on Him whom none can see without holiness, none but the pure in heart -and now the question is, how can we pray for it with sincerity?"[70]

The Advent sermon of 1836, from which the above quotation is taken, is entitled Shrinking from Christ's Coming. It continues the theme of the previous Sunday when Newman preached on the Day of Judgment, with Matt.25 as his text.[71] This text inculcates "a practical ruling conviction that every one of us must give an account of himself to God - a view fearful and solemn in itself." The certainty of the judgment is beyond question, and its nature is described under the image of fire to indicate the searching scrutiny of every man's work. Even though we now live under the dispensation of grace, no argument can be sustained on the grounds of God's infinite mercy, that justice and judgment will be waived. His justice is not absorbed by His mercy nor does His mercy absolve us from standing before Him in judgment. Each of God's attributes is as true as if its opposite did not exist. Hence His justice

"...is as true as if the other were not true. It must be as fully mastered and embraced, it must be as little encroached on or modified, as if no regeneration at all were made us about the efficacy of faith or the power of baptism."[72]

---

[70] P.P.S.v,4.

[71] We just have two sermons for Advent 1836. The unpublished sermon No. 435 is fragmentary. It was later combined with No. 400 and preached in Advent 1839.

[72] No. 435 p. 17.

While there is absolute certainty about the judgment to come, the Last Day is not meant as a message of doom and gloom. A miserable attitude arises from a neglect of true religion rather than as a result of it. Religion is fundamentally a blessing though it may appear at first sight as a severe and cheerless truth. The fear which it instils is not a slavish dread, but a deep reverence and acknowledgement of God's sovereignty. Despite, therefore, the anxiety at the thought of the Last Day, the Christian never loses the spirit of joy and gladness, and while we can never fully understand how joy and fear can be reconciled, the command to fear the Lord does not replace the Christian duty of ever rejoicing. On the surface they may appear contradictory, but at a deeper level they come together in the personal encounter with God.

> "...whatever be the duty of fearing greatly and trembling greatly at the thought of the Day of Judgment, and of course it is a great duty, yet the command so to do cannot reverse the command to rejoice; it can only so far interfere with it to explain what is meant by rejoicing. It is as clear a duty to rejoice in the prospect of Christ's coming, as if we were not told to fear it. The duty of fearing does but perfect our joy, which is informed and quickened by fear, and made thereby sober and reverent."[73]

An Anticipation of the Second Coming through Prayer

The mixed feelings of joy and fear may seem a paradox on the level of logical reason. Despite their apparent inconsistency, each emotion remains distinct and is not diluted by the other. Experience, however, takes us beyond the level of logic to an acceptance of matters we find difficult to reconcile. By simply trusting this fact of experience, we may acquire a deeper insight into these conflicting emotions. This is what happens when we come to pray. It is in this way that we are to approach the Coming of Christ, in which both joy and fear are intermingled. Hence we may anticipate what we shall feel *then*, by the mixed feelings we encounter *now* in our daily experience. The Coming of Christ is not only a future event but a present mystery which we can enter into through prayer. For prayer is the means par excellence by

---

[73] P.P.S.v,5.

38

which the object of faith is realized, while reason is a poor tool to convince us of the unseen world. It is not surprising, Newman observes, why we should have difficulty in believing in the next world, if we fail to pray.

> "Why? Because the next world is not a reality to him; it only exists in his mind in the form of certain conclusions and certain reasonings. It is but an inference; and never can be more, never can be present to his mind, until he acts, instead of arguing. Let him but give himself to such devotional exercises as we ought to observe in the presence of an All-Mighty, All-Holy and All-merciful God, and it will be a rare case indeed if his difficulties do not vanish."[74]

Prayer is a necessary means to maintain an eschatological perspective in daily Christian living. If we are to accustom ourselves to the realities of the next world it must be through the language of prayer, "for prayers and praises are the mode of his intercourse with the next world."[75] Like any other gift or talent it requires continuous practice. It is the way of sensitizing us to the reality of Christ's Coming and in detaching us from the gravitational pull of this world's pleasures.

> "Such is the effect of divine meditations; admitting us into the next world, and withdrawing us from this; making us children of God, by withal "strangers unto our brethren, even aliens unto our mother's children."[76]

Christians are commanded to pray continuously that Christ will hasten His kingdom and quickly bring to completion the number of the elect. This is not a selfish desire to bring this world to an end so that we may escape its present misery. It is not a rejection or a flight from duty, but an aspiration of hope in the prompt fulfilment of God's plan. There is an unavoidable conflict between the principles of this world and the next; so despite the efforts of Christians to promote the welfare of others, they will be seen as strangers and foreigners in the world's eye. Our prayer then must always be

---

[74] P.P.S.iv.15.

[75] ibid.

[76] ibid.

"that He would accomplish, - not curtail, but fulfil, - the circle of His Saints, and hasten the age to come without disordering this...When then we pray that He would come, we pray also that we may be ready; that all things may converge and meet in Him; that He may draw us as He draws near us, and make us holier, the closer He comes."[77]

In prayer we become conscious of the holiness of God and of our unworthiness before Him. This feeling of unworthiness in the presence of God should not however deter us from praying, for it is the means by which we are purified, and it is only the pure of heart who will see God. The process of purification continues until the Coming of Christ and the awareness of our sinfulness never fades. Praying therefore for His Coming is pursued, not in the complacent belief that we are ready for judgment, but in the hope of His grace that we may be prepared for it. In prayer we are but anticipating our encounter with Christ when we appear before the Holy One and are judged by Him.

"Consider what it is you mean by praying, and you will see that, at the very time you are asking for the coming of His kingdom you are anticipating that coming, and accomplishing the thing you fear."[78]

Anticipation through the Sacraments

Anticipating the future Coming of Christ becomes even more striking when we consider the significance of the Sacraments.[79] Though the final coming may be far into the future, Christ has left us means by which our present meeting with Him is an anticipation of our final encounter. Holy Communion "is in very form the anticipation of His coming, a near Presence of Him in earnest of it."[80] The sacrament is an encounter filled with joy and fear. For those who are unwilling to receive it, for fear of being condemned by an unworthy reception,

---

[77] P.P.S.v,4.

[78] ibid..

[79] This topic will be dealt with at some length in Chapter Six. However the Advent sermons contain references to it and can thus be briefly mentioned here.

[80] P.P.S.v,4.

40

Newman remarks that such fears will be exactly reproduced at the Second Coming. The order also in which we experience these feelings will be the same - fear first and then joy, sorrow and trial and then comfort and peace. At the Coming of Christ the encounter will be "fearful before it is ecstatic" and "as sudden as it is intimate." In the sacrament of the Last Supper we thus have a paradigm of the future emotions we will experience at His Final Coming.

Though the sacramental encounter is a form of anticipating Christ's Second Coming, it is not a direct manifestation. Newman reminds us that we are in the realm of faith and a veil separates us from Christ, who is present silently, hiddenly and secretly. But in the sacrament we gradually learn to bear the sight of Him, and steel ourselves before His future presence. Apart from being commanded to worship God, there is an internal rationale why we must do so. One day our very nature will be transformed, when we meet Him face to face. His judgment does not mean the mere passing of a sentence on our moral fitness, nor an impersonal application of reward and punishment. Something much more than a moral preparation is required. Unless we are accustomed to the outline of His face and are changed by it, standing before His presence will be a shattering experience. Hence Christ prepares us for this change through the sacraments, so that by drawing us gradually to Himself, we may not be overcome by His glory on the Last Day.

> "Why must they be partakers in what the Church calls Sacraments? I answer, they must do so, first of all and especially, because Christ tells them so to do. But besides this, I observe that we see this plain reason why, that they are one day to change their state of being. They are not to be here for ever. Direct intercourse with God on their part now, prayer and the like, may be necessary to their meeting Him suitably hereafter; and direct intercourse on His part with them, or what we call sacramental communion, may be necessary in some incomprehensible way, even for preparing their very nature to bear the sight of Him."[81]

---

[81] P.P.S.v,1.

Preparation of the Heart

Having considered something of the sacramental preparation for Christ's coming, Newman turns to the question of moral preparation.[82] Through the sacraments we become accustomed to the new state into which we are called; through obedience to conscience we are led to a radical conversion of heart. God has granted us privileged means of encounter through prayer and the sacraments. It remains for us to show our total surrender to Him by a single-minded desire to overcome our natural resistance to His call.

Sincerity and simplicity are the modern equivalents of what the Gospel means by "a perfect heart." If one could honestly say "I have not sinned against the heavenly vision", then one could look forward to meeting the Lord with great confidence and joy. If, however, we have failed to live according to our conscience, then it is with great anxiety that we approach the judgment-seat of Christ. The evidence of a good conscience is the testimony of our works; a mere profession of belief is insufficient proof of moral sincerity. We can never have certainty of our salvation, but if we have lived up to the light we have received, we can approach God's judgment with some measure of assurance.

> "Now I suppose, absolute certainty about our state cannot be attained at all in this life; but the nearest approach to such certainty which is possible, would seem to be afforded by the consciousness of openness and singleness of mind, this good understanding (if I may use such an expression) between the soul and its conscience, to which St. Paul so often alludes."[83]

Obedience to conscience is in Newman's words to have "a ruling sense of God's presence within", which allows Him to transform our mind and heart. What we lack is a willingness to be changed by God - a change which we cannot bring about solely by our own efforts. There is a natural reluctance to change for it ultimately means a complete surrender of oneself to God. The nominal Christian is one who pursues two ends - religion and the world. He wants to serve God and himself at

---

[82] The Advent sermons of 1838 may be divided into sacramental and moral preparation. No. 522 (P.P.S.v,1) is devoted to the sacramental side while No. 523 (P.P.S.v,17) and 524 (P.P.S.v,16) are concerned with the moral change necessary for encountering Christ at His Second Coming.

[83] P.P.S.v,17.

the same time, and does not allow God to penetrate his inner soul, for he has "a somewhat private hidden self at the bottom." The true Christian, however, has an awareness of God's presence within him, and, living by this conviction, each step of obedience is a step towards Christ. By living then according to our conscience, we have the moral preparation to sustain the scrutiny of the judgment, which the Coming of Christ entails.

A Spirit of Watchfulness

The Advent sermons of 1837 raise the question of how we are to maintain a living awareness of Christ's coming, in view of His prolonged absence. They are meditations on the Christian frame of mind which may be described as one of eschatological expectancy. Christ's visible departure at the Ascension was the start of His spiritual presence, which is no less real because it is unseen. To feel this presence requires a spirit of watchfulness and sensitivity.[84] Though He is hidden from the world,[85] we are in communion with Him in the Spirit.[86] In His absence we can prepare for His eventual return by dwelling on His words to watch and pray. We are in a state of ever waiting for Him, which only a lively faith can sustain.

> "...His prolonged absence has made it practically thought, that He never will come back in visible presence: and in the text he mercifully whispers into our ears, not to trust in what we see, not to share in that general unbelief, not to be carried away by the world, but to "take heed, watch and pray" and look out for His coming."[87]

This spirit of watchfulness, - whose New Testament term (γρηγορειν) Newman finds worthy of greatest attention, -is the characteristic which distinguishes the true Christian from the nominal one. In the manner of a parable, Newman enters into the feelings of one

---

[84] P.P.S.iv.22.

[85] P.P.S.iv.16.

[86] P.P.S.iv.15. These three sermons are numbered consecutively 486 (P.P.S.iv.22); 487 (P.P.S.iv.15); 488 (P.P.S.iv.16).

[87] P.P.S.iv.22.

who is eagerly awaiting a long-absent friend, on the assurance of his imminent return. Will not such a friend go through a whole range of feelings of expectancy? He will experience disappointment, sadness, boredom with the trivial, anxiety about the future, and at the same time suspense, joy, renewed hope and single-minded desire, anticipation of his arrival, all in the thought and affection of him. "To watch for Christ is a feeling such as all these; as far as feelings of this world are fit to shadow those of another."[88] It is the attitude of one

> "who has a sensitive, eager, apprehensive mind; who is awake, alive, quick-sighted, zealous in seeking and honouring Him; who looks out for Him in all that happens, and who would not be surprised, who would not be over-agitated or overwhelmed, if He found that He was coming at once."[89]

Such a vision of expectancy might be a dream, a contrived piece of make-belief, were it not founded on the solid ground of Christ's First Coming. It might be wishful thinking, the projection of our needs for fulfilment, the self-delusion of a fertile imagination, were it not for the certitude of faith formed in love. And with such faith, we do not look out *for* Christ on our own accord, but *with* Him through the spiritual presence He has left us. The ground for this lively apprehension of His return is our remembrance of His past mercy shown in His First Coming.

> "This then is to watch; to be detached from what is present, and to live in what is unseen; to live in the thought of Christ as He came once, and as He will come again; to desire His second coming, from the affectionate and grateful remembrance of His first."[90]

Watching is the acid test of the genuineness of our faith. Mere belief which is unaffected by love and expectation, untouched by hope or anxiety, is not real faith at all. Watching alone gives to our faith the living quality which captures the imagination and the affections. This is why detachment from the world is necessary, so as to resist its

---

[88] ibid.

[89] ibid.

[90] ibid.

44

secularizing power which "rusts the soul" and leaves us indifferent to the Coming of Christ. A mere "worldly religiousness", which is a "mixture of religion and unbelief", is grossly insufficient, though it is the commonplace experience of Christians. Without this eschatological stance towards the coming of Christ, our faith is little better than mere words. It is only the habit of watching that will keep our sensitivity to the next world alive, and lead us out of our ambivalence. Our temporizing with this present world and our standards of mediocrity weave a web of illusion, which one day will be swept aside with the manifestation of Christ.

We must therefore choose between two alternatives, either to live for this world or for the next. There is no easy compromise between the two, no middle ground where one can have a foot in both camps. This involves a gamble or a venture of faith which means placing the priorities of eternity over those of time. Our perspective has one fixed point, which is the Coming of Christ. This we must discern and prepare for, by detaching ourselves from this world. Commenting on this single-minded spirit of true Christians, Newman says:

"To one thing alone they are alive, His coming ...and when Christ comes at last, blessed indeed will be his lot. He has joined himself from the first to the conquering side; he has risked the present against the future, preferring the chance of eternity to the certainty of time; and then his reward will be but beginning, when that of the children of this world is come to an end."[91]

Newman illustrates the need for discernment in his comparison of the First and Second Coming. The First Coming differs from the Second in that Christ came in obscurity and hiddenness.[92] The example of His hidden life, His very ordinariness and even the contempt in which He was held by the world, confirm this truth. And what was true for Christ is true for us, and has been the condition of Christians ever since. Yet beneath this obscurity a training process is silently going on and a secret power is at work in preparing us for heaven. It is unobserved by the world and can only be recognized by the eyes of

[91] P.P.S.iv,15.

[92] The third sermon of this series, P.P.S.iv,16, entitled *Christ Hidden from the World*, was preached on the 4th Sunday of Advent and repeated the following day for the Christmas celebration.

faith. In Newman's view

> "..true religion is a hidden life in the heart; and though it cannot exist without deeds, yet they are for the most part secret deeds, secret charities, secret prayers, secret self-denials, secret struggles, secret victories."[93]

The commemoration of the birth of Christ reminds us that Christ has come into the world, that He has remained in it through His Holy Spirit, that He is to be found in the Church, in the poor and the afflicted, and particularly in the sacrament of Holy Communion, where we are specifically commanded to "discern the Lord's Body." But it is only by the power of discernment given us by the Holy Spirit that we will recognize His presence. It is to be found in the lives of holy people, who have a secret power and influence upon us.

A Spirit of Equanimity

Another feeling which Christ's Coming inspires, besides awe and reverence, is contentment and peace of mind. Newman's sermon on equanimity is an extended commentary on the epistle for the 4th Sunday of Advent.[94]He begins with an illustration in the life of St. Paul who, while in captivity and persecution, "should draw a picture of the Christian character as free from excitement and effort, as full of repose, as still and as equable, as if the great Apostle wrote in some monastery of the desert or some country parsonage."[95] Even in the most distressing situations the Christian lives with a serenity of mind because of his hope and confidence in the Coming of Christ.

Belief in Christ's Coming must create in us the mind of the pilgrim who is ready to depart at a moment's notice. It is to leave our material concerns behind and not be unsettled. Having no thought for tomorrow, however, is not to be confused with either passivity or fatalism. It means rather to look on the world in the light of eternity. It matters little whether Christ will come again in a short time or centuries from now.

---

[93] P.P.S.iv,16.

[94] The short verse from Philippians iv,4 prescribed as the first lesson for the day in the Book of Common Prayer.

[95] P.P.S.v,5.

46

What really matters is the kind of readiness and perception we have towards His Coming. It is this event which is our governing principle, a standpoint from which we may gain a true estimate of human life. The fact that He has come once is our assurance that He will come again, and has thrown a special light on our existence and final destiny.

> "One time or another Christ will come, for certain: and when He once *has* come, it matters not what length of time there was before He came; - however long that period may be, it has an end. Judgment is coming, whether it comes sooner or later, and the Christian realizes that it is coming; that is, time does not enter into his calculation, or interfere with his view of things. When men expect to carry out their plans and projects, then they care for them; and when they know these will come to nought, they give them over, or become indifferent to them."[96]

This calm frame of mind enables us to rid ourselves of the world of vanity and illusion. The values embraced by the worldly man will turn out to be as inappropriate "as faded flowers at a banquet". The Christian has a particular advantage over others for he sees things *now*, which will *then* be seen by all, as empty and fleeting vanities. At the core of the Christian life is an experience of peace. Though there are many things in the gospel intended to disturb and alarm us, the ultimate fruit of embracing it fully is "peace which surpasseth all understanding." There may be turmoil and confusion all around, but the Christian stands in the eye of the typhoon where calm and peace are found. The Second Coming of Christ may cause fright and anxiety, but the remembrance of His First Coming restores a spirit of equanimity and peace. Thus the Christian, in Newman's own words, lives between "...fearing and trembling, watching and repenting, because Christ is coming; joyful, thankful, and careless of the future because He is come."[97]

---

[96] ibid.

[97] ibid.

Part Three
The Delay of The Parousia

The long delay between the First and Second Coming and the consequent difficulty for Christians to maintain a state of expectancy is frequently considered by Newman. All the sermons on the apparent absence of Christ presuppose this dilemma of faith. In these sermons he studiously avoids directly answering objections to the belief in the Second Coming; his aim is rather to encourage and explain the dispositions of the heart which are implied in the belief. The Advent series of sermons in 1840,[98] however, while still retaining the practical objectives suitable to a parish congregation, are concerned more at meeting objections to the belief itself. They have an affinity with the University Sermons on the relation of faith and reason. In this series Newman proceeds in the argumentative style of an apologist to present a spirited defence of Christian belief in the Second Coming. He examines each of the objections against it and answers them with some telling argumenta ad hominem.

Waiting for Christ[99] begins with a highly condensed introduction on the question of Christ's promise concerning the Parousia. Either Christ gave a highly ambiguous statement about when He would return, or the early Christians grossly misunderstood His words. When He said He would come quickly He did not mean soon; He simply meant that it would be sudden, but gave no indication of the time. The early Christians were therefore mistaken in their belief regarding the time of His arrival, though not in its sudden and unannounced character. It is precisely because of its suddenness that His followers are to observe a constant readiness and look out for signs of His Coming. The Book of Revelation, which was written long after the expectation of His imminent return had subsided, still reminds us of the Christian duty to be alert for the Day of the Lord. St. Paul also, even though he found it necessary to dampen the enthusiasm of the Thessalonians, enjoins

---

[98] The first two, Nos. 570 and 571 are combined into one sermon published as P.P.S.vi,17 which falls naturally into two sections as originally delivered. The third is No. 572 (P.P.S.vi,18). Both published sermons were later ascribed to the Ascension, cf. Letter to Copeland on the rearrangement of the Parochial and Plain according to the season of the year, L.D., xxviii, pp. 250-256. The Ascension had a particular importance for Newman as marking the end of one era and introducing the age of the last times; the sermons were however originally written for Advent.

[99] The title of P.P.S.vi,17.

Christians to sustain an attitude of waiting and watching.

Nevertheless, eighteen hundred years of waiting is a long time for generations of Christians to be on the watch-tower. It places a heavy burden on reason to provide motives for a spirit of readiness. Christians of former times have been so ridiculously wrong in interpreting the signs of His Coming that reason would counsel prudence and moderation. Moreover, the alarmist calls so frequently heard during times of crisis have been discredited by history. It can be further objected that the recurring phenomenon of millenarianism[100] saps Christian energies, which could well be used in caring for the world, rather than living in indolence and superstition. Newman clearly states the objection in the following way:

> "...we cannot help using our reason: there are no more grounds to expect Christ now than at those many former times, when as the event showed, He did not come. Christians have ever been expecting the last day, and ever meeting with disappointment. They have seen what they thought symptoms of His coming and peculiarities in their own times, which a little more knowledge of the world, a more enlarged experience, would have shown them to be common to all times. They have ever been frightened without good reason, fretting in their narrow minds, and building on their superstitious fancies."[101]

This objection against the attitude of Christians in watching for the Second Coming overstates the case. It also contains a thinly disguised element of scoffing at their belief. Christians have doubtlessly been mistaken in the past, but better far to misread the signs of the times than never to expect Him. We must make a choice between what Scripture bids us and what a skeptical world would have us do. Nowhere does Scripture warn us against superstition, which is anathema to the rationalist mind, but against a high-minded complacency in our own powers. Moreover the argument may be turned around to show the credulousness of the objectors themselves:- have they not ever been expecting the demise of religion and of the Church? They argue in much the same fashion as they condemn, that religion has had its day

---

[100] Newman's own brother, Francis, fell under the spell of Darby's millenarianism and became a member of the Plymouth Brethren. He later became agnostic and a bitter foe of John Henry.

[101] P.P.S.vi,17.

and that its end is near. They believe in an age of enlightenment in which the march of intellect will put paid to religious superstition. And the signs and indications they allege are the ever-weakening position of the Church and the growing strength of reason. Until now however, their predictions and expectations have not been fulfilled.

What both sets of expectations have in common is a false interpretation of the times during a period of rapid change. Since both come to a similar conclusion i.e. that the end is near, and both parties hold a similar expectation, then "there cannot be anything very extravagant in the expectation itself."[102] Thus there is a case in principle for believing that either the end of the world or of the Church is imminent, since both positions are logically the same.

> "And God would have us give our minds to the latter side of the alternative, to open them to impressions from this side viz. that the end is coming - it being a wholesome thing to live as if that will come in our day, which may come any day."[103]

A Christian View of History

Before taking up the second objection, Newman gives an excursus on the Christian view of history, by contrasting it with the Jewish view. Both share a linear conception up to the point of the birth of Christ. For the Christian, however, history has reached its climax in the Christ-Event, and subsequent events may be considered as simply marking time. For the Jew on the other hand the line proceeds uninterrupted, since the coming of the Messiah is still awaited. Thus we have the contrast between a future which is as yet undetermined and one whose goal of history is now realized. The Jews could only look forward to the fulfilment of prophecy while the Christian Church has within it the experience of the mystery fulfilled. On this basis Newman argues that the nature of Christian and Jewish expectations is different. The Jews recognized the delay in His coming and lived in hope, but the delay of the Second Coming is not recognized in the Christian scheme. This view of Newman is equivalent to what modern theology describes by

---

[102] ibid.
[103] ibid.

50

saying that the End-time has arrived though the End has not yet come.[104] He sees the Christian as living more by faith than by hope, for the assurance of the future has been given, and the end of history in Christ is ever present.

> "Earth has had its most solemn event, and seen its most august sight; and therefore it was the last time. And hence, though time intervenes between Christ's first and second coming, it is not *recognized* (as I may say) in the Gospel scheme, but is, as it were, an accident. For so it was, that up to Christ's coming in the flesh, the course of things ran straight towards that end, nearing it by every step; but now, under the Gospel, that course has (if I may so speak) altered its direction, as regards His second coming, and runs, not towards the end, but along it and on the brink of it; and is at all times equally near that great event, which, did it run towards, it would at once run into. Christ then, is ever present at our doors; as near eighteen hundred years ago as now, and not nearer now than then; and not nearer when He comes than now."[105]

Newman reminds his congregation that Christians now live in a time when the fullness of revelation is made present. The history of the past and the future has now been absorbed into the mystery of Christ. Revelation has attained its definitive form and the future history of salvation is the unfolding of the mystery of Christ. Since we do not expect any further revelation, the end of history is already contained in what has been revealed; its consummation and goal are but the later manifestation of something already present. Hence the Christian perspective on history allows us to live and act as though the end has come.

The End-time has begun with the ascension of the risen Lord. The decisive victory has been achieved and all that remains is the history of gathering to the full the fruits of Christ's sacrifice on the cross. Our humanity is wrapped up in the risen humanity of Christ our Priest, who now makes intercession for us. Thus we are in a time of blessing which is made present sacramentally, in a manner befitting our condition of faith. This blessing is in substance the same as what it shall be, when we

---

[104] For the distinction between die Endzeit and das Ende cf D.S.Russell, *The Method and Message of Jewish Apocalyptic*, London, S.C.M., 1964, p. 24.
[105] P.P.S.vi,17.

meet Him face to face.

"Thus we are in all times of the Gospel, brought close to His Cross. We stand, as it were, under it, and receive its blessings fresh from it; only that since, historically speaking, time has gone on, and the Holy One is away, certain outward forms are necessary, by way of bringing us again under His shadow; and enjoy those blessings through a mystery, or sacramentally, in order to enjoy them really. All this witnesses to the duty both of remembering and of looking out for Christ, teaching us to neglect the present, to rely on no plans, to form no expectations for the future, but so to live in faith, as if He had not left us, so in hope, as if He had returned to us. We must try to live as if the Apostles were living, and we must try to muse upon our Lord's life in the gospels, not as a history, but as if a recollection."[106]

The Charges of Credulity and Superstition

Newman began his sermon on Waiting for Christ by defending the principle of looking out for Christ's Coming as an eminently reasonable attitude for Christians. Now he examines the charges of superstition and credulity which are alleged to be the practical result of such belief. He admits that through ignorance and enthusiasm, Christians have been mistaken in particulars, but not wrong in principle. But even in particulars he is ready to defend the recognition of God's providence in the events of history. Christians have not been deluded by imagining natural disasters or social revolutions were not intended by God as signs. These events have a purpose and are right to be considered. But we must dissociate ourselves from "enthusiasts, sectaries and wild presumptuous men." Though the Christian cannot identify any signs which may indicate that the end is near, it does not follow that he is wrong to discern God's hand in them. They are merely tokens, approximations, possibilities of the end, but signs nonetheless of God's presence.

"He still makes signs to us. But His voice is so low, and the world's din is so loud, and His signs are so covert, and the

---

[106] ibid.

52

world is so restless, that it is difficult to determine when He
addresses us, and what He says. Religious men cannot but
feel, in various ways, that His providence is guiding them
and blessing them personally, on the whole; yet when they
attempt to put their finger upon the times and places, the
traces of His presence disappears."[107]

However strong the evidence of God's personal providence may
appear to us, it is insufficient to convince others of it.[108] Nevertheless,
religious minds should not be put off from trusting in signs even to the
extent of appearing credulous, or perturbed by the fear of superstition.
It is better to have a devotional heart, which may exaggerate the signs of
His Coming, than a calculating mind which is impervious to belief. The
wild theories and alarmist calls come from those who have left the path
of true religion. Adherence to the revealed word of Scripture and
attendance at the Church's sacraments will be a sufficient safeguard
against adventist appeals. In a passage which could be applied to the
followers of Irving and Drummond[109] he says:

"Hence you find numbers running eagerly after men who
profess to work miracles, or who denounce the Church as
apostate, or who maintain that none are saved but those who
agree with themselves, or anyone, who without warrant of his
being right, speaks confidently. Hence the multitude is open
to sudden alarms.."[110]

The true Christian, however, is he who has found his stay in God's
revealed word, who has the equanimity and peace of the Gospel and is
not moved by the false prophets of the day.

---

[107] ibid.

[108] A good example of how deep Newman's belief was in God's providence can be
seen in P.P.S.iii.9. A firm belief in Special Providence was a strong feature of the
evangelical creed cf. Elizabeth Jay. *The Religion of the Heart*. Clarendon Press, pp. 97-
102.

[109] For an account of the millenialist religious groups of the period cf.
A.L.Drummond, *Edward Irving and His Circle*. London. J. Clarke and Co., 1938, pp.
126-135; W.H.Oliver, *Prophets and Millenialists, the uses of Biblical Prophecy in
England from the 1790s to the 1840s*, Oxford 1978, pp. 124-149.

[110] P.P.S.vi.17

Faith in Christ's Coming transcends Reason

Newman continues his defence of the eschatological temper of looking out for the Parousia, in the last of his Advent sermons of 1840. With a title reminiscent of his University Sermons,[111] he deals not merely with the relation of reason and faith but also with the role of the imagination in helping us to experience a vivid realization of the Second Coming. The starting point is similar to the previous sermon in that it begins with the objection that we have no grounds for believing in the imminent coming of the Lord. To work oneself into a state of expectancy and alarm would be a grave self-deception. It would be nothing other than mere pretence to make ourselves feel that the end is near, when we know that in all probability it is still far off. What the objection amounts to is that Reason must be the criterion and judge of belief and the authenticity of our feelings.

Newman flatly denies the premise. Not only is it possible to have aspirations and desires which reason regards with disapproval, but it is perfectly reasonable to have them. Reason rightly acts as a guide and check to the affective life, but it cannot dictate the feelings we can or ought to have. Our imagination and emotions have a life of their own and are not suppressed by rules of logical calculation. And so it is in religious matters; though we have no reason for believing in the imminent return of Christ on the grounds of probability - there are certainly no clear signs of it at present - it does not follow that hopes and desires for His speedy arrival are irrational, and that such feelings are thereby unauthentic. It is perfectly reasonable to trust in someone's word beyond what reason decrees. We are in fact commanded to do so in the case of Christ's promise that He will come again.

> "What Almighty God then requires of us is.... to hope, fear, expect our Lord's coming, more than reason warrants, and in a way which His word alone warrants; that is, to trust Him above our reason. You say, that it is not probable Christ will come at this time, and therefore you cannot expect it. Now, I say, you can expect it. You must feel there is a chance that He will come. Well, then, dwell on that chance; open your

---

[111] No. 572 (P.P.S.vi,18) is entitled *Subjection of the Reason and Feelings to the Revealed Word*.

mind to it..."[112]

This does not mean that we should be so excited as to be thrown into a frenzy over His coming, but that we should impress the image of it on our heart. This is what a spirit of faith demands. Once there are reasonable grounds for believing in His word, faith provides its own evidence and is not boxed in by a predetermined rationalism. For faith goes beyond reason and though not discounting or abandoning it, does not rest on the logical conclusion of a syllogism.[113]The same is also true for hope which is not determined by the evidence required for certainty.

> "..what is true of faith is true of hope.We may be commanded, if so be, to hope against hope, or to expect Christ's coming, in a certain sense, against reason. It is not inconsistent with God's general dealings towards us, that He should bid us feel and act as if that were at hand, which yet, if we went by what experience tells us, we should say was not likely to be at hand."[114]

We are not only to believe in the Second Coming but to live in a vivid realization of it. Even though the weight of probability is against the imminent return of Christ, the feelings it engenders can authentically be experienced now. There can be an immediacy of expectation and fear, even though the event is in the distant future. Moreover these feelings are not contrived but real, and are based on Christ's word that He will come and come suddenly. In fact we have a duty to allow the imagination to impress the thought upon our consciousness and act upon the knowledge of His coming. In this way we will have a living awareness, which moves us to hope and believe, rather than pay lip-service by notional assent.

It is precisely on this crucial point that the Christian rests his case for having a vivid apprehension of Christ's Coming. Acting on the truth to the degree of light that we have, is also the remedy against skepticism

---

[112] P.P.S.vi,18

[113] Cf. "The Tamworth Reading Room," *Discussions and Arguments, p.* 296: "It [Religion] never has been a deduction from what we know; it has ever been an assertion of what we are to believe. It has never lived in a conclusion; it has ever been a message, or a history, or a vision". This was written in February 1841, less than two months after the composition of the sermon.

[114] P.P.S.vi,18.

and the tyranny of reason. On the grounds of reason alone, skepticism in matters of faith would be the inevitable result, but our minds and hearts are formed differently. We may not have sufficient evidence to convince others, but we have sufficient for our own case to trust and to act upon the truth.

> "...the Christian's character is formed by a rule higher than that of calculation and reason, consisting in a Divine principle or life, which transcends the anticipations and criticisms of ordinary men. Judging by mere worldly reason the Christian ...ought to be doubting and hesitating in his faith, because his evidence for it might be greater than it is; he ought to have no expectation of Christ's coming, because Christ has delayed so long; but not so; his mind and heart are formed in a different mould."[115]

The End of the World

There is a symmetry in Newman's conception between the end of the world and the beginning of creation. As recorded in Scripture, both are the result of the direct intervention of God. Just as the world began in an instant by divine fiat, so will it end, if anything, with even more abruptness. It will not wither away, nor end with a whimper, but with the swift decree of God who calls a halt. All created things have a natural growth and decay subject to evolution. But evolution can no more explain the beginning as it can the end; it is simply concerned with the process within time. The end, in Newman's view, will also herald a new age of miracles, and here again we see the symmetry between the First and the Second Coming. Just as the beginning and the end are the two great sovereign acts of God towards creation, the First and Second Coming are His merciful acts of initial and final redemption.

> "Whenever He comes He will cut things short... And as He will end, so did He begin the world abruptly...and as He began without beginning, so will He end without an ending."[116]

---

[115] ibid.
[116] ibid.

56

God's sovereignty extends over the work of man's own hands. His overarching providence is the framework within which our contribution to life can be truly estimated. It is He who decides the value of our lives, whether they are long and rich in accomplishment, or short and meagre in fruit. The only true measure is how far we have been obedient to His will. Though Newman grants no excuse for idleness nor underestimates the value of work, he insists on the fact that human progress must be evaluated in the light of the Second Coming of Christ.

"...our efforts and beginnings, though they be nothing more, are just as necessary in the course of His Providence, as could be the most successful accomplishment... yet our work, finished or unfinished, will be acceptable, if done for Him. There is no inconsistency, then, in watching yet working, for we may work without setting our hearts on our work. Our sin will be if we idolize the work of our hands; if we love it so well as not to bear to part with it. The test of our faith lies in our being able to fail without disappointment."[117]

**Part Four
Sermons of the Day**

The Advent sermons during Newman's last two years at St. Mary's are marked by the note of poignancy as he is assailed by growing doubts of remaining in the Anglican communion.[118] In the aftermath of Tract xc, his constant preoccupation was to determine the degree to which the Church of his birth bore the signs of Christ's presence. Advent directs our attention to the Parousia, and this includes the notion of Christ's presence as well as His future arrival. In the season of 1841 and 1842[119] Newman thus applies the theme of Christ's

---

[117] ibid.

[118] Newman many years later describes this period as being "on my death-bed, as regards my membership with the Anglican Church." Apo. p 147.

[119] The Advent Sermons for 1841 are S.D. xii (583), xxii (584), xxiii (586) and xxiv (585). We have six sermons in 1842 on the Church as the Christian Empire which began two weeks before Advent and extended through the Advent Season viz. SD xiv (593), xv (594), xvi (595), xvii (596), xviii (566) and P.P.S.vii.3 (189). This later series will be considered in Chapter Four under the Church as Eschatological Sign.

Coming to recognizing the signs of His presence within the Church.

Despite his general aim to confine his preaching to moral and doctrinal instruction, Newman was aware of the tendency of these sermons to stir controversy. The Sermons of the Day are more closely affected by the circumstances[120] of the time; though admittedly controversial, the difference between the printed volume and his actual preaching should also be borne in mind.[121] When he published the sermons in 1843 he added a word of caution to the reader. The Advent sermons were not intended to undermine confidence where no doubt existed, but should be considered as retrospective essays addressed to those who had serious questions about remaining in the Anglican Church. These doubts were such as arise from a sincere search for truth, rather than the more common variety which result from defects of moral conduct.[122]

The Romeward march of Tractarians of the *Via Media* had already begun, and, though conscious of his influence on its younger members, Newman did not wish to promote any greater alienation than was already there. We have his word that he was addressing those who had begun to question the Anglican claims to be the Church of the ancient faith. But the real person to whom they are addressed is none other than Newman himself. Thus the sermons reflect the author's own search for Christ's presence in the Church, in the spirit of Advent waiting.

The Presence of Christ in the Church

Advent reminds us that Christ came "without observation" and that His presence among us is hidden. "The Kingdom of God cometh not with observation; neither shall they say, Lo here! or Lo there! *for* the kingdom of God is within you". This kingdom is unlike the kingdoms of the world, which are maintained by power and might. It began silently without force though with an inward power, but it will end triumphantly and be seen by all. Though it is "an inward and secret presence", Christ has given us external signs to guide us to Him. He

---

[120] "They have necessarily an historical and controversial aspect, though most of them treat of matters of deep and unfailing interest and of vast practical importance." Copeland, Preface to New Edition, Sermons of the Day, 1869.

[121] Appendix Note C in Apologia pro Vita Sua p. 312.

[122] Cf Note to Sermon xxi of Sermons of the Day, pp. 308-9.

58

has made the Church His appointed home and it is there that we must seek Him. It shall be known by the spirit of peace and equanimity it breathes; but when controversy and restlessness are rife,[123] there may be reason to doubt His presence and fear that He has abandoned it.

Since we need tokens and signs of God's presence, "Christ in mercy to all who seek Him, has been accustomed in all ages,... to hold forth certain plain and general tokens of His presence, to show the world where He is to be found."[124] He has provided two sets of signs, the external notes by which the Church is known, and the internal tokens of His grace within it. The external signs may fade and become barely visible, but while the inward signs remain, we have the assurance of His presence. The outward signs are supplementary and solely a means of leading us to Christ; they cease to be relevant once we have found Him. True religion is hidden in the heart and is found ultimately in our personal relationship with God. It is by the tokens of our interior life, rather than by our allegiance to an institution, that His presence is manifested to us at all times.

> "Now this is a distinction very necessary in all ages of the Church, for different reasons: when her outward glory is great, by way of turning attention to our own hearts, and our personal responsibility; and when it is obscured, in order to keep our faith from failing, and to revive our hope; at all times to hinder our being engrossed by what is external to the loss of what is inward to religion."[125]

Moreover, the public notes of the Church are not intended for its members, but for those outside it. They simply are meant to lead men to the decisively more important signs of its inner life, and for all practical purposes are superseded by them. Thus we must not be alarmed when the visible notes of the Church lose their shine. The external marks are not her only signs; should they disappear, the more significant proof of His presence still remains, in the personal experiences of His blessings. These "truer" and "more precious" tokens are worship and the sacraments through which Christ makes Himself present to us. With these means of grace and holiness in the Church, we do not have to look

---

[123] S.D. xxi; P.P.S.iv,12 *The Church a Home for the Lonely.*

[124] S.D. xxii.

[125] S.D.xxii, p. 328.

for other more dramatic signs of Christ's presence among us.[126]

> "It seems then, and it is a great source of comfort at a time like this, when the public notes of the Church shine so faintly and feebly among us to have cause to believe, that her private tokens are the true portion of Christians; that her private tokens are meant to guide them; and if these are vouchsafed to us they are God's guide to us and signs of His presence and that we need not look out for others."[127]

The Church will not Fail

The purpose of these sermons was to build confidence in the Anglican Church at a time when morale was low and defections to the Church of Rome were increasing. The loss, as he perceived, of the note of catholicity,[128] left him with a sense of abandonment that the Church of his birth had strayed from the path of Tradition. The apocalyptic texts of Advent reminded him of God's judgment on the Church falling into error "as if some abomination of desolation were coming upon us". As the foundations seemed to be crumbling he turned to the real reasons for remaining in the Anglican Community. These reasons, he admits, are often difficult to articulate and seldom satisfy the objections of enemies. But in being most personal, these inward signs of Christ's presence are the source of our hope in times of distress.

> "But still it holds good, that a man's real reason for attachment to his own religious communion, why he believes it to be true, why he is eager in its defence, why he feels indignant at being invited to abandon it, is not any series of historical or philosophical arguments, not anything merely beautiful in its system, or supernatural, but what it has done for him and for others; his confidence in it as a means by which men may be brought nearer to God, and may become

[126] Once again Newman is referring here to the extravagant practices of enthusiasts who sought the signs of the Spirit similar to pentecostalism.

[127] ibid. p. 332

[128] The recent appointment of an Anglican bishop of Jerusalem weakened the argument of the Via Media for the note of catholicity. Cf. Apo., p. 141-146

better and happier."[129]

The final sermon of this series is a brilliant piece of rhetoric which draws on the example of Elijah as the prophet of the latter days. Elijah is associated with delivering the Church from evil fortune and restoring it as the true Temple of God. He is the type of John the Baptist who is the herald of the Kingdom. But the role of Elijah is not exhausted by this partial fulfilment in the Baptist. He is the prophet associated with all moments of crisis in the Church. At such times the situation of the Church resembles the final period of apostasy, and thus the lesson of Elijah has a contemporary relevance for Newman.

"Whereas in one sense, all days resemble that last day, whereas Christ is ever coming, the love of many ever failing, and iniquity ever abounding - in this respect Elias is ever entering upon his mission, and in his power and spirit the ministers of Christ must ever labour."[130]

Newman develops several aspects of the history of Elijah and applies them to his own personal situation. The prophet was not in communion with the Church of Moses; he did not worship at the Temple and yet the Bible records that he was present with Moses on the mount of Transfiguration. The analogy is apt and encouraging for those who find themselves separated from the great body of Christians, and assures them that they may still remain in the presence of Christ. Secondly, Elijah's mission was limited - he did all that he could. He fulfilled the definite work that God has assigned to him, yet realized that he was not required to set everything right. He was not commissioned to restore all the privileges of the people of Israel, but to continue to teach them their duty within the system he had inherited. Being in despondency at the state of the Church, he withdrew in isolation and it was there that God spoke to him privately in the deep recesses of his heart. He heard God's voice, not in the strong gale, nor in the earthquake, nor in fire but in "a still small voice."

This account of the history of Elijah resonates with Newman's thoughts and feelings in the period which followed on the publication of the last Tract. The Via Media had become a paper theory; he feared separation from his Church, yet wished to retain communion with it.

---

129 S.D.xxiii, p. 347.

130 S.D.xxiv, pp. 368-9.

Moreover, he intended not to go beyond what God had asked him but to continue faithfully, though quietly, in his service as an Anglican priest. He saw the parallel of his predicament in each aspect of Elijah's life, and this confirmed and comforted him in his decision to remain in the Anglican Church. The Advent of 1841 was a time for being patient, for equanimity of spirit, for waiting and watching for that "still small voice" at the Lord's Coming.

A Summary of the Chapter

In the Advent sermons we have our first picture of the style and content of Newman's eschatology. It is marked by a tension between the "now" and the "not-yet" of salvation. To the left of the drawing lie two groups of sermons which depict a salvation of the "not-yet". In Parts One and Three, his attention has been drawn to the Second Coming. The unfulfilled prophecies of the end underline the idea of future judgment and the eschatological watching for His arrival presupposes that salvation is yet to come. To the right of the picture, there are two other groups of sermons in which Newman has portrayed the present state of our salvation. Parts Two and Four relate to the First Coming, when Christ brought salvation and offered us the means to encounter Him in mercy. In our spiritual preparation for the fulness of salvation, we have a present anticipation in the gift of the gospel. Likewise, His permanent presence in the Church is an assurance that He has already come and is known in the inward tokens of grace.

Having seen the general picture, we shall now look in some detail at each part of the diptych, beginning in Chapter Two with the left side of judgment. This will then be followed in Chapter Three with the bright side of the portrait of eternal life.

CHAPTER TWO

THE SEVERE SIDE OF ESCHATOLOGY

Introduction

The first chapter tried to show that Newman's eschatology was grounded on the governing principle of the Coming of Christ. His First Coming established a new creation, and His Return in glory will mark the return of creation to God, who will then be "all in all". This primary affirmation of Christian eschatology constitutes man's hope in the ultimately "friendly" nature of things. Without such a hope life could not be sustained, and human existence would amount to nothing more than a meaningless passion. By its very nature however, hope implies the possibility of missing the mark as well as the realization of a goal. It includes the note of uncertainty in the pursuit of future fulfilment.

This possibility of ultimate failure turns our attention to the dark or severe side of eschatology. It is based on the experience of evil which threatens our future fulfilment and is a permanent challenge to despair. At the root of all religious consciousness therefore, lies man's helplessness in the face of evil, which drives him to look beyond himself for redemption. He seeks a remedy for the conflict within and without, and hopes for the ultimate resolution of the problem of evil. Here we touch on the significance of eschatology for this is where the final issue of good and evil is addressed.

In its simplest terms, the Judeo-Christian tradition is a religion of deliverance from evil by the infinite goodness of God. According to it, evil exists as the result of a fall from grace made possible by the gift of freedom. Human freedom therefore stands as the backdrop to the moral structure of life in which the conflict of good and evil is waged. Our moral responsibility is the exercise of such freedom. It informs us that we are accountable human beings, and are to be judged accordingly. Being accountable means to count for something, and hence the value of human life is affirmed, a value which is deemed worthy of being weighed in an eternal balance. In Christian eschatology the Second Coming of Christ is attended by a universal judgment which is the ultimate criterion and sanction of our ethical nature. While God's sovereign design is to bring all things to fulfilment in Christ, human freedom retains its capacity to frustrate His plans. We have therefore the real possibility of the futility of human life which the doctrine of eternal punishment implies.

The present chapter examines Newman's treatment of the severe side of eschatology. It begins with a brief account of the human moral condition and its relation to evil. Only by understanding the roots of sin and guilt can we form an appreciation of the final judgment which is the main theme of the chapter. Inherent in the notion of judgment is some form of punishment, but the question of the eternity of punishment is an independent issue. Though connected with the Last Judgment it is therefore better to treat it separately, as is done in part three.

The severe side of religion permeates the whole of Newman's Anglican sermons. Unlike the theme of the first chapter where a well-defined genre, the Advent sermons, formed the basis of the analysis, the present subject does not lend itself to a similar method. It has been necessary to consider the complete sermon material, though certain courses such as his Lenten sermons have a special relevance to the topic.

Part One
The Roots of Severity

The Consciousness of Sin and Guilt

Newman's early sermons at St. Clement's contain earnest declarations on man's corrupt nature and the need for repentance. Though he did not subscribe to the belief in total human depravity, but recognized in the natural virtues firm evidence to the contrary,[1] he stressed that we are all sinners in the sight of God.[2] Human pride blurs an awareness of this deeper truth and blinds us to our real spiritual condition. To awaken us "from our insensibility" we must "be exposed to the wrath of God" for only then will we "feel the wound" of our

---

[1] Newman's religious conversion took place in an atmosphere of moderate Calvinism cf Apo. p. 4. His early sermons show that he did not accept the extreme Calvinist view of total human depravity cf No.21 preached on 19th Sept. 1824: "the doctrine of original corruption allows natural generosity, honour etc. - implying principally alienation from God."

[2] No.3.

damaged nature.[3] Our state of rebellion against God makes us "so corrupt and blind as to have no adequate feeling of the extent of odiousness and pollution conveyed by the word."[4] Moreover our natural tendency to attend only to the pleasant and bright side of the Gospel, leads to a form of denial about our real situation. Thus many people have "no abiding conviction of their own guilt and depravity, the need of a Saviour or the excellence of holiness."[5]

The immediate object of these early sermons is to conscientize the hearer into a personal realization of inner corruption. The process begins with the stirrings of conscience which gives us "an innate sense of weakness and guilt."[6] Its next stage is to uncover the secret faults which have lain dormant through want of seriousness or culpable ignorance[7] until one feels the pain and bitterness of human nature.[8] And finally it concludes with the recognition of the perilous condition in which we stand. In less startling language - which is such a feature of his "Scott and Newton days" - but losing none of their severity, the published sermons continue to underline the conviction about human sinfulness. He appeals for a root and branch examination of the heart.[9] Only by examining the structure of our minds and courageously peeling off the layers of self-deception, can we arrive at the core truth of our moral helplessness.

> "My object has been, as far as a few words can do it, to lead you to some true notion of the depths and deceitfulness of the heart, which we do not really know. It is easy to speak of human nature as corrupt in the general, to admit it in the general, and then get quit of the subject; as if the doctrine being once admitted, there was nothing more to be done with it. But in truth we can have no real apprehension of the doctrine of our corruption, till we view the structure of our minds, part by part; and dwell and draw out the signs of our

---

[3] No.4.

[4] No.10.

[5] No.18.

[6] No.133.

[7] No.19.

[8] No.74.

[9] Newman took the occasion of his birthday each year for such a thorough self-examination. Cf L.D., vol.ii p. 5.

weakness, inconsistency, and ungodliness, which are such as
can arise from nothing else than some strange original defect
in our moral nature."[10]

The fear of one's salvation as a motive for a change of heart can
scarcely be disguised in Newman's early sermons. Nevertheless he even
then averts to the danger of preaching a ministry of fear.[11] It is "a
comparatively grovelling or sordid way of serving God" but, he adds, "it
is the best, the only way for sinners to begin to serve God in."[12] Self-
interest is not to be despised as unworthy if it has the salutary effect of
getting one started on the road to true repentance. Fear in itself may be
inadequate and in retrospect appear unchristian, but it is a self-
authenticating truth of natural religion. Revelation completes rather than
substitutes for conscience[13] whose fearful voice is to be trusted,
precisely because it tells us of our guilt.[14]

While urging us to feel "the extent and depth of our guilt"[15] and
extremely conscious of his own acute fears for salvation,[16] Newman
clearly distinguishes between moral and pathological guilt.[17] Disturbing
emotions which come from an honest examination of conscience need
not be dismissed as unhealthy, or used as evidence of a sick mind.
Admission of guilt and self-condemnation cannot always be explained
away as arising from "affectation, or from a strange distempered state of
mind, or from accidental melancholy and disquiet."[18] Such feelings are

---

[10] P. P. S.i,13.

[11] No.26: "I would rather persuade you for love than urge you through fear."

[12] P.P.S.i,6.

[13] P.P.S.viii,14: "It would have been strange if the God of nature had said one
thing, and the God of grace another...all revelation is grounded on those simple truths
which our own consciences teach us in a measure, though a poor measure, even without
it."

[14] P.P.S.i,17.

[15] No.6

[16] No.285 p. 17 "Will not such an one, of tender conscience, with a profound view
of his own littleness and God's greatness, shrink through unbelief when he hears a message
of mercy? The more he advances in a right view of things, the more he will condemn
himself and the more this feeling of doubt concerning the possibility of his salvation will
haunt him."

[17] I prescind from the interesting question whether Newman himself was plagued
with guilt. That would require a psychological analysis. What is more ad rem is whether
the sermons promote a salutary moral sense or a destructive one.

[18] P.P.S.i,4; ii,15 Newman puts such occurrences down to the consequences of self-
contemplation, "a deranged state of the mental powers," rather than a true understanding

not to be confused however with the substance of religion, which is to instil a settled conviction based on conscience and reason that bears fruit in amendment.[19] "Feeling guilty even when we are not is a ploy of Satan," in having us contemplate ourselves rather than the sufferings of Christ.[20] Moreover all our feelings should not be imprisoned in the thought of guilt. In the very moment of repentance feelings of peace, joy and hope will also be present to the sinner. Guilt therefore which arises from our moral weakness is entirely different from that which results from one's morbid concentration on self. The latter finds no sanction in the Gospel.

> "Now no one will fancy, I should trust, that I am saying any thing in disparagement of such feelings [of moral guilt]; they are very right and true. I only say that they should not be the whole of man's religion. He ought to have other and more cheerful feelings too... Sins of infirmity then, such as arise from the infection of our original nature, and not from deliberation and wilfulness, have no warrant to keep us from joy and peace in believing."[21]

Raising an awareness of sin and guilt is not, however, the ultimate objective of Newman's preaching. It is but the means, though an essential one, for appreciating God's blessings. Even in his most trenchant mood Newman invariably calls forth feelings of gratitude and recalls the mercy of God.[22] Scripture states the fact of our corruption "not for its own sake, but to introduce a message of mercy."[23] But it is only in proportion as one realizes the depth of one's sinfulness can one understand the meaning of pardon and sanctification, which would otherwise be mere words.[24]

---

of the Atonement; In P.P.S.iii,11 he also refers to guilt feelings as the result of self-introversion arising from an erroneous use of the mystery.

[19] P.P.S.i,9.

[20] P.P.S.vi,1.

[21] P.P.S.iv,9.

[22] Nos.3,4,26,27; "It would be a cruel act of mine to awaken you to a sense of your misery had we no means of rescuing you from it." Cf No 27.

[23] No.192 p. 5.

[24] P.P.S.i,4. Secret Faults is one of only five sermons from St.Clement's (if one includes No. 50 which was rewritten and given a new number No. 327) which were later published. The other sermons are No. 53 (P.P.S. vii.5), No. 124 (P.P.S. viii, 8) and No. 125 (P.P.S. viii, 17). In its published form No.83 still retains the sermon structure modeled on

The Meaning of Evil and Human Corruption

The paramount importance which Newman attached to the doctrine of human corruption is seen by the place it holds in his very first course of sermons.[25] The corruption of our nature can be assumed as a self-evident principle of the moral order. There is certainty about "the awful fact" though it is more difficult to ascertain "the degree of our guilt and the extent of the punishment it deserves."[26] What first strikes Newman, however, is the all-pervasiveness of the disorder.

" Now, let us see, what has our examination suggested about the extent of our disobedience to the will of God. That it is according to all appearance *continual* through our lives, imperfection staining almost everything we do; and that sin is seen, not here and there, but universally (more or less) in every age and nation; and that its tendencies, when encouraged, are towards indefinite and (as far as we can see) unlimited wickedness."[27]

It was only at a later date[28] that Newman attempted to describe the nature and the origin of the evil. A world permeated by sin was an overwhelming idea which required time to reflect calmly upon. Having considered the full extent of the disease he then defined what is meant by corruption.

"The corruption of our nature, and our extreme peril in consequence of it, may be proved as matters of fact and of moral certainty from what we see within and without it. By corruption I mean our not having the inclinations, desires and judgments which God approves: and by our consequent peril I mean that which arises from the prospect of passing from this life into God's presence, without loving what He loves and hating what He hates, and thus not being able to

---

Simeon and represents a bridge between the early and the mature Newman.

[25] Course i: *The Trinity and Man's Salvation.*

[26] No.19 p. 5.

[27] ibid. p. 22.

[28] The manuscript of No.19 is that which was rewritten for St.Mary's Chapel in Brighton on Jan.18 1829, five years after its first composition. The important redactions on the nature of original sin are much later additions but undated.

68

take pleasure in His presence."[29]

He goes on to describe more fully that "this corruption is not a mere misfortune," "not a mere accident of our nature such as want of ability might be, or bodily infirmity." He also notes that "corruption" may be misunderstood as though it referred only to the wicked. To avoid such misunderstanding, human corruption is also called "birth sin" or "original sin." Thus by birth all human beings share in the sin of Adam and bear responsibility for it, even though we do not know how each person can be held responsible.

Newman avoids the pitfall of pessimistic determinism which the doctrine of total human depravity implies.[30] God's grace is sufficient for us "however deep and far-spreading is the root of evil in us." But we are to accept the fact of our own nothingness and inquire less about "the over-subtle questions" of "the exact limits and character of our natural corruption."[31] Despite the fact that "the very taint of birth-sin admits of a cure by the coming of Christ" and "that all our sorrow and corruption can be blessed and changed by Him,"[32] the doctrine of the fallen nature of man is the only true introduction to the Gospel.[33] Though not in itself the foundation for a theology of salvation, the "certain" belief "that the present nature of man is evil and not good" is the only valid ground on which such a theology can be laid.

> "This is the great truth which is at the foundation of all true doctrine as to the way of salvation. All teaching about duty and obedience, about attaining heaven, and about the office of Christ towards us, is hollow and unsubstantial, which is not built *here*, in the doctrine of our original corruption and helplessness; and in consequence, of original guilt and sin. Christ indeed is the foundation, but a broken, self-abased, self-renouncing heart is (as it were) the ground and soil in which the foundation must be laid; and it is but building on the sand to profess to believe in Christ, yet not to

[29] ibid. A later redaction which forms a new introduction to the sermon.

[30] No.192 p. 6: "There are writers who have openly asserted that human corruption is so entire that amendment and sanctification are impossible...."

[31] P.P.S.ii,11.

[32] P.P.S.ii,12.

[33] P.P.S.i,7.

acknowledge that without Him we can do nothing."[34]

The manuscript of Newman's sermon on The Corruption of Human Nature reveals the stages of logical development in his thinking on the subject.[35] Having described the extent and the nature of human corruption, he then considers the effect of original sin in the baptized. Despite the true regeneration[36] which takes place in baptism, original sin "is still sinful though qualified [and (as it were) pleaded for and (if I may use the word) sanctified by the principle of grace, by the presence of the Holy Spirit in the heart]." These qualifying clauses reflect the struggle in Newman's mind to avoid articulating a view which might seem to diminish the power of this evil principle. "It is still sinful - it is still powerful - it is still in many cases victorious over the grace of God." Original sin in the baptized may "be subdued and modified"; we may no longer be in such a hopeless condition but the evil root of corrupt human nature is still present.[37]

Our present condition has not been changed even though Christ has come. Each of us is burdened by Adam's fallen nature and it is only by appropriating the grace of Christ's redemption in each individual case that our will can be transformed. The race of man remains the same though Christ has died for sin, for His death is not the waving of a magical wand over corrupt human nature.

"We have Adam's nature in the same sense as if Christ had not come to the world...We are changed *one by one;* the race of man is what it ever was, guilty; - what it was before Christ came, with the same evil passions, the same slavish will...the

---

34 P.P.S.v.10.

35 There are two very important redactions, one defining what he means by corruption, the other pointing out the difference made by baptism, which are written in Newman's later smaller script. It is difficult to determine the chronological order of these redactions. The sermon was preached seven times. The redactions most likely come later than 1835, most probably in 1838 or 1841.

36 Hawkins thought that Newman's sermon No.2 implied a denial of baptismal regeneration, cf. Pett p. 24. There was a clear tendency in evangelicalism to undervalue the sacrament though Newman believed his early sermons were only "mildly evangelical." The question of baptismal regeneration arose from Newman's reading of Sumner's Apostolical Preaching in 1824. This was also the occasion for his rejection of the distinctive Calvinist beliefs. L.D. Vol.1 p. 185, 206; AW p. 78, 230ff.

37 When the uniform edition of his sermons was being edited, Newman wrote to Copeland about his misgivings on his Anglican views of original sin. Cf. L.D. xxviii, 250 -256.

Gospel has not annulled -our corruption."[38]

The early sermons generally present a picture of sin and evil as one amorphous whole without distinctions.[39] While he retained a horror of even the slightest sin, he drew the distinction in his later work, between wilful transgressions (which forfeit the state of grace) and infirmities (which do not), "without drawing a line between them."[40] Infirmities are those sins which arise from weakness and of these original sin is the principal one. By baptism "the curse is removed and we are no longer under God's wrath; our guilt is forgiven us but still the infection of it remains."[41] A new spiritual principle is imparted to combat the force of evil inherited from our corrupt human nature. A hidden power, greater than evil has been given to enable us to choose the good and to restore "to a certain extent the gift of free-will."[42]

Before concluding this introduction, it is important to note the power which Newman attributes to the principle of evil. It is "active and obstinate and tyrannizing in its operations" and capable of limitless growth and influence.[43] Its power is demonstrated by the endless suffering we find in the world.[44] The Bible from beginning to end records an unbroken line of human misery due to sin. It begins with the history of a curse on creation, and ends with the most threatening of prospects. The Word of God puts before us this severe truth "which is ultimately the true view of human life."[45] Evil is on all sides for "the world lieth in wickedness - it is plunged and steeped in a flood of

---

[38] P.P.S.i,7; No.197: "that root of corruption remains in all of us, in spite of our baptism."

[39] The concept of parvity of matter or the distinction between imperfection, venial and mortal sin is absent in the early sermons. cf No.10: "In itself the smallest sin will undo a man as well as the greatest." For a view of how real sin was for Newman cf J.A.Froude, *The Nemesis of Faith*, London, The Walter Scott Publishing Co., Ltd., 1904, pp. 160 -161.

[40] P.P.S.v,14 ; v.15 Newman lists eight kinds of infirmities which recall the course *on Sins*, No.vi(a), he delivered in 1824.

[41] P.P.S.v,15.

[42] P.P.S.v,24.

[43] No.19 pp. 32-33.

[44] No.93 p. 2:"No doubt all suffering (as has already been observed) ultimately arises from sin - if we were not in a fallen state we should not be afflicted."

[45] P.P.S.i,25. This sermon on *Scripture A Record of Human Sorrow* has the same aim as the preceding one of challenging *The Religion of the Day*. Its leading idea was already contained in No.19 p. 35.

sin."[46] Even the bright side of the Gospel is manipulated by Satan to lure us into a shallow optimism and have us forget the unpleasant truth.

Evil moreover has a power of possession over the world and holds fast its conquest. Nothing but a long drawn out battle will get it to yield its spoils. It has had a head start over the principle of good which can only proceed slowly and secretly against it. Its most important source of strength is its internal ally in the human heart.[47] So as long as man lives "the mystery of iniquity will continue on till the Avenger solves it once for all."[48] This world, once created good but now saturated with evil, awaits destruction when sin is brought under subjection. Then the apocalypse will come and Christ will crush the evil power.

> "When our Saviour comes, He will destroy this world, even His own work, and much more the lusts of the world which are of the evil one;...and we shall perish with the world, if on that day its lusts are found within us."[49]

Part Two
The Last Judgment

The Certainty of a Universal Judgment

Newman's intense awareness of the nature and extent of corruption leads him to emphasize the importance of the Last Judgment. It is only then "that we will better understand the nature of evil."[50] Moreover, it is unconscionable that evil should escape with impunity; there must be a time of reckoning when all things will be set at right. Even though the sentence on evil is postponed in the present life, the Day of Judgment is the assurance that truth will ultimately triumph.[51]

The fact of a judgment to come is assured by both conscience and

---

[46] P.P.S.vii,3.

[47] ibid.

[48] P.P.S.ii,31.

[49] P.P.S.vii,3.

[50] No.19.

[51] P.P.S.ii,1: "The triumph of truth in all its forms is postponed to the next world."

72

Scripture. There is sufficient evidence on the face of nature for conscience to grasp the truth, though the state of darkness of the heathen blinded them to the future judgment.[52] Nevertheless by the weight of its own authority, it tells us "of an unseen but accurate Judge"[53] who will one day call for an account of our stewardship.[54] Conscience may be neglected and smothered but its voice cannot utterly be silenced. It still reminds the sinner of God's anger and the threat that some time or other He will come to judge.[55] We have only to search our hearts to understand what is meant by an Infinite Governor and Judge[56] and it is mere self-delusion to forget the judgment day.[57] Conscience "assuredly forebodes ill to the sinner"; it is the voice of God in consonance with His justice and moral governance.[58] And what conscience suggests Christ Himself has sanctioned. He did not come to gain us easier admittance into heaven but to enable us to bear the burden of conscience more responsibly.[59] Both Scripture and conscience tell us that we are answerable to God who is a righteous Judge.[60] Hence the revealed fact of the Last Judgment is grounded on our nature as morally accountable human beings.

> "The law of his nature is urged upon him, by the Creator of that law; a sort of uncontrollable destiny is represented as encompassing him; the destiny of accountableness, the fate of being free, the unalienable prerogative of choosing between life and death, the inevitable prospect of heaven and hell."[61]

Newman stresses the universal nature of the Judgment. No one is exempted from having to render an account, and all will be found

---

[52] No.106.

[53] No.135.

[54] No.119 p. 15.

[55] P.P.S.vii,13.

[56] P.P.S.i,4.

[57] P.P.S.i,10.

[58] P.P.S.ii,23.

[59] P.P.S.viii,14.

[60] P.P.S.i,2.

[61] P.P.S.iv,4 , first delivered at Oriel Chapel.

wanting in the balance.[62] It is only the self-righteous who by definition have no fear of the judgment.[63] Every sin shall appear before God, every man according to his work, all Christians.[64] Even sins that have been forgiven in the past will not escape God's judgment, for we have no assurance that the debt of sin has been completely paid up.[65] This universality is particular in its application; we are judged one by one and while we have some responsibility for the sins of others while we live, we bear our own sin alone on that day.[66] Thus, Newman rejects the evangelical view that only the wicked will be judged, for such false assurance leads to a virtual antinomianism.

> "It is certain, however startling it is to reflect upon it, that numbers do not in any true sense believe that they shall be judged; they believe in a coming judgment as regards the wicked, but they do not believe that all men, that they themselves personally will undergo it."[67]

The Last Judgment will be particularly severe on Christians. In an early sermon stressing the need for separation from the world, he has especially harsh words for "ungodly Christians" who "will be especial objects of divine punishment at the last day." They could have been preeminently holy but "they will be condemned with a ten-fold damnation."[68] Later in more moderate tones though no less clear, Newman reminds those who neglect or abuse their birthright that the judgment will be more awful than if they had never been baptized.[69] Christians will have more to answer for and their doom will be two-fold, though they have double grounds for hope.[70] Since they are capable through God's grace of rising to the heights of sanctity, their neglect of

---

[62] No.343.

[63] P.P.S.iv,5.

[64] No.435.

[65] P.P.S.iv,7.

[66] No.332 *On National Sins - for the Fast Day*. Newman gives a good description of what today would be called "social sin." Cf. also the notion of National Sin in No.376 on *the Feast of King Charles the Martyr*.

[67] P.P.S.iii,6.

[68] No.135 p. 19.

[69] No.118 p. 4 ; P.P.S. iv,3 : "We have reason for saying that those who sin, after grace given are, as such, in a worse state than if they had not received it."

[70] No.360.

the Gospel privileges is an added reason for fear at the Day of Judgment.[71] To despise God's gift and not to use the grace of the Gospel is to increase our future punishment.[72] Christians can expect "a judgment heavier than the plagues of Egypt" if despite repeated opportunities for repentance they continue in their sinful ways.[73]

> "If, as I truly believe, Christians of the Church's forming rise to a height and stature in Christ unknown to all other systems (communions) what will be our (overwhelming) guilt at the day of judgment if, though born within its fold we have neglected our privileges."[74]

The Time of Judgment

Before entering into the question of the time of judgment it is relevant to note Newman's remarkable freedom from passing judgment on others. Judgment is the unique prerogative of God and must be left solely in His hands. "Man can only judge from externals, hence he cannot separate the tares from the wheat which agree in externals but differ in essentials."[75] We simply do not have the competence to judge, for all we see is the external, which is not a sufficient means for knowing the heart.[76] No one has the right to inquire into the spiritual state of his neighbour or make judgments on his character.[77] We have enough difficulty understanding our own minds, not to speak of the mind of others. Hence it would seem "the height of madness" to presume to estimate the value of anything and how God will finally account it.[78] Human judgment is so much the child of ignorance and

---

[71] No.270.

[72] P.P.S.viii,4.

[73] P.P.S.vii,9.

[74] No.270 p. 27.

[75] No.30. Only an abstract of this sermon is extant. Newman may have learned this principle from Hawkins who criticized his evangelical tendency to divide the world into the sheep and the goats.

[76] P.P.S.vi,2; viii,7: "so little may we judge of God's love or displeasure by outward appearances"

[77] The sermon is unidentified but was preached on 9th Sept. 1827 at Well Walk Chapel.

[78] P.P.S.v,18; i,4; iv,3.

prejudice that if we must judge, let it be confined to ourselves. While not discounting the need for correction we should not fear the judgment of others. It is only God's just assessment that we can depend upon, not the judgment of the world.[79]

If judgment then is to be left entirely to God, when may we expect it to occur? The question is not as straightforward as it looks for it involves the providence of God and its relation to eschatology. Does the justice of God, which is a principle of providence, manifest itself in the present time, or is His judgment postponed until the Last Day? It is further complicated by the notion that judgment commonly denotes punishment and thereby raises the problem whether temporal affliction is an instance of God's present judgment.[80]

With regard to the time of judgment Newman's sermons provide an illustration of the eschatological tension between the "now" and the "not yet." In his early period he unambiguously states that the time of God's judgment is in the future and that present afflictions should not be regarded as judgments. Unlike the Jewish dispensation with its temporal rewards and punishments, the Christian era is a time of salvation, judgment being deferred to the end.

> "In my present discourse I have insisted principally on two things - 1st on a point which has also come before us the last two Sundays - viz that the judgment punishment and satisfaction for sin is not in this life, but in the next - 2ndly and more especially, that since God does not usually judge and punish us here, but hereafter, we ought not to call afflictions judgments."[81]

The context of the sermon makes clear that Newman adopts this general principle partly to remove the danger of superstitious belief in natural disasters. No one is to be alarmed or driven to suppose that God exacts vengeance by sending calamities. Nonetheless he does not rule out or deny that "judgments *sometimes* occur - but they are *extra-*

---

[79] P.P.S.i,10; vii,4.

[80] "By the term *judgment* is commonly understood all affliction which happens out of the usual course of things in consequence of some particular sin committed" No.92 p. 1. The significance of affliction will be treated in the next section.

[81] No.92 p. 11. The sermon is marked "Whateleyan" but Newman does not explain why. The term may simply note a stage of development or may be used pejoratively to illustrate the liberal views he once held, but now rejects.

76

ordinary, they are *exceptions* to the general rule."[82] However, in the very next sermon he preached,[83] he lists three such exceptions which considerably modify his initial view. One such instance is judicial blindness which is the penalty for sins against conscience.[84] As a spiritual penalty it is a hidden judgment which does not give us any basis for declaring it to be divine retribution.[85]

In his farewell sermon at St. Clement's, he refers again to the question of God's judgments in this life. God's temporal punishment for sin was a feature of the Jewish dispensation but it is not so in the Christian system. We should not trouble ourselves with the superstitious belief that present afflictions are evidence of God's wrath.

> "In the gospel there is no declaration of present vengeance, but of *future*.... We must not look out for judgments, we must not expect them, fancy we see them, form our opinions of the spiritual state of others by their worldly success or misfortune or direct our own conduct *as if* God punished us here."[86]

The deferment of God's judgment to the future may be found in Newman's later sermons but never in the same exclusive sense. The idea of something which is totally future seemed to make irrelevant the present operations of God's justice, and to create a spirit of indifference towards the need to live constantly under His judgment. It would lead to a false security and undervalue the severe side of religion. There still are however, examples reminding us that now is not the time of judgment but of mercy, and that we should "forebear anticipating the next world." Judgment is to be left to the end "till the Judge shall come."[87] Then and only then will secret faults be manifest; the Day of the Lord will declare them.[88]

---

[82] ibid. p. 5.

[83] No.93.

[84] On judicial blindness cf P.P.S.i,17; ii,9

[85] No.93 p. 6 "while in many cases, as in those of judicial blindness, not knowing the heart, we can say nothing at all."

[86] No.150 p. 10. A few weeks later we find in No.154 "He has changed His mode of governing the Church."

[87] P.P.S.ii,31.

[88] P.P.S.i,4; v,9; viii,3.

In general however there is a marked shift of viewpoint from the future to the present judgment of God. God's judgment is neither dormant nor suspended until the Last Day, but is acting in the present, though in a hidden manner. In his University sermon *On Justice, as a Principle of Divine Governance*, Newman retracts his former opinion as part of the false optimism of the age. Not that he ever espoused the view which he now attacks, that of God's unmixed benevolence. The postponement of God's judgments to the next world simply runs against the facts "seeing we have actual evidences of His justice in the course of the world." There are "visible consequences of single sins, as furnishing some foreboding of the full and final judgment of God upon all we do; and the survey of such instances is very striking." So judgment is present now and we may "all through life suffer the penalty of past disobedience." Newman still recognizes the danger of superstition in attributing natural disasters to the wrath of God but such superstition is less harmful than the view which ignores altogether the present consequences of sin. "Those who are not superstitious without the gospel will not be religious with it."[89]

The Last Day is the climax of a process, the definitive moment which puts the seal on what has already occurred. Time and eternity are not disconnected for the judgment of the next world has already effectively entered into the present. Every event and decision has a bearing on the ultimate outcome and the Last Judgment is already operative in everyday life. Thus while we wait for the final sentence and the definitive separation on the Last Day, the process has already silently and invisibly begun.

> "Every one of us here assembled is either a vessel of mercy or a vessel of wrath fitted to destruction; or rather, I should say, *will* be such at the Last Day, and now is acting *towards* the one or the other. We cannot judge each other, we cannot judge ourselves...Still it is true that the solemn process of *separation* between bad and good is ever going on. The net has at present gathered of every kind. At the end of the world will be the final division; meanwhile there is a gradual sorting and sifting, silent but sure, towards it."[90]

The "now" and the "not yet" of judgment are illustrated in a

---

[89] U.S.vi, p. 117.

[90] P.P.S.iii,15.

sermon on chastisement in which Newman combines the notion of correction, which is appropriate to a dispensation of mercy, with the idea of punishment which reflects God's present justice. During the Whateleyan period he was at pains to free his congregation from superstition and dread but now he feels it necessary to underline the present reality of judgment. At the same time he reaffirms his belief that though punishment is a natural consequence of sin even in this life, serious Christians should not give way to a state of alarm, for the day of judgment is in the future. They have the twofold experience of accepting the penalty and being conscious that they are being supported by God's grace.

> " I know it is sometimes said that such trials are to the true Christian not judgments but corrections; rather they are judgments *and* corrections; surely they are merciful corrections, but they are judgments too."[91]

Both points of view can also be seen when he contrasts the final state of glory and wrath with the present state of grace and sin. Though we cannot determine the spiritual state of any individual, it is nevertheless true that the final state is already proleptically present. It is therefore inadequate to speak of sinners being "in danger of hell" when their real state is actually one of God's judgment and wrath.

> "We are in error if we mean, as is often the case, to deny thereby that irreligious men, as such, whether man can ascertain them or not, are at this very time, not only in danger, but actually under the power of God's wrath."[92]

Present Affliction

The Last Judgment and the real possibility of eternal punishment mark the final resolution of the problem of evil. Present affliction is linked to these final realities as a process is to its termination. When the goal has been attained, or kept in sight, it throws a retrospective light on what has gone before, thereby illuminating the meaning of the process.

---

[91] P.P.S.iv,8.

[92] P.P.S.iv,6.

In the light therefore of future judgment and punishment, affliction can be seen as an integral part of the continuous conflict between good and evil, which works its way through history. It arises from sin[93] and is part of the mystery of suffering through which redemption is achieved. We do not know *how* suffering is necessary in God's plan; we only know *that* it follows the law of redemption and is in conformity with the paradigm of Christ.

The theme of affliction is one of the most frequent subjects in Newman's sermons. He treats it under two main aspects, its significance as a present punishment for sin, and as an instrument of God's merciful purification. Through affliction we participate in Christ's redemptive work in both the dark side of bearing suffering for sin and in the bright side of training for future glory. Newman treats the theme dialectically, emphasizing at one time the aspect of judgment upon sin, at another the instrument of mercy. There is however a general trend towards recognizing in present suffering the merciful design of God to have us endure the lesser punishment here than the future punishment in store for sin.[94] In this way Newman redirects the severe side of eschatology from the future horizon and plants it in the present soil of our spiritual lives.

The connection between present and future punishment is made by Newman in one of his first sermons in which he notes the paradox that good men suffer while evil men escape visible punishment. The difficulty is only partly resolved by the knowledge that there is a future punishment in store for the wicked; it does not explain by what law present suffering falls upon the upright. He gives two reasons: first, as even good men sin, their affliction is meant as a warning to us and second, it is a merciful chastisement so that we may not be condemned with the world in that future day.[95]

This first mention we find regarding chastisement is on an Old Testament figure and it is in the context of Jewish history that Newman develops the theme. For him the Old Testament prophets are the model par excellence of the meaning of affliction. They bore their trials both as

---

[93] "No doubt all suffering (as has already been observed) ultimately arises from sin - if we were not in a fallen state we should not be afflicted." No.93.

[94] Present Affliction is treated under the rubric of Judgment and not of Eternal Punishment. The latter has no analogue in the present life. Present punishment is not the realization of eternal punishment for we cannot have a realized eschatology of hell symmetrical with the experience of eternal life.

[95] No.10.

a punishment for sin and as the instrument to prepare for the innocent suffering of Christ. From their example we learn that those whom God chooses to carry out his mission are first chastened "with a kind severity" since a preparation "is needed whether for this world's glory or the next."[96] All the great characters of the Old Testament were "made so by a long discipline."[97] Thus the prophets were in their turn able to chastise and instruct a sinful people and their mission "may be called the greatest instance of God's mercy."[98] Affliction therefore, is an example of God sparing His servants on account of His promise, and at the same time a presage of future punishment. It combines the elements of a present punishment which is less than what sin deserves, and a preparation for future glory. But the prior element is that of punishment, as affliction always remains "a sign of God's power, holiness and severe justice." From all of this Newman draws the lesson that God's chastisement on the just is mild when compared with the final punishment reserved for the wicked.

> "If God so punish his own children, what will be the final, though delayed, punishment of the wicked? If the righteous scarcely be saved, where shall the ungodly and the sinner appear?"[99]

Esau had no fear that God would punish him. He was profane and then presumptuous. He trifled with God's mercies and tried to regain them when it was too late. Here also we have a lesson that "we cannot escape punishment, here or hereafter; we must take our choice, whether to suffer and mourn a little now, or much then."[100] The fact that God sends affliction is a sure sign of His love by rescueing us from an infinitely greater punishment, despite ourselves. This is to be our personal attitude towards trials of any kind without passing judgment on the affliction of others. "We indeed cannot decide in the case of others, when trouble is a punishment, and when not; yet this we know that all sin brings affliction."

---

[96] No.208.

[97] No.210.

[98] No.253.

[99] P.P.S.iii,5.

[100] P.P.S. vi,2.

"I recommend them to look on all pain and sorrow which comes on them as a *punishment* for what they once were; and to take it patiently on that account, nay, joyfully, as giving them a hope that God *is* punishing them here instead of hereafter."[101]

The prophet Jeremiah[102] is taken as the most eminent representative of "suffering affliction and patience." His spirit of resignation is "a more blessed frame of mind than sanguine hope of present success, because it is the truer, and the more consistent with our fallen state of being, and the more improving to our hearts." In this he illustrates the great rule "that they who sow in sorrow reap in joy" and teaches us to "prepare for suffering and disappointment, which befit us as sinners, and which are necessary for us as saints."

In the figure of Job Newman finds the classical case to illustrate the state of things "of our being actually under punishment for our sins." Though he was innocent Job had to wait in darkness "till God revealed why He chastised as a sinner." Likewise we are to concur with God's chastisements by trusting that He knows what is best for us. With the hopeful assurance "that we are not in a desperate state" we are still conscious of "evil behind us, and that through our frailty ever increasing, and a judgment before us." Thus affliction is a constant reminder of sin but also a reason to rejoice, "thinking it better to be punished in this life than in the next."

"God is our merciful Father, and when He afflicts His sons, yet it is not willingly; and though in one sense it is in judgment, yet in another and higher, it is in mercy. He provides that what is in itself an evil should become a good; and while He does not supersede the original law of His just government, that suffering should follow sin, He overrules it to be a healing medicine as well as a punishment. Thus, "in wrath," He "remembers mercy."[103]

Having thus seen how Newman considered the Old Testament message of affliction we can now turn to the significance of suffering in the Gospel. Newman constantly stresses the unity of the two

---

101 P.P.S.vi,2.

102 P.P.S.viii,9.

103 P.P.S.iv,8.

dispensations and the element of continuity. Without such continuity with the revealed past, the new dispensation could not effect an authentic transformation. Affliction remains what it has always been, a consequence of sin; by the mystery of Christ it is transformed into an instrument of God's grace. The innocence of Job is radically changed by the innocence of Christ.

On the feast of the Holy Innocents Newman preached on the relation between virtue and suffering.[104] The feast reminds us that Christ is not only the perfect example of innocent suffering but also the cause of suffering for all whom He loves. Though it is a "strange" fact that the virtuous should be afflicted, it is "in the order of Providence that the mediators of blessings between Him and mankind suffer." This law is most clearly fulfilled in the mediation of Christ Himself. His atonement for sin does not explain the mystery but confirms the law of grace through suffering, and is an inward consolation to believers.

In a later redaction[105] of the sermon Newman adds that there is no necessary connection between virtue and suffering. The link is due entirely to the historical order of a world "crowded with evil which is not of God's making." In this "system of confusion" we are under the inscrutable mystery "that the present course of things is under the direction of another master, Satan, who is called by St. Paul, "the god of this world." Moreover, in the present state of conflict virtue is a provocation to evil and brings down upon its own head its share of suffering. Hence all of us must in some way bear the burden of "punishment of the evil within us. Let us take it as such when we suffer."

Bodily pain is an instance of innocent suffering for it comes upon all whether they have sinned or not, and on the whole of creation which is a stranger to Adam's nature. In itself bodily suffering has no intrinsic value; it gives us no grounds for believing it can expiate sin or bring us closer to God.[106] It is an evil which in fact has the tendency to turn us in on ourselves and make us selfish. Its power however lies in its ability to remind us of our individuality. Pain is not a spiritual experience as such, but through faith it becomes the gateway to redemption.

---

[104] No.279 first delivered in 1830 and subsequently used every two years on the feast day.

[105] ibid. There are seven pages of redactions to this sermon.

[106] Only the sufferings of Christ have the power to expiate. Our present afflictions have no expiatory value. This is a constant thought of Newman cf.No.54, his first sermon on *The Blessedness of Affliction*, and No.92.

"This, then, is the effect of suffering, that it arrests us: that it puts, as it were, a finger upon us to ascertain for us our own individuality. But it does no more than this; if such a warning does not lead us through the stirrings of our conscience heavenwards, it does but imprison us in ourselves and makes us selfish."[107]

Love for Christ is the only thing which turns suffering into a redemptive experience. A mere negative asceticism is not only worthless but positively harmful. Suffering of itself is no sure test of holiness and often leads to morose and self-centred contemplation. Hence self-imposed affliction is to be discouraged when it is not accompanied by love. The early Christians endured their trial for the love of Christ and not from "superstitious alarms, or cowardly imaginations, or senseless hurrying into difficulty." Unless the austerity of Christians is joyful, it is not Christian austerity at all.

"Affliction, when love is away, leads a man to wish others to be as he is; it leads to repining, malevolence, hatred, rejoicing in evil."[108]

If suffering has not come our way through bodily infirmity or other involuntary means, then self-denial and fasting must take its place. There must be some form of suffering in our lives to remind us of our sinfulness and of the need "to complete the remnant of His sufferings in [our] own flesh."[109] It is no great thing to suffer here instead of suffering in the future world. A life of comfort and pleasure is sufficient of itself to expose us to the danger of eternal misery. With the proper disposition of faith self-mortification both joins us to Christ in suffering and keeps before our minds our deserved punishment for sin.

"Let us never forget in all we suffer, that, properly speaking, our own sin is the cause of it, and it is only in Christ's mercy that we are allowed to range ourselves at His side. We who are children of wrath, are made through Him children of

---

[107] P.P.S.iii,11: "There is the selfishness of worldly pleasure but also the selfishness of worldly pain."

[108] ibid.

[109] No.351 p. 21. Both self-denial and fasting are frequent subjects of Newman's preaching. Self-denial is the substitute in a time of peace for the mark of persecution which was the test of the genuineness of faith, cf P.P.S.i,5.

84

grace; and our pains - which are in themselves but foretastes of hell - are changed by the sprinkling of His blood into a preparation for heaven."[110]

Voluntary penance however is not to be assumed lightly. The spiritual weapons of fasting and mortification run the gauntlet of challenging the powers of evil. They are not mere exercises of spiritual preparation but are "in good measure" the very cause of the conflict. Fasting "is therefore to be viewed, chiefly as an *approach* to God - an approach to the powers of heaven - yes and to the powers of hell. And in this point of view there is something awful in it."[111] The significance and the implications of fasting are spelled out for us in the temptation of Christ in the desert. Here we see and should expect in our own lives an engagement with our spiritual enemy.

> "...it is plain from the sacred history, that in His case, as in ours, fasting opened the way to temptation. And perhaps this is the truest view of such exercises, that in some wonderful unknown way they open the next world for good and evil upon us, and are an introduction to somewhat of an extraordinary conflict with the powers of evil."[112]

With the idea of chastisement Newman has been able to retain the notion of present punishment as an instance of God's judgment upon sin and clothed it in the mantle of mercy. He has integrated suffering which is the token of evil into the mystery of redemption in Christ. These two elements are neatly summed up in one of his Sermons of the Day.

> "When His children go wrong they are, in St. Paul's words, "judged." He does not abandon them, but He makes their sin "find them out." And as we well know, it is His merciful pleasure that this punishment should at the same time act as a chastisement and correction so that "when they are judged they are chastened of the Lord, that they should not be condemned with the world." But still their visitation is of the nature of a judgment; and no sinner knows what kind, what

---

110 P.P.S.iii,11.

111 P.P.S.vi,1.

112 ibid.

number of judgments, he has incurred at the hands of the
righteous Judge."[113]

The Relation between God's Justice and Mercy

It has already been noted that the Last Judgment is seen by
Newman as an event which evokes mixed emotions of fear and joy. He
believed that, however difficult it is to reconcile such feelings, both are
experienced fully without any dilution or mutual absorption. This
instance is part of a general pattern Newman adopts towards the
resolution of apparently incompatible elements. In all such cases he
aims to preserve the integral truth in the face of inconsistency, which is
often more logical than real. This is true not only of emotions but also
of contrary virtues and truths which seem at first sight to be in
opposition.[114] He permits no reduction of the truth which is to be
found in the whole, not in the apprehension of its individual parts.

We have a similar case in trying to reconcile God's justice and
mercy. Even at the purely human level the two are incompatible to
reason. When we hold therefore that God is infinite justice and at the
same time infinite mercy we cannot argue or explain how they are
reconciled. "The difficulty it is plain lies in our words, in our
conceptions, not in divine truth."[115] Moreover our knowledge of God
comes to us through two distinct channels. His justice is a truth of the
natural order, though only fully disclosed in revelation, whereas His
mercy is known by revelation alone.[116]

The starting point for Newman is the principle of justice for it is
logically prior to revelation and is never superseded by it. The history of
revelation itself follows the same pedagogical line by emphasizing first
the justice of God and progressively unfolding His mercy.[117] The

---

[113] S.D. ii, p. 20.

[114] P.P.S.ii.23: "The very problem which Christian duty acquires us to
accomplish, is the reconciling in our conduct opposite virtues" ; No.404 :"But whatever
we decide about it (reconciling opposite truths) so much is quite plain there is a limit
beyond which we may not attempt to reconcile".

[115] No.603 p. 12.

[116] No.119 where he makes the distinction between natural and revealed truths
and chooses justice and mercy respectively as examples.

[117] We see the beginnings of Newman's attempts to construct a theory of development
of doctrine based on the history of salvation. There is a progressive unfolding of doctrine but the

Jewish Law was a system of temporal rewards and punishments based on the rule of justice; the New Covenant in Christ and the promise of eternal life is founded on mercy.[118] God does not cease to be just when once we learn of His mercy, nor do the laws of His providence become obsolete when the order of redemption is established. Doctrines may change as revelation progresses but the principles and feelings produced in its various stages remain constant.[119] His providence "moves by great and comprehensive laws"[120] and He has "so clearly shown us from the beginning, that His own glory is the end, and justice the essential rule of His providence."[121] Hence Providence is the infrastructure on which Christ's redemption is laid. So what may appear to us as two parallel orders, of justice and mercy, have the same origin and the same goal.

In one of his University sermons of 1832, in the context of liberal cries for Church reform, Newman issued a warning against a shallow and superficial view of human nature based on the benevolence of God.[122] This optimistic and laissez-faire philosophy of utilitarianism implied the denial of God's justice and contained a false idea of freedom. "Our very consciousness of being free, and so responsible, includes in it the idea of an unchangeable rule of justice, on which judgment is hereafter to be conducted; or rather excludes, as far as it goes, the notion of a simply benevolent Governor."

But a view of justice as the sole attribute of God is equally wrong. If it were a case of God's "unmixed justice" our present human condition could lead to nothing but despair. However, the assurance of His unchanging rule of justice is a fixed guarantee for us to rely upon His benevolence. It gives a certainty and character to the course of Divine governance.[123] As far as reason goes we cannot show that

---

principles of revelation remain constant. This series of sermons on the *History of Gospel Doctrines* are numbered Nos. 104-123. Numbers 108, 110 and 112 are particularly important.

[118] This is the core of his *Course on Jewish History* which followed soon after. It consists of Nos.133,135,138,139,142,143, 145,149 and 150.

[119] On the continuity of principles cf Dev. pp. 178-185.

[120] P.P.S.ii,8.

[121] P.P.S.ii,11.

[122] U.S. vi, *On Justice, as a Principle of Divine Governance* It was preached on April 8, two months before the third reading of the Reform Bill was passed in the Lords. See also Newman's correspondence to Froude in which he gives a detailed account of it, and Froude's suggestions regarding the ordering of his points. L.D. Vol.iii, pp. 35-37.

[123] This is also stated in P.P.S.iii,7

mercy has substituted for justice as the governing principle.

> "Nothing however is told us in nature of the limits of the two
> rules, of love and of justice, or how they are to be reconciled;
> nothing to show that the rule of mercy, as acting on moral
> agents, is more than the supplement, not the substitute of the
> fundamental law of justice and holiness."[124]

This need for certainty which the fundamental law of justice
provides, is taken up again in a context which would seem to undermine
it, the manifestation of God's mercy to the prodigal son. The traditional
reading of the parable is from the standpoint of the younger brother but
it may also be considered from the elder son's point of view. Here we
have an apparent failure of justice and a feeling of being treated
shabbily for a life of unbroken fidelity. It is natural for him to feel hurt
for such indignation comes from an instinctive demand for justice.[125]
Though not justifying the elder brother's resentment, Newman's
sympathies clearly lie with him. He wishes to assure himself that even
in this display of mercy God's rule of justice is not contravened. If
fickleness and favoritism were God's way of acting there would be no
stable anchor for the perplexed mind, and without justice the moral
order would collapse. Newman finds in the Father's reply to the elder
son's expressed indignation an answer to his difficulty.

> "It is to meet this difficulty that Almighty God has
> vouchsafed again and again to declare the unswerving rule of
> His government - favour to the obedient, punishment to the
> sinner...Accordingly, when we witness the inequalities of
> the present world, we comfort ourselves by reflecting that
> they will be put right in another."[126]

Up to this point of the discussion it may seem that Newman's
constant stress on justice relegates mercy to a subordinate role. Mercy
is for him a supplement to justice rather than its substitution. Newman's

---

[124] U.S.vi, p. 114

[125] Newman mentions resentment as a natural consequence of a failure of justice
in U.S. vi, p. 106. "If it be natural to pity and wish well to men in general....it is natural to
feel indignation when vice triumphs, and to be dissatisfied and uneasy till the inequality
is removed."

[126] P.P.S.iii.8. Newman's identification with the elder brother lends some support
to Henri Bremond's charge of resentment against him.

88

stress however is aimed at defending the severe side of the gospel against the religious enthusiasm of the day. In a context where a sentimental view of faith prevails, he emphasizes its practical expression in works of obedience. Likewise, where the gospel promises are exclusively recalled, he reminds us that such promises entail commands. There is substantially no difference between faith and obedience or promise and command, and any subordination of one to the other is due to one's perspective. Newman is concerned about the state of mind which puts in jeopardy the hard truth by unduly dwelling on the bright perspective. Likewise in the relation of God's mercy and justice we have a parallel case of two dimensions to something which is essentially one. Just as faith is preeminently proclaimed in the gospel, so also is God's mercy, but without in either case diminishing the aspect of our obedience or His justice.

> "The gospel being preeminently a covenant of grace, faith is so far of more excellence than other virtues, because it confesses this beyond all others. Works of obedience witness to God's just claims upon us, not to His mercy."[127]

The essential unity in God of justice and mercy is to be held despite the difficulty we have in reconciling them. Though the higher order of revelation tells us of His mercy, it does not suppress the truth of justice. How the reconciliation takes place we do not know for we cannot understand a love in which justice and mercy are harmonized. What we do know however is that the truly penitent are forgiven, and are now in God's favour. But we have no reason to state with certainty that no further debt remains for their sins.

> "His love then does not necessarily exclude His anger, nor His favour His severity, nor His grace His justice. How He reconciles these together we know not; this much we know, that those who forsake their sins, and come to Him for grace, are in His favour, and obtain what they need for the day; but that they are forgiven at once for all the past, we do not know."[128]

---

[127] P.P.S.iii,6. P.P.S.iii,6-10 reflect an arrangement in which the dialectic of justice and mercy are highlighted.

[128] P.P.S.iv,7; No.175.

Christ the Merciful Judge

The role of Christ in the Last Judgment has an inauspicious beginning in Newman's sermons. A theology of satisfaction interpreted in a juridical manner leads him to assign a subordinate role to Christ before an offended Father.[129] He is merely the advocate, pleading His client's case before the Almighty Judge and having "to acquiesce in the sentence of condemnation."[130] Nevertheless Newman's compassionate nature is not entirely absent in the early sermons as is shown by his sympathy for the unfortunate Judas.[131]

The case of Judas is referred to again in a much later sermon when Newman deals with belief in God's personal providence. If Providence were simply understood in its universal sense "as manifesting itself in general laws [and] moving forward upon the lines of truth and justice" it would provide cold comfort, being nothing more than an abstraction or a theory. But far from being abstract, it is universal precisely as being found concretely in each particular instance of His care for all mankind. "He is a merciful God, regarding them individually, and not a mere universal Providence acting by general laws." Moreover, any perplexity which may remain from a theoretical debate on divine mercy and justice, is dispelled by the mystery of the Incarnation.

> "He has taken upon Him the thoughts and feelings of our own nature, which we all understand *is* capable of such personal attachments. By becoming man, He has cut short the perplexities and the discussions of our reason on the subject, as if He would grant our objections for argument's sake, and supersede them by taking our own ground."[132]

To underline the depth of God's providence, Newman recalls the plight of Judas and the attitude of Christ who is now no mere advocate

---

[129] Nos.25,46 and 51 *on the Mediatorial Kingdom* represent Christ in an inferior role to the Father (the party offended). This tendency was pointed out by Whateley and Hawkins in the Oriel sermon No.160. A change can be noted in No.175 p. 10 where he carefully notes that "all the mercy of the Son is the Father's too."

[130] No.28. ."..the most awful circumstance in their abandonment is that Christ, their Saviour, their Intercessor and advocate, Yea mercy itself, acquiesces in the sentence of condemnation."

[131] No.74 In words of sympathy he laconically remarks that "life had become a burden for him."

[132] P.P.S.iii,9.

but has been appointed Judge.[133] No longer is it a question of acquies-
cence in this tragic case nor a sentence of condemnation passed by an
offended God. The gospel does not speak of Judas's condemnation but
of his hatred for the light and his going "to his own place." Judas's fall
into the abyss was not the inexorable result of general and abstract
principles but of his rejection of a Judge whose fundamental attitude
was one of compassion, seeking to find the least shred of evidence in
favour of acquittal. In Newman's touching description, judgment is
handed down

> "...not by the mere force of certain natural principles work-
> ing out their inevitable results - by some unfeeling fate,
> which sentences the wicked to hell, but by a Judge who sur-
> veys him head to foot, who searches him through and
> through, to see if there is any ray of hope, any latent spark of
> faith; who pleads with him again and again, and at length
> abandoning him, mourns over him the while with the
> wounded affection of a friend rather than the severity of a
> Judge of the whole earth."[134]

Since Christ's care extends, as we see, even to the case of betrayal
and rejection, we can depend upon His mercy on the Day of Judgment.
Instead of a mass condemnation of the wicked, each case will be treated
individually and with the utmost care of a Judge "who would fain make,
if He could, the fruit of His passion more numerous than it is."[135] The
Judgment can no longer be regarded as an impersonal application of
eternal decrees but an encounter with God in human form. It must now
be seen in the new light of the mystery of the Incarnation. Though
God's justice still requires satisfaction for sin it is accompanied by the
love of Christ manifested in His humanity. Hence Newman reminds us
of the Person who will be our judge at the Last Day.

> "...for Man has redeemed us, Man is set above all creatures,
> as one with the Creator. Man shall judge man at the last day.
> So honoured is this earth, that no stranger shall judge us, but
> He who is our fellow, who will sustain our interests and has
> full sympathy with all our imperfections. He who loved us,
> even to die for us, is graciously appointed to assign the final

---

[133] P.P.S.ii.3.

[134] P.P.S.iii.9.

[135] ibid.

measurement and price upon His own work. He who best knows by infirmity to take the part of the infirm, He who would fain reap the full fruit of His passion. He will separate the wheat from the chaff, so that not a grain shall fall to the ground. He who has given us to share His own spiritual nature. He from whom we have drawn the life's blood of our souls. He our brother will decide about His brethren. In that His second coming, may He in His grace and loving pity, remember us, who is our only hope, our only salvation."[136]

The humanity of Christ therefore changes the Day of Judgment from an event of unmitigated dread to a personal encounter filled with hope. The image of a tribunal at which all must plead guilty, is transformed into a seat of mercy. There is also a change in the relationship between the Judge and the accused for it is the Judge's own work that will be assessed. He will judge according to His love and His love will be the guardian of His justice.[137] Thus the Day of Judgment becomes the Day of the Lord. When He comes it will be in human form.[138] Though it is as Judge of all the earth, His humanity is the assurance that we could not wish for any more favourable treatment. No human friend or love could fill us with greater hope than the desire to fall into the hands of Christ.

"Therefore though I am in a great strait, I would rather fall into His hands, than into those of any creature. True it is I could find creatures more like myself, imperfect or sinful; it might seem better to betake myself to some of these who have power with God, and to beseech them to interest themselves for me. But no; somehow I cannot content myself with this; terrible as it is, I had rather go to God alone, I have an instinct within me which leads me to rise and go to my Father."[139]

This hopeful vision of the Last Judgment is based on Christ's atonement. This is the heart of religion without which no other doctrine

---

[136] P.P.S.ii,3.

[137] Newman's view anticipates the famous aphorism that "any justice which is only justice soon degenerates into something less than justice. It must be saved by something which is more than justice." R.Niebuhr, *Moral Man and Immoral Society*, SCM, 1963, p. 258

[138] P.P.S.vi,10.

[139] P.P.S.v,4.

may be held profitably. The Judgment to come is an untrue belief if it is not linked to the sacrifice of Christ.[140] His merits enable us to raise our hearts to God in hope.[141] We must not worry therefore about the future of where our path leads as long as it leads to Him. Why trouble ourselves with thoughts of the terrors in store if Christ is present to protect and strengthen us?[142] He is the only one who can do us any good or bring us comfort on that day for He "was born into this world for our regeneration, was bruised for our iniquities, and rose again for our justification."[143]

Newman's Anglican sermons begin with "the two grand doctrines of justification and sanctification." These doctrines which are at the core of the Gospel scheme of salvation, are the means by which the mystery of the Trinity is revealed.[144] Newman at this early stage however, approached the mystery in a juridical frame of mind. Judgment belonged to the Father and subsidiary roles were given to the Son and Holy Spirit. In his later sermons a great change can be seen and the influence of the Church fathers is evident. In a rich development of Trinitarian theology, all three Persons complement each other in the Last Judgment. Heaven and earth are linked in the one solemn act. The Father remains in heaven, the Son comes as Judge and the Holy Spirit speaks from within the world.

"God is mysteriously threefold; and while He remains in His highest heaven, He comes to judge the world; - and while He judges the world, He is in us also, bearing us up and going forth in us to meet Himself. God the Son is without, but God the Spirit is within, - and when the Son asks, the Spirit will answer. That Spirit is vouchsafed to us here; and if we yield ourselves to His gracious influences, so that He draws up our thoughts and wills to heavenly things, and becomes one with us, He will assuredly be still in us and give us confidence at the Day of Judgment."[145]

---

[140] P.P.S.vi.7. Here Newman integrates all the Christian mysteries around the mystery of the Cross of Christ. For a description of how the mysteries are related to each other cf. Nos.402-408.

[141] P.P.S.v,22.

[142] P.P.S.v,6.

[143] P.P.S.vii,1.

[144] No.23.

[145] ibid.

div align="center">/div>

Part Three
Eternal Punishment

Introduction and Context

There are but few examples in the history of theology which can
match such a radical reversal in the reception of doctrine, as that which
occurred in the case of eternal punishment in 19th century England.
What was all but universally believed at the beginning of the century,
was all but universally denied at its close.[146] Changing social structures
such as the growth of the middle class, reforms in the criminal and
penal system,[147] and the prevailing philosophy of Bentham and Mill
greatly influenced the religious values of the time. The attitude towards
punishment changed from a punitive view where the satisfaction of the
offended party was the primary purpose, to a remedial view which
aimed at the reform of the offender. Corporal punishment still
functioned as a social deterrent - it was a common feature both in family
and school - but no longer needed the religious sanction of eternal
punishment.[148] As a crusade for civilized values took the foreground,
doubts gathered around the doctrine for reasons of its moral
unacceptability.

In the midst of such changes, Newman retained to the end his
belief in eternal punishment.[149] However, it was not from obstinacy or
any reactionary spirit that he did so. More than most he felt the
intolerable burden of the belief, but he strove to defend it, combining a
care for the Word of God with sensitivity for the perplexed religious
mind. A mere rejection of eternal punishment on moral grounds was all
too facile for him, for it ignored the density of the revealed fact. Its
literal and plain disclosure in the New Testament seemed to him all too

---

[146] G.Rowell, *Hell and the Victorians*, Oxford, 1974.

[147] In 1818 there were more than 200 capital offences on the statute books. Such
deterrents to crime only diminished after Robert Peel established an efficient police-
force. Cf. L.E. Elliot-Binns, *Religion in the Victorian Era*, London, 1946, p. 16.

[148] The role of religious beliefs in sanctioning social values can be shown in the
case of F.D.Maurice who was dismissed from his chair of theology at London University
in 1853 for his public denial of the belief in eternal punishment. cf. Elliot-Binns, op. cit.
p. 281.

[149] In W.Ward's life of Newman which covers his Catholic period there are many
letters attesting to the Cardinal's belief in his old age. See also Newman's article in *"Stray
Essays"* 1884.

obvious to be denied.

Newman saw the belief in eternal punishment as the most vulnerable of the mysteries of religion open to a liberal attack. It was the exposed flank of the Christian system of doctrine which could be most easily penetrated. A doctrine so inherently abhorrent to the human mind could not be but at variance with the benevolence of God. A rejection of it, however, implied the denial of the Atonement, "the keystone of Christianity"[150] which when undermined would herald the collapse of the whole dogmatic system. Hence it was for him "the great crux in the Christian system as contemplated by the human mind... it is the critical doctrine - you can't get rid of it - it is the very characteristic of Christianity."[151] If the doctrinal thread of eternal punishment were withdrawn it would unravel the whole pattern of revealed truth.

Eternal Punishment as a Revealed Fact

In contrast to the moral certainty we have from conscience of future judgment, the belief in eternal punishment arises solely from revelation. It is a doctrine "peculiarly Christian and is to be received by Christians entirely on faith and not as if they could understand why God has declared it."[152] It is unknown among the heathens "yet our Lord, in His account of the Judgment when "all nations" shall be gathered before Him, does not except them from the risk of it."[153] The doctrine is made known to us as the underside of the mystery of the Atonement. It is "the appalling light" which Christ's death throws upon the mystery of sin and the punishment it deserves.

"...since sin is thus odious in our Maker's sight, thus inherent in the very constitution of our minds, and thus paramount and engrossing in its workings within us, we may be somewhat prepared to contemplate the extent of punishment which Scripture declares to be its due. This is an awful, an incomprehensible subject. We receive the doctrine

---

[150] L.D. Vol.i, p. 68 ; AW p. 38.

[151] L.D. Vol.xi, p. 318, Dec.2 1849.

[152] No.269 p. 12.

[153] P.P.S.iii,20.

in faith because God has revealed it, and are sure the Judge of all the earth does right - A punishment of eternal misery awaits it from the hands of God. Sin is said to expose us to His wrath, His never-dying wrath."[154]

Newman's sermons are a continual reminder of the doctrine. By His death Christ took upon Himself "the punishment which we had deserved."[155] He has paid satisfaction to an offended God and thus relieved us from the curse which our natural disobedience merits.[156] By nature "we tend to God's wrath everlasting - we are in the way to the pit of destruction."[157] Though eternal punishment is "inconceivable," the penalty for sin is a second death of "unutterable suffering."[158] The curse has been removed by the sacrifice of Christ yet the choice remains whether to "gratify yourself now and perish for all eternity" or "suffer a little now and enjoy eternal bliss."[159] To choose the former is to live "in peril of eternal ruin."[160] If we were left to ourselves we would grow up to hate God and eventually arrive at "that inward fire of hell torments, maturing in evil through a long eternity."[161] All of this is due to that "fearful root of sin which is sure in the event of reigning and triumphing unto everlasting woe."[162] Conscience can inform and alarm us about evil "but how sinful sin is, must be a matter of revelation." He is a God of love and cannot take any pleasure in the misery of His creatures, yet He has declared in the clearest possible terms the fact of eternal punishment.

"...in the plainest terms He declares the wicked shall go into everlasting fire. Again and again is the future punishment of sin declared to be eternal - and lest, through our ignorance of ourselves and of true holiness we should proudly refuse to

---

[154] No.19 pp. 36-37.

[155] No.27.

[156] No.4; No.6.

[157] No.562.

[158] No.70.

[159] No.26. The option is also mentioned in P.P.S. viii,11: "Sorrow here or misery hereafter; they cannot escape one or the other."

[160] P.P.S.vii,1.

[161] P.P.S.vii,15.

[162] ibid.

admit this teaching, and ...try to explain it in a sense more favourable to our wishes these declarations have frequently a caution added to beware of deceiving ourselves."[163]

Unfounded Notions and Errors

Once the belief in eternal punishment is accepted as a datum of revelation, reason can proceed to assess its significance. From Newman's earliest days the incomprehensibility of the doctrine was perceived as a challenge to faith.[164] Immediately following upon his sermon on Human Corruption, he lists the reasons brought against the doctrine and attempts to show their inadequacy. Since our original corruption has entirely alienated us from God "eternal punishment should not be reckoned unjust and unmerciful and improbable."[165] Newman's defence is per viam negativam; there is nothing to be said on the grounds of antecedent probability - reason could not argue towards it - but there is nothing in it against reason, once we accept in faith the mystery of the atonement and its shadow side, which is the mystery of sin. His argument starts by first reminding us that "there are many things in nature and providence [which] are contrary to our a priori ideas." Moreover, there is a natural bias within us to reject the doctrine since we cannot view it dispassionately, and our condition as guilty persons renders us unfit to be proper judges of guilt. Our tendency to consider sin a light matter runs contrary to the evidence, for even in this life we see that it is punished heavily. In the light of this evidence "future misery seems to be the natural consequence of sin." Finally, he surmises that "eternal punishment may be necessary to God's moral government." The hereditary nature of our guilt, and attempts to repair the offence of sin, may seem to diminish the threat of eternal punishment but such reasons are inadequate to satisfy the just demand of an offended God. A punishment which is eternal would alone appear

---

[163] No.192 p. 17.

[164] The doctrine was one of the reasons for his brother Charles's rejection of Christianity and can be seen from the long correspondence between the brothers in L.D. Vols.i and ii. A resume of the arguments is found in Newman's long letter to Charles, L.D. ii, 266-281 and in his memorandum on Revelation which immediately follows.

[165] No.21 *The Corruption of our Nature [continued]*. The manuscript is missing but the abstract of the sermon is extant. The nine points of the argument are outlined in this sermon abstract and are similar to the account of Newman's conversation with a friend on their walk from Turnham Green to Knightsbridge, cf AW p. 192 .

to do justice to the enormity of our transgression.

In many of his sermons Newman looks at the doubtful arguments which are brought against the doctrine. He points out that such errors all stem from a defective notion of sin. On the analogy that temporal punishment is a satisfaction for offences against society, it is often wrongly assumed that such suffering can atone for "our sins *against our Maker.*" There is in fact no proportionate relation between temporal suffering and the enormity of sin for "the least sin deserves ... a punishment greater than the greatest temporal punishment."[166] Our present suffering can in no way be an expiation for our guilt since "the satisfaction for sin is not in this life but in the next." Hence nothing we can do by our own efforts can substitute for the inherent penalty of eternal punishment as the just reward for sin. In fact Newman asserts that "...the whole scheme of Christian doctrine was in direct variance with the notion of temporal affliction atoning for sin and being put in the place of eternal punishment."[167]

Another error is to assume that since Christians now live under a dispensation of mercy, the threat of eternal punishment should no longer be taken seriously. Newman counters this by saying that though Christ has removed the *curse* of eternal punishment, He has not taken away its sanction and the real possibility of eternal misery.

"Many persons indeed talk of the Christian covenant as being less terrible in its punishments than the Jewish - and imagine because it contains more mercy that therefore it contains less severity on the offender. But I confess, I cannot see that it is less fearful in its denunciations, because the fulfilment of them is unseen not seen, future not present nor can I comprehend how it can be said to have softened the rigors of the Jewish Law when Christ denounces not a mere temporal punishment (as Moses did) but an eternal punishment...let no one then flatter himself with vain and unfounded notions of what he calls the mercy of God or fancy that He will not punish."[168]

It is also argued in objection to the doctrine, that life is miserable enough without the prospect of further misery in the next world. But

---

[166] No.92 p. 3.
[167] No.90.
[168] No.143 pp. 18-19.

this is merely an argumentum ad hominem based on conjecture and hope, with no substantial evidence to support it. The burden of proof is not on those who rest their argument on the express declaration of Scripture, but on those who would contest it. Moreover the experience we have of God's dealings with sin would support rather than contradict the doctrine of eternal punishment. Though we believe rightly that Christ has stood in the place of our suffering, it is plainly obvious that it does not mean our present troubles, which we must bear alone. It can therefore only refer to our future suffering, which is the natural consequence of sin, had not Christ intervened on our behalf.[169]

> "In support of their doctrine they will bring mere conjectures and hopes and doubtful arguments. And can it give any stable comfort to a mind conscious of sin, to have at best merely the surmise that perhaps God will allow his present sufferings to atone for his offences."[170]

It is also sometimes alleged that it is unjust of God to punish us when our guilt is merely the result of following our nature. Such an argument, however, fails to distinguish between the law of our old nature and the new creation. We are not told about the doctrine of eternal punishment until we first learn of our regeneration, so in arguing against it we must do so on the basis of our new nature. The argument would have some substance if we were condemned without any recourse to the means of salvation but that is not now the case. Even then however it would be a specious argument.

> "We were meant to follow the law of our nature; but why of our old nature, why not of our new? Were we indeed in the state of our first nature, under the guilt and defilement of our birth-sin, then this argument might be urged speciously, though not conclusively of course then; Now that God has opened the doors of our prison-house, and brought us into the kingdom of His Son, if men are still carnal men, and the world a sinful world, and the life of Angels a burden, and the law of our nature not the law of God, whose fault is it?"[171]

---

[169] No.180.

[170] No.175 p. 5.

[171] P.P.S.iv,1.

All objections to the doctrine really boil down to a personal conviction that it is inconceivable that God should punish and condemn. It is impossible to believe that any great number of the elect should be lost, and hence it is reasonable to take the practical gamble that one will be counted among the vast majority who have nothing to fear in this regard.[172] Human experience simply cannot contemplate the thought of anyone, not least oneself, being condemned for all eternity. This is precisely where faith and human experience are in opposition to each other.[173] Our reason can only be baffled by the idea. Yet in spite of all the arguments which reason can bring, in spite of the feelings of abhorrence and the realization that no human being is entirely bereft of goodness, Newman puts his reliance on the revealed word. He eschews the doctrine of the predestination of the damned and the right to judge any person as condemned, but He holds the doctrine of eternal punishment on the Word of God.

> "We have no right indeed, surely not, to say absolutely that this or that man whom we see and can point at, is destined to future punishment. God forbid! for we can judge by outward appearance, and God alone seeth the hearts of men. But we are expressly told that there are persons so destined; and whatever the sight of things may tell us, however the weaknesses and waywardness of our hearts may plead against such awful truths, however our feelings, and imaginations, and reason may be assailed, yet "let God be true, and every man a liar;" let us believe Him, though the whole world rose up and with one voice denied His words. Let us accept the truth, as an act of faith towards God, and as a most solemn warning to ourselves"[174]

The Fate of the Damned

Newman's belief in the existence of Hell does not entail the denial of God's universal salvific will. "It must not be for an instance supposed that I am admitting the possibility of a person being rejected by God,

---

[172] No.319.

[173] S.D.vi entitled *Faith and Experience*. The doctrine of eternal punishment is one of four instances where faith and experience are in opposition and where a revealed doctrine constitutes a trial of faith.

[174] S.D.iv p. 76-7.

who has any such right feelings in his mind."[175] Damnation is entirely due to human freedom which has the power to resist the grace of salvation. Hence human beings are capable of ultimately determining their destiny, and should the gift of salvation be rejected, must bear the whole blame for their damnation.[176] Moreover, our freedom can be so totally perverted by sin as to render "God's glory irreconcilable with the salvation of sinners."[177] He believes therefore that hell is not empty, though we can never discern nor judge whether any particular person has been committed to it.[178]

Despite the often intense severity of the Anglican sermons, there is an absence of any gruesome details of the place of damnation.[179] The scant references to the torments of the wicked is in strong contrast to Newman's portrait of the blessed in heaven. These occasional allusions to hell underline the spiritual nature of the torment and avoid any conjectures about the physical condition of the damned. The picture Newman presents is one in which the souls in hell gain a full knowledge of evil[180] without any of its pleasures, and where human feelings of sympathy do not exist.[181] They are condemned to a fate of their own making, a state of wilful obduracy which imprisons them in the frustrated company of each other.[182] It is a withering experience, a "living death of eternal torment" for which annihilation would be a mercy.

Though God "laid the foundations of the eternal prison where lie the fallen angels"[183] and is "intimately present *with* evil"[184] thereby sustaining it in existence, He has not predestined or condemned out of hand the souls of the impenitent. The misery of the damned, like the

[175] P.P.S.i,18.

[176] P.P.S.ii,28.

[177] P.P.S.ii,31.

[178] ibid; P.P.S.v,18.

[179] "I have tried in various ways to make the truth less terrible to the imagination." Apo. p. 6.

[180] P.P.S.viii,18.

[181] P.P.S.iv,6; S.D.vi.

[182] No.109; P.P.S.iv,4. "the horror of finding themselves without bodies, without anything to touch, anything to turn upon and wreck their fury upon...."

[183] No.95.

[184] P.P.S.viii,18.

great part of all human misery, arises from within themselves. It is not a punishment externally imposed, but "an inward fire" of personal sin. Hell is not a place of fatalism but the creation of an evil self-will, which resolutely remains at variance with the will of God. It is the place of rebellious spirits, conscious of their destructive power and energetic in their determined hatred of God.

> "And in hell they will still be tormented by the worm of proud rebellious hatred of God! Not even ages will reconcile them to a hard endurance of their fate; not even the dry apathy in which unbelievers on earth take refuge, will be allowed them. There is no fatalism in the place of torment. The devils see their doom was their own fault, they are unable to be sorry for it. It is their *will* that is in direct energetic variance with the will of God, and they know it."[185]

The most characteristic feature of hell is the total absence of human affection. History has witnessed evil and wicked persons but never to the degree where there were no redeeming qualities. Thus the mind cannot envisage a situation in which people whom we have known are condemned to a place where "human feelings cannot exist." We cannot understand what is meant by the company of fallen spirits "who have no sympathies, no weaknesses, but are impenetrable and absolute evil, even though they suffer."[186]

> "There is no man but has some human feelings or other: and those very feelings impress us with a sort of conviction that he cannot possibly be the destined companion of evil spirits. Hell is the habitation of no human affections"[187]

A Trial of Faith

The doctrine of eternal punishment is an instance, by no means rare, of something relatively unimportant assuming a significance far beyond its proper sphere. It has a peculiar power to involve us

---

[185] P.P.S.iii,7.

[186] S.D. p. 75.

[187] ibid. There is a parallel passage in P.P.S.iv,6.

102

personally in the issue and to stimulate deeper questions. It cannot be regarded as central to Christian belief, yet it raises the essential nature of revelation and of our assent to it in faith. By posing the threat of possible damnation, it provokes an entirely personal response, which puts in sharp relief, one's real rather than one's notional views of revealed truth.

The doctrine highlights two important elements which together constitute a supreme trial of faith. In common with the other mysteries of religion it contains the element of obscurity, since the notion of eternal damnation is inconceivable to the human mind. However, unlike the higher mysteries such as the Incarnation and the Trinity, which are indeed much more obscure, it provokes a sense of revulsion at the prospect of eternal misery. These two dimensions of intellectual darkness and inner revulsion make the doctrine of eternal punishment the example par excellence of religious perplexity, though not exclusively so.

In his sermons Newman frequently has recourse to eternal punishment to illustrate the nature of revealed truth and the state of mind we should have in approaching the mysteries. Here we find his use of the dogmatic principle in opposition to rationalism,[188] and the principle of reserve[189] as the means of protecting and transmitting revealed truth. These three elements, dogma, reserve and perplexity are interwoven into his treatment of the doctrine of eternal punishment. To show however the function they play, they will be examined separately, beginning with the immediate trial itself of religious perplexity.[190]

---

[188] For Newman's defence of dogma against the attack by Rationalism cf his Tract LXXIII written in 1835 and later republished in an essay entitled *On the Introduction of Rationalistic Principles into Revealed Religion,* in Essays Critical and Historical, Vol.i pp. 30 - 101. See also Note A, No.5 on the denial of eternal punishment as a consequence of Liberalism, Apo. p. 294.

[189] Cf. R.C. Selby, *The Principle of Reserve in the Writings ofJohn Henry Cardinal Newman,* Oxford, Oxford University Press, 1975. The author provides many examples of Newman's use of reserve, but no example regarding eternal punishment.

[190] No adequate account of any of the three elements can be given in this thesis. The goal is simply to show how the doctrine of eternal punishment is an example illustrating them.

Religious Perplexity

All three elements first appear in a short course Newman gave in January 1825 on the Hiddenness of God.[191] God reveals Himself enough for us to seek Him but not enough for us to control or presume equality with Him. We must seek Him in a certain way and with a certain frame of mind. Our knowledge of Him is but partial and this implies a search and a trial of our sincerity to take Him at His Word. The open door of skepticism is often entered by Satan "suggesting unbelieving thoughts and wicked doubts, confusing and overpowering the mind with a variety of temptations." However sufficient knowledge has been revealed for salvation "even supposing the difficult passages which cause perplexity were not written..."[192]

Newman returned to the theme of perplexity five years later in his course on Seeking and Finding which he gave again in 1833 with two notable changes.[193] He first notes that intellectual ability is of a different order from moral and spiritual excellence and revelation is intended to promote the latter. "Faith is one thing and ability is another; because ability of mind is a *gift* and faith is a *grace*."[194] Only moral earnestness and humble inquiry can bring us under God's grace to religious truth; we cannot decide a priori what is "trifling or extravagant or irrational" in revealed doctrine. We must simply act upon the partial light[195] we have and in this way of obedience, more light will be given. For obedience is the remedy for all perplexity.

> "Seek truth by the way of *obedience*; try to act up to your conscience, and let your opinions be the result, not of mere chance reasoning or fancy, but of an improved heart...God surely will listen to none but those who strive to obey

---

191 No.47,48,49.

192 No.48 p. 6.

193 Course xxxiii, 1830 consisted of Nos. 263 (P.P.S. viii,13), 264 (P.P.S. i,17), 265 (P.P.S. viii,14), 268 (P.P.S. i,18), 269, 270 and 272 (not exstant). The two notable additions were No.304 (P.P.S. vii,5) and 231 (P.P.S.vii,18) which both underline the principle of reserve.

194 P.P.S.viii.13. The distinction between blessing, a natural gift, and grace was made in No.88. The danger of intellectual ability divorced from faith can also be seen in P.P.S.i,17.

195 No.404 p. 2: "It is not easy in an educated age to acquiesce in partial knowledge yet act upon it."

Him."[196]

Newman compares the attitudes of two classes of men in their search for religious truth. The first class are the rationalists, the "self-wise inquirers" who trust their own reasoning powers instead of taking what God has already revealed. They do not acknowledge that reason is "weak in all inquiries into moral and religious truth" and "in questions connected with our duty to God and man is very unskilful and equivocating."[197] The second class are the honest inquirers, who seek religious truth in a spirit of faith. But even though they accept what God has revealed, difficulties do not disappear. Quite the contrary, their faith creates even greater problems.[198] However, they manfully bear the difficulties and doubts as a test of their sincerity and eventually arrive at a settled state of mind.

Every doctrine has its prescriptive as well as its cognitive side and "doubts in religion do not interfere with practical obedience."[199] The remedy therefore in times of doubt is to "embody [the general doctrines] in those particular instances in which they become ordinary duties." Thus the doctrine of eternal punishment contains a warning on the consequences of sin and embodies the general obligation to avoid it. In proportion as we follow this duty in each instance of temptation, greater light is thrown on the meaning of the doctrine. Hence the more we actually avoid sin the less distracted and disturbed we are by "vague fears and uncertain indefinite surmises about the future." It is a practical wisdom to deal with the present implications of the doctrine rather than to allow the imagination and feelings of despair to overpower us.

> "Nay though it is shocking to set before their minds such a prospect, yet even were they already in the place of punishment, will they not confess, it would be the best thing they could do, to commit then as little sin as possible? Much more then, *now*, when even if they have no hope, their heart

---

[196] ibid. P.P.S.viii.14 continues the theme of obedience; obedience to conscience leads to obedience to the gospel

[197] P.P.S.i.17.

[198] P.P.S.i,18; No.269 p. 10; P.P.S. iv.2: "Revelation has added to our perplexities, not relieved them!"

[199] The title of No.269.

at least is not so entirely hardened as it will be then."[200]

Increase in knowledge is not the way of getting rid of difficulties in religion. These trials however can not be blamed on the work of Satan instilling doubts in our minds, (as he suggested in his earlier sermon). Christ Himself did not hide trials from us. He did not deceive us by offering a message of mercy and then leaving us to find out the difficulties for ourselves afterwards. Moreover, the revelation of God's mercy is accompanied by the incomprehensible doctrine of eternal punishment, and like two sides of a coin must be taken as one.

"The grant of mercy is conveyed by means of incomprehensible doctrines. The doctrine of the Incarnation is a mystery and peculiar to Christianity yet it is the medium through which the joyful news of redemption is conveyed to us and the promised reward is itself revealed, not without the companionship of a fearful doctrine, that of eternal punishment..."[201]

The perplexity which arises from the doctrine of eternal punishment is not something to be wondered at. It comes from the nature of revelation itself which has an illuminated side, which is the revealed message itself, and a dark side in which the mystery consists.[202] We cannot discard one without the other but must be content with the measure of religious light we gain at the cost of increased intellectual darkness. By humbly accepting the dilemma we discover more about the mystery and "prove *the reality of our faith*."

"We gain spiritual light at the price of intellectual perplexity; a blessed exchange doubtless, (for which is better, to be well and happy within ourselves, or to know what is going on at the world's end?) still at the price of perplexity. For instance, how infinitely important and blessed is the news of eternal happiness? but we learn in connexion with this joyful truth, that there is a *state of endless misery* too. Now how great a

---

[200] P.P.S.i.18.

[201] No.269 p. 12 ; P.P.S.i.16 "not merely do the good tidings and the mystery go together, as in the revelation of eternal life and eternal death...."

[202] *Essays Critical and Historical*, vol.i, p. 41: "A Revelation is religious doctrine viewed on its illuminated side; a Mystery is the self-same doctrine on the side unilluminated. Thus Religious Truth is neither light nor darkness, but both together."

mystery is this! Yet the difficulty goes hand in hand with the spiritual blessing."[203]

A Doctrine of Faith

We have seen that Newman regards intellectual difficulties as a necessary consequence of the nature of revelation. It would in fact be surprising, he says, if there were not something mysterious in revealed truth. Such mysteriousness is indeed a recommendation for it, not in the sense "that it *is* true, *because* it is mysterious; but that if it *be* true, it cannot help being mysterious."[204] Hence revelation implies some trial of faith and the doctrine of eternal punishment is one clear instance of such a trial. If we refuse to be tried we are making ourselves the centre and the judge of truth and putting God on trial instead. This is the presumptuous spirit which characterizes rationalism; it exalts reason and reverses the role of the Creator and the creature. Newman thus defines presumption as the sin of

."...seeking God beyond or beside His own revealed word - of acting without Him - or forgetting that He has to speak before we act - that He has to speak and we to listen - that we are to follow not to lead"[205]

Our refusal to take God at His Word on the question of eternal punishment is an example of such presumption. We either go "beyond it" by exaggerating His attribute of mercy or "beside it" by our indifference, but do not listen and follow its injunction.

"Others again presume on God's mercy - imagine mercy to be the sole attribute of God - they think it is impossible He can punish sin as He said He will - they pretend to honour Him by making Him more merciful than He really is - This is of course dreadful presumption - This is gross unbelief -

---

[203] P.P.S.i,16.

[204] P.P.S.vi,23.

[205] No.95. The handwriting in this passage is of the later Newman, possibly in 1841 when he repeated this sermon.

for these men affect to think so highly of God's love, as to doubt His truth. He hath said and shall He not do it?"[206]

We have also seen that obedience to conscience and the Word of God was the unique remedy for religious perplexity. Obedience likewise to the voice of the Church complements this practical rule. Despite its fallibility and corruptions, the Church is to be taken as a reliable "guide in the search for truth and as a rule for practice till they can prove it is mistaken."[207] In its creeds and liturgy we have the testimony of what Christians have always believed. The object of such belief is to inspire holiness and virtue rather than add to the store of intellectual knowledge. This might seem to question the need for orthodoxy or whether there is any point to an enlightened faith. Orthodox belief however, is as necessary for holiness as the observance of the commandments, for faith is "the only way to become holy."[208] Receiving the faith promotes a life of holiness and neglect or ignorance of it tends to lower moral standards for "a defective faith is attended by a defective obedience."[209] Hence a severe doctrine such as eternal punishment cannot be dismissed as irrelevant to the growth of holiness since it instils the dispositions required for it, by teaching us abhorrence for sin and fearful awe of God. It is a "holy doctrine for it provides for our pardon without dispensing with our obedience."[210]

"When I am asked how is a man better for believing in the creed, I answer he is evidently better in this respect - it has taught him awe and strictness ... religion in its essence is subordination to a law; this is what the world, the flesh and the devil in every age have striven against. Evil takes many shapes but insubordination is its essence."[211]

What Newman has said on believing in the creed has a particular relevance to eternal punishment which is explicitly professed in the

---

[206] ibid. p. 12.

[207] No.270 p. 23. This sermon entitled *The Church a Guide and Refuge to those who are perplexed with Doubt* is thematically similar to P.P.S.iv.12.

[208] No.155 p. 6 *On the Creeds* .

[209] No.518 p. 11.

[210] P.P.S. v.14.

[211] No.518 p. 21.

Athanasian creed.[212] A movement of disenchantment with the metaphysical language on the Trinity, and a repugnance towards its two anathemas, was gathering strength to have it no longer required in public worship.[213] Such anathemas offended the tolerant mind which opposed them "on the ground that none but senseless bigots contend about points of faith." The creed was also regarded as authoritarian and inconsistent with the freedom of the gospel. Newman had before the age of sixteen drawn up a series of texts on each verse of the Athanasian creed[214]; in his sermons he regards it as a true development of the baptismal and Nicene creeds in "fuller and more accurate form."[215] Toleration of error was a false form of charity and revealed doctrine could not be accommodated to satisfy liberal wishes. Since intolerance was now seen as "the chief of sins" the Apostles must be regarded as the most intolerant of men for they anathematized with the curse of eternal punishment those who did not obey the Gospel.[216]

> "...and when they find offence taken at the Church's creed, they begin to think how they can modify or curtail it under the same sort of feeling as would lead them to be generous in a money transaction...Thus, for instance, they speak against the Anathemas of the Athanasian Creed, or of the Commination Service, or of certain of the Psalms, and wish to get rid of them."[217]

One of the features of rationalism in religion is the principle of expediency, which measures the truth of revelation by the success it has to influence and convince the liberal mind.[218] Without reference to the

---

[212] The Athanasian creed, also known as the 'Quicunque Vult', was recited on 13 feast days of the year including the Feast of SS.Simon and Jude on which this sermon was preached. The Athanasian authorship of this creed has generally been abandoned.

[213] The liberal movement for the removal of it from the Prayer Book was in its infancy at the time of this sermon. The movement came to its head with the rejection by Convocation of the liberal view in 1873, largely by the forceful intervention of former Tractarians, Pusey and Liddon. Cf S.C.Carpenter, *Church and People, 1789-1889*, SPCK, 1937, p. 353f.

[214] Apo. p. 5.

[215] P.P.S.ii,26; No.226, p. 11; No.408: "I do not know anything which strikes a young mind sooner and makes it feel inquisitive than the Athanasian creed."

[216] P.P.S.ii,31.

[217] P.P.S.ii,23. The two anathemas are contained in vv.2 and 42.

[218] P.P.S.ii,22.

clear and definite statements of the creed it considers faith to be " a mere temper of mind or principle of action, [or] much less vaguely, the Christian cause."[219] Rationalism leads to a partial selection of revealed truth based on pre-conceived notions and ideas acceptable to the age. This can be illustrated by its rejection of eternal punishment as inconsistent with the notion of Infinite Love. It seeks moreover an accommodation of religious truth with reason and sentiment. If however we began, by first taking the voice of Scripture and the Church at their word, we might then learn the true accommodation the doctrine makes to our infirmity.

> "Many schools of Religion and Ethics are to be found among us, and they all profess to magnify, in one shape or other, what they consider the principle of love; but what they lack is, a firm maintenance of that characteristic of Divine Nature, which in accommodation to our infirmity, is named by St. John and his brethren, the wrath of God."[220]

Allied to the spirit of benevolence was a humane view of punishment which considered it to be essentially intended for the reformation of the offender. On this basis eternal punishment served no purpose for the possibility of reform was over. It could only mean therefore a form of punitive retribution for the satisfaction of a vengeful God. If punishment was purely remedial the doctrine of eternal punishment had no longer any validity. By invalidating its purpose, however, a knock-on effect occurs which undermines the doctrine of the Atonement, since there is no longer a need to be saved from the curse of eternal death. Denying any part of revealed truth therefore, affects the integrity of the whole system of doctrine.[221]

> "Hence, they consider all punishment to be remedial, a means to an end, deny that the woe threatened against sinners is of eternal duration,[222] and explain away the

---

[219] P.P.S.ii,26.

[220] P.P.S.ii,23.

[221] P.P.S.ii,22; ii,25.

[222] Newman does not consider in his Anglican sermons the essential question of the duration of punishment. As far back however as 1823 the question was in his mind. We can understand what is meant by punishment but not what is meant by it being eternal. Cf AW p. 192. Later in life he writes: "Before we say it we must know what eternity is. We only know the negative side, not the positive. 'Punishment *never* ends' - This proposition

doctrine of the Atonement."[223]

The Principle of Reserve

It has been clearly demonstrated by Selby how Newman used reserve as "a principle not of concealment, but of sensitivity"[224] in communicating the Christian mysteries. Many illustrations of the principle can be found in the sermons, particularly with regard to the Incarnation and the Trinity. However, the reverence and awe which are preeminently associated with these mysteries, also extend to the lesser doctrines such as that of eternal punishment. Although there is no example we can quote in which reserve is explicitly applied to eternal punishment, there are several allusions in his sermons which suggest that Newman intended it to be so.

The need for reserve is mentioned specifically in moments of temptation to unbelief. Newman notes how doctrines - and here we may include eternal punishment - are frequently a subject for ridicule. Such ridicule first shocks and offends but later leaves its mark. Having become the target for cleverness and wit, the doctrines soon lose their power to inspire us with their awesomeness. The ultimate result is that "when we begin to make up our minds which way lies the course of duty on particular trials," we become morally infeebled and unable to act upon the doctrine. Our only recourse is to resist intellectual curiosity, that is, to exercise reserve with the mysteries of faith. "Heaven and hell are at war for us and against us, yet we trifle, and let life go on at random...."

"Speculating wantonly on sacred subjects, and jesting about them, offend us at first; and we turn away: but if in an evil hour we are seduced by the cleverness or wit of a writer or speaker, to listen to his impieties, who can say where we shall stop? Can we save ourselves from the infection of his profaneness? We cannot hope to do so."225

    The principle of reserve can also be seen in the kind severity which Christ showed towards his disciples. His command to Peter to wash His feet was "calculated (assuredly it was) to humble, to awe, and subdue the very person to whom He administered." He brings a message of mercy, but His conduct also teaches us not to presume on His dignity. He did not try "to gain anyone over by smooth representations of His doctrine." So while He showed us love, it was a "love sobered by our fear of Him." The severe doctrine of His wrath is intended to preserve this sense of reverence towards Him for "He draws us on with encouraging voice amid the terrors of His threatenings."

> "Though He is our Saviour, and has removed the slavish fear of death and judgment, are we, therefore, to make light of the prospect before us, as if we were sure of that reward which He bids us struggle for? Assuredly, we are still to "serve the Lord with fear, and rejoice with reverence" - to "kiss the Son, lest He be angry, and so perish from the right way, if His wrath be kindled, yea but a little""226

    One of the practical consequences of reserve, which led to a great deal of objection and misunderstanding, was the rule never to expose the Christian mysteries to argument and debate. Controversy and public dispute tended to debase the currency of sacred doctrine which should properly be communicated to those "who can bear them; not being eager to recount them all, rather hiding them from the world."227 Scripture being a record of faith testifies and confirms doctrine "to those who believe it already" rather than offers any proof. If we approach doctrine in a critical and argumentative fashion, we may be able to "dispute acutely and to hit objections, but not to discover truth."228 The doctrine of eternal punishment is a case in point. It should not be discussed in the abstract but treated, as it was intended, as a matter for personal conversion and repentance.229 Our attitude to it

---

225 P.P.S.viii,5.

226 P.P.S.i,23.

227 ibid.

228 P.P.S.vi,23.

229 Cf Letter of 3rd July 1867 quoted by Dessain in "Cardinal Newman and Eternal Punishment," *Beiträge Zu Einer Hermeneutik Des Theologischen Gesprächs,*

112

must be similar to the reserve in which we hold all the doctrines of faith. If we find them too severe to our reason and imagination we must bow before His revealed word and reverently "impress it on our hearts."

> "If we find it tries, and is too severe whether for our reason or our imagination, or our feelings, let us bow down in simple adoration, and submit to it each of our faculties in turn, not complain of its sublimity and its range."[230]

Summary of Chapter Two

The chapter showed that the severe side of Newman's eschatology had its roots in an intense conviction about the reality of sin and guilt. Though he did not subscribe to a belief in the total depravity of mankind, he laid great emphasis on the depth and extent of human corruption. Only by admitting our human condition as permeated by sin, could one build a solid theology of eternal life through Christ's redemption.

The mystery of the Atonement formed therefore the background to Newman's preaching on the Day of Judgment. In the cross of Christ, God's judgment on a sinful world was definitively declared, but the time for its execution was mercifully deferred until the Last Day. However, though the present was a time of salvation, the principle of God's justice was already operative, albeit in a hidden manner. Christians could regard present affliction as both a penalty for sin and a healing medicine to prepare them for the Day of Judgment.

The dread of future judgment was greatly reduced when Newman turned to consider the mystery of the Incarnation. God's judgment was then seen, not as the impersonal application of eternal decrees, but as the compassionate assessment by a merciful Judge of the fruit of His redemption. Though the fundamental law of justice was not abrogated by the mercy of God, the divine prerogative of passing judgment belonged to Christ who was no stranger to human weakness.

In the last part of the chapter we saw Newman's defence of the

Verlag Styria, 1972, pp. 715-719 .

[230] P.P.S.vi,24. Isaac Williams, who was once Newman's curate, wrote the Tract on Reserve. The principle is recommended for the imprecatory psalms against the wicked, as bound up with the doctrine of eternal punishment. By considering these psalms as offensive, i.e. not holding them in reserve, we may be led to reject the latter.

doctrine of eternal punishment. Though this belief was impalatable to the moral sense and inconceivable to the human mind, the density of the revealed word could not be ignored. Newman thus approached this severe truth with the reserve which must accompany a "holy doctrine", combining at the same time a sensitivity for the perplexed religious mind. He described hell as "the habitation of no human affections" but spared his congregation from gruesome images of fire and brimstone. For Newman, however, the doctrine underpinned the tragic reality of evil in the world and the real possibility of human futility.

CHAPTER THREE

ETERNAL LIFE

Introduction

Newman presents his phenomenology of religion under two aspects, a severe side and a bright side. He first takes the dark side since the encounter with God is initially one of fear and human unworthiness. But this is followed by an inner and more important aspect, that religion both natural and revealed is fundamentally a blessing.[1] In Chapter Two we considered the severe side of eschatology; now we must turn to the heart of the Christian message of salvation, which is the bright prospect of eternal life.

This aspect of blessing however, is less obvious to the naked eye, and the deficiency of natural religion in this respect is all the more apparent. While reason, aided by grace, has some intimation of a future existence where the human heart may find rest, it cannot argue in any sense to the doctrine of eternal life. Only revelation could inform us of such a future destiny. Thus we are utterly dependent on revelation and are totally within the realm of faith in understanding the nature of our final salvation.

The source of our belief in eternal life is the mystery of Christ's resurrection from the dead. If Christ is not risen, we are still in our sins and our hope is in vain. Christ's rising from the dead, however, is seen by Newman, not as an isolated event, but as a particular moment within the Paschal mystery. His death and His ascension are also integral parts of the drama of redemption, in which Christ's sacrifice for sin is transformed into the new life of the Spirit. By His death Christ won our salvation, and His ascension marked the completion of His work. Upon His return to the Father a new era began under the ministration of the Spirit. It was the closure of Christ's manifestation, and the start of an indefinite period under the veil of faith, until He shows Himself again in His Second Coming.

---

[1] This is described most explicitly in the *Grammar of Assent* pp. 386 ff. but the paradigm of severe and bright sides can also be seen in the sermons. The bright side is the more fundamental of the two: "All religion, so far as it is genuine, is a blessing. Natural as well as Revealed" G.A., p. 395.

The core of the doctrine of eternal life may be found in Newman's sermons on the Resurrection and Ascension. The Easter period is the season of faith, and salvation is essentially a hidden reality. Hence we must first consider the nature of faith and the unseen world in which we live. All that we know about eternal life is strictly limited to what revelation tells us, and so a preliminary brief account of Newman's approach to statements of faith, seems necessary. The invisible blessing of eternal life is not something however which begins only after death, but is already given in the present state of salvation. This is a real beginning as well as a preparatory stage of our ultimate fulfilment in Christ. On this new mode of existence Christian hope is founded, a hope which will bear its ultimate fruit in the resurrection of the dead. Salvation, hope and final resurrection thus form the structure of this chapter on eternal life.

Part One
The State of Salvation

The Invisible World

The idea which Newman conveys in his description of the invisible world is both simple and complex. It is simple in the direct and immediate image it imprints on the mind, but complex in the range of problems it raises concerning the reality and knowledge of faith. In this respect however, it is not unlike the physical world we take so much for granted. Both of them imply the element of trust in the reliability of evidence, whether of sense or the testimony of faith. Moreover, the idea of a world of any kind, requires the active involvement of a human subject and the existence of an objective reality which it perceives, and in this lies its complexity.[2] Mercifully however, this questioning of reality only arises on the second level of reflection, and must always be preceded by a common-sense acceptance of something existing outside

---

[2] The epistemology of faith which Newman deals with in his university sermons and later develops in the Grammar of Assent is beyond the scope of this thesis. Nevertheless it is essential to the hermeneutics of eschatological statements which I will briefly touch on here. For an account of Newman's thought on the subject, cf. T.Vargish, *The Contemplation of Mind*, Oxford 1970, pp. 25-72.

116

ourselves. We have an instinct within us - what Newman later called an illative sense - forcing us to trust the evidence of sense and the voice of conscience and revelation.

> "We have an instinct within us, impelling us, we have external necessity forcing us, to trust our senses, and we may leave the question of their substantial truth for another world, "till the day break, and the shadows flee away." And what is true of reliance on our senses, is true of all the information which it has pleased God to vouchsafe to us, whether in nature or in grace."[3]

The unseen world which Newman vividly describes is a world in which the objects of revealed truth are known in a personal and concrete way. Though it cannot be verified empirically, the act of trusting in such a world is no different from the reliance we place on our everyday experience.[4] Though we may be deceived by our senses and credulous in our belief, trust is a basic element of life common to reason and faith. A skeptical attitude is legitimate in matters of opinion when decisive evidence is required. But in things which touch our personal lives and are of supreme practical importance, it is perfectly reasonable to act on limited information, even though "higher and fuller evidence of its truth might be given us."[5] In matters of faith we have sufficient light to go by, and revelation conveys its message in a human way, by facts and actions, while at the same time impressing itself on our mind. In this respect it is a direct and simple disclosure.

> "Here, then, Revelation meets us with simple and distinct facts and actions, not with painful deductions from existing phenomena, not with generalized laws or metaphysical conjectures, but with *Jesus and the Resurrection;*...Facts such as this are not simply evidence of the truth of revelation, but the media of its impressiveness."[6]

Though the unseen world is not a figment of the imagination or a

---

[3] U.S.xv p. 349.

[4] P.P.S.i,15: "It is (I repeat) the things believed, not the act of believing them, which is peculiar to religion."

[5] P.P.S.ii,2.

[6] U.S.ii p. 29.

projection of wish fulfilment, it is indeed a hidden world of symbol.[7]
Our senses impress upon us the reality of the external world, and we
not only see things, but know that we see them. But the invisible world,
though it acts upon us, does so without "impressing us with the
consciousness that it does so."[8] Yet it exists as truly as the physical
world, if for no other reason than the reality of God Himself, whose
presence has never been "perceptible to the senses." Just as our material
world is not a world created by our consciousness - but exists prior to it
and through it we become conscious - the invisible world in which God
exists is fully real. It is by faith and the religious imagination, stamping
its impression on our minds, i.e. by realizing things unseen, that we gain
a living apprehension of it.

> "Almighty God, we know, exists more really and absolutely
> than any of those fellow-men whose existence is conveyed
> to us through the senses; yet we see Him not, hear Him not,
> we do but "feel after Him," yet without finding Him. It
> appears then, that the things which are seen are but a part,
> and but a secondary part of the beings around us...."[9]

Human existence then, is living both in a world of sense and in a
world of spirit. This spiritual world however, is not something which
begins only after death when the material world has passed from sight,
but exists at present and surrounds us. "The world of spirits then,
though unseen, is present; present, not future, not distant. It is not above
the sky, it is not beyond the grave; it is now and here; the kingdom of
God is among us."[10] Hence any knowledge we have of the last things is
not information obtained from the after-life - something at present
totally beyond our experience - but a knowledge, however limited, given
to us by revelation. What we therefore affirm about eternal life, is
derived from, and confined to, the limits of our present faith experience.

Though religious impressions of revealed truth are real, they differ
"from those of material objects, in the mode in which they are made.
The senses are direct, immediate, and ordinary informants, and act

---

[7] Newman's strong imaginative powers from his earliest childhood (cf.Apologia p.
2 re.Arabian tales) can be seen in the role he attributes to the religious imagination to
impress upon us the truths of faith so as to realize things unseen.

[8] P.P.S.iv,13.

[9] ibid.

[10] ibid.

118

spontaneously without any will or effort on our part; but no such faculties have been given us, as far as we know, for realizing the Objects of Faith."[11] Since the mode of communication is different,"we put the latter into language in order to fix, teach, and transmit them, but not the former."[12] Revealed truth is received by hearing and not by sight, and thus our only access to it is by way of language. Thus dogma plays a crucial role in providing us with such a means of knowing, though it can never unravel the mystery, or give us its inner meaning. As Newman remarks, "...there is no such inward view of these doctrines, distinct from the dogmatic language to express them...[for] our ideas of Divine things are just co-extensive with the figures by which we express them, neither more nor less, and without them are not."[13] Hence statements of eschatology are no more illuminating than the light of faith itself. They are navigational buoys directing faith through narrow water, safeguarding it from the rapids of enthusiasm and the sands of skepticism.

"Our lives are hid with Christ in God" is the leitmotiv of Newman's sermons on the mystery of salvation. This element of hiddenness is the note he constantly stresses in all the Christian mysteries. Christ "is a hidden Saviour...whatever be the tokens of His Presence, still they must be of a nature to admit of persons doubting where it is." "True religion is a life hidden in the heart."[14] All God's visitations are shrouded in secrecy[15] and the privileges of the Gospel are invisible. Even nature itself is full of hidden powers and as spring comes but once a year, an Eternal Spring awaits us, which was once made manifest in Christ's resurrection. Since then He has lodged new life in His kingdom "and as it is now hidden, so in due season it shall be revealed."[16] The life of grace and future glory therefore, are under the veil and perceived only by the infra-red light of faith. Christians then are those whose "thoughts...contemplations...desires and hopes are

---

[11] U.S.xv. p. 334. Newman states the purpose of this sermon which is "to investigate the connexion between Faith and Dogmatic Confession, as far as relates to the sacred doctrines...and to show the office of Reason in reference to it."

[12] ibid.

[13] ibid.

[14] P.P.S.iv,16.

[15] P.P.S.ii,10; viii,13; vi,9: "The Annunciation was secret; the Nativity was secret; the miraculous Fasting was secret..."

[16] P.P.S.iv,13.

stored in the invisible world."[17] Such was Newman's own hidden life of faith which was so aptly described in his epitaph: *ex umbris et imaginibus in veritatem*

A New Heavens and a New Earth

In Newman's first Good Friday sermon in 1825, the new order of the resurrection is introduced and anticipated. Christ's death "has opened a new prospect...put things in a new light,... given me new relations, objects and motives...a new life."[18] This new state of things is described symbolically "under the figure of a new heavens and earth."[19] However, when we look around for signs of the new creation, our immediate feelings are those of disappointment; clearly nothing has changed, and the old world order has remained the same. The newness of the world is not seen on its visible surface, but can only be discerned by the eyes of faith. Christ has made it new "not in *altering the actual* state of it, but the *use* of it, not altering the natural form of it but adding a secret power."[20] He has wrought a change in *us*, not in the external world, and addressed it to faith and not to sight; "It is not new, except to new hearts...by the presence of the Holy Spirit in our hearts."[21] Thus Newman describes salvation as personal and spiritual, as a new reality hidden within an old external framework.

> "...though salvation be of faith, and religion be spiritual, and old things be passed away, and all things have become new, yet the old framework remains... the Gospel though it be light and liberty, has not materially altered things here."[22]

---

[17] P.P.S.iv,20.

[18] No. 74.

[19] No. 114 p. 1. This sermon, preached twelve times in all, serves as a guide to Newman's development on the theme of salvation in his published sermons. The important redactions on various occasions, such as Christmas, Easter and the beginning of the year, illustrate how the theme of the new creation branches out and forms a synthesis of the Christian mysteries.

[20] ibid. pp. 2-3.

[21] ibid. p. 22.

[22] P.P.S.v,12.

120

Though no material change has occurred in the world, a moral transformation has taken place by radically changing our relationship to it. By leaving things as they were, but imparting a new inward power to man, God has created a world best suited to the development of our moral character. In His wisdom He has chosen the very means which spelled disaster to be the instrument of our recovery, "making the consequences of sin a medicine for sin." The world of toil and suffering, which was the result of the Fall, has been preserved, but can now be put to a new use. It serves the purpose of training us in holiness by being the testing ground of faith and obedience. The call to duty remains as it ever was, but a new path has been chartered enabling us to attain our goal. Moreover there is now an in-built power in life, a self-correcting mechanism which directs our efforts towards good and away from evil - "the perplexed and corrupted system of human affairs has, when divine grace is once given as an element of improvement, a tendency to right itself."[23] It is truly a new world when seen by faith, but an old world as regards obedience. Newman concludes by saying

> "The Gospel Covenant, then, is both a new way and not a new way. It is not a new way, seeing it is in works: it is a new way, in that it is by faith. It is as St. Paul words it, "the obedience of faith;" - new because of faith, old because of obedience."[24]

This world then is the means through which salvation is to be accomplished. Despite the apparent lack of change and the continued outward misery, everything is in our favour, the trial and the test, temptation and affliction all conspiring to bring about the plan of redemption. The whole face and aspect of the world has been transformed from one of sorrow and despair, to one of promise and eternal life. Though the fullness of the promise has not yet been accomplished, the gift of the Spirit has been received, and with it the capacity and motivation to work out our salvation.

> "He is brought into a new world, and, as being in that new world, is invested with powers and privileges which he

---

[23] No. 114 p. 19.

[24] P.P.S.v,12. God's part and man's cooperation in the work of salvation are summed up in the image of the gate and the road. God's gift of faith is the gate to heaven while our obedience is the road which takes us there.

absolutely had not in the way of nature...peace, hope, love, faith, purity he had not; nothing of heaven in him. But in Christ all these blessings are given:.. As far as a being can be changed without losing his identity, as far as it is sense to say that an existing being can be new created, so far has man this gift when the grace of the gospel has its perfect work and its maturity of fruit in him."[25]

The State of Grace and The State of Glory

Our salvation in Christ comes about in two phases. We are brought first into a state of grace, "the new world of religious privileges, hopes and aids, which is the *present* possession of all Christians," and then to a state of glory, "that future world of eternal life which is the *inheritance* of them all."[26] The first phase is a preparatory stage and an essential condition for future glory. "Those who are to be saved hereafter are (to speak generally) those, and those only, who are placed in that saving state here."[27] We have not been directly transplanted from the state of nature to the state of glory, but pass through a stage of gradual transformation by grace. Though Christ's redemption was complete and perfect in itself, and needs no further addition, it requires time to work its saving power in us, and bring our salvation to the full. His death did not at once transform the whole world, but the fruit of His redemption is applied to each of us individually.[28] However, this does not minimize the significance of our present state, which is "a kind of type, pledge, forerunner" of the state of glory.[29]

Since salvation has been accomplished and made perfect in Christ, the present state of grace and the state of future glory are in their nature,

---

[25] P.P.S.v,13; S.D. v,p.61.

[26] No. 114 p. 7.

[27] P.P.S.v,13.

[28] P.P.S.v,10: God "did not once for all restore the whole race, and change the condition of the world in His sight on Christ's death."; P.P.S.i,7: "It *has* come to all the world, but the world is not changed thereby as a whole - that change is not a work done and over in Christ...."

[29] No. 114 p. 7. In his sermons Newman uses a variety of terms, such as "portion", "earnest", "title", "promise", "pledge" and "token", to describe the intrinsic relation between glory and grace. "Portion" and "earnest" are the strongest terms and underline the aspect of present possession, while the other terms point to the future prospect. In P.P.S.ii,19 he distinguishes between a pledge and an earnest.

one and the same.[30] They can be considered as one since "Christ makes but one new world, and He will not need to repair His work. Only He works slowly."[31] The only real difference between them is the gap in time, not in substance, for grace is glory in exile and glory is grace at home. So even "though Christians are now in a very far inferior state of blessedness to that which they will enjoy hereafter, yet in all essential matters, they are in the very same state."[32] The fulfilment in glory has already begun and all true Christians "are tending to it; are growing into it, and are pleasing to God because they are becoming like Him...."[33] Though the "new heavens and new earth" seems to speak about a future state, it can legitimately be applied, both individually and collectively, to the present state of Christians. Newman therefore observes that those who regard it as a mere metaphor, fail to express adequately the blessedness of the Gospel dispensation or appreciate the real meaning of it in their lives.[34]

Nevertheless, though we live under the dispensation of grace, the Gospel "calls our attention to things invisible and future." It has been founded on better promises, of which we enjoy the earnest, but "the fulness is yet to come." Hence our state is still a time of labour and self-discipline, of living in hope and preparing for the next world.[35] Though Christians have crossed the Red Sea, they still have, like the Jews before them, to spend some time in the desert.[36] Unlike the Jews, however, they are already in possession of the promised land. Hence the state of salvation in which they live is both a state of faith and of possession, which Newman describes as follows:

"We Christians,... are at once in the wilderness and in the promised land. In the wilderness because we live amid

---

[30] This can be seen also in another sermon where Newman states that holiness here and holiness in heaven are one and the same cf No. 97.

[31] No. 114 p. 7.

[32] ibid. p. 8.

[33] P.P.S.v,10; v,11: "and now that perfection is beginning in them, now they have a gift in them which will in due time, through God's mercy, leaven the whole mass within them."

[34] No. 389 pp. 1-2.

[35] No. 99 p. 1; No. 102 p. 2.

[36] No. 563 p. 2. In this sermon Newman stresses our cooperation with grace as necessary for final salvation, while in the next Littlemore sermon No. 565, he emphasizes the absolute need of being saved only by Christ.

wonders; in the promised land, because we are in a state of enjoyment. That we are in a state of enjoyment is surely certain, unless all the prophecies have failed; but that we are in a state where faith alone has that enjoyment, is plain from the fact that God's great blessings are not seen...."[37]

Christ and the Ministration of the Spirit

We have seen that "the new heavens and a new earth" is an internal transformation of our world, and that the world becomes new to us by the presence of the Spirit.[38] As the Spirit once hovered over the first creation, turning chaos into cosmos, so now it transforms the world into a new creation in Christ. Since "He has ever been the secret Presence of God within the Creation,"[39] the Holy Ghost is the source of new life, won for us by Christ's death and resurrection. It is this gift of the Spirit which sets the Christian dispensation apart and is the mark and privilege of the state of salvation in Christ. From this time forward "in some sense or other God has come down and ever since dwells upon earth differently from what He ever did before." Though there never was a time when God did not make Himself known,[40] and even displayed His glory in the Old Testament, His presence in the new dispensation is more glorious still. If the "ministration of condemnation was glorious, much more is the ministration of the righteous Spirit rather glorious."[41]

Christ first accomplished in Himself the work of our Redemption by becoming at His resurrection a life-giving Spirit. It is through the same Spirit that He now communicates Himself to us. What He did outwardly in the flesh, He conveys inwardly by His Spirit. The great end of Christ's coming was the renewal of our nature[42] which He provided for by His passion, but could not give us individually until the Spirit came. He "did not finish His gracious economy by His death; viz.

---

[37] P.P.S.vii.12.

[38] No. 114.

[39] P.P.S.ii.19.

[40] U.S.ii p. 19: "No people (to speak in general terms) has been denied a revelation from God, though but a portion of the world has enjoyed an authenticated revelation."

[41] No. 389.

[42] No. 33.

124

because the Holy Spirit came in order to finish it." The latter came "to finish in us what Christ had finished in Himself, but left unfinished as regards us. To Him is committed to us severally all that Christ had done for us."[43] Though Christ has died and left this world, He is still present with us "by the substitution of His Spirit for Himself."[44] Thus in receiving the gift of the Spirit, which is eternal life, Newman underlines the truth that we receive none other than Christ Himself.

> "Thus eternal life is identified with Christ -Christ is eternal life - The giver and the gift are not separated - as He was known, it was known - The Christian Church knows it fully, as knowing Him fully."[45]

The presence of the Spirit within us is neither an alternative nor a supplement to the presence of Christ.[46] He is present in all His substance, but in a new manner, in the form of His Spirit. He is present "personally, as the Christ, as God and man; not present to us locally and sensibly, but still really, in our hearts and to our faith. And it is by the Holy Ghost that this gracious communion is effected."[47] Through the Spirit He brings about in us the same transformation which He underwent in His death and resurrection. This change took place in Christ by a succession of events, but its fruit is effected in us by one simultaneous action of the Holy Spirit.

> "Christ Himself vouchsafes to repeat in each of us in figure and mystery all that He did and suffered in the flesh...not by a succession of events, but all at once, for He comes to us as a Spirit, all dying, all rising again, all living."[48]

In coming to us as a Spirit, Christ is present in a way which far surpasses His communion with man during His earthly life. Precisely because it is a spiritual presence it is more intimate and pervades our

---

[43] P.P.S.v,10.

[44] P.P.S.ii,19.

[45] No. 99 p. 6.

[46] P.P.S.iv,17; vi,10. "Thus the Spirit does not take the place of Christ in the soul but secures that place to Christ."

[47] P.P.S.vi,10.

[48] P.P.S.v,10. It is on this basis that quoad nos the resurrection and ascension are considered as two moments of one event.

whole being.[49] Paradoxically the very hiddenness of His presence makes it all the more real and substantial. It is no longer an external communication but an inward one raising us to a new form of being.[50] Christ has regenerated us in the Spirit, and thus "implants the seed of eternal life and promises us glory and bliss everlasting."[51] By this divine indwelling we have the warrant of future glory. Since His image has been stamped on us, He will recognize His property, and claim what is His on the last day.

> "His whole economy in all its parts is ever in us all at once; and this divine presence constitutes the title of each of us to heaven; this is what He will acknowledge and accept at the last day. He will acknowledge Himself - His image in us - as though we reflected Him, and He on looking round about, discerned at once who were His; those namely who gave Him back His image."[52]

Justifying Faith and The Principle of New Life

We have seen in Chapter Two that the roots of future judgment and punishment are planted in corrupt human nature, and that the state of nature is a state of wrath and condemnation. Sin was described as not merely an accident, nor extrinsic to our nature but a deeply seated principle within us. Since however, eternal life is our future destiny, some provision must be made to counteract this evil tendency. Our justification[53] can only be achieved by an inward power more effective than sin. For Newman the doctrine of original sin could clearly be found in Scripture, and human experience confirmed what he

---

[49] P.P.S.ii,19; S.D. xi, p. 141.

[50] P.P.S.ii,19; iv,17: "...inasmuch as the Divine Spirit is more than flesh and blood; inasmuch as the risen and glorified Saviour is more powerful than He was in the form of a servant...He who glorified Christ imparts Him thus glorified to us."

[51] No. 385 p. 9.

[52] P.P.S.v,10; No. 533 p. 7.

[53] This brief section on justification is limited to the one point that the life-giving principle of the Spirit is the ground for future glory, just as the principle of evil was the ground for eternal death. The 14 lectures on justification began on 13th April 1837, cf L.D., vol.vi,p.57. There was one more lecture than the number of chapters contained in his later published work, making it difficult to define the exact relation between the original lectures and the volume. The sermons are numbered 447,454,455,456,457,458,461,448, 463,465,452,467,469 and 470.

considered a self-evident moral truth. But he also found a greater truth, more generously affirmed in the New Testament, of belief in the life-giving grace of Christ. Contrasting the truth of our original sinfulness with the truth of our inward righteousness, he says:

> "It is as easy, by some evasion, to explain away the Scripture proofs for the doctrine of original sin, as to get rid of those which Scripture furnishes us for the doctrine of implanted righteousness, and that through the Spirit."[54]

"To die from wrath and rise to God's favour" is how Newman defines justification in one of his first Easter sermons.[55] These sermons were immediately preceded by a series on Faith[56] in which his early view of justification is found, and from which the development of his thought can be traced. In them a predominantly Lutheran view prevails despite the emphasis on works as the evidence of "living faith."[57] It is clear at this stage, that Newman makes faith the unique principle of justification. Salvation is a holy salvation and faith "is the foremost principle of holiness."[58] It is "the sure ground of confidence for eternal life,"[59] "the evidence and principle of newness of heart, the evidence of regeneration, the principle of sanctification and the hope of eternal glory."[60] All depends on faith - "what indeed is it to us whether or not Christ rose from the dead, unless we believe in it?" His resurrection meant both our justification and new birth to holiness, and since "both are inseparably connected with faith, they are inseparably connected with each other."[61]

---

[54] P.P.S.v,11.

[55] No. 70.

[56] Course iv: Nos. 57,59,61,63,65 and 67. Much later Newman described the Easter season as "the season of faith", P.P.S.vi,11; here at this early period we find how he instinctively chooses the theme of faith in preparation for the feast.

[57] On Newman's controversy with the Evangelicals on the doctrine of faith alone, cf D.Newsome, "Justification and Sanctification - Newman and the Evangelicals," *Journal of Theological Studies*, Vol.xv, Oxford, 1964 pp. 32-53. For an account of the development of Newman's view on justification cf. Sheridan, T., *Newman on Justification, A Theological Biography*, New York, Alba House, 1967.

[58] No. 57.

[59] No. 61.

[60] No. 63.

[61] No. 70.

"Faith cannot wash us from guilt without also cleansing us from sin for if it does not sanctify, it is but pretended faith and therefore cannot justify - Again, if our faith sanctify us, it must justify...."[62]

We see from the above that faith was for Newman not merely a title to justification, but the very principle of it and the means of sanctification. Moreover justification was described not as man's being made righteous, but as "a state of acceptance" into which we are brought by faith. On these two crucial points the future development of Newman's view changed radically. Though he continued to stress the essential role of faith, he now identifies the indwelling of the Holy Spirit as the formal cause of our justification. The Old Testament was a dispensation of faith but it is "the one great distinction of Gospel times, that that original righteousness which is so necessary for us and from which we are so far gone, should be vouchsafed again to us, and that through the Spirit." As the principle of sin, coming from us, is the cause of eternal death, the principle of justifying grace by the Holy Spirit, is the cause of eternal life.

"When I speak of righteousness I speak of the work of the Spirit, and this work, though imperfect considered as ours, is perfect as far as it comes from Him. Our works, done in the Spirit of Christ, have a justifying principle in them, and that is the presence of the All-Holy Spirit."[63]

Righteousness is not of us but in us.[64] It is Christ through the Spirit, who has made a new beginning in us, and faith which receives it. However, the latter "is the only principle which can do this."[65] Faith gives access to the new life and is itself the "first fruits" and "pledge" of perfection "which it for certain will end in."[66] It is with faith where one begins one's recovery from sin because it "is itself of a holy nature, and the first fruits and earnest of holiness to come."[67] But the first gift of

---

[62] ibid.

[63] P.P.S.v,11.

[64] The title of P.P.S.v,10.

[65] P.P.S.v,12.

[66] P.P.S.v,11.

[67] P.P.S.vi,9.

faith "does not give the second gift [justifying grace], it does not involve it; it does but prepare for it, it does but constitute a title to it."[68] It is one thing to have a title and quite another thing to be in possession. Faith gives a title to the gift of the Holy Spirit, but the gift itself is received in baptism. "Faith gave a title: baptism gave possession. Faith procured... what nothing else could procure, and baptism conveyed it."[69] In the ordinary means of salvation therefore, it is by the sacrament of Christ's death and resurrection that we are justified, and by which the Gift of the Spirit, is conferred.[70]

Though justification is not our own doing however great our faith, Newman stresses that it is implanted within us as our personal possession. It is not a mere imputation or accounting us as righteous; a real internal change is effected in our corrupt human nature. Justifying grace is "not merely nominally given to us and imputed to us, but really implanted in us by the operation of the Holy Spirit."[71] It is not a legal semblance in which our intrinsic sinfulness is overlooked for the sake of Christ, but "a real and true righteousness, which approves itself to God. They are able to stand before God and yet not be condemned."[72] Hence the state of salvation is not merely one of acceptance on account of our faith, but of "substantial holiness." In a clear rejection of the Lutheran doctrine of faith alone, Newman chides those who think "that the only business of a Christian is, not to be holy, but to have faith, and to think and speak of Christ." He rejects the phrase "justified sinner" as a contradiction in terms, and notes that the "Gospel only knows of justified saints."[73]

The power of evil seemed overwhelming to the young Newman driving him to an excessive fear of damnation. Though he was conscious of the Holy Spirit's power as the remedy for sin and the source of sanctification, it was not until studying the Greek Fathers that he found the full measure and significance of justifying grace. The new

---

[68] P.P.S.vi,12.

[69] ibid; No. 577 the unpublished companion sermon to P.P.S.vi,12 (No. 575) also makes the same points.

[70] Newman succinctly draws together the various dimensions of his teaching on justification in the sentence. "Justification comes *through* the Sacraments; is received *by* faith; *consists* in God's inward presence, and *lives* in obedience." Jfc. p 278.

[71] P.P.S.v,10.

[72] P.P.S.v,11.

[73] P.P.S.v,13.

creation was not merely a moral but an ontological change, putting man into a higher order of being. A new capacity was conferred by the gift of the Spirit and justification became the possession of the Christian. While the tendency to sin remained, he could act with a power that was truly his to work out his salvation. Referring to this new change, Newman tells us

"...there is another reason why, for Christ's sake we are dealt with as perfectly righteous, though we be not so. Not only for the Spirit's presence within us, but for what is ours - not indeed what is now ours, but for what we shall be. We are not unreprovable, and unblemished in holiness yet, but we shall be at length through God's mercy...They will one day be presented blameless before the Throne, and they are now to labour towards, and begin that perfect state. And in consideration that it is begun in them, God of His great mercy imputes it to them as if it were already completed. He anticipates what will be, and treats them as that which they are labouring to become."[74]

Part Two
The Principle of Hope

A Dialectic of Hope and Despair

Newman's theology of hope can perhaps best be read against the background of a mind ever alert to the danger of self-deception. Hope could so easily be mistaken for unreal dreams and superficial optimism. It also seemed to him a weak word to express the depth of confidence and entire dependence on Christ, to which Christians are called. Faith formed in love offered a surer path to certitude than hope could provide, and became the leading principle of his life.[75] In his sermons therefore, hope is inseparably linked with faith, and shares in the same darkness which surrounds it. As faith has to be tested by doubts of unbelief, hope likewise is subject to feelings of despair. Fears and perplexity are thus

---

[74] P.P.S.v.11.

[75] The law of probability became a "guide to life" and certitude could be attained by faith formed in love cf. Apo.p.19.

130

an essential component of its authenticity, for without them Christian
hope loses its real significance. Hope then emerges, through grace, at
the point where natural hopes fail, and rising above them, is transformed
into Christian joy.

In Newman's early sermons at St. Clement's, one is struck by a
general feeling of cheerless severity. Though this feeling is later
substantially changed, the principle of hope appears all too muted.[76]
We are seldom allowed to bask in bright sunlight under cloudless skies.
In these his evangelical days, hope is generally refracted through a haze
of anxiety but finally breaks through as a hard-earned reward from the
struggle between faith and skepticism. This dialogue between hope and
despair can be seen quite clearly and is a feature of the early Newman.
First he observes that it is sheer presumption to think that future glory
is as automatic "as succeeding to an earthly inheritance," as if "there
were no more doubt or difficulty as regards obtaining it."[77] For one so
conscious of guilt, it should not be surprising, that despite the
knowledge of Christ's power to forgive, he doubts "whether He is
willing to forgive sinners such as us."[78] "There are few men indeed,
who do not feel at least occasional misgivings within them" about their
future hope, for "we are by nature through our manifold sins in a
kingdom of despair."[79] We live in a world where "there is no respite
but wave succeeds to wave, sweeping away our fair hopes and earthly
prospects - All human helps are failing...."[80] Even the promise of the
Gospel at times appears as little more than a mere declaration of intent.
Though it is reliable on divine authority, it still leaves us open to doubt.

> "Now, supposing, we had only God's simple word that He
> would forgive all penitent sinners - I know we ought to
> believe it by itself - but still would not the very depths of our
> self-knowledge drive us from God...No one of them [true
> penitents] so to say would have faith enough to overcome

---

[76] Of all the sermons in the Anglican period there are only two which could be
described as treating the theme of hope in an explicit way. No. 230 is entitled *The
Liturgy, second, forms the character viz. to hope.* and No. 73 on *The Theological
Virtues* has a section on hope in pages 8-10.

[77] No. 47 p. 4.

[78] No. 48 p. 6.

[79] No. 175 p. 9.

[80] No. 180 p. 22. One could read an allusion here to Mary who died ten months
before the sermon was preached - "the dearest earthly joys are but for a time."

his despair."[81]

Doubts therefore continue to persist and no amount of increased knowledge will dispel them. Even the Church, that "refuge for inquirers" has itself become "a question of controversy" and cannot relieve us of the burden.[82] Its very preaching "is a work of faith in the first instance, not of hope"[83] and thus the individual Christian must be content "with that imperfect knowledge which is the lot in his life."[84] Christ did not dissimulate or paper over these difficulties, but showed us instead the way of hope through darkness and abandonment.

"...on the cross He thought that God had forsaken Him. What is this but to be laden with doubt and gloom?"[85]

Doubt and perplexity then, is the normal precondition for the attainment of mature Christian hope. The request of the apostle Philip to be shown the Father "puts before us the state of all religious minds, the state of doubt and restlessness, before the glorious gospel shines upon them."[86] Creation is not a sufficient instrument in itself for revealing God's presence or give "the soul an anchor in the storm." By nature we are born into a state of guilt and misery - "we have no hope, we have no prospect but evil before us."[87]

However, Newman reminds us that we are no longer in a state of nature but are now under grace. We have a light in the darkness which is always sufficient to calm fears and overcome despair.[88] We may be "troubled on every side, yet not distressed - perplexed but not in

---

[81] No. 285. Newman substituted this sermon for No. 180 when he repeated course xxiii *on the Offices of Christ, Christ the One Mediator between God and guilty man.* He attached to the manuscript the following note: "from p. 16 is entirely in *matter*, the greater part in words as No. 180."

[82] No. 270 p. 19.

[83] No. 267 p. 3.

[84] No. 269 p. 3.

[85] No. 269 p. 29.

[86] No. 337 p. 2.

[87] No. 562 p. 3.

[88] No. 49 p. 19: God "is always revealed sufficiently for the salvation of every one of us."

132

despair...."[89] Though we are humbled, such humiliation is "with hope, not despair, in gratitude; not merely in sorrow."[90] And thus "the Christian even in his gloomiest days experiences feelings of ...hope vastly more pleasurable...than mere worldly gratifications."[91] We have been given more than the broken mirror of creation to recognize God's presence and sustain our hope. This is the revelation of Christ Himself in whom "we gain all the knowledge of God we can have here, all we want for our need." Hence

> "We gain comfort and hope - for we see things are not going on at hazards, but that there is one who orders them - we gain a rest for our faith, a direction to steady its course while we look at Christ."[92]

Christ is our Almighty Stay

It is clear then that reason alone cannot provide us with hope, and that revelation must come to the rescue. The condition of the heathen was "a state of doubt and gloom," which illustrates man's instinctive need for divine instruction "and our earnest wishes and continual hopes that such an instructor would at length arrive."[93] Hope thus begins with revelation, and the Bible, which in another context Newman described as a record of human sorrow, is equally a record of human hope. Immediately upon the Fall a promise of deliverance was given, which suggested to our first parents "a hope that they might still be spared by Him." "Though there was nothing explicitly declared," by this first promise, "there was much implied - and though there was nothing to impart certainty, there was much to sustain hope."[94] As further revelation was disclosed, hopes began to rise, but the hope of the Patriarchs could never reach the level of confidence and assurance. Though the Jews were given glimpses of a future Messiah, and were

[89] No. 48 p. 21.

[90] No. 4.

[91] No. 48 p. 17.

[92] No. 337 p. 11.

[93] No. 106 p. 15.

[94] No. 112 pp. 6-7.

thus never "actually in that entire state of gloom,"[95] no guarantee was accorded to their hope, and so uncertainty and anxiety was their lot.[96] Even their prayers in the messianic psalms "would rather raise hope than inspire confidence."[97] Their hope then, was deficient, for the Old Testament "revealed more evil on the whole than it promised good."[98] Hence, Jewish hope was little better than human aspiration, until a sacrifice for sin had been offered, and transgressions wiped out; till then it was at best uncertain, and dependent upon an event which had not yet been accomplished.

> "Yet this hope I would strongly urge, is after all a faint hope till a sacrifice for sin is revealed to the inquirer, till the weight of transgression is shown to have been borne by another and put away, he will receive very little pleasure or rather much fear, from turning his thoughts to a future life or inquiring into the hidden purposes of God."[99]

The Atonement of Christ therefore, "is the only warrantable foundation on which man can establish his hopes of future life."[100] By His sacrifice " a new beginning of hope" was inaugurated.[101] Though we do not know why Christ's death was necessary as an atonement for sin,[102] we can be content in the knowledge that "it is the only doctrine which can subdue our alarms and bring peace to our conscience."[103] Through His death "we have our peculiar and better promises, which the Jews had not - we are elected into nobler hopes and more glorious prospects and what these are, we must learn from the New Testament,

---

[95] No. 197 p. 23.

[96] No. 115 p. 15.

[97] No. 117 p. 15.

[98] No. 187 p. 2.

[99] No. 119 p. 18. While laying the foundations of hope in the Old Testament revelation, Newman insists on its deficiency. Here and in similar passages we see the word hope used in a minimalist sense: "what they were assured of and what they merely hoped."

[100] No. 117 p. 5.

[101] No. 175 p. 9.

[102] In his earlier sermons Newman follows a line of argument on the necessity of the Atonement. When he later accepts the principle of reserve towards the sacred mysteries, he disclaims any such argument. The difference can be seen by comparing No. 180 and No. 285; in the former the principle of reserve is absent but clear in the later sermon which replaced it.

[103] No. 285.

and not from the Old."[104] Moreover we no longer have a mere promise but a fact on which to rest secure. "It is God's deed, which is (to a weak heart) far beyond His word. In it we have a pledge of the reality of God's purpose towards us."[105]

> "The bare promise that Christ should die for us would be an evidence of God's merciful intention, but the fact that Christ has died, is a proof that He has forgiven us and gives us the certainty that we may gain all blessings from Him."[106]

Christ is our only hope of glory; our assurance rests on His sacrifice which is the fulfilment of earlier promises.[107] His holiness "is a ground for hope and confidence...a strong ground of trust."[108] The state of the Christian therefore is one in which a reliable principle of hope is established.[109] Our doubts which at first appeared so overwhelming, are by the light of faith irrational, and our attempt to appease God with self-inflicted penance is mere superstition.[110] Hence though we may cry out in distress "Who shall save us!" we can confidently say that "We have but one stay, but He is almighty."[111]

The Nature and Object of Hope

Newman considers the nature of hope as something essentially practical. It is a principle of action, a virtue to be exercised, rather than a sentiment or desire. Secondly, while hope involves the moral virtue of fortitude, it is strictly theological in both its origin and object, which is God Himself.

Newman begins however by pointing out that hope implies an

---

[104] No. 99 p. 8.

[105] ibid.

[106] No. 180 p. 16.

[107] No. 66.

[108] No. 533 pp. 14-15.

[109] No. 389 p. 2: "Alas, is our hope in Christ so uncertain? yet if such promises have no meaning at all now, how can they grow into a meaning then?"

[110] The genesis of superstition is often seen by Newman as the alternative proposed by the religious mind in its recoil from skepticism cf.No. 106; P.P.S.ii,2,;U.S.xii.

[111] No. 180.

element of desire, for without desires there can be no human life, and "without hope religion cannot exist."[112] Human desire, then, is at the very root of hope: "hope would seem a thing to be desired as a reward, rather than a virtue."[113] But being rooted in nature, desire is open to the danger of wish-fulfillment. Newman therefore shifts our attention from self-regarding advantage, to the practical end for which the reward of heaven was promised. The object of such a promise was "to cheer" and "to animate" us in the work of our sanctification.[114] The comfort contained in the Old Testament predictions of a Saviour was so "that they might receive the principle of hope sufficient to animate them in doing the will of God."[115] Hope therefore is an animating principle to be exercised, rather than a desire to be passively gratified.

The principle of hope originates with God alone. It is "not of our own obtaining" but God "forms it in us [and] that we might have a right and title to this spiritual help" which Christ won for us on the cross.[116] Hope therefore is not to be confused with the natural blessing of a sanguine temperament or cheerful disposition. It is an infused grace, independent of psychological factors, which like other Christian principles, has a particular tendency "to produce a steadfast and vigorous hope," even among the despondent. It enables the Christian "to see good in every event, so firmly to take hold of the divine promises...as to triumph in the God of salvation even when outward circumstances are against us."[117] It is directed to this world as well as the next. By the grace of hope we have the sustaining power in present trials, which both enlightens and motivates the Christian. By it he discerns the good which is derived from suffering, and is ready to undergo trial and pain in the service of others. Hence the Christian vocation, in Newman's view, is marked by cheerfulness and confidence.

"We see in him no gloom, moroseness, mortified pride, sullenness - his heart is not hardened and rendered callous

---

[112] No. 230 p. 25.

[113] No. 73 p. 8.

[114] No. 69. This is a one-page fragment on *Consolatory Truths implied in Resurrection* in which "we shall confine ourselves to some of the consolatory truths it was intended to convey to us."

[115] No. 112 p. 6.

[116] No. 73 p. 10.

[117] ibid.

by affliction - it is soft and tender and he can pity others though in distress himself - so far of hope with reference to the present world."[118]

Although hope "is the great incentive to all action" it is not confined or even principally related to the present world, but to the world to come. The Christian is to look forward constantly to the next world for "it is the promise of Christ's eternal love and the future presence of God which abundantly sustains him."[119] It is natural for the young and the childish to place their hopes in this world, but mature Christians realize "that our treasure is not here, but in heaven with Him who is ascended thither."[120] Thus they are prepared to bear manfully their present sorrows and exchange their earthly ambitions for "a truer and holier hope."[121]

It is in the liturgy that Newman sees the theological nature of hope most clearly expressed.[122] Each of the virtues which the liturgy teaches and promotes, has a special point of reference in the formation of Christian character. While faith is exercised by self-denial, and charity in our relations with others, hope is uniquely related to God Himself. "In our relation towards God its distinguishing property was hope - towards man love and in our duties towards ourselves self-denial."[123] Almighty God then is the principal object of our hope. Christian hope however, differs in its object from Jewish hope, which was generally directed to this world. Though they are the same in nature and in their mode of operation, the Jewish people sought "the temporal deliverances of their Church," while the Christian object of hope is the future Coming of Christ.[124] This object is neither a temporal desire of fulfilment nor a private and individual one. Its goal is the eternal destiny of the Church as a whole. Christian hope is thus directed not to any personal reward we may obtain at the moment of death, but to the

---

[118] ibid.

[119] No. 102.

[120] P.P.S.i.26.

[121] P.P.S.ii,16. Both these sermons on *Christian Manhood* and *Religious Cowardice* are Easter sermons in which the theme of hope as manly virtue is considered.

[122] Course xxx *on the Liturgy* consists of ten sermons numbered consecutively from No. 224 to No. 233.

[123] No. 233 p. 4; No. 232 p. 3. Self-denial is the test of faith cf.P.P.S.i.5.

[124] No. 230 p. 25.

corporate fulfilment of the Body of Christ when He comes in glory.

> "Above all our hope is perfected by its peculiar Christian
> object. Its object is one of common interest to the *whole*
> Church - the coming of Christ suggests a personal but not a
> solitary consolation. *This* is why we are bid to look forward
> to Christ's coming rather than each of us to his own
> *death.*"[125]

Looking at hope in this way frees us from the prison of our own private concerns and enables us to look to the Church's joys and sorrows. It releases us from anxiety and produces the spirit of equanimity. But this sure confidence is the privilege only of confirmed Christians and comes "when humility, patience, self-denial have had their perfect work."[126] Patience, in the mind of St. Paul, "must precede the gift of hope,"[127] which gives rise in turn to motives for further self-denial.[128] We have a poor conception of hope if it does not strengthen us to "submit ourselves with composure to the ills of this life." Hence hope becomes "a subdued temper, not a passionate longing, an intemperate or rash emotion."

The Relationship of Faith and Hope

While Newman fully acknowledges the proper character of Christian hope, he incorporates it in a quite distinctive manner, with the virtue of faith. "Hope" he says, "is a form of faith" but then quickly adds, "though something more."[129] With the coming of the Gospel "hope is the temper especially addressed and satisfied." We are saved by hope; the gospel " gives hope - its very motto and badge is "therefore there is no condemnation...ye prisoners of hope."[130] Before the time of the Gospel however, the two virtues were not only distinct

---

[125] ibid.
[126] No. 197 p. 27.
[127] No. 230 p. 27.
[128] P.P.S.i,5.
[129] No. 233 p. 5.
[130] No. 197 p. 23.

138

but separate; now they have become one, though hope retains its own special character.

> "Faith is not hope - but in the New Testament the two are united again - God is reconciled to man and faith and hope become one. Accordingly St. Paul says we are saved by hope."[131]

This view of regarding hope more as a constituent part of faith than as a separate virtue, is particularly evident in the period of his maturity. As his eschatology becomes more and more realized, the future, to which hope is always directed, diminishes in significance, and is eclipsed by the importance of the present life of faith. Two other tendencies directly related to this change in perspective can also be observed. The anxiety which was a dominant feature of the early sermons is greatly reduced, and a greater certitude of faith is found. Since the future by its very nature is beyond man's control, and essentially unknown, it is prone to inspire fear and doubt, rather than instil security. Hence the assurance of our hope is better sought for in the present promises of the gospel, and grounded in the past ages of faith. A second tendency is the growing emphasis on Christian joy, which virtually replaces the role of hope in highlighting the bright side of religion. Joy is attached to the notion of a present blessing in possession, while hope signifies a longing for a future good.[132]

The interplay between faith and hope can however, be seen already in his early sermons, and the primacy of faith noted. Hope is something secondary to faith for it is dependent on it and follows it. Without faith, hope would be impossible for it is only by faith that we have access to the future promises.

> "We first believe the riches stored up in Christ and then hope that they may be stored up for us. Faith brings us into the grace of the Gospel and thus gives a hope of future glory. As the Apostle says "we have access by faith into our present state of favour and rejoice in hope of the glory of the

---

[131] No. 233 p. 5.

[132] This I believe is the explanation why there is such a scanty treatment of hope in the published sermons while there is an abundant reference to joy.

Lord.""[133]

There still remains a sense in which faith may be regarded as hope. This can be seen by comparing the faith of Abraham with Christian faith. In one sense, they are the same, not only in the act of faith (fides qua), but in the object of faith itself (fides quae). The faith of Abraham looked almost entirely to the future; it was exercised by looking forward to an object "which was not only unseen but unknown." Though Christians have a greater knowledge, and know that eternal life is the object of their hope, they still do not understand what eternal life means. Like Abraham therefore, they "must move at first simply by faith -obeying God not with definite knowledge of your reward but on the promise with the vague hope of a future heaven."[134] In another sense however, there is a great difference. The future promises to the Jews were primarily objects of hope, but having been fulfilled, they have now become objects of faith as well. As Newman observes, "...then the doctrines of the gospel were chiefly objects of hope - now they are objects of faith also because actually promised."[135]

In comparing the faith of Abraham with that of Jacob, Newman illustrates the difference between a future-oriented faith, and the faith of one who has inherited the promises. At the same time he provides a portrait of his own development from anxious longing to composed belief. In Jacob he finds a similar character to his own, and identifies closely with his experience of deepest fears concealing deepest desires. Abraham gives a picture of hopeful faith rejoicing in the future, but Jacob is "more interesting and winning in the eyes of us common men"; his faith "seems to show a fear and anxiety, gentle indeed and subdued, and very human." Jacob was of a more skeptical temper than Abraham, and "like St. Thomas perhaps, anxious for sight and possession from earnest and longing desire for them." Moreover he "seems to have had a gentle, tender, affectionate, timid mind - easily frightened, easily agitated, loving God so much that he feared to lose Him." But all is changed when, after wrestling with God, Jacob sees in a dream a ladder let down from heaven, symbolizing a privileged and lasting communication with the invisible world. Jacob then, and Newman in like manner, inherits the promises and is content with faith.

---

[133] No. 73.

[134] No. 202 p. 32.

[135] No. 115 p. 2 redaction.

140

"Abraham appears ever to have been looking forward in
hope, - Jacob looking back in memory: the one rejoicing in
the future, the other in the past; the one setting his affections
on the future, the other on the past; the one making his way
towards the promises, the other musing over their
fulfilment."[136]

Newman thus closely binds the virtue of hope to faith, and moves
away from unanchored desires of the future. Christian memory, rather
than flights of fancy, is the key to a comfortable hope. Christian
believers are those "who expect no new revelation, and who, though they
look forward in hope, yet see the future only in the mirror of times
past."[137] The divine favours of the past are the pledge of the future and
hope is grounded on God's former mercies, which we know by faith.
The fulfilment of God's promises to Abraham and Jacob "were the
objects on which hope dwelt and were made the types and blessings in
prospect." It is the grateful remembrance of the past which Newman
regards as providing the surest token of our hope for the future.

"But further, to bind them to the observance of this duty, the
past was made the pledge of the future, hope was grounded
on memory; all prayer for favour sent them back to the old
mercies of God."[138]

Though hope appears as a secondary, though distinctive and
irreplaceable element of faith, both faith and hope are under the primacy
of love. They are the ways of expressing love and the instruments of
charity. Behind this synthesis of the theological virtues, lies Newman's
search for certitude and his epistemology is summed up in the principle,
fides formata charitate.[139] Love is the fuel which drives the engine of
faith and hope. Faith and hope are subordinate and owe to love all that
is of value in them. The object of both faith and hope is a Person and
not a proposition, and it is only a person who can be believed and hoped
in, in a real, and not merely notional way. Hence both faith and hope are

[136] P.P.S.v.6; No. 209 pp. 21-22.

[137] P.P.S.vii,18.

[138] ibid.

[139] U.S.xii,p.228; Apo.pp.19-21. Newman makes the distinction between
certitude, which is "a habit of mind" and certainty which is "a quality of propositions."
He came to this distinction through Butler's principle of probability.

formed in love of that Person on Whom our heart and mind are fixed.

> "Faith and hope are means by which we express our love;
> we believe God's word, because we love it; we hope after
> heaven, because we love it. We should not have any hope or
> concern about it, unless we loved it; we should not trust or
> confide in the God of heaven, unless we loved Him. Faith
> then and hope are but instruments or expressions of
> love...."[140]

Christian Joy

As Newman's perspective moves from the future horizon to the
present blessings of salvation, the spring of hope changes course, and
runs into a river of joy.[141] Hope however, is not entirely submerged, for
Christian joy is not yet full, and final salvation is yet to come. Christians
have not been promised everything - there is no assurance of final
perseverance[142] - though they are in a state of enjoyment of the Gospel
privileges. This is a state of possession and not merely of promise, of
grace, which is the earnest of future glory. Hence though the future is
unknown and remains a cause of anxiety as well as an object of hope,
Christians have reason for rejoicing in the present blessings of eternity.

> "In spite then of all recollections of the past or fear for the
> future, we have a present source of rejoicing; whatever
> comes, weal or woe, however stands our account as yet in the
> books against the Last Day, this we have and this we may
> glory in, the present power and grace of God in us and over
> us, and the means thereby given of victory in the end."[143]

The present possession of Christians is none other than Christ
Himself. His presence, however, may not always be felt, - for various

---

[140] P.P.S.iv,21. Here we have one of the few extended passages on hope in
Newman's published sermons. It is significant that while Faith and Love are in the title of
the sermon, the third theological virtue of Hope is absent.

[141] We have seen in Chapter One that hope and fear are the dominant feelings at
the Second Coming. We cannot strictly speak of joy in this future event, except by
anticipation, for joy is always associated with the present possession of a good.

[142] P.P.S.iv,9; P.P.S.iv,8: "We will not cease to rejoice in what God has given,
because He has not as yet promised us everything."

[143] ibid.

reasons; psychological depression, or sins of infirmity, or a general lack of sensibility to the unseen world, hinder the expression of joy, and deliberate sin excludes His presence altogether.[144] This lack of any feeling of joy is generally due to our human limitations rather than to any defect in the reality of Christ's presence. Newman however did not always see things that way; in his early period his lack of joy troubled him. With anxious concern of the future and inadequate appreciation of present blessings, he concluded that "Spiritual joy then comes only at times and for a season...here it cannot be found - we cannot hope to sit down with the possession of it - we must seek it in another world - all we can do here is to prepare for it, and to get ready."[145] Joy was not an infallible sign to him of Christ's presence, and so he comforted himself with the thought that "by itself [it is] no test of spirituality, nor is it the invariable portion of every believer." Nevertheless he even then recognized that the presence of Christ had a natural tendency to effect joy,-"where it does attend upon holiness (as is generally the case) it affords a strong confirmation to the truth of the Word of God."[146]

The presence of Christ is the thread linking all the variations on the theme of joy in Newman's sermons. Though His presence is universal, Newman underlines three particular ways in which Christ is present, and from where he draws the lesson of joy. He is present to us by virtue of the incarnation, and here one can include natural joys, for in Christ's birth all creation is blessed. This is the joy which is attached to the feast of Christmas. Then we have a more complex experience of joy associated with the Paschal mystery, which Newman treats in his Resurrection and Ascension sermons. Finally, Christ has left us the presence of His Spirit, and the Law of the Spirit in our hearts is a spirit of joy. By observing this Law the Christian finds a true sense of freedom and the result of such freedom is joy.

The incarnation reminds us of the simple but profound truth that life is intended for our enjoyment, and that our highest good is to be found in the acceptance of a gift, rather than in the restless pursuit after happiness. Christ has graced our world so that "we may enjoy His temporal bounty and partake of the pleasant things of earth with Him in

---

[144] P.P.S.iv,9; iv,1: "wilful sin, if it is habitual and deliberate, of course destroys his hope" and therefore a posteriori, his joy. The reasons for not experiencing joy though we are in a state of grace will be considered under the heading of realization in Chapter Six.

[145] No. 99 p. 14.

[146] No. 67 p. 19.

our thoughts." Moreover, it tells us that religion is primarily a consolation rather than a dread or burden. "Far from inculcating alarm and terror" the Angel's announcement of His birth is one of joy and the calming of all fear.

> "We are reminded that though this life must ever be a life of toil and effort, yet that, properly speaking, we have not to seek our highest good. It is found, it is brought near us, in the descent of the Son of God from His Father's bosom to this world."[147]

A more positive evaluation of creation is one of the developments to be noted in Newman's sermons as the mystery of the Incarnation becomes a central theme. The early dichotomy between the material and the spiritual is abandoned,[148] and temporal blessings are now seen as a cause for joy and thanksgiving, rather than looked on as occasions of sinful pleasure. The early puritan view which stressed that natural blessings were not guaranteed by the Gospel promises, is contrasted with his later declaration to the contrary. "Life consists in things pleasant; it is sustained by blessings. And moreover, the Gospel by a solemn grant, guarantees these things to us...Here then surely is a matter for joy and thankfulness at all seasons."[149] Grace is built on nature, and God found it worthy enough to assume it in Christ. It therefore follows that "Gloom is no Christian temper...We must live in sunshine, even when we sorrow; we must live in God's presence...."[150]

Newman distinguishes two kinds of joy - the joy of Christmas which is "natural and unmixed," and "the highly wrought and refined" joy of Easter. As Christmas reminds us of Christ's presence in creation, Easter joy in the new creation "is so much the child of sorrow." But precisely because it is born of suffering and atonement "it is a joy only the greater from the contrast."[151] An unalloyed sense of joy is possible in only two states, the state of original innocence, which Christmas

---

[147] P.P.S.viii.17. This sermon was first composed in 1825 but then rewritten for publication in 1843. Though the original manuscript is lost, it may reasonably be assumed that the full implications of the Incarnation had not yet been grasped.

[148] cf No. 88 where grace and blessing are not only distinguished from each other but are antithetical.

[149] P.P.S.v.19.

[150] ibid.

[151] P.P.S.iv.23. This is an Easter Day sermon in 1838.

144

symbolizes, and the state of final resurrection, sealed for us by Christ's
rising from the dead. In the in-between time we have the earnest of joy,
but not its fullness. Christian joy is a joy in repentance, not the
exuberance of the enthusiasts, but one "marked with much of
pensiveness and tender and joyful melancholy." It differs from a
worldly joy which takes no account of past sins. It is a "manly joy, not
so manly as to be rude, not so tender as to be effeminate," but
combining the highest qualities of male and female nature. Though
Christian joy is quiet and reserved, (as reflected in Newman's own
personality), it outweighs the weight of sorrow. The Church sets aside a
longer period of celebration for Easter than for Lent "as if to show that
where sin abounded, there much more has grace abounded."[152]

This complex joy is illustrated by the mixed feelings of the
apostles during the interval between Easter and the Ascension. This was
a period of recollection; they had the experience of Christ's appearance
from the dead, and only gradually understood its meaning.[153] Christ's
return to the Father meant His absence, and every departure brings
sorrow, but His spiritual presence among them was a source of even
greater joy. Hence we have the surprising response of the apostles
when, at the Ascension, He was removed from their sight. "How was it,"
Newman asks, "that when nature would have wept, the Apostles
rejoiced?"[154] From then on, they could rejoice, like their Master, in trial
and persecution. "Christ suffered and entered into joy; so did they in
their measure, after Him. And in our measure so do we."[155]

"Thus Christ's going to the Father is at once a source of
sorrow because it involves His absence; and of joy, because
it involves His presence. And out of the doctrine of the
Resurrection and Ascension, spring those Christian
paradoxes, often spoken of in Scripture, that we are
sorrowing, yet always rejoicing; as having nothing, yet
possessing all things."[156]

The third form of Christ's joyful presence is in the Law of the

<hr>

152 ibid.

153 P.P.S.iv,17.

154 P.P.S.vi,16.

155 ibid.

156 P.P.S. vi,10.

Spirit. It is the joy which comes from perfect freedom. This connection between freedom and joy can be seen in an early Easter course where he includes a sermon on the Holy Spirit and one on the liberty of the Gospel.[157] The renewal of the Spirit is to lead to joy which is found in Christian freedom. Newman's view of freedom at that time however, was of the liberal kind, under the influence of Whateley - a view he later rejected.[158] In a published sermon on the same subject he insists that "strictness is the condition for rejoicing."[159] To believe that we are the slaves of no one is a false idea of freedom, for our human condition is one in which we are never our own masters. Our true freedom really consists in being servants of Christ. It is by conforming to His Law, that Christians tend to a state of "utter and absolute captivity of their own will to His will," which is "the fulness of joy and everlasting life."[160]

Law is intended paradoxically, as a liberating force rather than a restriction on human freedom, and so the liberty of the Gospel is mediated to us through a Law. Moreover, joy comes when one's duty and one's pleasure coincide. This was not possible under the Old Law for we were then incapable of fulfilling it, however much we desired to do so. Hence it was an experience of frustration and bondage. But now that we are under the power of grace, we are enabled to do so, and find freedom, not *from* the law, but *in* it.[161] Such freedom to live according to the new Law of the Spirit tends to the end for which it was given, which is a state of rejoicing.

> "We are under grace. That law, which to nature is a grievous bondage, is to those who live under the power of God's presence, what it was meant to be, a rejoicing."[162]

---

[157] Course xxi. *Christ by His Resurrection renews all things*, contains No. 33 *on the Holy Spirit*, which is followed by No. 161 *on the New and Spiritual Law of Christ or Christian Liberty*.

[158] The manuscript of No. 161 bears the note "Whateleyan" and the liberal spirit can quite easily be seen.

[159] P.P.S.iv.1.

[160] P.P.S.iv.1.

[161] P.P.S.iv.9: "The message of the gospel is glorious, not because it releases us from the law, but because it enables us to fulfil it...not that it *destroys* the law, but that it makes it *cease* to be a bondage; not that it gives us freedom *from* it, but *in* it."

[162] P.P.S.iv.9.

146

Christian joy however must not be identified with the peace of mind one gets from a clean conscience, or the satisfaction of fulfilling a moral code. It goes far beyond morality and consists in the possession of privileges we cannot merit. It is not the result of upright moral behaviour but a gratuitous gift, in spite of our shortcomings. If it were otherwise it could only lead to despondency, for the Law of the Spirit sets standards far beyond our natural reach. Hence the joy of the Gospel is one which surpasses a religion of rights and duties. Referring to the "high and dry" religion of the Established Church, Newman remarks:

"Under such circumstances, religion becomes little more than a code of morals, the word and will of an absent God, who will one day come to judge and to recompense, not the voice of a present and bountiful Saviour."[163]

Newman has shown that Christian joy is of a higher order than a good moral life by itself can produce. The difference may be seen in his description of the early Christians. Their joy was not due to any merit on their part, but to the grace they had received. They went beyond the call of duty by unreservedly giving up the world, and embracing a life sustained by prayer and watching. Besides these two characteristics of the early Christians, there was a third distinguishing mark, which was that of "joy in all its forms."

"This, then, is the third chief grace of primitive Christianity - joy in all its forms...joy, if it be Christian joy, the refined joy of the mortified and persecuted, makes men peaceful, serene, thankful, gentle, affectionate, sweet-tempered, pleasant, hopeful; it is graceful, tender, touching, winning. All this were the Christians of the New Testament, for they had obtained what they desired."[164]

Finally, Newman reminds us that it is as much an obligation to be cheerful as it is a Gospel privilege. We are commanded to rejoice, for it is the sure witness of Christ's presence among us. With His presence in mind, the Christian will recall that there are no circumstances in life, however distressful, which can deprive him of the gift of joy.

---

[163] P.P.S.iv.9.
[164] S.D. xix pp. 286-7.

"Rejoice in the Lord always. That sorrow, that sollicitude, that fear, that repentance, is not Christian which has not its portion of Christian joy."[165]

Part Three
Immortality and Resurrection of the Dead

The doctrine of the immortality of the soul has come to be regarded among some authors, as incompatible with the Christian belief in the resurrection of the body.[166] No such radical opposition can be found in Newman's sermons. Though he recognizes the difference between them, not merely of expression but of meaning, Newman shows no great reluctance to employ both terms to denote the life hereafter.[167] While he presents the Christian doctrine of bodily resurrection in all its startling novelty, he does not discard the insights of natural religion and philosophy as unworthy of our attention. Natural religion, as a practical creed, and philosophy under the aspect of wisdom, have never been entirely unaided by God's grace.[168] Hence the intimations of an after-life, which reason has intuitively felt, have not been quenched by the new knowledge of revelation. Revelation however, is the decisive criterion for belief in human immortality, and the perspective from which Newman considers the question.

The Development of the Idea of Immortality

Following the principle of antecedent probability, as illustrated in natural religion, Newman shows the development of the idea of immor-

[165] S.D. xxv p. 384; P.P.S.v.19.

[166] O.Cullmann's influential work, *Immortality of the Soul or Resurrection of the Dead?*, London, Epworth Press, 1958, is based on the mutual exclusivity between the Platonic doctrine and primitive Christian belief: "in realtà non è neppure un legame, ma una renuncia all'una in favore dell'altra..." of the preface to the Italian translation, Paideia Editrice, Brescia, 1986.

[167] P.P.S.i.2 and P.P.S.i.21 are respectively entitled *The Immortality of the Soul* and *The Resurrection of the Body*.

[168] U.S.ii.

148

tality through the various stages of revealed religion.[169] He begins however with the state of natural religion, as illustrated in the writings of pagan philosophers.[170] Though they had a high regard for virtue, "their sentiments regarding future life were quite as dark as those concerning God [and] did not go farther than to say there might be"[171] a hereafter. This rather negative evaluation is considerably modified five years later, in a sermon which compares the influence of natural and revealed religion. Here he speaks of "the presentiment of a future life...which forms an article, more or less distinct, in the creed of Natural Religion."[172] Though the knowledge of immortality was not actually attained, the instinct of "a general connection between right moral conduct and happiness" indicates that the human spirit was set on line to receive the explicit revelation about everlasting happiness hereafter. The attempt to establish the doctrine failed, for it was based on a theory, but the instinct was correct and was later confirmed by the revelation of a personal God.

> "...the philosopher saw clearly the tendencies of the moral system, the constitution of the human soul, and the ways leading to the perfection of our nature."[173]

The possibility of a future life becomes clearer in proportion as the knowledge of a personal God is revealed. Even before the special history of revelation is formally begun in Abraham, we have illustrations in the case of Abel and Enoch, of Providence preparing the ground for the doctrine of a life after death. In this future existence "the inequalities of the present life were to be rectified, and the present tendencies towards holiness and happiness perfected and completed."[174] Since "the Revealed system is deeply rooted in the natural course of things" these illustrations confirm the intrinsic connection between immortality and

---

[169] Course vii *On the Revelation and Knowledge of the Gospel*, consists of Nos. 104,106,108,110,111,112,115,117,119,123,124.

[170] Newman has principally in mind the Stoic philosophers who drew a connection between virtue and immortality.

[171] No. 106 p. 6.

[172] U.S.ii.p.20.

[173] U.S.ii.p.30. A year or so before, Newman had set himself an examination of Cicero's proof for the immortality of the soul in *Tusculanae Questiones*. cf. L.D., Vol.ii. p. 106.

[174] No. 112 p. 13.

holiness.[175]

> "There is much in nature, much in the events of life to render
> it *probable* that God intends the soul to live on through
> death into another state of being - but the *certainty* in this
> matter we can only learn from His own mouth."[176]

With Abraham we have the disclosure of a personal God, promis-
ing "some spiritual and future salvation, and not merely temporal
blessings." This further confirmed the hopes of a future existence after
death and is corroborated by the way in which God described Himself
to Moses. By saying that He *is*, rather than He *was*, the "God of
Abraham, Isaac and Jacob," the revelation implied that the patriarchs
were still alive, though they had long since died.[177] Though we are now
reading retrospectively into how this revelation was then received,
Newman surmises that the patriarchs themselves "might believe in a
future life, without believing it to be eternal" for the doctrine was not yet
"openly promised."[178] As well as the disclosure of the personality of
God and the promise of future spiritual salvation, there is also the first
indication of how such a promise would be made. The covenant with
Abraham was "a covenant *upon a sacrifice*," a type to "usher in the
revelation of a covenant laden with an eternal promise."[179]

The prospect of eternal life becomes clearer still under the Mosaic
covenant. Throughout this stage of revelation, a general principle can be
seen that "as more and more was disclosed about the sufferings and
sacrifice of Christ, more also was spoken of the glory which was to
follow."[180] What began therefore as an inference and presentiment,
breaks into the pledge of future immortality as the atonement of the
Messiah is gradually unfolded. Summing up this development Newman
concludes:

---

[175] No. 119 p. 18: "..it does seem more consistent with the usual dealings of God
to permit those who have in this world begun through grace to purify themselves, to grow
into perfection in some future state of being."

[176] ibid. p. 16.

[177] No. 115 p. This is the introductory idea to Newman's sermon on *The
Resurrection of the Body*, P.P.S.i,21: "Abraham *shall* rise from the dead, because in truth,
he *is* still alive."

[178] ibid. p. 7.

[179] ibid. pp. 15-16.

[180] No. 117 p. 4.

150

"Thus while the Messiah continued veiled under the types and obscure prophecies of the Law, the doctrine of immortality was veiled also. When He is described more minutely by the prophets, it is revealed more openly. And lastly, the veil of mystery is rent in twain, and the Messiah fully known, then also the doctrine of a future life is explicitly promised."[181]

In a progressive manner, through Moses, David, Hosea and Isaiah, light is thrown by the messianic prophecies on the three-fold Gospel privilege of pardon, sanctification and eternal glory. The last age of the prophets anticipates the doctrine even more clearly. Daniel explicitly speaks of the resurrection of the dead, though no assurance or warrant can be given, until Christ's own resurrection has occurred and the gift of the Holy Spirit given.

"...the doctrine of pardon on repentance, sanctification through a spiritual influence and everlasting life are plainly taught by Zechariah, Jeremiah and Malachi - and by Daniel is even mentioned the resurrection of the dead, a doctrine most intimately connected with the history of Christ, as the pledge and certainty of it depends upon the fact of His resurrection."[182]

Christ is the Origin of our Immortality

The possibility of life after death is one thing, but the secure promise of it is another.[183] Such a guarantee did not come until the Spirit was given upon Christ's resurrection. "St. Paul expressly assures us that Christ brought life and immortality to light through the Gospel."[184] Moreover, our future existence is not one which takes place outside of Christ. His death and resurrection was not an extrinsic cause of our immortality, inasmuch as it satisfied the condition by which heaven is now open. It means rather, that Christ alone is the Immortal One, and it is by sharing in His immortality, that we are made immortal.

[181] ibid. pp. 4-5.
[182] No. 117 pp. 19-20.
[183] No. 187 p. 12.
[184] No. 150 p. 4.

Our life becomes the life of Christ and is impregnated by the same power which raised Jesus from the dead. Thus the idea of our immortality must be conceived as one of insertion into Him as members of His mystical body. Newman describes the effects of this union with Christ as a transformation from death to new life:

> "...but when knit unto Christ's mystical body and made one of His spiritual members we die unto all these sinful prospects and purposes.. thus we are dead and our lives are hid with Christ in God - our life becomes Christian life - we are risen to a new mode of existence - as Christ rose from natural death, so we rise from spiritual death - it is a resurrection of the soul - a new creation - and manifests the same Almighty power which effected Christ's resurrection."[185]

How then is immortality communicated to us? Clearly by Christ, but in Newman's complex thought, it is by virtue both of the Paschal mystery and of the Incarnation. For while it is true that our redemption was accomplished historically through His death and resurrection, the principle of an immortal human nature originates and depends on the Incarnation. Thus Newman combines both mysteries, not without some difficulties, in his description of Christ as the origin of our immortality.

In his evangelical days the mystery of Redemption was foremost in his preaching. He first links the source of our immortality to the sacrifice of Christ.[186] The atonement and resurrection is the one and only evidence for belief in eternal life. By means of this paschal event, we are brought into "an immortal and eternal Kingdom, not of this perishable world but of the immortal soul and therefore may last forever."[187] Hence Christ's resurrection is "made the assurance and evidence of our future resurrection and present pardon."[188] Unless we die to sin and are justified by the Holy Spirit, we cannot partake of resurrection at the last day.[189] This constant referral to the Atonement linked with the resurrection is for Newman the source and origin of our immortality. "The death and resurrection of Christ is ever a call upon you to die in time,

---

185 No. 70 p. 7.

186 No. 27.

187 No. 36; 139 p. 20.

188 No. 78.

189 No. 145 p. 22.

152

and to live in eternity."[190]

The history of our immortality begins with our regeneration in Christ. This seed of new life is implanted at the moment of our incorporation into Christ at baptism. From that moment forward we have received a life which will last forever. Natural death does not interrupt this process of growth into the fullness of Christ, but is simply a transition from a period of probation to maturity, from the chrysalis to the butterfly.

> "For Christ Himself has died, and His followers are to live forever; and between these two great truths, before and after it, His death and our immortality, our soul's separation from the body is an inconsiderable event."[191]

Christ's atonement was a death to sin, His resurrection a spiritual regeneration of our nature. When however Newman wishes to describe our solidarity with Christ, which is the ground of our immortality, he turns to the mystery of the Incarnation. Christ is the Second Adam in Whom our nature is reborn. The universality of our corrupt nature in Adam is transformed by the universality of a new creation in Christ.[192] As Adam "is in us as the original cause of our nature and of that corruption of nature which causes death, Christ is the cause original of restoration to life."[193] It is in Christ's incorruptible human nature, which He communicates to us, that we find the source of our immortality. "Adam spreads poison, Christ diffuses life eternal. Christ communicates life to us, one by one, by means of that holy and incorrupt nature which He assumed for our redemption."[194] Moreover it is our whole nature, body and soul, which was assumed by His being born in the flesh. The incarnation therefore is the basis on which the resurrection of the body can be affirmed.

> "Our corruptible bodies could never live the life they shall live, were it not that *here they are joined with His body*

---

[190] S.D.viii,p.110.

[191] No. 174 p. 10.

[192] P.P.S.v.9.

[193] No. 348 p. 15. This is a quotation from Hooker which refers to the Eucharist as the bread of immortality.

[194] P.P.S.ii,13.

which is incorruptible, and that His is in ours as a cause of
immortality, a cause by removing through the death and
merit of His own flesh that which hindered the life of ours.
Christ is therefore, both as God and as man that true vine,
whereof we *both* spiritually *and corporally* are
branches."195

We have seen how the intimations of immortality were linked with
the human spirit's search for perfection, through virtue and holiness. It
is now linked decisively and explicitly to the holy and incorruptible
human nature which Christ assumed at the Incarnation. What our nature
in Adam could not achieve because of corruption, the nature which
Christ assumed did not only "abhor corruption" but was incorruptible
in itself. He was "immortal even in His mortal nature" and thus "His
rising from the dead may be said to have evinced His divine original."
At the very moment of the Annunciation "His incorruptible and
immortal nature is implied," and the resurrection simply manifests the
inherent power of immortality present to Him from His birth. Thus we
can "observe how Christ's resurrection harmonizes with the history of
His birth."196

The harmony which Newman seeks in the Person of Christ is not,
however, one which can be established by historical means. The identity
between the Christ of faith and the Jesus of history forever remains a
mystery, known only retrospectively by faith in the resurrection. To
concretely enter history Christ assumed man's fallen nature, and not a
hypothetical humanity of original innocence.197 But, in his desire to
find the theological basis of immortality, particularly in the form of
bodily incorruption, Newman takes Adam's original state before the Fall

---

195 No. 348 pp. 15-16.

196 P.P.S.ii,13. The influence of Alexandrian theology and the high Christology
of the Anglican divines of the 17th cent. is very clear. The tendency towards a docetic
Christology arising from Neo-Platonism can be found, e.g. "His personal appearance
seems to have borne the marks of one who was not tainted with birth-sin."; "as if there was
some hidden inherent vigour in Him which secured His manhood from dissolution";
though Christ had "a real body" it was fully a "partaker in the properties of His soul", a
spiritualizing and Platonic implication.

197 No. 352 p. 5: "..of course He could not take upon Himself that corrupt nature
of Adam's race, but He took upon Himself the sinless nature in which Adam was
created...." In another sermon, No. 533 Newman is less forthright:- "Whatever the nature
He assumed in addition to His original Godhead, He could not but bring His ineffable
and infinite glories into it though it was in itself an imperfect nature, such as the human
is."

154

as the type on which the Incarnation was modelled.[198] It is then by virtue of the "purity and incorruption" of Christ's human nature that He can "leaven the whole mass of human corruption and make it live." This leavening takes place at the resurrection and thus the mystery of regeneration is incorporated into the prior mystery of the incarnation.

> "Such then is our risen Saviour in Himself and towards us:- conceived by the Holy Ghost; holy from the womb; dying, but abhorring corruption; rising again the third day by His own inherent life; exalted as the Son of God and Son of man, to raise us after Him; and filling us incomprehensibly with His immortal nature, till we become like Him; filling us with a spiritual life which may expel the poison of the fruit of knowledge, and restore us to God."[199]

The Body, The Soul and The Self

Before considering the Christian belief in the resurrection of the body, it is important to describe briefly Newman's view of the body-soul relation. Since "the immortality of the soul" is frequently used by him as an expression of the life hereafter, it may easily give rise to a misinterpretation of his meaning. Newman takes a common-sense approach to words and the meaning intended by them. He notes that on one level we understand perfectly well what is meant by "body" and "soul," but in another sense the meaning of these words is quite beyond us. Experience tells us that man is "one and indivisible," and though we may distinguish between spirit and matter, their union and how it is achieved in the human person, is quite a mystery.[200]

While spirit holds the primacy over matter, there is no implied negative value of the body in Newman's anthropology.[201] He combines

---

[198] Though Christ was without sin, the human nature He assumed was subject to temptation to sin. Newman confronts the difficulty of whether Christ's humanity was in itself sinless or sinful; in No. 405 he seems to be referring to the case of Irving who stressed Christ's solidarity with sinful man. For a discussion on this point cf R.Strange, *The Gospel of Christ*, Oxford, pp. 79-84, and a shift in the author's position in his recent article in *Newman after a Hundred Years*, eds.I.Ker-A.G.Hill, Oxford 1990, pp. 323-336.

[199] P.P.S.ii,13.

[200] P.P.S.iv,19.

[201] P.P.S.i,21: "Among the wise men of the heathen, as I have said, it was usual to speak slightingly and contemptuously of the mortal body; they knew no better. They thought it scarcely a part of their real selves, and fancied they should be in a better

the biblical concept of man's unitary nature with the empirical philosophy of Aristotle. The union of body and soul is of a unique kind and unlike any other thing made up of parts. The body is united not *to* the soul but *in* the soul, which is the common term for denoting the individual self.[202] Hence it is not an instrument, which can be taken up or laid down. "Every part of it is part of himself; it is connected into one by the soul which is one."[203] The body then is not simply extended matter, but an essential principle of the whole person.[204] What we see is merely the outward expression of the body principle, without understanding exactly what the body is.

> "We are apt to talk about our bodies as if we knew how and what they really were; whereas we only know what our eyes tell us...we have no direct cognizance of what may be called the substantive existence of the body, only of its accidents. Again, we are apt to speak of soul and body, as if we could distinguish between them; but for the most part we use words without meaning."[205]

A logical analysis of the body-soul relation would seem to lead to an impasse of linguistic knots and contradictions, forcing one into a form of dualism. But "experience outstrips reason" and intuitively grasps the unitary nature of the human being. It is the human being, whole and entire, which is the subject of redemption and immortality. Redemption is of the person and not of any one single dimension, whether material or spiritual. "He blessed Abraham and gave him eternal life; not to his soul only without his body, but to Abraham as one man. And so He is our God, and it is not given to us to distinguish between what He does for our different natures, spiritual and material. These are mere words; each of us may feel himself to be one, and that one being, in all its substantial parts, and attributes, will never die."[206] Hence the bible, while acknowledging the different dimensions of our

---

condition without it."

[202] It is human selfhood and individuality which Newman is underlining in such sermons as P.P.S.i,2 and iv,6, which he denotes by the term soul.

[203] P.P.S.iv,19.

[204] Hence arises the distinction between a body and a corpse. P.P.S.iii,16: "when the soul leaves the body, it ceases to be a body, it becomes a corpse."

[205] P.P.S.i,21.

[206] ibid.

nature, invariably and without exception, proposes a salvation of the whole person, body and soul.

The Resurrection of the Body

In Newman's reflections on the resurrection of the body, two general characteristics of his theology may be found. The first of these is his fidelity to the revealed word as expressing truths above reason, where reason has "nothing to argue upon." The second is his respect for reason as a marriage partner to faith, which involves both the use and rejection of philosophy in coming up to the standard set by revelation. While Platonism is rejected because of its dualistic view of the body-soul relation, Aristotle's natural anthropology is less inimical to matter and the body. Both however are incapable of offering any positive contribution to the doctrine of bodily resurrection, which is totally within the realm of faith.

> "Philosophers of old time thought the soul indeed might live for ever, but that the body perished at death; but Christ tells us otherwise, He tells us that the body will live forever. In the text He seems to intimate that it never really dies; that we lose sight indeed of what we are accustomed to see, but that God still sees the elements of it which are not exposed to our senses."[207]

Newman thus dissociates himself from the conception of immortality as propounded by Greek philosophy. Moreover he declares that it was precisely the question of existence after death, that distinguished Christian faith from pagan belief, and overthrew the latter. Though the resurrection of the dead is not the whole of Christianity,[208] "it will be said, and said truly, that this doctrine of a future life was the doctrine

---

[207] ibid. Here and in the earlier quote, Newman seems to be alluding to the Aristotelian distinction between prime matter and secondary matter. What is visible is secondary matter; prime matter is "not exposed to the senses."

[208] No. 404 p. 5: "They have...this preconceived theory in their minds, that the substance of the Gospel lies in the immortality of the soul and the resurrection - this is their orthodoxy - they think nothing else important...The resurrection of Christ and our resurrection in consequence is a true, a glorious, a most consoling, a most momentous and mysterious doctrine. The fault of these men is that they assume it is the whole of the Gospel, whereas though an important part, is but a part of it."

which broke the power and fascination of paganism."[209] Hence to talk of "the immortality of the soul" may cloud the very originality of the message the apostles preached, which was "was contrary to all their native prejudices and original habits."[210] For a Christian to speak of the soul's immortality, does not entail the acceptance of any theoretical platform, but is aimed at the practical conviction that our personal identity, once given by God, will never cease. However, we do not positively know what immortality consists in, for it is a negative word, though a little more intelligible than the resurrection of the body.[211] Though we have no way of determining in what sense our bodies are to rise, we have the revealed word, addressed solely to faith, to assure us of our integral and complete glory.

> "Far different is the temper which the glorious light of the Gospel teaches us. Our bodies shall rise again and live for ever; they may not be irreverently handled. How they will rise we know not; but surely if the word of Scripture be true, the body from which the soul is departed shall come to life. There are some truths addressed solely to our faith, not to our reason; not to our reason, because we know so little about "the power of God" (in our Saviour's words) that we have nothing to reason upon...And so, as regards the resurrection of the dead, we have no means or ground of argument. We cannot determine in what exact sense our bodies on the resurrection will be the same as they are at present, but we cannot harm ourselves by taking God's declaration simply, and acting upon it."[212]

As the incarnation and resurrection are events totally beyond the power of anticipated reasoning, the ground for our belief in the resurrection of the body can be found only in the mystery of Christ. The mystery is conveyed to us in and through the power of the Spirit. As Christ became a life-giving spirit, and communicated new life to us in His resurrection, our bodies become sacred. "They are not ours; they are Christ's; they are instinct with that flesh which saw not corruption;

---

[209] P.P.S.i,2.

[210] No. 78 p. 5.

[211] P.P.S.i,2: "We never in this life can fully understand what is meant by our living for ever, but we can understand what is meant by this world's *not* living for ever, by its dying never to rise again."

[212] P.P.S.i,21.

they are inhabited by His Spirit; they become immortal."[213] This presence of the Holy Ghost is not simply a spiritual influence within us, to be seen only in its effects as a life of holiness, but a mysterious indwelling, touching body and soul. The Spirit, moreover, not only bestows His gifts, but gives Himself. Hence the body's immortality is not some miraculous or moral transformation, which could occur without the Spirit Himself being given. It is rather the hallowing of a temple by His inward presence. As the flesh of Christ was essentially penetrated and possessed by the life-giving Spirit,[214] so also in our degree our bodies become temples of God. They are sown with the seed of immortality, which organically grows to its full fruit, in the resurrection of the dead.

> "...is the gift of the body's immortality miraculous or moral? Neither, in the common sense of the words; yet it is a gift bestowed on us in this life, and by the power of the Holy Ghost, according to the texts "Your body is the temple of the Holy Ghost;" and "He that raised up Christ from the dead shall also quicken your mortal bodies by His indwelling Spirit."[215]

Summary of Chapter Three

In contrast to the previous chapter where sin and the dark prospect of eternal death abounded, Chapter Three showed that grace and the bright promise of eternal life were more generously affirmed in the Gospel. The chapter began with Newman's account of the new creation, which though invisible to the senses, was present to the eyes of faith. The state of salvation into which we were redeemed was a true beginning and first installment of our future state of glory. Newman described this state as constituted by the indwelling of the Holy Spirit, who was the formal cause of our justification to eternal life. This was the central affirmation of Christian eschatology which fundamentally transformed our human condition into one of hope and joy.

In Part Two of the chapter, we saw that Newman's theology of

---

213 ibid.

214 No. 406 p. 12.

215 P.P.S.iii,18.

hope did not appear on the surface of his sermons but was hidden deep within them. He did not confuse Christian hope with shallow optimism or identify it with the natural gift of a cheerful disposition. Hope was a grace whose warrant and foundation was the sacrifice of Christ. Its origin and object was God alone and the Second Coming of Christ was the goal to which hope was directed. Though it included the element of desire, Newman saw hope more as a virtue to be exercised than a wish to be gratified. While hope looked to the future, it was grounded on the past mercies of God. The past then became the pledge of the future and faith formed in love the assurance of our hope.

Hope implied the absence of Christ while joy signified His spiritual presence among us. Newman thus attached to the death of Christ the symbol of our hope, and to Christ's birth, His resurrection from the dead and the gift of the Holy Spirit, the joy of His presence and possession. Thus the paradox of Christ's absence by His death was the condition for His spiritual presence and illustrated the mixed economy of hope and joy in a salvation which is "now" but "not-yet".

In the final section on Eternal Life we had Newman's treatment of immortality and the resurrection of the dead. Newman dealt first of all with the intimations of reason regarding the after-life and then followed the thread of development of life after death in the Old Testament. This led him to the startling and distinctive Christian belief in the resurrection of the body, a belief which was totally beyond the range of reason. Christ alone was the source and origin of immortality and it was precisely by being inserted in Him, through the instrumentality of the Holy Spirit, that the dead shall rise again. By being made temples of the Holy Ghost, members of Christ reap the final fruit of redemption in the resurrection of the body.

CHAPTER FOUR

THE CHURCH AS ESCHATOLOGICAL SIGN

Introduction

In the first three chapters, our account of Newman's thought has revolved around the axis of the Christ-Event, which is the source and origin of eschatology. We have considered the Coming of Christ and its related themes of judgment and salvation to eternal life. Christ came in the flesh to inaugurate God's plan of salvation, which was definitively sealed in His death and resurrection. His cross signified the divine judgment on the world and His rising from the dead the new creation to eternal life. At the end of time He will come again to mark the completion of His reign on earth. Then He will clearly manifest what He has already begun in mystery; a general judgment will be seen by all and the fulness of salvation will be gloriously revealed.

We must now look at what Newman had to say about the in-between time, between Christ's First and Second Coming, which is the time of the Church. At His resurrection, Christ became a life-giving Spirit and this transformation of His humanity enables us to share in His risen life. It was the Spirit's task to create a community of believers in which the new creation would be formed. This community we call the Church, which is the Sacrament of Christ, in whom the end of all things has been revealed. The mystery of the Church is thus derived from the eschatological event of Christ and is the sign of His risen presence. Being the historical fruit of Christ's resurrection, it is also the instrument by which the mystery of salvation is proclaimed.

Newman suggests three ways in which the Church reflects the eschatological event of Christ's death and resurrection. As a divine institution, it represents the end-time in being the fulfilment of prophecy. In this Body we have the embryo of the Reign of God, which reached its fulness in Christ, and is now symbolized in the glory of the Christian Church. The Church is also the Body of the Elect, of those who are predestined for the blessedness of heaven. It is the sign of Christ's atonement and the countersign to a sinful world. Like its Saviour it will suffer persecution; it is the little flock, the holy remnant which is meant not for this world but for the next. Lastly, the Church

forms part of the Communion of Saints which is the fruit of Christ's
resurrection. It thereby anticipates its future perfection and is the sign of
the heavenly New Jerusalem.

Part One
The Kingdom of Heaven

The Mediatorial Kingdom

It is significant[1] that the beginnings of Newman's theology of the
Church is marked by a forthright distinction "between the absolute
kingdom of Christ as God, and His mediatorial kingdom as man."[2] The
Church, which is identified with the mediatorial kingdom, is a remedial
institution. In contrast with the absolute kingdom of God's eternal
sovereignty, in which Christ shares by His divine nature, the kingdom
of the Mediator is "relative," "temporary" and "changeable." Since it
had a beginning, it will also have an end, when it attains its full stature at
the day of Judgment.[3] It is the kingdom prophesied by Daniel which
will grow into a universal empire, until Christ's reign returns to His pre-
existent, absolute reign as God.

"Then He will resume His eternal reign as one with the
Father. His kingdom will spread and spread like Daniel's
stone until the earth is His."[4]

The extension of this kingdom is dependent on the degree of

---

[1] It is significant for two reasons. First, Newman's early conception of the Church is
dominated by the mystery of the Atonement. His soteriology is so accentuated as to put
him later in difficulties on Christological grounds. Secondly, his starting point, which is
human corruption, can be compared with his contemporary F.D.Maurice, whose theology
of the Kingdom begins with creation, not redemption. For a comparison between
Newman and Maurice cf E.Vidler, *F.D. Maurice and Company*, London, S.C.M.
Press,1966, pp. 37ff.

[2] No. 46.

[3] No. 51. The last of Newman's sermons on the mediatorial kingdom, No. 175
makes the same point on p. 19.

[4] No. 51.

holiness within the Church. While the principle of holiness has been
implanted by Christ, it is nonetheless subject to human freedom. As the
result of man's sin, a wide gap occurs between God's design and the
actual reality of the Church. In the plan of God however, the kingdom
of the Mediator is "a universal Church... pure and holy... blessed with
peace and unity... secure and prosperous ... the Church is to be
glorious."[5]

Newman then adds the missing note of apostolicity as an element
of the Church's identity.[6] But for the moment, he is more concerned
with the spiritual nature of the kingdom and the need for holiness,
which alone brings to fulfilment the prophecy of a universal reign.[7]
However, the four notes of the Church, which are the ways by which it
is a sign to the world, have been mentioned at this early stage, with
reference to its final accomplishment.

The mediatorial kingdom as the fulfilment of Daniel's prophecy is
considered a year later in a sermon preached on Christmas Day.[8] Once
again we see a sharp distinction within Christ with respect to His
authority. In His divine nature, He shares a role with the Father in the
absolute Kingdom, but in his human nature he presides over a kingdom
within the Kingdom of God. An important development, however, takes
place by introducing the priestly prayer of intercession over the
Church.[9] Three special blessings have been conferred by Christ on the
mediatorial kingdom - holiness, unity and eternal life - and "it is the
possession of these privileges which makes us the favoured people of
God, elect, beloved."

Newman's next sermon on the theme of the kingdom was
preached the following Easter at Oriel College and greeted with some
dismay. It opened once again with the prophecy of the eschatological

---

[5] ibid.

[6] This note was to become of greater importance to him in asserting the claims of
the Anglican Church as the Via Media. In it he saw the strength of the Anglican position
vis-à-vis the Roman communion, whose catholicity outshone his own branch of the
Church.

[7] The third sermon in this Course xii. *On the Mediatorial Kingdom* is No. 52.
Only an abstract remains of it, but the emphasis on the spiritual covenant between the
Mediator and the Christian, is clear. The other two sermons are No. 46 and 51.

[8] No. 158. The inappropriateness of the theme for this day confirms the view that
the Atonement was so dominant as to drown out the mystery of the Incarnation. The next
time he came to preach on the subject he chose the more suitable time of Easter Day.

[9] This Johannine text, Jn.xvii, is found in Nos. 158, 160 and 175, which are all on
the mediatorial kingdom

messiah, who would herald a universal kingdom. This had been fulfilled in Christ, who upon entering into His glory, commissioned His disciples to extend it to the whole world. This sermon was to prove a watershed in Newman's Christology as a result of the severe criticisms of Hawkins and Whateley, the latter charging him with Arianizing. The greater part of his address was devoted to "several texts relating to our Lord's person, character and office" connected with the nature of His mediatorial kingdom.[10] From there on, Newman dropped the term "mediatorial kingdom," which had created difficulties in exposition. It had led him into too neat distinctions of a speculative kind which implied a form of subordinationism. Thereafter, we see the development of the category of "mystery," which Newman applied to revealed doctrine including the nature of the Church.[11]

Before passing beyond this landmark, a brief mention must be made of the Church's note of universality, which was an important concern for him in his early preaching.[12] Though the promise of the kingdom's ultimate extension to the whole world is a source of comfort,[13] the fact that it is not so extended after 1800 years, raises the question of why the prophecy is as yet unfulfilled. In trying to resolve the dilemma, Newman notes that Scripture looks to the distant horizon of God's design, and in so doing passes over the intervening history as though it were already accomplished.

> "In these then and many other passages in the prophets the nature of Christ's kingdom, its eventual extent, its full perfections and finished glories are spoken of, what it should be now and will be *hereafter*, passing over the fact of

---

[10] Newman kept the Oriel address in a packet of four sermons marked "personal." Extensive comments by Hawkins and Whateley are written on the side together with Newman's own reflections on the criticisms they made. On this sermon cf Newman's Memorandum, L.D., Vol.ii, pp. 15-16.

[11] No. 175 still keeps to the old terminology of "a mediatorial kingdom" but this sermon is substantially the same as No. 158: "from p. 7 onwards this sermon is the same as No. 175." No. 175 however was preached six times in all up to 1836. We have an example of "some strong sentences" on p. 17 of No. 175, which Newman thought ought to be added to No. 160 to dispel an Arian interpretation.

[12] No. 104, 164, 267 on the extension of the Kingdom, reflect Newman's original desire to be a missionary. He was secretary of the Oxford branch of the Church Missionary Society and his first public address was delivered under its auspices. cf L.D. i Appendix..

[13] No. 104 also outlines the advantages to the Church, by the delay in the fulfilment of prophecy. The Church has need for purification and time to truly appropriate the gospel.

its gradual extension and actual history."[14]

The promise of "a new heavens and a new earth," is considered by Newman in a later sermon. He notes that it may be understood in two senses, either as referring to the setting up of the kingdom at Christ's resurrection, or to its termination.[15] As regards the end of the kingdom, which he describes apocalyptically, he surmises if a time will come when the whole earth shall become Christian. Its triumph is assured in the next world, but no such assurance is given in the present order of things. Christianity is indeed fitted to be the religion of the world, but the Scripture passages predicting Christ's universal reign "cannot be taken to imply more than will or design." Prophetical texts have an inbuilt uncertainty in them and it is more likely that the eschatological kingdom they refer to, is a description of heaven rather than of earth. Millenarian dreams[16] are the result of too literal and partial an interpretation of Scripture; the revealed word "gives us no expectations, rather the contrary, that the Church, however widely extended, will on the whole be very much purer than it is at the present day."[17] But as far as the hope of universal holiness is concerned, Newman's characteristic realism appears:

"... but will flesh and blood ever inherit so blest a kingdom? will mortal man in his best estate ever be thus holy? we dare not anticipate it... The notion of every individual upon the face of the earth being at some future day converted to the spiritual worship of God and real faith in Christ, is not countenanced by Scripture. Not that we have any authority for saying positively that the Christian Church will not hereafter be much purer than it is, as well as more extended; only, it is not revealed, and it is not antecedently probable."[18]

---

[14] No. 116 p. 11.

[15] No. 164 p. 1.

[16] The 1820s when this sermon was preached, were rife with interest in prophecy. Pre-millenialists and post-millenialists contested with each other. Though Newman's earliest views on the matter are ambiguous, his sermons take the Augustinian view that the millenium has already come in the form of the Christian Church. For an account of the context cf. W.H.Oliver, *Prophets and Millenialists...*, Oxford, 1978, pp. 144-149.

[17] No. 164.

[18] ibid.

The Imperial Church

The Church as the fulfilment of prophecy is treated in a sermon entitled The Kingdom of the Saints.[19] The providential history of the spread of the gospel all but confirms Daniel's prophecy of the Fifth Kingdom, "which is fulfilled among us at this day." Without discounting the human factors involved,[20] the growth of the Church was primarily due to "an internal development of one and the same principle... suitably called invisible, and not of this world." Even apart from any reference to prophecy, its beginnings and subsequent history were unprecedented in the world; we are thus forced to consider more than purely human reasons to account for its success. At the very infancy of the Church, Jesus and the apostles spoke "confidently, solemnly, calmly of its destined growth and triumph," and Christ Himself contemplated "the overshadowing sovereignty of His Kingdom." He foretold that its rule would be attended by the breakdown and destruction of all earthly kingdoms. Moreover, God's providence, seen in the light of history, goes hand in hand with the prophecy of Daniel. It has been verified in the fall of the Roman Empire, which marks its partial fulfilment. Prescinding from the chronology of future events, the "recognized prophetical symbols"[21] predict the fullness of God's sovereignty and hence the "destruction sooner or later, of existing political institutions." Despite the persecutions and the attempts to destroy it, the Church can rest confident that it has inherited a kingdom which cannot be moved.

"Now, if we had nothing more to bring forward than the two considerations which have been here insisted on, the singular history of Christianity, and the clear and confident anticipation of it by its first preachers, we should have

---

[19] This is one sermon but published in two parts, P.P.S.ii,20-21. Like four other sermons in Vol.ii, dating from Jan-Feb.1835, it was never preached, a practice which Newman never again followed. Cf. F. Rogers' enthusiastic comment on the sermon as "an essential theory in the Anglican system." L.D., Vol.vi, p. 121.

[20] Newman depends on Gibbon's *Decline and Fall of the Roman Empire* for his factual information on the period.

[21] The underlying apocalyptic view in Newman's sermons is confirmed by L.Bouyer: "A plus forte raison, ces considérations s'appliquent-elles à un autre aspect des sermons de Newman, qui met dans une lumière particulièrement vive ce qui est peut-être l'aspect le plus profond du mouvement d'Oxford. Je veux dire ce qu'ils ont et qu'il faut qualifier hardiment d'apocalyptique." L.Bouyer, *Newman sa Vie et sa Spiritualité*, Paris, Les éditions du Cerf, 1952, p. 235.

enough of evidence, one would think, to subdue the most difficult inquirer to a belief of its divinity."[22]

The Church then is invested with an invisible, divine source of life; it is not a kingdom of this world. Earthly kingdoms have arisen and failed because they had not the power and sanction of prophecy. But the Church's roots are planted deep beneath the surface and despite the twists and turns of fortune, it will finally attain its goal, as Christ intended, in becoming the spiritual empire foretold in prophecy.

"If the Christian Church has spread its branches high and wide over the earth, its roots are fixed deep below the surface. The intention of Christ and His Apostles, on which I have dwelt, is itself but the accomplishment of ancient prophecy."[23]

A long intervening period of almost eight years passed before Newman took up again the theme of the Church as the fulfilment of prophecy.[24] From the middle of November in 1842 till the second Sunday of Advent, he preached six sermons on the Church as the fulfilment of the spiritual empire promised in the Old Testament.[25] His stated purpose for these sermons was to "remove some difficulties in the way of looking at the prophecies" regarding the Church, by showing that they have been "literally fulfilled in gospel times."[26] Though the language of prophecy is conveyed in symbols, it is meant to refer to some real object, and hence "where a literal meaning will stand, the furthest from the letter is usually the worst." Hence the prophecies regarding the Church should be given a literal, and not merely a metaphorical interpretation. They do not simply refer to the moral influence which the gospel exerts on the world, but are found concretely, really, and visibly in the Christian Church itself. When asked then whether the kingdom is already present or yet to come, Newman's answer is that the kingdom is now realized in the Christian Church.

---

[22] P.P.S.ii,20.

[23] P.P.S.ii,21.

[24] From Jan/Feb 1835 when the Kingdom of the Saints was written, but never preached, and the Advent Sermons of 1842 on the Spiritual Empire.

[25] These sermons are S.D. xiv, xv, xvi, xvii, xviii and P.P.S. vii,3.

[26] S.D.xiv p. 196.

"Has this promise yet been fulfilled or no? and if fulfilled, in what sense fulfilled? Many persons think it has not yet been fulfilled at all, and is to be fulfilled in some future dispensation or millenium; and many think that it has been fulfilled, yet not literally, but spiritually and figuratively; or in other words, that the promised reign of Christ upon earth has been nothing more than the influence of the Gospel over the souls of men, the triumphs of Divine Grace, the privileges enjoyed by faith, and the conversion of the elect. On the contrary, I would say that the prophecies in question have in their substance been fulfilled literally, and in the present Dispensation; and if so, we need no figurative and no future fulfilment."[27]

In Newman's view we see that the Kingdom of God is in substance identical with the Church. While the Jews had a Church, the Christian antitype becomes what it had never been before - it becomes an empire or a kingdom; "and hence so much stress is laid upon its being a kingdom, and Christ a King." It is meaningless however, to speak of an invisible kingdom, for by a kingdom is meant an organized society with a head of government. The visible Church is such a body, though it has an invisible King. "Christ is the *invisible* King of a *visible* kingdom."[28]He rules His kingdom by regents, but has not abandoned it. What He gives it, is of Himself, and as He is King, His Church is thereby His Kingdom.

The Christian Church differed from the Jewish, inasmuch as it is a Kingdom; it still retained however its identity as a Church. Daniel saw in vision the empires under which the Church was subject, and to which it succeeded as the Fifth Empire. But in succeeding to them, it became an empire of a different kind, run on different principles from the kingdoms of the world. Like all other empires, it is a kingdom in the world, but not of it. It is a spiritual empire and in this respect it remains a Church.

"As then it may be shown that the Church of Christ, though one church with the Jewish, differs from it as being a Kingdom; so now let me dwell on this point, that though a kingdom like empires of the earth, it differs from them in

[27] S.D.xiv pp. 180-1.

[28] S.D.xvi p. 221. This is also clearly brought out in No. 389 p. 2.

being a Church i.e. a kingdom of truth and righteousness."29

Since the Church is the realization of the messianic kingdom it has
a similar "inward and characteristic structure" to the Jewish Church. In
being the continuation of the latter, it did not reject its origins in the plan
of God, which was fulfilled when all things were made new in Christ.
For genuine continuity, similarity as well as difference is required.30
This element of continuity can be seen between Jewish rituals and
Christian sacraments, but the mark of difference is all essential. Unlike
the rituals of the past, the ordinances of the Church are life-giving, being
grafted into Christ and sanctified by Him.

Though Newman believes that the imperial nature of the Church
may be inferred from the Gospel, he finds the more striking
announcements of its spiritual dominion in the Old Testament
prophecies. By its very nature an empire must extend itself, it must
conquer and subdue, live by aggression or die. This is true in substance
for the Kingdom of Christ as well. It is ever advancing and confronting
earthly kingdoms, raising up and pulling down by its spiritual weapons
of divine power. Such is the vision of the Christian Church as pictured
in the prophecies of the Old Testament. Through them we are assured
that it is the sign of the last times, until all the world is Christ's.

"What is wanting in such passages to the picture of a great
empire, comprising all that a great empire ordinarily
exhibits? Extended dominion, and that not only over its
immediate subjects, but over the kings of other kingdoms;
aggression and advance; a warfare against enemies; acts of
judgment upon the proud; acts of triumph over the defeated;
high imperial majesty towards the suppliant; clemency
towards the repentant; parental care of the dutiful."31

---

29 S.D.xvii p. 238.

30 S.D.xv. Two objections are met with in this sermon. The most common one was
the charge of "Judaizing" against the Tractarians from men like Arnold. An emphasis on
Church rites and laws, was perceived as directly at variance with the freedom of the
gospel, which differentiated it from the Jewish Law. The second objection from men like
Milman, erred by stressing too much the similarity between the Jewish and Christian
Dispensation, without noting their essential difference.

31 S.D. xxi, p.234.

The Glory of the Christian Church

Looking back on Newman's early sermons on the mediatorial kingdom, we see the Church described in functional terms as the means to future glory. For the most part his sight was trained on the distant horizon of unfulfilled prophecy, with little attention paid to its present realization. It is natural to expect, however, that the means should somehow prefigure and contain the end to which the Church is called. In this respect we see a development in Newman's sermons with his focus on the present realization of the Kingdom in the glory of the Christian Church.

To account for the gap between the actual condition of the Church and what it is to become, Newman had introduced the distinction[32] between God's design revealed in Scripture and historical fact. In his earlier sermons, the design had not yet been realized, but now he applies to the Church a measure of the final glory which one day will be hers to the full.

"In like manner the Christian Church had in the day of its nativity all that fullness of holiness and peace named upon it, and sealed up to it, which beseemed it, viewed as God's design - viewed in its essence, as it is realized at all times, and under whatever circumstances - viewed as God's work without man's cooperation - viewed as God's work in its tendency, and in its ultimate blessedness; so that the titles given it upon earth are a picture of what it will be absolutely in heaven."[33]

We have also seen the failure of the Church to realize its note of universality because of its lack of holiness. But now he shows how in both respects the promises were fulfilled in the very beginnings of the Church.[34] Regarding the note of catholicity, Newman sees it as satisfied by the Church's mission as universal witness, however much the world may remain unconverted. Catholicity is what distinguishes the Church

---

[32] This distinction first introduced in No. 116 is even more clearly brought out in P.P.S.ii,8 with an emphasis on the present realization of God's design in the Church.

[33] P.P.S.ii,8.

[34] P.P.S.ii,8: Newman's romanticism is shown by his attributing perfection to the beginnings or birth of the Church. Likewise, the Transfiguration is described as the childhood innocence of the Church. "Here was a pledge of eternal blessedness, the same in kind as a child's innocence is a forerunner of a holy immortality."

170

from its Jewish antecedent, and is the distinctive note manifesting God's outward glory.[35] The glory of God was confined to the Jewish Temple, but in the new dispensation it is disseminated throughout the world, by means of the Christian Church. Moses asked to see the glory of God and was granted a glimpse of "the skirts of His glory," but "the glory of the New Covenant is so much greater that in comparison of it, the Law was as nothing."[36] Though as yet we have but a measure of future glory, our present state far exceeds that of the Jewish covenant.

"Yet though the glory which is to come so far exceeds the present glory, we *have* somewhat in common with the future, which the Jewish covenant had *not* with us"[37]

Moreover, the Covenant on Mount Sinai was a mere shadow of the glory on the Mount of Transfiguration. Here Christ had gathered the representatives of His Church and anticipated the glory which He was about to bestow on it.[38] What the apostles experienced was "the earnest of what one day will be perfected."[39] It was Christ's way of showing His apostles the glorious Church, which lay on the other side of the resurrection. The significance of this Gospel story was not incidental to the nature of the Church; though it was revealed privately to the few, it was meant for all to deepen their understanding of the mystery.

"surely, it is of a doctrinal nature, being nothing less than a figurative exhibition of the blessed truth contained in the texts under review, a vision of a glorious Kingdom He set up on the earth on His Coming."[40]

Newman had earlier distinguished two kingdoms, one absolute, the

---

[35] ibid. No. 388 p. 2: "The Jewish Church was local - the Christian Catholic i.e. universal."

[36] No. 485 pp. 1-2.

[37] ibid. p. 2 In this sermon Newman strongly warns against expressions of enthusiasm. The supernatural gift given to the Church is perceived by faith, not by sensible manifestations. In the conclusions to both P.P.S.ii,8 and iii,18 where the glory of the Church is described, we find the same admonition.

[38] For references to the Transfiguration in the sermons cf Nos.102; 251; P.P.S.ii,8; iii,18; vi,10; vi,15; vii,6

[39] P.P.S.ii,8.

[40] P.P.S.iii,18.

other relative, one of God Himself and the other of the Mediator. At the
end of time these two kingdoms would come together when the
mediatorial would fuse into the Kingdom of God. A radical change in
Newman's conception is now seen when he considers the gift of the
Spirit, which inseparably and for all time binds the two kingdoms
together into one. By the reconciling blood of Christ, Almighty God,
"who had retreated from the earth as far as His kingly presence was
concerned" had returned, so that heaven and earth have been reunited.
The Church thus "became once more an integral part of the unseen, but
really existing world, of which the Lord is the Everlasting Light." The
earlier distinction is thus put aside, and the Church, which he had called
the mediatorial kingdom, is now identified with the Kingdom of God.

> "Since then the Christian Church is a Heaven upon earth, it is
> not surprising that in some sense or other its distinguishing
> privilege or gift should be glory, for this is the one attribute
> we ever attach to Heaven itself, according to the Scripture
> intimations concerning it. The glory here may be conceived of
> by considering what we believe of the glory hereafter."[41]

As catholicity signifies the outward manifestation of glory, holiness pertains to the greater inward glory of the Church. We can speak
of glory even under the Law, but properly speaking, it "belongs exclusively to the promised blessedness hereafter."[42] There is however "a
peculiar and sufficient sense" in which it can be ascribed to the
Christian Church. This is essentially due to her mark of holiness, which
is the presence of the Holy Spirit within it.

> "And further, the Church as being thus honoured and exalted
> by the presence of the Spirit of Christ, is called "the Kingdom
> of God, the "Kingdom of Heaven" as, for instance, by Christ
> Himself... I propose now to make some remarks on the
> peculiar gift of the Gospel Dispensation, which, as in the
> foregoing passages, is spoken of as the gift of "the Spirit," the
> gift of "glory," and through which the Church has become
> what it was not before, the Kingdom of Heaven."[43]

---

[41] P.P.S.iii,18.
[42] ibid.
[43] ibid.

172

Though the Jewish Church showed the presence of the Spirit in the miracles and the means of sanctification, it fell far short of the Gift of the Spirit itself. This Gospel privilege imparted to the Church is "something deeper, wider and more mysterious, though including both miracles and graces."[44] The essential difference lies in this Gift by which the Church becomes the dwelling-place of God. Hence all former expressions of glory, whether miraculous or moral, are surpassed by the glory of the Christian Church.

> "Such reflections as these are calculated, perhaps, to give us somewhat of a deeper view than is ordinarily admitted, of the character of that gift which attends on the presence of the Holy Ghost in the Church, and which is called the gift of glory."[45]

The nature of the Church cannot be described as anything less than a mystery. This notion was conspicuously absent in Newman's earlier sermons on the nature of the mediatorial kingdom. The church was then defined in functional terms as a remedial institution. However, he now admits the futility of defining something which must "embrace what is incomprehensible and unfathomable," and would "fain keep from making the same mistake." Only an enlarged view can give some idea of the nature of the Church, and "mystery" is the only adequate tool of description. He therefore views the Church as inserted into two great mysteries, first of the Incarnation and that of Regeneration in the Holy Spirit. Christ Himself linked admittance to the Kingdom of heaven with His own Person. He also revealed that the glory He had from the Father, has now been given to His Church, through baptism in the Spirit.

> "Thus the greater Mystery of the Incarnation is made to envelope and pledge to us the mystery of the new birth. As He was in heaven in an ineffable sense, even "in the days of His flesh," so are we, in our degree;"[46]

---

[44] P.P.S.iii.18. This sermon, No. 390, on *The Gift of the Spirit* is thematically linked to two unpublished sermons, viz No. 389 on *The Kingdom of Heaven or The Church as Mysterious* and No. 388 on *The Sanctity of Churches*

[45] ibid.

[46] P.P.S.iii,18.

Though no single term can express the glory of the Church, various combined descriptions may give some idea of "that unspeakable Gospel privilege, which is the earnest and portion of heavenly glory." Clear definition is impossible, for it implies putting limits and control on the Church's Gift of the Spirit. It is described as "illumination, the heavenly gift, the Holy Ghost, the Divine Word, the powers of the world to come." But in essence the Church's glory is its sharing the life "of the Word Incarnate, ministered to us by the Holy Ghost." It has been formed "in the image of Christ"[47] in whom "the whole exceeding and eternal weight of glory is hid."[48] As the Church grows in the holiness of its Head, its glory within is gradually realized, until such time as all its members share the fullness of Christ.

> "Such is the Kingdom of God; Christ the centre of it, His glory the light of it, the Just made perfect His companions, and His apostles His witnesses to His brethren. It realizes what the ancient Saints saw by glimpses - Jacob at Bethel, Moses on Sinai. Such then, being the especial glory and "dreadfulness" which attaches to the Christian Church."[49]

Part Two
The Church of the Elect

> "Calvinists make a sharp separation between the elect and the world; there is much in this that is cognate or parallel to the Catholic doctrine."[50]

This tantalizingly brief comparison between the two systems, Catholic and Calvinist, indicates the importance Newman attached to the idea of Christian election. Though he explicitly states that, by the age of twenty-one, he had abandoned his belief in final perseverance, he

---

[47] P.P.S.ii,8.

[48] No. 458 p. 2.

[49] P.P.S.iii,18.

[50] Apo. p. 6.

174

acknowledges the enduring influence of God's initial choice in his conversion. This signal assurance of divine mercy was later accompanied by a conviction that he was called to a single life, as the means best suited to an exclusive devotion to God.[51]

The feeling of detachment, indeed of separation from the things of sense, exercises a major influence on Newman's concept of the Church. It is a Church of the Elect, a sign of the next world and a countersign to this. By God's design, it is predestined to glory, but not without passing through persecution and hostility from the world. The Church is "a little flock," "a holy remnant," sustained by the grace of Christ against principalities and powers. Its unique task is to generate and nourish holiness in its members and rise above the mediocrity of the world.

Separation from the World

The need for separation from the world is a recurring theme in Newman's sermons at St. Clement's. "Come out from among them and be ye separate,"[52] rings like a clarion call warning Christians to resist the temptation to present forms of idolatry.[53] They are to preserve "their exclusive privilege and peculiar excellence" and "to keep themselves at a distance."[54] Only then can the identity of the Church as a "peculiar people" be guarded and maintained. To this end, Newman devotes a course of sermons, in which he draws parallels between the Jewish and Christian election.[55] Circumcision is "an emblem of the devotion of the heart to God," in much the same way as baptism is now regarded by some evangelicals.[56] The Sabbath is a lasting sign of creation, while the Lord's Day is the sign of Christian redemption. It is also the way by which Christians celebrate their new election to glory, which entails

---

[51] ibid. pp. 4-7.

[52] 2 Cor.vi,7.

[53] No. 10.

[54] No. 16.

[55] Course ix entitled *The Jewish Law useful in checking idolatry.* It consisted of Nos. 133, 135, 138, 142, 143, 145, 149, 150.

[56] No. 135 p. 9. Newman had at this time begun to change his view on regeneration by baptism but had not yet relinquished the language of the peculiars.

separation from the world.[57]

> "Nothing is more constantly impressed upon the Israelites
> than this, that they were a distinct, a separate, a peculiar, an
> elect people... To us equally with them may be applied the
> words of the text <Eph.6>... we too are exposed to the
> snares of spiritual idolatry."[58]

Such separation is not, however, an end in itself, but the necessary
prior condition for holiness; something more positive than mere
withdrawal is required.[59] Nevertheless, as the Jewish was a type and
preparation for Christian election, a similar detachment obtains. The
essential difference, however, between the two, was that one was for a
temporal glory, the other for an eternal one. "All the glories of the law
were for the sake of the gospel"[60]- "a kingdom of heavenly blessings
succeeds an earthly one."[61]

By the force of these parallels one gathers the distinct feeling of
spiritual apartheid in the early Newman. Something close to such a
charge is confronted by Newman some ten years later, in a sermon
which contains a note of self-accusation; he rejects the allegation yet
maintains as separatist a view as is found in his evangelical days.[62] By
distinguishing between a rule of discipline and an ideology, he insists
on the need of dissociating from wicked men, without the presumptuous
speculation that "they are partly or wholly destitute of God's grace." By
that time his Calvinist views had toned down, though his letters of the
period show a burning zeal for purity in the Church and apocalyptic

---

[57] No. 145 p. 4.

[58] No. 135 pp. 3,14. Newman later notes a number of points he omitted regarding
the nature of Jewish election and the laws prescribed for maintaining strict separation. He
mentions the precept of iconoclasm, the rules for admitting non-Jews to the community,
the prescriptions on travel and attendance at Jerusalem, for all of which evangelical
parallels can be found.

[59] No. 19 "ye have been severed from the world, but for holiness - severed you
must be; it is done - you cannot undo it - be sure then, if it be not unto holiness, it is unto
wrath."

[60] No. 149, p. 3.

[61] No. 139. The antimonies between temporal and eternal, material and spiritual,
local and universal, run through this course.

[62] No. 347 delivered at the Ambassador's residence in Naples in 1833. Here he
defends the Church's power of excommunication so as to maintain discipline and purity
in the Church.

visions of the future in store for it.[63]

This note of separation and distinction can also be illustrated in his published sermons. To prepare the Church for its final destiny, God first delivers it from this sinful world. Christ did not pray for the world, but for those He had chosen from it. Hence St. Paul reminds us that

"Christ came, not to convert the world, but "to purify unto Himself a peculiar people, zealous of good works"; not to sanctify this evil world, but to "deliver us *out* of this present evil world according to the will of God and our Father"; not to turn the whole earth into a heaven, but to bring down heaven upon earth."[64]

Once again he deals with the charge of exclusivism and singularity, to which the Christian Church "must ever be exposed," when it remains true to its origins. It is condemned for leading people away from the world, and for its isolation and rejection of contemporary life.[65] Singularity, he assures us, is no criterion of authenticity, though the authentic "will invariably differ from the common." His dislike, however, for pretentiousness of any kind, is equally matched by his disdain for populist pressure - "it would seem" he says, "to be certain that those opinions which are popular will ever be mistaken and dangerous as being popular opinions." At the same time he condemns the attitude of false otherworldliness,[66] and shows the futility of thinking it possible for the Church to expel all traces of the world from within it.[67]

The idea of being set apart is combined in a more positive manner with the sign of virginity, a value which Newman held from the very outset of his ministry. Indeed this is shown by his sermon on the Parable of Ten Virgins, in which we find the earliest reference to the elect. The image of the virgin wife waiting for the bridegroom to come,

[63] e.g. Letter to Pusey, March 19 1833, L.D. Vol.iii, pp. 259-26.

[64] P.P.S. iv,10.

[65] P.P.S. v,18. This charge was brought against Newman when he sought to set up his community at Littlemore. He was reported to the Bishop of Oxford for his extravagant plan to build a monastery

[66] P.P.S. viii,11. The Christian is to glorify God in the world. "that *while* in it he is to glorify God, not *out* of it, but *in* it and *by means* of it.

[67] P.P.S. vii,3 ."..how vain in consequence, the attempt is (which some make) of separating the world distinctly from the Church."

and the marriage of the Lamb, is the first image of the Church Newman gives us, thus highlighting its eschatological dimension.

> "In this psalm too we have mention of "the *virgins* that follow the King's daughter (or the Church of God) - (as in the parable before, the ten virgins. - These virgins are Christians considered *individually*, or one by one: *altogether* they make up the bride, the Lamb's wife; - who wait for the bridegroom's coming, to conduct home his wife. - They are called *virgins* among other reasons, to signify the profession of every Christian, who is in baptism set apart for his God and Saviour, as holy unto the Lord."[68]

Discipleship with Christ is linked with purity of heart symbolized by virginity. Chastity is related to a holy separation from the world for an entire life of devotion to God. The Chaste Spouse is the symbol par excellence of the future purity of the Church. Christ Himself was a virgin on whom all virtue is modelled, and by her virginity, Mary became a type and image of His Church. Thus, in an introduction to the feast of the Annunciation, Newman recalls the perfection to which the Church is called.

> "There is no image in Scripture which so forcibly presents to us what we are called to than the image of the Virgin Bride of the Lamb; -such should be every elect soul, holy as a virgin, faithful as a Wife, after the pattern of its immaculate Saviour."[69]

Citing passages from St. Paul, from the Book of Revelation, and in particular from the Canticle of Canticles, Newman notes that this sign of virginity points to the "perfection of the company of elect souls, which is the Church." Moreover, when God decided to take to Himself a people, He "began by first of all separating therefrom as a type[70] of the

[68] No. 8 p. 3.

[69] No. 494 pp 1-2. This sermon has the same number as P.P.S. v,14 on *Transgressions and Infirmities*. The link between the two may be seen in the contrast between the perfection of Mary and the sins of the elect, which is then followed up in the published sermon.

[70] P.P.S. vi,22: "What God began in her was a sort of type of His dealings with His Church."

Church, a virgin of the House of David whose name was Mary." This was to indicate that we are all called to a heavenly state "which the Virgin Mary typifies, and which she realized above others."[71]

This grace of virginity stands in special contrast to the Jewish Dispensation. It is a charism within the Church which signifies that we have received the promise of eternal glory. It is not for every member, but a property held by the Body. But if it were to cease altogether, it would mean that the Church has fallen back into the Jewish state.[72] This would still be a state of faith, but a faith without possession of the promise.

The Nature of Christian Election

As far as separation from the world is concerned and the need for the Church to be a holy and distinct people, the Calvinist and Catholic systems run parallel. When we come however to consider the nature of Christian election, their paths diverge. Both views agree that Christian election can only be understood by referring to the earlier Jewish one, but where the Catholic recognizes continuity in change, the Calvinist confuses and identifies the two. The latter fails to see the radical difference, largely because Scripture describes both elections in similar terms.

"A Calvinist will be unwilling to admit the difference of the Jewish and Christian promise, because it affords so satisfactory an explanation of the words "election" etc. in the

---

[71] ibid. We have four sermons in the Anglican period devoted to the place of Mary in the Church. Nos.137, 291, 333 (P.P.S. ii,12) and 494. P.P.S. vii,10 on *The Crucifixion* also mentions the place of Mary since Good Friday fell on March 25, 1842. Newman's first sermon on *The Faith of Mary* No. 137, was preached on 19th Feb. 1826. It is to be found in a packet with the following note attached: "I put this sermon into the packet as showing how I speak of the Blessed Virgin two years after FWN accuses me of arguing in defence of her invocation."

For an account of Newman's Mariology cf. L.Govaert, *Kardinal Newmans Mariologie und sein personlicher Werdegang,* Salzburg-München, Universitätsverlag Pustet, 1975. In this thesis, the date given for Newman's first sermon on Mary is actually the date of his second.

[72] P.P.S. vi,13. Newman's letter to Henry Wilberforce clearly shows how he regarded celibacy as a higher calling. L.D. Vol.iii, pp. 33-4.

epistles."[73]

In his farewell sermon at St. Clement's,[74] Newman examines the account of Christian election on which Calvinists base the doctrine of predestination. Expressions such as the "elect" and the "chosen" must, he reminds us, be put in context before being applied to the new dispensation. These words were written at a time of discouragement for converts from Judaism, who were taunted by fellow Jews as being no longer God's chosen people. It was alleged that their present suffering and persecution was evidence that God had retracted His favour. Hence the apostles had to insist so much on the fact of election, but of a different nature from that of the Jews. They pointed out the spiritual nature of the promises which lay in the future, and explained the present hardships of Christians as meant to purify them for heaven.

While the similarity of the two elections is obvious, and is found in the unconditional gratuitousness of God, the difference between them lies in the nature of the privileges bestowed. To Christians, gifts of a spiritual nature are granted; to the Jews, worldly blessings. The object of their election differs respectively in the same way as this world differs from the next.

> "In the Jewish election *this* world is the prize; in the
> *Christian* the *next* world - this world being considered
> important not in itself but as preparing us for another."[75]

Jewish converts therefore were made to realize clearly, that they had given up the promises of earthly blessing in exchange for an eternal crown. They experienced more forcibly a trial of faith by persecution, in a way which Christians today have lost or fail to recognize. Christians should not expect worldly blessing, for it is no longer promised; the order of values between the two elections has been reversed. On the spiritual plane however, there is no loss, but only gain. The Church of the elect can both rejoice in present suffering, in conformity with Christ, and look with a spirit of hope for a future reward, which was prepared

---

[73] No. 99 p. 8.

[74] No. 150. Newman had already treated the theme of *Jewish election* in a course by that name. It consisted of three sermons, Nos. 127, 129 and 131. Unfortunately, none of the manuscripts is extant.

[75] No. 200 p. 5. This is part of Newman's course *on the Romans* in which the doctrine of election is prominent.

180

for them from the beginning of time. Their election was not an afterthought but the design of God from the start. It had been "forecontemplated, devised and planned... He had not cast off one people, and taken another who might perhaps in turn be rejected -He had never intended the election of the Jews to last beyond that "fullness of time" when Christ was to appear."[76] Thus the past and the future are gathered together in the present Christian election.

A Persecuted Church

By putting Christian election in its original context, Newman underlines the note of persecution as an integral part of the Church of the Elect. Christian election can only be explained in connection with this fact, and only properly understood from this perspective. Though not a necessary note of the Church, persecution is a permanent historical feature, an appropriate badge symbolizing its character of holiness in an evil world. A holy and elect Church is a Church marked by suffering. When overt persecution is no longer inflicted on the Church, this sign is kept alive in its internal life of penance.[77]

> "This then is the principal point of view in which the doctrine of election is mentioned in the epistles viz. as connected with the fact of the persecutions. Keeping this in mind we shall be prepared to enter into and rightly understand the texts in which Christian election is spoken of."[78]

It has already been shown that one of the preeminent signs at the time of the Antichrist will be the persecution of the Church.[79] This final assault has its tokens and precedents throughout the history of the Church, beginning with the early martyrs. Circumstances have changed

[76] ibid. p. 21. In his next sermon, No. 201 and in No. 256, Newman states that God did not take back His gift of election from the Jews. "Thus in the case of the Jews, God cast not off His people whom He thus foreknew" No. 201, p.20. The sermon also mentions the restoration of Israel as part of the prophecy of the last times.

[77] Self-denial substitutes for the absence of persecution in times of peace. Faith is nothing if it is not tested, and self-denial is such a test cf. P.P.S. i.5.

[78] No. 200 p. 12.

[79] Advent sermon No. 395 in Chapter One.

the Church's fortune but the principle has remained the same. Christians however, must not seek direct confrontation with evil, or play the martyr, yet the same frame of mind which motivated the early Church must be preserved. A willingness to endure persecution "is a constituent part of that mode of thinking and acting, which belief in the gospel of Christ naturally produces."[80] Even when external hostility has ceased, internal distress often takes its place. A house divided against itself is a new form of persecution, which equivalently advances the march of evil against the Church.[81]

In his sermon at Christ Church on the ordination to the priesthood, Newman first reminds the candidates of their election to "the Church of the first born which are written in heaven," but then goes on to dwell more realistically on what they can expect to find - a little flock, reviled and attacked.[82] Christ's ministers will be threatened, rather than obeyed by the world,[83] and should they look for leadership, all they will find is a Church lacking in discipline and authority.[84] Liberalism has crept into the very sanctuary of the Church and waged war against its purity. It has tried to make the Church keep pace with the march of mind,[85] and spread the contaminating influence of the world within it. Against this subtle form of persecution, the Church must arm itself with the spiritual weapons of prayer and penance.

If we wish to understand the true condition of the Christian Church, we must look for it in her public prayer.[86] The psalms hold a special place in the Church's life of prayer. In great part they express the lament, the entreaty and the hope of the Church over the world, which is poised to attack her. It is surely no accident that her empire will

[80] No. 194 p. 25.

[81] No. 281. This is an Epiphany sermon of 1831. It contrasts the future glory of the Church, which the feast foreshadows, with the present discord and internal crisis.

[82] No. 323. The sermon illustrates Newman's awareness of the impending crisis. The later redactions of 1836 and 1840 on feast days of apostles, underline the note of persecution.

[83] Ministers of the Church must bear in a special way the opposition and subtle persecution of the world, and be a sign of the world hereafter cf P.P.S.viii,10.

[84] This lack of discipline is the main reason for the distressing condition of the Church - "evil times when the Church and the world are mixed together and the power of our rulers is lost by some sad misfortune, or rather by some melancholy sin." No. 347 p. 1.

[85] No. 474 p. 19. The permanent conflict between the Church and the World forms a backdrop to Newman's ecclesiology.

[86] This theme will be considered in Chapter Six.

182

be resisted and her fortunes marked by persecution. However, in the measure that she is true to herself, she will consider such suffering her very portion and lot.

> "What will be the fortunes of such an empire in the world? persecution; persecution is the token of the Church; persecution is the note of the Church, perhaps the most abiding note of all."[87]

Persecution arises both from the very claims of the Church and also from its frailty. Her claim to a spiritual dominion over the world provokes the world's anger. Her internal weakness, caused by sin and schism, invites the power of evil to renew its onslaught in the hope of conquering the Church. In both cases there is a common cause; it is the Church's nature as a holy and elect body that is the reason why she suffers persecution and distress.

> "Now, is it not just the peculiarity of the Christian Church, not only that it is slandered, scorned, ill-used by the world, but that all this happens to it *because* it is holy, - for its righteousness' sake?"[88]

Election to Glory

Newman gingerly approaches the question of predestination[89] for the first time in his last sermon at St. Clement's. He notes that while this was antecedently possible and may be true, the doctrine as propounded by Calvinists, cannot be defended on Scriptural grounds.[90] They had

---

[87] S.D. 18, p. 261.

[88] ibid. p. 270.

[89] I can only touch here on predestination in so far as it relates to ecclesiology. The topic is an important one in the sermons and may be found in the following unpublished manuscripts Nos.150, 200, 569, and also in P.P.S.ii,8; ii,11; ii,15; ii,26; iii,20; iv,9; v,18.

[90] No. 150 p. 14: "But this at least I must say that I cannot see it in the Bible, and if it is not in the Bible, it *may* be *false*." For his hesitancy and growing clarity on the question of election and predestination cf. L.D. Vol i, p 211: "I have come to no decision of the doctrines of election etc. but the predestination of individuals seems to me hardly a Scriptural doctrine." Later he adds, "I am almost convinced about predestination in the Calvinist sense, that is I see no proofs for them in Scripture" op.cit. p. 277.

taken certain passages out of context which referred to final salvation, and have misapplied them; they have also attributed to individuals what properly belongs to the Body of the Elect as such.[91] Their misuse of these texts has led many Christians to be wary, and deprived them of the comfort which they were intended to convey. Since these parts of Scripture are meant for the whole Church, they must not be allowed to be the sole property of a false theory.[92]

Besides the misapplication of the doctrine, Calvinists also confuse the two senses in which election can be understood. They fail to distinguish between regeneration and final salvation, both of which are incorporated in the meaning of "election." The first privilege is given with a view to its future realization in eternal life, but it does not provide any assurance of the gift of final perseverance. This confusion is the result of failing to recognize the manner in which Scripture discloses the plan of God. Rather than being a description of the actual measure of fulfilment, Scripture simply informs us of the the nature of God's design, which will ultimately be accomplished.

> "And hence it happens that the word "elect" in Scripture has two senses, standing both for those who are called *in order* to salvation, and for those who at the last day shall be the *actually resulting fruit* of that holy call."[93]

Admission to the Church takes place by baptism, which is the sacrament of election in Christ. Through it we are brought into a condition which is different in kind, vis-à-vis salvation, from the non-baptized.[94] It is a privileged state consisting of three distinct though

---

[91] P.P.S. ii,26 ; ii,11: "in this election of us, He does not look at us as mere *individuals*, but as a body."

[92] P.P.S. iv,9 ."..better men are robbed of their portion; their comfortable texts are gone, they acquiesce in the notion (too readily) that these texts are *not* theirs."

[93] P.P.S. ii,8. This distinction is also made in No. 169 p. 13, a sermon *on Infant Baptism Part ii*. It also occurs in No. 347. The same principle of Scripture interpretation is applied the prophecy concerning the universality of the Church e.g. in No. 164.

[94] No. 118, p. 4; No. 228 p. 9. Newman's position, like that of De Lubac, Küng and Von Balthasar, is opposed to Rahner's Anonymous Christian. However, his implication that the salvation of the heathen is something other than Christian salvation, raises serious difficulties: ."..their salvation is (as far as we know) a very different, far inferior benefit, to ours. Ours is Christian salvation - we do not know fully what this is - we know not what we shall be. But we know it is something different from that of all others."

interrelated gifts viz. regeneration, sanctification and eternal glory.[95] In its nature and tendency therefore, baptism is related to the end; it confers the means and is the earnest of future glory.

> "... not, indeed, as if grace had done its perfect work within them, or all had a good hope for salvation, but because there had been a *beginning* and thus there was a *hope* of them because they were within Christ's kingdom... "[96]

To avoid an antinomian interpretation, Newman stresses that no assurance of final perseverance is thereby given. What is past and conferred but once only, is no guarantee for the future.[97] Nevertheless, baptism bestows "the principle of holiness" and "the nature of godliness," which is fully realized in heaven. The promise of eternal glory which we receive, constitutes the ground of hope in final salvation. It is that "great gift [which] may be made the cause,... of our gaining eternal life... "[98] Hence membership of the Church through baptism is a participation in its final glory.[99] By God's design a first instalment is granted, which is the same in nature as the eternal life hereafter. As far as God is concerned, He has willed our final salvation, though we may forfeit it through sin. In Newman's words, "Man then, as far as God's part is concerned, is perfectly and irrevocably saved on his first justification... "[100]

Like the Jewish election, baptism is an unconditional gift of God which is given independently of any merit on our part. Whether it is

---

[95] No. 118; 170.

[96] No. 118 p. 4. This sermon represents a breakthrough in Newman's understanding of Baptism.

[97] In other sermons Newman modifies this axiom by saying that the past is all we can lean on for the future, e.g. P.P.S. i,13: "Nothing but *past* acts are vouchers for *future*" and reminds us that "the past is the mirror of the future."

[98] P.P.S. vii,16. This is the first part of three sermons on Infant Baptism given in his first course on the Sacraments. It is No. 168. Nos.169 and 170 are parts two and three. cf also No. 328 p. 12 : "we ought to pray God by His promise in baptism" which is our ground for future glory.

[99] No. 328 *On the Epiphany, as the Commemoration of our Baptism*. It was preached on the feast in 1832, 1834, 1837 and 1841. No. 360 *on Regeneration*, which was first preached in November 1834, was later transferred to the season of Epiphany in 1838 and 1840. In this way Newman illustrates the liturgical significance of baptism by including it in the season of glory. *The Glory of the Christian Church*, P.P.S. ii,8 (No. 361) immediately follows his sermon on Regeneration (No. 360).

[100] No. 169 p. 12; No. 170 p. 4.

received fruitfully or not is another question, but there is nothing impossible in the notion itself, of a new birth being accorded even to impenitent sinners. When received in its fullness, it "includes in it perfect happiness and holiness, to which it tends from the start."[101] If we were therefore to preserve our baptismal innocence, final salvation would be assured.

Though administered to individuals, the sacrament is a social sign since it is the admission of a member to a Body, which is the Church.[102] The Church claims the baptized as her own, and bestows on him the privileges which were primarily granted to her.[103] Hence the intrinsic relation between the first and final election pertains, properly speaking, to the Church as a body. She is the Church of the Elect, not by virtue of the individually elected souls within her, but of herself, as a people specially chosen by God.

> "... still, looking at Christians through the ages as one vast body, we may consider the first chosen and the finally saved in one sense the same. Who in victory dwells upon the numbers that fell in the fight and does not rather account the whole body conquerors who engaged? and so the Church militant and the Church triumphant may be counted as one and the same when we look abroad in the history of that extended warfare which Christ through many ages carries on against the powers of evil"[104]

A Holy Remnant

The term "remnant" or "the few" does not appear in the sermons until 1829, but from then on occupies an increasingly prominent place in Newman's preaching.[105] The belief, however, that the number of true

---

[101] P.P.S. iii.16.

[102] No. 213 p. 11: ."..are they (the ordinances) private or are they social and public?...Baptism is a social rite because in it we are incorporated into Christ - we are brought into His spiritual body."

[103] P.P.S. iv.11: "When a child is brought for baptism, the Church invisible claims it, begs it of God, receives it, and extends to it, as God's instrument, her own sanctity."; P.P.S. ii.8.

[104] No. 169 p. 14; P.P.S. ii.8.

[105] The first mention I can find is in No. 201, 28th June 1829.

Christians is small, is present from the beginning. Newman first drew a sharp division between the elect, who showed evidence of the Spirit, and those, who, though baptized, had forfeited their election.[106] As his understanding of baptismal regeneration grew, the division between the visible and invisible Church was abandoned,[107] and the elect became simply an equivalent term for the Church. Nevertheless, the idea that true members among the elect of God are small in number, was retained.

The idea of a remnant is a distinctive feature which highlights the eschatological dimension of the Church. It is "the few" who truly represent the Body of the Elect on its journey heavenwards. This feature of the chosen few is developed from two points of view; first by considering God's plan as understood in the doctrine of predestination, and then by seeing it in the actual history of salvation. On the theological level, there is an unresolvable dilemma between God's sovereignty and the power of human freedom to frustrate grace.[108] Moreover, the predestination of the elect appears at variance with God's universal salvific will. However, in the light of the history of salvation, God provides an instrument in the form of a remnant, to ensure that His plan is substantially accomplished. In the process, from a human point of view, there is loss and gain on God's part. He gains His coveted object of bringing the elect to glory, by forfeiting His prior wish to accomplish the salvation of all.[109] Newman completes the circle by showing that doctrine and history are at one in declaring that "many are called but few are chosen."[110]

It is significant that the first mention of the remnant occurs when Newman's preaching moves from a doctrinal viewpoint to the

---

[106] No. 8 p. 4; No. 135 p. 18: "His true children Christ will bring all to heaven - but directly we depart from grace and make shipwreck of our faith, we cease to be His children and those to whom He has promised glory."

[107] The clearest refutation of this division is found in P.P.S. iii.16.

[108] P.P.S.ii.26. The question of predestination is always in the background of the discussion on the nature of election. God's grace and human freedom are on two different planes and "incommensurable."

[109] No. 202 p. 13 Newman adds the following note: "and of course in overcoming resistance something must be expended e g at least power or wisdom. i.e. something (according to our ideas) lost in all His appointments whether of this world or the next, while the course of Providence moves on to its destined end."

[110] P.P.S. v.18: "So certain, so uniform is the fact, that it is almost stated as a doctrine."

perspective of the history of salvation.[111] In the history of Israel, there were but few who remained faithful to the Covenant, but this was sufficient to carry forward God's plan of salvation. Despite many shortfalls His plan was not defeated, for He had foreseen the partial success of His system. It was in the representative portion of His Church i.e. the elect, that He substantially achieved His object. Even though many were lost, it was for the sake of the faithful remnant that the whole House of Israel was promised restoration. In like manner so will it be with the Church, whose future glory rests with the Christian remnant. As Newman observes "... at the present time also there is a remnant according to the Christian election - a Christian 'remnant'."[112]

The principle of selection in the accomplishment of God's design is found "in the very birth of the Church," when Jacob was chosen contrary to the natural course of heredity. Christ's own saying about the many and the few is an instance of this general law concerning the role of the elect. Jacob was chosen by God for the sake of Abraham; in like manner the few are chosen for the sake of Christ. The many could not ensure the completion of God's work in Christ.[113]

The same was also true of the prophets. Despite widespread corruption, God's grace had done its work and a remnant sprung up as the fruit of His continual toil. The pattern of the Christian Church is similar to the role of the prophets. It is exemplified in the ministry of St. Paul, whose toil and endurance was "for the sake of the elect."[114] The fruit will be small but worth all the effort; a harvest of "all that was precious and excellent among them" will be gathered in.[115]

In several sermons Newman presents a picture of the Church as a mosaic - it is made up of discrete particles whose individual brilliance casts a glorious light over the whole Church. These are the saints of God who appear "from the dark multitude, here one and there

---

[111] Course xxvi(a) in 1829 *On the book of Genesis*. He had already considered the stages of revelation in Course vii, from the point of view of doctrine and principles. He now looks at revelation during the patriarchal period, from the aspect of history. It is the *history and character* of the patriarchs which is considered in this course.

[112] No. 201 p. 22. This is a fragment consisting of pp. 19-24 and 27-32.

[113] No. 202 p. 14.

[114] No. 253 p.222; P.P.S. iv,10 is parallel to this sermon.

[115] ibid. p. 27; No. 256 p. 20: "there was a conspicuous remnant of a different make...."

another."[116] They are like the stars of heaven creating a Milky Way; their light "really streams from apertures which might be numbered," as "scattered witnesses."[117] Each of them is a living stone, showing forth the glory of the Church as the place where the Spirit dwells.[118] Their holiness is the evidence of the Church's power to create saints, a power which only a Body destined to glory can give.

> "It has made men saints, and brought into existence specimens of faith and holiness, which without it are unknown and impossible. It has laboured for the elect, and it has succeeded with them. This is as it were, its token.[119] An ordinary kind of religion, praiseworthy and respectable in its way, may exist under many systems; but saints are creations of the gospel and the Church."[120]

The fewness of the true members of the Church is not something accidental or the result of chance, but part of God's design. Not only is God content with "a little flock,"[121] but He shows a predilection for the few.[122] Newman offers an explanation for such a divine preference, based on preserving excellence, which might otherwise be lost. Quality is maintained at the expense of quantity, for holiness can not be mass produced. It requires a certain character which few are capable of attaining. This character of holiness "will be the peculiarity of the scantiest portion of all."[123] Thus the few in number is a natural consequence of the demanding requirement to be holy. When God therefore calls the many to holiness of life, He recognizes the inbuilt limitation of His desire, but the precious fruit of His grace He tends

---

[116] No. 253 p. 20.

[117] P.P.S.iii,17; iv,15: "a starry host or (if I may say so) a milky way of divine companions."

[118] P.P.S.iv,11.

[119] Newman develops this idea in S.D.xvii, pp. 242-3, entitled *Sanctity, the Token of the Christian Empire*. The indefectibility of the Church is due to its note of sanctity which is her proper claim to glory.

[120] P.P.S. iv,10.

[121] No. 354 p. 12. God also wills His Church to be universal, but universality is substantially achieved by the few witnesses scattered throughout the world cf.P.P.S. ii,8.

[122] P.P.S.i,22 where the witnesses to the resurrection are few, and P.P.S.iii,14 where the few are favoured for the good of the many.

[123] No. 569 p. 10 preached on All Souls Day 1840. It is closely related to P.P.S. v,18 (No. 477).

with care and devotion.

> "For so it has pleased the Dresser of the Vineyard, who seems to have purposed that His own should not grow too thick together; and if they seem to do so, He prunes His vine, that, seeming to bear less, it may bear better. He plucks off some of the promise of the vintage; and those who are left, mourn over their brethren whom God has taken to Himself, not understanding that it is no strange providence, but the very rule of His government, to leave His servants few and solitary."[124]

Towards the end of his Anglican sermons, Newman reviews the history of the Church as the history of God's favour to a remnant. It is the few who inherit the promises and "the phenomenon of a remnant has been a sort of law of the Divine Dispensations ... and is declared, especially by St. Paul to be such."[125] He concludes by saying that the same mode of divine operation is continued in the New Dispensation, and that the remnant is the sign of the Church's identity. By thus characterizing the Church as the remnant who will inherit the promises, he underscores its eschatological dimension. "I consider then,"he says, "that the word "remnant," so constantly used in Scripture, is the token of the identity of the Church, in the mind of her Divine Creator, before and after the coming of Christ."[126]

Part Three
The Communion of Saints

The influence of the theocentric world of the Old Testament is evident in Newman's vision of the Christian Church as the Body of the Elect. God's sovereignty and transcendence is deeply engraved in its identity as a Church, not of this world, but set apart for a predestined glory. It is as pure from the world's sin as the holiness of its Redeemer, and though it must not become an exclusive body, it is removed from

[124] P.P.S. iii,18.
[125] S.D. xiv, pp.193-196.
[126] ibid.

190

the many by the very nature of its excellence. This is the Church of the Apocalypse, which hopes for the end of the present world order of persecution, and trains its sight on the next world.

Newman's eschatology of the Church is not however confined or adequately treated in these severe terms. It is also a Church of present blessings from above, the Sacrament of Christ under the ministration of the Spirit. While the idea of election is common to Jews and Christians, the doctrine of the Communion of Saints is radically new. Though the Jews lived in the hope of a Messiah and were led by the Spirit, the fullness of time had not yet come. But now that Christ is risen, He has lodged in His Church "the powers of the world to come,"[127] which are realized in a sacramental communion with Him. The distance between man and a remote God has been bridged in the incarnation of His Son; the transcendence of the Father is softened by the immanence of the life-giving Spirit of Christ. Thus the largely theocentric view we find in the Church of the Elect, is exchanged for a Christocentric and pneumatological one. What tended to be a separate and exclusive Church, now manifests its assimilative and inclusive nature. This is the Communion of Saints in which the fullness of the Church dwells.[128]

The Foundation in Christ and the Spirit

Though traces of the doctrine of the Communion of Saints may be found in Newman's first sermons,[129] it is not explicitly referred to until he comes to preach on the New Creation.[130] As new creatures in Christ,

---

[127] P.P.S. iii,16. The Church bestows "a great gift, an initiation into the powers of the world to come."

[128] My attention is here confined to the pilgrim Church as part of the Communion of Saints, and inasmuch as it bestows on the visible Church of Christ its eschatological dimension. The Church at rest and the Church in glory will be treated in the next Chapter.

[129] E.g. No. 24 *On The Lord's Supper.* The Eucharist is intrinsically connected with the Communion of Saints and should be treated under this head cf. Newman's letter to Manning, June 6,1838, L.D., Vol.vi, p. 255. It will however be left until Chapter Six when it is considered under the *Liturgy and Christian Life.*

[130] No. 114 pp. 11-12. I have noted the importance of this sermon which was first preached in November 1825. It became the introductory sermon to Course xxi *on Christ by His Resurrection Renews All Things.* In this course it was immediately followed by No. 120 on *The Communion of Saints.*

we have "an eternal tie of union instead of a temporary [one]." Christ has "so knit us together in His mystical body" that we hold with fellow members of Christ "a spiritual communion ... amid all that variety of changes and chances which disquiets this mortal life."[131] Both here and in his subsequent sermon on the Communion of Saints, his focus is clearly on the moral implications of such a bond, without any further development.[132] But the intrinsic connection between the resurrection and the Communion of Saints, which he significantly began with, later comes into the foreground.[133] The unity of fellowship is grounded more theologically in the eschatological event of Christ's resurrection. This union which is characterized by the Communion of Saints, is the fruit of the new order established by the risen Christ.

> "... believers in Christ are represented as becoming new according to the declaration of the text "behold I make all things new" when they become one - they cannot become one without becoming *new*... they could not then become *one* except they first were changed and became *new* even in Christ - that blessed change has been wrought in them etc... "[134]

The change which Newman speaks of may at first seem a purely moral one, and the bond with Christ and among the members of His Body based on a conversion of the heart. However, even during his early period, Newman saw in the Communion of Saints something more profound than the evangelical sentiment of a union of heart and mind.[135] A new objective reality had been brought into being by the resurrection of Christ. Though perceived only by the eyes of faith, it constituted a radically new identity for Christians. In speaking therefore of the new creation and the resulting fruit of it in the Communion of

---

[131] ibid.

[132] There is no mention of the saints in heaven or the saints at rest at this stage in his description of the Communion of Saints.

[133] In his revised introduction to the 1828 version of No. 120 he opens with the text of Rev.xxi,5 ."..behold I make all things new."

[134] No. 120 p. 7. This quotation is made up of two later redactions on the margin of the page.

[135] Much later he expressly criticizes such an attitude. P.P.S. iii,14:"Now let it be carefully noted, that if order is to be preserved at all, it must be at the expense of what seems to be of more consequence viz. the so-called communion of the heart between Christians."

Saints, Newman is struck by the extraordinary way it is described in the New Testament.

> "The sacred writers forcibly describe their own views of it by presenting it, not merely as a union, but a sort of oneness of heart and spirit. They seem hardly to acknowledge the distinction of Christian from Christian but exhibit all as forming *one* new man, *one* body, one soul living in them all, connecting them with each other by a kind of identity, in the same way that the different members of the human body are animated by one and but one sentient principle."[136]

Though Christians are joined together by an unseen bond, this privilege is invested in a visible body, the Church. It is a real gift sacramentally bestowed by means of the public rite or institution of Baptism.[137] It is a transformation in Christ which breaks down all the divisions and enmity between man and man.[138] By it all human differences are wiped out, revealing one and one only consuming object of faith, the mystery of Christ in His members. Hence the first Christians saw in each other the image of Christ and their communion with Him in the New Covenant.

> "They had been begotten again unto new hopes, baptized unto new prospects - and these were the same to all. They looked upon each other clothed in His excellence and partakers of His salvation. They were to each other the essence of Christ."[139]

To complete this picture, which shows the Christocentric light in which Newman saw the Communion of Saints, we have his description of the one unique and total sign of Christ-in-the-Church. From the moment of Pentecost onwards, there is but one new phenomenon, in which we see that the future of the members of the Church is entirely the future of Christ Himself. The eschatological dimension of the

---

[136] No. 120 redaction on p. 8.

[137] P.P.S. vii.17.

[138] In his first course *on the Sacraments*, Newman describes the bond of unity through baptism as stronger than any natural ties. It is intended to banish all differences of class and rank cf. No. 170 p. 19; No. 114 p. 11; No. 389 p. 12.

[139] No. 120 p. 8.

Church, its future glory, is tied intrinsically to the glorified humanity of Christ, made present through the work of the Holy Spirit. It is this new reality of the Communion of Saints which makes the Church the sign of the heavenly kingdom.

> "So that in a true sense it may be said, that from the day of Pentecost to this hour, there has been in the Church but One Holy One, the King of kings, the Lord of lords Himself, who is in all believers, and through Whom they are what they are; their separate persons being but separate developments, vessels, instruments, and works of Him who is invisible. Such is the difference between the Church before the Spirit of Christ came, and after."[140]

Though the doctrine of the Communion of Saints is centred on Christ, the gift itself is of the Holy Spirit. This emphasis on the Spirit is evident from the very beginning, and throughout Newman's treatment of the theme.[141] It is the Spirit who first directs us to the reality of Christ and is the agent of Communion with Him. Thus the arrangement in the Creed illustrates the order of the economy of Christian salvation.

> "This mystical fellowship of Christians in common hopes, privileges and graces is in the creed called the communion of Saints - it is *through* the Church and *by* the Holy Spirit - and hence the arrangement in the Apostles' creed"[142]

Speaking of the Communion of Saints, Newman reminds his congregation that the office of the Holy Spirit is not confined to the growth in grace of individual Christians, but is primarily given for the building up of the general body. Christians are baptized by one Spirit into one Body, and have all been made to drink in the one Spirit.[143] St. Paul seldom refers to the gift of the Spirit without attaching it to the

---

[140] P.P.S. iv,11. The living members or saints of the Church are models of the One Holy One. Christ is the one pattern which is diversified cf P.P.S. ii,32.

[141] No. 118 on *Our Admittance into the Church, Our Title to the Holy Spirit*, is a prelude to his first sermon on *The Communion of Saints*, which was preached the following Sunday.

[142] No. 120 p. 3. The sermon was preached six times in all. There are four different introductions in the extant manuscript of 1827. A four-page introduction on the office of the Holy Spirit is attached to the sermon when it was preached in 1831.

[143] No. 120 p. 6.

194

whole body of Christ of which the individual members partake.[144] Thus
without the Holy Spirit there could be no true communion with Christ.
It was only when Christ came in the Person of His Spirit, that He could
exchange for an external and apparent unity, an internal and real
communion.

"He who came for ever, came as a Spirit, and so coming, did
for His own that which the visible flesh and blood of the
Son of man, from its very nature, could not do, viz. He came
into the souls of all who believe, and taking possession of
them, He, being One, knit them all together into one. Christ,
by coming in the flesh, provided an external or apparent
unity, such as had been under the Law. He formed His
apostles into a visible society; but when He came again in
the Person of His Spirit, He made them all in a real sense
one, not in name only... Thus Christ came, not to make us
one, but to die for us; the Spirit came to make us one in Him
who had died and was alive, that is, to form the Church."[145]

The Church therefore is ontologically grafted unto Christ who
became a life-giving Spirit at the resurrection. Though Christ now lives
"in His own incommunicable glory,"[146]He has left a sign in the world
of His presence. The Church as the mystical Body shares in its measure
the glory of the risen Lord, which is dispensed to it by the Holy Spirit.
Thus it can rightly be described as the sign of the eschaton.

The Church as The Sacrament of The Communion of Saints

The earnestness of evangelicals for a spiritual gospel led many of
them to attach a relatively unimportant place to the Church as a visible
institution.[147] A doctrine like the Communion of Saints, was eminently
suited to promote this view of a great invisible Church, paying scant
attention to its embodiment in an organized society. Though no less

[144] No. 162 p. 6.

[145] P.P.S.iv,11.

[146] P.P.S. ii,32.

[147] Cf G.F.A.Best, "The Evangelicals and the Established Church in the Early
Nineteenth Century," *Journal of Theological Studies,* Vol.x Part 1, pp. 63-78, 1959.

earnest for the things of the Spirit, Newman had come, under the influence of Butler[148] and Whateley,[149] to recognize the Church as a divine appointment with institutional laws and structures. He was aware then, that his first sermon on the Communion of Saints could be dangerously misunderstood. To correct such an impression was the immediate aim of his next address.[150] It had to be made clear that the visible Church is the body anchoring the invisible communion of Saints.

> "The message of salvation however glorious, is not alas so grateful to the human heart, that it was unlikely to be received and to gain ground by itself. To prevent then the loss of this best of gifts (vid.Butler) appears to have been one reason why a visible church was instituted... till the whole earth is turned over to God... quickening men unto a life of holiness."[151]

It has been noted that the subject and sign of eschatology, which we are concerned with in this chapter, is the historic Church of Christ on its pilgrim journey. This dimension is illustrated by reference to the Communion of Saints, of which the visible Church forms a constitutive part, and a witness to its future perfection. Without the note of visibility, the Church could not be a sign, but without the invisible principle of life within her, she ceases to be a Church or have any meaning or relevance to eschatology. She is however the Sacrament of the End-time, in being a visible sign of the invisible grace of Christ.

> "The Church of Christ, as Scripture teaches, is a visible body, invested with, or (I may say) existing in invisible

---

[148] From Butler's Analogy Newman learned the Sacramental Principle which he applied to the Church. Butler's "inculcation of a visible Church" is "economically or sacramentally connected with the more momentous system" or Invisible Church. Apologia p. 10.

[149] Whateley's anti-Erastian views were published anonymously in "Letters on the Church by an Episcopalian." Newman remembered Whateley's taunts that such a book "would make my blood boil." He also mentions being "somewhat impatient" when he was first introduced to the doctrine of Apostolical Succession in 1823. cf Apologia p. 10-12.

[150] No. 121 On the Visible Church. There is a clear structural pattern in Newman's sermons on this theme viz. an invisible principle (No. 120) invested in a visible body (No. 121) with the practical task of edification (No. 122). This same pattern is maintained in P.P.S.iii,16-17-18, and in P.P.S.iv,11-10-12 in that order.

[151] No. 121 p. 5. In a later sermon, No. 157, which marks his espousal of High Church principles, he gives four reasons for the need of a visible Church.

privileges... So the Church would cease to be the Church,
did the Holy Spirit leave it; and it does not exist at all except
in the Spirit."[152]

As the Church is simultaneously a visible institution and a divine
mystery, it may be considered under different perspectives. From one
point of view it may be called an invisible church, since the greater part
of its members live in the unseen world, and the visible portion finds its
identity in an unseen communion. It can also clearly be seen as the
Church which Christ founded on the apostles and continues to exist as
a fact of history. However, these are merely different aspects of one and
the same reality, a Church which is indivisible.

Without making two churches, a visible Church and an invisible
one, it is still quite legitimate to consider the Christian Body under the
invisible aspect of the Communion of Saints. We can speak of it as the
community consisting of "what all Christians are intended and ought to
be, and all that would remain of the Church visible, did the Day of
Judgment suddenly come."[153] It has the present privilege of
communion in Christ, which is the earnest of its future consummation
in heaven. Within it there exist elect souls, unknown to themselves or to
others, who are "the ripening fruit of holiness, which grows on the stem
of the Church Visible."[154] The Church as viewed by faith is a body
formed on a new relationship, as yet but partially disclosed, but steadily
advancing to its fulfilment in the New Jerusalem."[155] Then, and not till
then, will the doctrine of the Communion of Saints be plain and
intelligible - till then it is a mystery."[156]

"The body of the elect, contemplated as it will be hereafter,
nay as it already exists in Paradise, we may, if we will, call
the Church, and since this blessed consummation takes place
in the unseen world, we may call it the Invisible Church.

---

[152] P.P.S. iii,17.

[153] ibid..

[154] P.P.S. iii,17. In this very context he explicitly warns against the view of an
invisible church as a reality separate from the visible: "there is no Invisible Church yet
formed; it is but a name as yet...."

[155] Cf. Tract LVIII *On the Church as Viewed by Faith and By the World,* written
by a layman. Newman invited his friend Bowden to compose this tract in which the
eschatological dimension of the Church is prominent.

[156] No. 389 pp. 10-11.

Doubtless, we may speak of the Invisible Church in the sense of glory, or the Church at rest. There is no error in such a mode of speech. We do not make two Churches, we only view the Christian Body as existing in the world of spirits; and the present Church visible, so far as it really has part and lot in the same blessedness."[157]

A Secondary Stay

Newman derives inestimable comfort from the doctrine of the Communion of Saints. Its practical import is the hope and encouragement it gives to the Christian on the journey of faith. Our struggle is not a solitary one, for we advance as "one great body journeying on to heaven."[158] Though Christ is the primary source of our reliance, being the "Author and Finisher of Faith," He has given us a secondary support in the companionship of the saints. Though His presence is all-sufficient, in His accommodating mercy He recognizes our need for strength from fellow human beings like ourselves. Christ does not withdraw His presence from us, but extends it to include, together with Him, the members of the Church in glory.

"So, in mercy to us, without withdrawing His presence, He has included within it, His Saints and Angels, a great company of created beings, nay of those who once were sinners, and subjects of His Kingdom on earth; and thus we may be encouraged by the example of others before us to look upon Him and live."[159]

The persecuted Church of the Elect is at once turned into the joyful company of the Communion of Saints. Though evil has assailed her, a bulwark and a remedy has been provided. If the faithful are but few in number, they have the consolation of "a cloud of witnesses, an

[157] P.P.S. iii.16.

[158] No. 122 p. 14. This aspect of mutual encouragement and confirmation in the faith is likewise seen in P.P.S.iii,17 and P.P.S.iv,12. It is closely related to the subject of Christian education, whose religious basis is the Communion of Saints. This declared goal of Christian education found Newman in trouble with Hawkins over his understanding of the role of tutor. Cf L.D. Vol.ii,202. For his sermons on Christian "education," cf. Nos.122,128 and 162.

[159] P.P.S.iii,17.

august assemblage." It is not enough to say that such consolation is reserved for the hereafter; it would be an empty promise which offered no real comfort in the present. A naked faith in an invisible privilege is scarcely assurance enough in our trial. Hence God intends to give us a present realization of being citizens of heaven through the sensible support of the Communion of Saints. We are one with the saints perfected and have "come unto Mount Zion, and unto the city of the living God...." Otherwise, one may rhetorically ask with Newman what support and companionship does the Church offer?

> "... in such circumstances what shall we say? Are they but solitary witnesses, each in his own place? Is the Church, which they really see, no consolation for them at all, except as contemplated by faith in respect of invisible gifts? or does it, after all, really afford them some sensible stay, a vision of heaven, of peace and purity, antagonist to the world that now is, in spite of the evil which abounds in it, and overlays it? Through God's great mercy, it is actually, in no small degree, a present and sensible consolation."[160]

We enjoy this added assurance not by dwelling on the future, which is unknown to us, but on the past. We have history on our side as shown by the example set before us in the lives of the saints.[161] Here we have a "sensible" consolation, for their lives "are sealed up," giving us some sure evidence and knowledge. As we are one of their company, the memory of them puts firm ground under our feet. In them we have a pledge that we are not alone, and that our victory over the world is assured. This assurance however is not confined to the past, but can be seen in the present life of the Church, in the lives of holy people. Even if there were but one living saint, it would be a sufficient guarantee to us "of the whole Church invisible."[162] In meditating therefore on the history of the saints and the holy examples of our times, we have a ground of hope and models to imitate. "What a world of sympathy and

---

[160] P.P.S.iii.17.

[161] ibid: "In spite of the variety of books now circulated among all classes of the community, how little is known about the lives of the saints." This great need for the edification of the faithful was soon remedied by Newman when he set about providing Lives of the Saints cf.also P.P.S. ii.32. There is a sharp contrast here with his former fear of idolatry which was noted in the Church of the Elect.

[162] ibid.

comfort is thus opened to us in the Communion of Saints."[163]

Not only can we draw strength from our brethren in the faith, who have now received their reward, but also from the angels who minister to the Church on earth. They, too, are part of that one Communion. Every society is constituted on the principle of inter-dependence, and there is no part that has not a social need for the other. We are never our own masters, but in one way or another, are under the protection and the guardianship of others. By analogy, this is as true of a heavenly society as it is of an earthly one. The Christian finds little comfort and fellowship in the present world but looks out for support from another "which is filled with saints and angels." In this other world of faith, the angels have been assigned the guardianship of the Christian Church.[164]

If the Church of the Elect is characterized by the fewness of its numbers, the Communion of Saints in contrast represents a vast multitude. A cup is either half empty or half full, depending on how we look at it. With the diminishing eye of sorrow, its deficiency will appear, but seen in the light of hope it will be a cause for rejoicing. The Communion of Saints is the bright vessel of glory, while the Church of the Elect is the cup half filled with grief. In the light of the Communion of Saints our numbers are ever increasing, the cup is filling up. It is a hopeful and positive sign of the Church's future harvest.

> "They are the true Church, ever increasing in number, ever gathering in, as time goes on; with them lies the Communion of Saints; they have power with God; they are His armies who follow the Lamb, who overcame princes of the earth, and who shall hereafter judge Angels."[165]

Though the Communion of Saints is a privilege of the Church upon the resurrection, and was unknown before Christ came, Newman finds a foreshadowing of it in the Old Testament. In desolation Elisha was given assurance and granted the promise of victory by the pledge of

---

[163] ibid.

[164] No. 540 p. 16. The Sermon is for the *Feast of Michael the Archangel.* Newman lists seven ways in which the angels minister to the Church. He himself had a special devotion to the Guardian Angel. cf VV.clxvii. For another sermon on the angels, see P.P.S. ii,29.

[165] P.P.S.iv,10. The elect are few relative to the many who take the broad way. They are innumerable when viewed in themselves, for they include all the saints of every age. No. 569 p. 12: "Nay, though a little flock in every age, on the whole they will form a large company. God's purposes we are told, is to bring "many sons to glory....Rev.7."

a remnant.[166] The remnant would remain and form a great host. In this way the prophet was introduced to the future promise of the Communion of Saints. He "had the privilege of knowing he was one of a great host who were fighting the Lord's battles, though he might be solitary on earth. To him was revealed in its measure the comfortable Christian doctrine of the Communion of Saints."[167] This promise has now been fulfilled in the Church, through which we have access to "a heavenly home in the midst of this turbulent world." The Christian remnant is no longer bereft of comfort, but derives its strength from being part of the Communion of Saints.

> "This is the Church of God, which is our true Home of God's providing. His own heavenly court, where He dwells with His Saints and Angels, into which He introduces us by a new birth, and in which we forget the outward world and its many troubles."[168]

The Notes of the Church

The notes of the Church as one, holy, catholic and apostolic, have commonly been used for apologetic purposes. They have been taken as the criteria for identifying the one true Church of Christ, and are the test of its credibility. However, the notes form part of the profession of faith and have a dogmatic rather than an apologetic significance. They are primarily concerned with the Church as a mystery and in a secondary way with the visible institution. The notes are thus related to the Church's identity, first internally as the invisible communion in Christ, and then externally in the visible body of the Church.

Since we have been concerned with the question of the Church's identity, we should expect to find evidence of her characteristic notes in the Communion of Saints. This doctrine has highlighted the new relationship on which the Church is formed; it has provided her with an identity which she shares with the saints in glory. When she has accomplished her work, she will dissolve into the fullness of

---

[166] The prophets Elisha and Elijah are contrasted in two sermons in Sermons of the Day. The first represents the bright side of present privileges of the Church, the second the dark side of future judgment.

[167] S.D.13 p. 170.

[168] P.P.S.iv.12.

communion with Christ. The notes of her identity will then be brought to their completion, and hence her present signs are tokens of her future blessedness. Through them the eschatological dimension of the Church is revealed.

The tension between the now and the not yet, which has been a feature of Newman's eschatology, can be seen also in the notes of the Church. Her insertion into Christ is an instance of the paradox of God's mercy in uniting a sinful people to an immaculate Head. By this union the Church "gains somewhat of His excellence by the glorious fellowship, and receives the foretaste of those divine joys which we hope will be our eternal portion in heaven."[169] Her present notes are imperfect but full of promise, and the measure of their realization is a presage of their future fulfilment.

The note of unity is self-evidently disclosed by the Communion of Saints. Though the Church's visible unity is racked by schism, internally it is "the invisible Body of Christ Mystical."[170] If Christians therefore believe in an unseen unity, and that "hereafter they will be one blessed company in heaven," the Visible Church must image and anticipate such a state. It should conform as far as possible to the eschatological Church and represent it in its pilgrim stage. The very design of Christ for unity is seen in the visibility of a single rite of incorporation by baptism. It was founded upon one Person and brought into one body, which is the Communion of Saints.

"When, then, I am asked, why we Christians must unite into a visible body or society, I answer, first, that the very earnestness with which Scripture insists upon an unseen unity at present, and a future unity in heaven, of itself directs a pious mind to the imitation of that visible unity on earth."[171]

Of all the notes of the Church, holiness was for Newman the most characteristic and essential. It is the very raison d'etre of the Church, the

---

[169] No. 120 p. 24.

[170] P.P.S. vii,17. This sermon is really a composite of Nos.215, 216 and 217 which were part of Course xxviii *On the Church and Public Worship*. The condensed sermon still retains the aims of the three sermons which are illustrated by their respective titles: *The Unity of the Church, and the Bishops the principle of it* (215); *On Church Union and the Sin of Schism* (216); *Permanence of the Church how secured* (217).

[171] ibid.

note of Life itself.[172] The Church's task is "to elicit, foster, mature the seeds of heaven, which lie hid in the earth, to multiply images of Christ"[173] and thus to make a holy people. The Christian Church has been divided by schism, her universality is far from complete, her apostolic claims sometimes feeble and frayed, but she has continued to exist throughout the ages. But if the note of holiness were absent, her very life would cease and she would fail, not in this or that note of identity, but altogether. When the Church comes to her final destiny in the Communion of Saints, her deficiencies in unity and universality will be rectified, but no remedy will be found for a Church without the note of holiness.

> "In the next world this whole Church will be brought together in one, whenever its separate members lived, and then, too, all its unsound and unfruitful members will be dropped, so that nothing but holiness will remain in it."[174]

The universality of the Church was a pressing concern for Newman in the early days of his missionary dream. He quickly saw the dilemma which this note presented, as a prophecy perhaps never to be fulfilled in history. We have seen the dialectical relationship in which universality stood with regard to holiness, and the way in which Newman tried to account for it as a realized note of the Church. In his later sermons, however, Newman thought of the Church's catholicity, not so much in geographical terms, but in terms of history. The Church's universality is not so much its extension to every place, but an extension in time. Even then, however, its spatial universality can be accounted for by its witnesses to every nation and culture, though they be but few. But its note of catholicity is shown more decisively in its history, for there has never been a time from the moment of its birth that the Church has not existed.

In the light of the above, it is significant to see how Newman attaches the note of universality to the Communion of Saints. When preaching on the mediatorial kingdom at Oriel, he alludes to it as being realized in the unbroken link of faith between the ages, connecting us "and the unseen communion of spirits with those successive

---

[172] In the Apologia Newman defines the holiness of the Church as the Note of Life, cf p. 150 ff.

[173] P.P.S.iv,10.

[174] P.P.S. iii,16.

generations of saints... "[175] It is a sign of the Church's glory, for Christ "has engaged to bring forward unto glory this universal Church."[176] Hence when viewed by the eye of faith, the Church appears as catholic by virtue of the Communion of Saints, stretching from the distant past to the future shore.

> "See what a noble principle faith is. Faith alone lengthens a man's existence, and makes him in his own feelings, live in the future and in the past... The Christian throws himself fearlessly upon the future, because He believes in Him, which is, and which was, and which is to come. He can endure to be one of an everlasting company while in this world, as well as in the next."[177]

Of the four notes of the Church, apostolicity seems the least amenable to being interpreted in an eschatological sense. Its sign-value is turned more to the Church in its origins than to what the Church is to become. However, apostolicity is that note which gives the official stamp whereby the Visible Church may consider itself the Church of Christ. By its apostolic mandate it is identified with the body Christ will bring to glory. Moreover this note ensures the unity of the Church in its journey through history.[178] The Church at the beginning is one and the same as the Church at the end. It is this, and only this Church, which will display fully the marks of the New Jerusalem. The Church which has a part in the Communion of Saints will be recognized as the Church of Peter and the apostles. "While St. Peter and St. Paul still live among us though unseen in the fullness of their apostolic <spiritual> authority,"[179] the Church can not be moved.

After years of controversy and apologetics on behalf of the Catholic and Apostolic Church, Newman finally resorts to the inward signs of the Church as the truest tokens of her identity.[180] Though it is a social body whose signs must be visible, its real life lies in the invisible world of faith. The public marks are intended for those not yet

---

[175] No. 160 pp. 2-3.

[176] No. 120 p. 7.

[177] P.P.S.vi.19 .

[178] P.P.S.iii.14; vi.14.

[179] No. 402 p. 11.

[180] S.D.xxii entitled *Outward and Inward Notes of the Church.*

part of her; but for those within, she has more reliable and lasting tokens. She is one, holy, catholic and apostolic in her internal identity, for she is the Sacrament of Christ who has called her into the mystery of the Communion of Saints.

The Indefectibility of the Church

Because of the "eternal tie" with which it is bound to Christ, the Church will last until the end. The feast of All Saints celebrates and anticipates the end to which the Church is tending - to the fullness of the Communion of Saints. "This is the blessed company which today meets the Christian pilgrim in the Services of the Church."[181] But the Church's end, Newman notes, will mean the end of the world, for it is only the continuance of the saints on earth which prevents this world from folding up. All Saints Day therefore is "a kind of memento to us that this world is coming to an end" since it commemorates the passage each year of a portion of the elect into heaven.[182] While there remain saints on earth, the Church is indestructible, and cannot be moved.[183]

> "Christ's Church is indestructible, and lasting on through the vicissitudes of this world, she *must* rise again and flourish, when the poor creatures of a day who opposed her, have crumbled into dust."[184]

In its relation to the world it is called the Church militant, for it is an army at war. Though there may be temporary changes of fortune, its final victory is assured. Those who remain within its ranks can boast of belonging to no mean city, for "nothing so elevates the mind than the consciousness of being one of a great and victorious company."[185] The Church is invincible because of the gift of immortality lodged within her. When one of her members dies, he "goes to form part of a new society... to join the company of Saints... " and hence "there is but one

---

[181] P.P.S.ii.32.

[182] A summary which Newman gives to No. 163 for All Saints Day,1836. The same idea is found in No. 332: ."..did the Saints fail this world would end," and S.D.8 p. 101: "but we know that when it dies, at least the world will die with it."

[183] No. 402 p. 12.

[184] P.P.S. ii,32.

[185] P.P.S.iii,17; ii,8.

body on earth which has immortality, and that is the Church."[186]

The link between the Church's indefectibility and the Communion of Saints was a common theme in Newman's sermons at Littlemore. Here he had built a church in 1836 and commemorated the anniversary each year with a sermon.[187] The building of the church was a source of great pride and comfort for him. He shared his joy with his parishioners telling them that "you have been admitted to the truest symbol of God's eternity. You have built what may be destined to have no end but in Christ's coming."[188] The sight of ancient cathedrals reminds us of the faith of past generations, and our participation in the Communion of Saints. "What a visible, palpable specimen this, of the communion of saints."[189] The Jewish Temple was local and temporary; it was merely a type which has been fulfilled by "the True and Spiritual Temple, the Communion of Saints."[190] It is the Christian boast and privilege then, to be part of a universal and everlasting company.

"O happy they, who, in a sorrowful time, avail themselves of this bond of communion with the saints of old and with the universal Church... Happy they, who when they enter within their holy limits, enter in heart into the court of heaven... In heaven is the substance, of which here below we are vouchsafed the image; and thither, if we be worthy, we shall at length attain. There is the holy Jerusalem, whose light is like unto a stone most precious.."[191]

---

[186] No. 174 p. 15.

[187] No. 425 was preached on the day of inauguration, 22 September. New sermons were composed for the anniversary in the next three successive years: No. 479, 516 (P.P.S.v,6); 539 (P.P.S.vi,21). In the chronological list of sermons in *John Henry Newman: Sermons 1824-1843*, Vol. I, edited by P. Murray, Nos. 539 and 540 have been inadvertently ascribed to the month of June instead of the correct month of September.

[188] P.P.S.vi,19. This sermon was originally written "for the Churches and chapels under the King's letter" in Nov. 1836. It was later preached at the Littlemore commemoration in 1841. It is related to P.P.S.vi,20, which may also have been preached on the anniversary in 1840 cf Pett p. 429.

[189] ibid.

[190] S.D.xv p. 211.

[191] P.P.S.vi,19 .

A Summary of the Chapter

In this chapter we have seen how the mystery of the Church reflects the eschatological event of Christ's death and resurrection in three ways. First, the Church is the seed and the beginning of the Kingdom of God; it contains the embryo of the new creation in Christ. Secondly, it is the community of believers which has been redeemed from the sin of this world and destined for the world to come. Thirdly, in being part of a Communion which extends beyond its pilgrim way, it shares in the blessedness of the saints in heaven. In each of these ways, the Church is the corporate sign of the glory of Christ and His mystical Body on earth. We will now consider, in the next chapter, how this sign of the Church is concretized in the life of its individual members.

CHAPTER FIVE

INDIVIDUAL ESCHATOLOGY

Introduction

The collective eschatology of the Church, which was treated in the last chapter, in no way obscures the life of the individual Christian in relation to his final end. It is only the individual who is concrete and real, while the collective as such is an abstraction. As the body exists only in its members, the universal sign of the Church is realized only in its particular parts, which are joined to each other in Christ. Being a living part of a living body, each member therefore shares in the glory that will one day be revealed.

In its present form as a visible body, the Church is on pilgrimage towards the New Jerusalem. Each step of this spiritual journey is concretely enacted in the personal life of the Christian. As the Church makes herself ready to meet the Bridegroom, each member of the body is engaged in the task of sanctification. This is a process which continues until the Day of the Lord, when Christ will come to gather into glory the members of His Body. The way of the pilgrim passes through the portals of death, which marks the end of a period of probation. This is a point of transition to a new stage of purification, in which the fruit of grace is matured, before entering into full communion with Christ.

Newman's individual eschatology is considered under three headings which represent the stages of growth of each member of the Church into the fulness of Christ. First, we have his theology of death which he treats on two levels. On the natural level it is experienced as the end of all things and thus has a significance for all, irrespective of faith. But in the light of revelation, death is seen as a moment of change, not the termination of Christian life. It is the passage to a new form of existence between our earthly departure and the general resurrection of the body. This intermediate state is a school of contemplation mercifully designed to complete the process of sanctification, until God will be all in all. The end of the journey is the bliss of heaven where Christ in his glorified humanity awaits us. Thus the present chapter is divided into three parts: Newman's theology of death, his inquiry into the nature of the Intermediate State and his view of our eternal reward in heaven.

Part One
Newman's Theology of Death

Introduction

The author of "The Dream of Gerontius" has left us a vivid picture of Christian death which has been an inspiration to his contemporaries and to succeeding generations.[1] It is the longest of his poems, and like most of them, was written at a time of inactivity, which, on this occasion, gave him some relief from the mental strain of the *Apologia*.[2] Newman scribbled it on scraps of paper and first considered it to be of no great significance.[3] Several of his poems are on the subject of death[4] and his many letters of condolence bear testimony of his deep compassion for the bereaved.[5] Though he believed that his own age gave too little thought to the dead,[6] the Victorian period was in fact a time of frequent remembrance and respect for the departed.[7]

It is rather surprising therefore when we come to his Anglican sermons to find relatively little treatment of the theme. There are only four sermons[8] which are directly concerned with the question of death, though there are frequent allusions to it in his other sermons. These

---

[1] General Gordon at the seige of Khartoum was greatly affected and comforted by it. It is chiefly recalled today through the music of Edward Elgar.

[2] Before the controversy with Kingsley, Newman had written a private memorandum in prospect of his own death which continued to fill him with apprehension during the writing of the Apologia. G. Rowell, 'The Dream of Gerontius', *The Ampleforth Journal*, Vol. 73, 1968, pp. 184-192.,

[3] L.D., Vol.xxii, p. 72. Newman did not attach too great importance to his verses. Verse-making was a means of quiet recollection of private thoughts meant for himself, rather than a serious mode of communicating his ideas to the public.

[4] e.g. the poems on the death of Mary his sister VV.ix, x, xiii, xvii, as well as cx, *Hora Novissima*, and cxv, *Separation of Friends*.

[5] On his own bereavement over Mary's death vid. his letter to R.I.Wilberforce, L.D. Vol.i, pp. 48-51.

[6] "There have been times, we know, when men thought too much of the dead. That is not the fault of this age. We now go to the opposite extreme. Our fault surely is, to think of them too little." P.P.S. iii,25.

[7] Death was a popular subject for poets e.g. Tennyson and Arnold, and death-bed scenes a common device used by preachers for moral admonition. In 1828 Newman read the four-volume work of John Warton D.D. entitled *"Death-bed Scenes and Pastoral Conversations."* Cf.L.D. Vol.ii, p. 94ss.

[8] No. 50 was later rewritten and was considered by Newman as a new sermon, being numbered No. 327. No. 163 was on the death of Walter Mayers and No. 174 "is a commune for the end of the year, Advent and St.John's Day".

brief references however, do not indicate either a lack of reflection on his part or an insignificant contribution to the theology of death. By the very brevity of his treatment Newman underlines, on the contrary, an important principle on the meaning of Christian death.

Newman's first sermon on death was preached on New Year's Day in 1825, an appropriate time for a moral reckoning of the past year.[9] It is based on the text of Ecclesiasticus ix,10. Here the sacred writer's horizon is bounded by the belief that there is nothing beyond the grave, and thus he admonishes the reader to make full use of the present limited time. The moral for Christians, in the new horizon of immortality, is to consider the present time a period of probation, and not to procrastinate in matters where their eternal salvation is at stake. Time is short, eternity is long and our future destiny depends on how we prepare for the inevitable moment of death. When he preached the sermon again in 1831 he rewrote it, giving it the title "Preparation for Death,"[10] but retaining the same general ideas.[11] Prior to this first sermon, death is mentioned briefly on two occasions, when it is described as the moment of truth when we stand naked before God, and when the delusion of the world is unmasked. Then it will appear whether we have built our lives on quicksand or on the Word of God.[12]

The remaining two sermons on death are more clearly written from a Christian perspective in which we move beyond the level of reason to an understanding of death grounded on faith. The occasion for the first of these sermons was the funeral service of Walter Mayers[13] who had shepherded Newman during his conversion at Ealing and for whom Newman had preached his very first sermon as a deacon.[14] The second

---

[9] No. 50 is included in Newman's list of 46 sermons of which he made the following comment. "None of these sermons are worth anything in themselves but those preached at St.Clement's up to No. 150 inclusive will show you how far I was an evangelical when I went into Anglican orders."

[10] No. 327. This was later published under a new title, *The Lapse of Time*, as P.P.S.vii,1. Volumes vii and viii of Parochial and Plain Sermons were originally one volume of 36 sermons which Newman unsolicitedly offered Isaac Williams as a contribution to the latter's project of Plain Sermons.

[11] The earlier sermon was written in the style of Simeon and was rather diffuse. Newman dropped section two of the composition and shortened the application. Cf. Pett.p. 161ff.

[12] These sermons are No. 36, *God's Word a Refuge in Trouble* and No. 38, his first Advent sermon.

[13] No. 163 is entitled *"On the death of a very dear friend"*. Newman kept it in a packet of four sermons marked personal (Box A.50.5).

[14] The first sermon he preached is No. 2 entitled *Waiting on God*. Newman alludes

210

is a sermon written as a "commune for the end of the year, Advent, St. John's Day and the Sunday after Ascension." Though first preached in 1831, the extant manuscript is clearly a much later composition which shows a great development in his view of the Christian meaning of death.[15]

Newman's theology of death may be considered on two levels, first in its most general nature as it affects everyone, and second in the special significance which it has in Christian faith. On the natural level, death is an enigma which fills us with a deep anxiety from which no one is immune. The gospel does not take away the mystery involved or propose a false transcendence; it builds upon our human experience, and complements it with the light of faith. By looking first at an understanding of death on this human level and appreciating the universal dilemma it presents, we may then examine the added, and indeed transformed, significance it has in Christian revelation.

Section One
The General Significance of Death

The general significance of death is covered by Newman under four main aspects. He first of all sees death as a uniquely personal event by its very nature; it is the only thing we can be fully certain of and the event in which we suffer utterly alone. Secondly, it epitomizes the human condition as one of anxiety, for it is from the prospect of death that all our fears are ultimately derived. It is also the moment of moral accountability by providing us with a standard of judgment and discrimination between the values of the world and those of eternity. Finally it has the nature of a religious experience since it carries the mind beyond the reality of sense and time to the unseen world. These considerations are meant to influence our life at present rather than at the moment of death itself, when the significance it ought to have will have escaped us.

---

to it and remarks on how appropriate the theme is for his present address.

[15] Newman had difficulty numbering this sermon. He finally decided it was not No. 181 but No. 174. Cf. his comment on the cover of the manuscript which was newly transcribed, probably in 1840.

A Uniquely Personal Event

Newman stresses that there is but one proper way of entering into the meaning of death and that is by contemplating our own personal demise.[16] To think of it as something that only happens to others, is to treat it as an abstraction and to deprive it of its essential meaning. The death of a friend or relative drives home the truth of our own individuality by reminding us of the irrevocable sentence that some day we too will die. Each of us has his own personal history and is really a microcosm to himself, which testifies to the unfathomable mystery of the human person. At death this whole personal world to all appearance comes to an end and the question of life after death is sharply raised. The contemplation of death thus enables us to recognize our uniqueness in the world and the thought of "two and two only absolute and luminously self-evident beings, myself and my Creator."[17]

"He has his own hopes and fears, desires, judgments, and aims; he is everything to himself, and no one else is really anything. No one outside him can really touch him, can touch his soul, his immortality; he must live with himself for ever. He has a depth within him unfathomable, an infinite abyss of existence; and the scene in which he bears part for the moment is but a gleam of sunshine upon its surface."[18]

The Anxiety of Death

Death brings the ultimate questions of the meaning of our existence into sharp focus.[19] The fear of the unknown future is the most frightening of all, since it is something which is beyond our power to name and control. We are thrown upon "the immense and boundless and fathomless futurity."[20] The threat of our annihilation, or the kind of existence we face after death, or whether indeed there is any connection

---

[16] No. 50 p. 7; P.P.S. vii,1 mentions the need for a personal conviction of our own death saying that an awareness which is general and abstract it is not real knowledge of death at all.

[17] Apo. p. 4.

[18] ibid. P.P.S.i,2 .

[19] P.P.S.vii,5.

[20] No. 50 p. 1.

between this life and the next fill the mind with anxiety. Newman observes that "Questions such as these on the most momentous of all subjects naturally crowd upon the mind -and must at times create an anxiety which no effort can dispel."[21]

We naturally shrink from the thought of death but the pain and suffering it may bring is nothing compared to the consequences implied in it.[22] For those who live without any knowledge of their future destiny, of why we are here and what there is to hope for, only sadness, melancholy and gloom are the natural result. It is this perplexity and ignorance of the hereafter which was so overpowering as to lead to despair in the case of the heathen.[23]

A Time of Moral Accountability

Death also reminds us that our personal responsibility is something which cannot be transferred to another. The distractions of the world create a cloud of illusion which conceals this truth from us, but when death comes the illusion will be shattered. All that will then remain is to wait for the judgment, to stand before God with no one but ourselves to give an account. The day of death is the day when the account books[24] will be closed, never to be opened again until the Last Day. In bringing to mind the thought of death, Newman issues a solemn observation that

> "...in that awful period, when the fever of life is over, and you are waiting in silence for the judgment, with nothing to distract your thoughts, who can say how dreadful may be the memory of sins done in the body?"[25]

The values we have lived by and the real objects of our affections

---

[21] ibid. p. 2.

[22] ibid.

[23] P.P.S.iii,25.

[24] The image of God as a Divine Accountant is found in the Book of Revelation. Its appeal for Newman is reflected in his experience as assistant treasurer at Oriel as well as being bursar and superior of the Birmingham oratory. His background as being the son of a banker may also be noted.

[25] P.P.S.iv,6.

will become crystal clear when death comes. The worldly person thinks principally of death as the termination of pleasures and faces it not only reluctantly, but even in a spirit of rebellion against God, whom he sees as a cruel tyrant. Those who have found their security in the world and not from the venture of faith, cannot but turn in horror from the thought of death and judgment. The real danger of attachment to riches lies in the fact that they make a true disposition of surrender almost impossible:

> "...and these all turn the mind from religion and fasten it on the objects of time and sense:- and death is regarded not as the entrance to a heavenly life, but as the termination to the joys they at present have, and Christ is regarded not as a gracious Saviour but as an austere Master who calls them from the pleasures of sin to thoughts of God and eternity."[26]

A Sense of Reverence upon Death

The air of mystery surrounding death often causes it to be seen as a taboo so that it is not "a welcome subject of thought"[27] or conversation. This feeling of awe with which we regard the dead arises from a religious experience in which we come face to face with our own utter helplessness and dependence on God. Bereavement and death can therefore be the instrument through which the unseen world is brought to our attention.

> "There is a peculiar feeling with which we regard the dead. What does it arise from? - that he is absent? No, for we do not feel the same towards one who is merely distant, though he be at the other end of the earth...Surely it is the passing into another state which impresses itself upon us, and makes us speak of him as we do, - I mean with a sort of awe."[28]

We may try to suppress this feeling on the pretext that nothing is known of the hereafter, but this is a subterfuge for avoiding the

---

[26] No. 90 p. 9; P.P.S.ii,28.

[27] P.P.S.ii,28.

[28] P.P.S.v,2.

implications of the invisible world. Even if someone did come back from the dead, what more could he tell us other than what we already know? Our difficulty in taking seriously the truth of the unseen world does not arise from lack of knowledge. It is primarily due to our unwillingness to accept the consequences of acting upon the truth.[29]

Section Two
The Christian View of Death

Up to this point the meaning of death has been considered from the standpoint of natural religion. Conscience, the universal testimony of mankind and the history of the world are the sources which inform us about its general significance. Beyond these natural views on death there are also attitudes, which though derived from a Christian culture, fall far short of Christian faith. It is very common in fact to find among Christians a strict moral preparation and a religious view of death which bears little relation to the mind of Christ. Faith is a personal habit acquired by years of prayer and obedience, not a custom or fashion unconsciously absorbed from a social environment.[30] Without this distinct element of faith death will remain a frightful experience, without ever having the comfort of seeing it as dissolving into Christ.

Death as a Gracious Deliverance from a Sinful World

An example of such a custom is to speak of death as a happy release from suffering. This indeed is true, since death is a release which puts an end to human anguish. There is however, nothing specifically religious in such an attitude since a deliverance from pain may simply be desired as such. It becomes a religious act only when it is seen in the light of God's merciful providence. A true disposition of faith is one in which death is perceived as the fulfilment of God's promise of deliverance, and embraced as a gracious gift coming from His hands. Just as in the case of freedom from persecution promised to the Church, death is likewise a liberation for the individual Christian.

---

[29] P.P.S.viii,6.

[30] P.P.S.i,6.

This is the spirit in which Newman spoke at the funeral of Walter Mayers, of one who had waited on Christ and was now reaping the fruit of His promise.

> "[It is] a *promised* deliverance. This is what invests the waiting for it with a religious character - it is promised, and as such connected with the name, the attributes and the providences of God. Every deliverance must in itself be pleasant; there is nothing then necessarily religious in desiring it. It was natural for the Christians under persecution to wish to be released from it - but it became a religious wish, when deliverance was viewed as the gracious gift of God and as already promised by Him."[31]

Death then is to be awaited in a spirit of faith and self-renunciation. It is the final act of turning over everything to Him and implies an attitude in which "we feel ourselves to be nothing, and God everything" - an evangelical tenet he learned from Mayers himself. The Christian simply casts himself upon the mercy of God, and thus acknowledges that death is both a debt for sin as well as a deliverance promised by God from a sinful world.

> "With reference to the particular deliverance just spoken of, death, a holy justifying faith is shown in acknowledging it on the one hand to be the just desert of sin, in regarding it on the other to be a merciful deliverance through Christ from this sinful world, in meditating upon it, in preparing for it, in praising God for it."[32]

Death in itself is an evil and a curse. It is experienced as a human tragedy, a negation of life signalling the victory of the forces of evil over good. It is a unique sign that God's creation has been marred. To those who believe in God's goodness death therefore presents a permanent trial of faith, - to all appearances evil has the last word. The significance of this mystery of evil was fully understood by Christ when he was confronted with the death of Lazarus.

> "What was it He saw? He saw visibly displayed the *victory*

---

[31] No. 163 p. 5.
[32] ibid. p. 11.

of death ... Here then was the Creator surrounded by the work of His hands, who adored Him indeed, yet seemed to ask why He suffered what He Himself had made so to be marred. Here was the Creator of the world at a scene of death, seeing the issue of His gracious handiwork."[33]

Death is the culminating debt for sin. It is the expression of sinful nature's dominion over us and all that we can do is to keep silence before it. This is the lesson Christ Himself taught us by His silence before the grave of Lazarus. He offered no explanation for the death of His friend, but stood in awe before it. He knew what He was about to do in His own death, but as the time had not yet come, He could only grant a temporary respite over the power of evil. This "inscrutable law" would again soon have its day and claim its victory. Newman notes that there is but one exception to this law and that is Christ Himself, who was without sin and over whom death had no dominion. No one could take His life from Him; He gave it voluntarily and could take it up again.[34] But in all other cases the victory of evil is embodied in the event of each one's death. This victory however is not an absolute one, for Christ has taken upon Himself the full brunt of sin and conquered it by His resurrection.

Christ's Death transforms the Meaning of our Death

The significance of Christ's death is first understood by Newman as "the most convincing proof of the malignity of sin."[35] In his evangelical days Newman seems to argue to the necessity of the Incarnation, inasmuch as nothing less than the Saviour's death could satisfy God for the enormity of sin. But even in his early preaching a more positive note is given. It was not just an event for Christ but for every Christian. Though "in Him we died and suffered and paid the penalty of our transgressions," it was also for us the gateway to new life. This he explains by paraphrasing a passage from St. Paul to the Galatians:

---

[33] P.P.S.iii,10.

[34] No. 352 p. 8.

[35] No. 27 p. 14.

"as if he [St. Paul] said, the death of Christ for human sins has opened a new prospect and world of thought upon me - it has put things in a new light, it has given me new relations, objects and motives - I am constrained to enter upon a new life for I find myself bound to my God and Saviour by a stronger tie than any which binds me to any other thing in the whole world."[36]

Since Christ identified Himself so totally with the human condition, the sense of ultimate human futility implied by death has been overcome. Our death has already taken place, not just metaphorically speaking, but in reality. Its sting has been removed by Christ's taking upon Himself the natural consequences of sin. We have passed beyond death to a new life and nothing but the second death should hold any real fear for us. Our mortal death has lost its threat of annihilation, since we are now joined to the Risen Christ in an eternal union. Thus the mystery of death has been demythologized and its ominous significance diminished by the death of Christ. Here Newman observes that

"... the same undervaluing of death, considered as a break in our existence, and a severance of us from the world, is conveyed in what is said concerning our union with Christ our Saviour. Christ died once, then rose again; that time of death may truly be counted the time of our death, as far as the real evil of death is concerned. Our baptism has made it such for us. Then we died in Him, when He died, not when our bodies die. He suffered the real agony of God's wrath, not we in our natural death; and as death has no more dominion over Him so in any fearful sense it has as little power over us either. Death is passed, life is begun, we are complete in Him."[37]

This fundamental union with Christ in his death and resurrection changes our whole conception of death. We now see that our lives are committed to His safe keeping, and as we belong to Him on earth, we cannot be any more than His in heaven - so death makes no difference to our union with Christ. This union also implies a bond with each other, for we are all joined together as members of His mystical Body.

[36] No. 74 p. 4. The sermon was preached on Good Friday 1825.
[37] No. 174 pp. 10-11.

Hence faith in the Communion of Saints provides great comfort at the time of bereavement, in the knowledge that our departed friends are still united with us. Since we have been joined once in Christ there cannot be any final separation. Death then is not just a time of sorrow and loss, but also a sign of victory that one of Christ's elect has been gathered into His rest. It is an occasion for giving thanks, knowing that the condition of the deceased is more fortunate than our own. We who are left behind still live in darkness and in a troublesome world, while no further harm can befall those who die in Christ. Their days of trial are over and they wait in confidence for the day of resurrection. Newman reminds his congregation of this truth at the funeral of Walter Mayers, of whom he says:

> "Nor is he really taken from us, it is the privilege of faith to be the substance of things hoped for and unseen. To the eye of faith he still lives and is present with us -We loved him in the Lord, we were knit together unto him in the Lord - the Lord that bought both him and us, has joined together all his Saints in a mystical body. Who can ever separate us from Him and from each other?"[38]

Death is a Point of Transition

From the standpoint of nature death spells the end of human existence, and the natural man will understandably be filled with "dreary miserable feelings" at the thought of it. Sinful human nature can guarantee nothing beyond the grave or grant any hope of immortality. But by the Incarnation our nature has been renewed by sharing in the incorrupt nature which Christ assumed. This is the basis and the promise of our immortality. In the light of faith the character and meaning of death has been transformed. It no longer marks the end of our existence but stands for something different now that Christ has come.

> "That nature, thus renewed, He communicates to us. He raises our souls to eternal life now -He will raise our bodies hereafter. Death stands for a different thing since Christ has

---

[38] No. 163 p. 24.

come - It is no longer a break, or a catastrophe, to the Christian it is an era, though a solemn and momentous era, in the history of our immortality."[39]

Newman's theology of death is set within a Christological framework and developed in accordance with the paradigm of Christ. The work of salvation through Christ is defined by two events which mark its beginning and its end, viz. His First and Second Coming. Since Christ is the very raison d'etre of faith, these two events constitute the parameters of the spiritual life of the Christian. His First Coming marks our new birth and His Second our bodily resurrection on the last day - they are the terminus a quo and the terminus ad quem of the Christian life. Our lives are a process of sanctification which is not complete until it is perfected by Christ at the Second Coming. Hence death, which we so often think of in human terms as the end, is on this scheme simply a point on the spectrum of the spiritual life. It is a point of transition, a change of phase, not an end to the process of perfection in Christ. It denotes the end of the period of probation but not the closure of our sanctification, which continues until the full measure of grace is manifested in the resurrection of the body.

"This indeed, is our Saviour's usual doctrine as well as that of His apostles. I mean, it is His custom to insist on two events chiefly, His first coming and His second - our regeneration and our resurrection - throwing into the background the prospect of our death, as if it were but a mark of distinction (however momentous a one), not of division, in the extended course of our purification."[40]

By locating death within this Christological framework Newman makes the further point that salvation in Christ is the salvation of a community, and not just of one individual. Thus the day of general judgment, rather than the day we die, marks the definitive moment of salvation. He thereby rescues his theology from a privatized view of death, by subordinating the event to the day of the general resurrection of the dead. He likewise considers the stress on the moment of death as the goal of Christian life, to be theologically misplaced and a "strange fact." Making the death of the individual the primary focus of attention

---

[39] No. 174 p. 5.
[40] P.P.S.iii,25.

220

is at variance with the principles of Christian faith. When examined closely, it will be seen to arise from judgments other than those of Christian theology. It implies that we are placing ourselves rather than Christ at the centre of things, and thereby elevating our own personal experience, however momentous, above the Coming of Christ. In so doing there is a shift in focus from the primary consideration of Christ's Coming to the secondary one of our own death. This may arise from self-deception or undetected cultural values not grounded on faith, which derogate from Christ the supreme importance which He has attached to His Coming.

> "Now if the sacred writers uniformly hold out Christ's coming, but we consider death, as the close of all things, is it not plain that, in spite of our apparent agreement with them in formal statements of doctrine, there must be some hidden and undetected difference between them and ourselves, some unfounded notion on our part which we have inherited, some assumed premiss, some lurking prejudice, some earthly temper, or some mere human principle?"[41]

Relativizing death is not the same as belittling it. By changing its significance Newman has not thereby robbed it of its importance. Far from believing that death loses its meaning because it loses its sting, the Christian sees it as acquiring a new importance in the light of faith. It is not the end of all things but simply the end of our trial. It marks the end of our training period but not our spiritual growth. Training is a means to an end, not an end in itself, so our period of probation is an apprenticeship into spiritual maturity. Its consequences for the future however, are momentous, for it is the initiation into eternal life or eternal misery. At that moment a definitive character is formed within us, either for good or for evil.[42] The thought of death therefore sharpens our perception of the need of preparation on which our final destiny depends.

> "This life compared to our future destinies as the redeemed of Christ, is what a child's schooling time is to his manhood. Now who dwells on it for its own sake and does not pass on to the consideration of the real life of action which is the end

---

[41] ibid.

[42] No. 174 p. 6.

of his early education."[43]

The Implications of the Christian View of Death

In his sermons Newman has shown how very different the Christian view of death is from any conventional wisdom on the subject. Such a difference is consistent with the general nature of Christianity which so often upsets some of our most cherished ideas. Were the Gospel not "a strange thing in the world" we should in fact have doubts about its authenticity. From this distinctive understanding of death Newman derives some uncompromising conclusions about the Christian's relation to the world. If death is the ultimate horizon there is every reason to be committed to temporal things, but if the horizon is eternity, temporal concerns must be subordinated to eternal interests. If our souls are immortal, "nothing is really important but our own personal prospects and our own history, past and to come."[44]

It is therefore inconsistent on the basis of this principle to invest all our energy in temporal matters which bear little relation to eternity. Excessive concern for politics or an exclusive interest in the welfare of the world is tantamount to denying the primacy of the spirit. If we must be involved with the world we should first see it in relation to the Church. For the Church is the only body in the world that has the mark of eternity on it, while everything else perishes.

> "There is but one body on earth which has immortality, and that is the Church. The Church will last forever; its members will meet again on the other side of the grave....Parties of this world, political, philosophical, religious, have in them no seed of eternal life. But the Bride of the Lamb is destined for the Marriage Supper."[45]

---

[43] ibid. p. 7.

[44] ibid. p. 13.

[45] ibid pp. 15-16.

Preparation for Death

Newman's views on preparing for death are the fruit of his reflections on pastoral experience. He was greatly affected by his visits to the sick and the dying while at St. Clement's.[46] On one occasion he recalls in his diary his conversation with a man in declining health, in which he records "the awful state of those, who having left religion to their death-bed, could give no *evidences* of their sincerity."[47] One's death-bed therefore is clearly not the place or the time for sudden conversions, or for the choice of fundamental options. It is then too late to change the habits of a life-time, or to summon enough energy as the body steadily weakens. Repentance is the work of a lifetime, not of a few fleeting moments, no matter how important they may be. Merely to profess amendment even at so crucial a time as death is not the same as having the true spirit of repentance. Speaking of death-bed conversions, Newman adds the sobering thought:

"It is, indeed, easy enough to have good words put into our mouths, and our feelings roused, and to profess the union of utter self-abandonment and enlightened sense of sin; but to claim is not really to possess such tempers. Really to gain these is a work of time."[48]

Even the committed Christian must assume in his last hours the attitude of the prodigal son. The moment of death is the opportunity for him to fulfil his role by an act of complete surrender to God. Though he has sincerely made an effort throughout life, it would be self-deception not to be conscious of the mixed motivations and half-hearted amendments of the past. Being all too aware of his sinfulness, the Christian finds his comfort in the remembrance of God's mercy than in a vain trust in his own good deeds.

"Under these circumstances, how vain it is to tell him of his own good deeds, and to bid him look back on his consistent life! This reflection will rarely comfort him; and when it does, it will be the recollection of the instances of God's

---

[46] L.D. Vol.i, pp. 196ff.

[47] ibid. p. 252.

[48] P.P.S.iii,7. The points made in this sermon are very similar to the account in his diary of his conversation with the dying man.

mercy towards him in former years which will be the chief ground of encouragement in it."[49]

The dying Christian has the comforting picture of the tears of Jesus at the grave of Lazarus. When one considers that Jesus was bound by ties of blood to no one but His mother, the depth of His compassion is all the more revealing. For there we see not just the finite sympathy of one human being for another, but "the love of God, the bowels of compassion of the Almighty and Eternal."[50] This is the true ground of confidence for the Christian on his death-bed; with the story of Lazarus in his mind, the believer draws assurance that Christ stands present with him.

"There our Lord vouchsafes to stand, though unseen - whether over the bed of death or over the grave; whether we ourselves are sinking or those who are dear to us. Blessed be His name! Nothing can rob us of this consolation: we will be as certain through His grace, that He is standing over us in love, as though we saw Him."[51]

Part Two
The Intermediate State

Introduction:

Newman's reflections on the Intermediate State may be regarded as the outcome of a theological inquiry. The investigation is prompted by the incomplete account in Scripture of the condition of the souls departed. The Bible gives little by way of direct knowledge about their plight, other than to say that they are "at rest." Beyond this revealed truth there is a lack of hard information, which stimulates rather than curtails further inquiry. We are left therefore with many open questions on the nature of their state, which may thus be pursued in the spirit of theological investigation.

---

[49] ibid. The same idea is expressed in P.P.S.iv,20.
[50] P.P.S.iii,10.
[51] ibid..

The Beginning of the Inquiry

The inquiry begins with the intriguing question about the state of the just who died before the time of Christ. It is then followed by the parallel question about the condition of all the departed who have known Christ, but whose salvation is not complete until the day of bodily resurrection. Newman bases his inquiry on two main principles, the doctrine of the Communion of Saints and the need of spiritual purification. These are the two chief pillars he depends upon for the development of his views on the nature of the Intermediate State.[52]

The first reference we have to the Intermediate State, though it is not so named, is in a sermon given at St. Clement's on the 16th October 1825.[53] It is in the context of sanctification as a basic element common to all forms of revelation. The holiness of God is an elementary truth, which requires a corresponding need on man's part "to seek after a transformation into His likeness." Though the patriarchs died before the full revelation in Christ was disclosed, they can still be held up to Christians as models of holiness.[54] They have passed into another world, and the question now arises whether Christ has revealed Himself to them. We have no clear information from Scripture however, as to whether or not this full disclosure has been made, but we can feel certain that they share the lot of "the just who rest from their labours."

> "Where they are now we know not - nor what their state, their employments, their thoughts, their knowledge - whether they yet know the glories of redemption through the Son of God, we cannot tell - Scripture is silent, and it is perhaps rash to inquire and conjecture - we know they are at rest that they have ceased from their labours and that is all we know. Yet assuredly whether the gospel be already revealed to them or whether it be reserved to the time of the body's resurrection from the grave, still sooner or later the disclosure is to be made to them."[55]

The fear of trespassing beyond the express declaration of

---

[52] The lines of this inquiry are limited to the scope of the thesis which is Anglican sermons themselves.

[53] No. 110.

[54] Newman returns to this idea in P.P.S.iii,18.

[55] No. 110 p. 15.

Scripture is a real one for Newman, though it does not prevent him from continuing his inquiry. In a sermon on the Feast of All Saints[56] he notes that there are various opinions held on the question "in which some persons take a particular interest." He cautions restraint and the need to confine discussion to a simple presentation of the view of Scripture. This should have the effect of stemming idle curiosity and of relativizing the importance of the Intermediate State. Scripture, after all, declares the Second Coming and the final resurrection to be the primary goal which Christians must look out for; the intervening time between death and the last day is of secondary importance and should therefore cause no anxiety.

> "...if we accustom ourselves to think much of Christ's coming and the day of judgment, not only things of this world, but even the intermediate state of the disembodied soul, will employ little of our thoughts and our anxiety."[57]

Having said this, Newman nonetheless disingenuously proceeds to examine the text of Scripture in such a way as to reveal his own interest and curiosity in this intriguing question. He notes that anxieties do arise about the invisible world, and about the nature of the soul, particularly in the disembodied state. Moreover the pain of permanent separation from our loved ones with so little knowledge of where they have gone, naturally provokes an inquiry into the condition of the departed. But before the question is looked at, it is necessary to see first what revelation tells us about the fact that they are alive.

Life is not ended but changed

We have seen under the section on death the emphasis Newman places on the immortality of the soul and the life of the world to come. Our mortal life comes from God and death is but the soul's separation from the body as it returns to Him.[58] Hence all the millions of human

---

[56] The two sermons which are entirely devoted to the Intermediate State were preached on this Feast Day. No. 266 was preached on November 1.1830 and No. 393, which was published as P.P.S.iii.25, on the same day in 1835.

[57] No. 266 p. 6.

[58] Newman is fully aware that the Greek division into body and soul does not truly represent the biblical view of man's unitary nature. He simply uses the word "soul"

beings who ever lived, are kept in existence beyond the gate of death. Their individual identities are not destroyed, but the core of their personality is preserved to the last day. Until then they all live and are kept safe in God's remembrance. Newman thus reminds us that

> "Every one of those souls still lives. They had their separate thoughts and feelings when on earth, they have them now. They had their likings and pursuits; they gained what they thought good and enjoyed it; and they still somewhere or other live, and what they then did in the flesh surely has its influence on their present destiny. They live, reserved for a day which is to come, when all nations shall stand before God."[59]

The existence of the departed is also affirmed by our belief in the Invisible World.[60] Just as the visible world is filled with objects known to us through the senses, there are higher objects, no less real, which are known through the eyes of faith. Faith tells us of a spiritual communion between the living and the dead in Christ, but gives us no grounds for belief in any form of psychic communication with them, mediated through the senses. They no longer have the normal means of contact but are still present to us in faith.

> "And in that other world are the souls also of the dead. They too, when they depart hence, do not cease to exist, but they retire from this visible scene of things; or, in other words, they cease to act towards us and before us *through our senses....* They remain but without the usual means of approach towards us, and correspondence with us."[61]

---

as a term by default to describe the core of the human person. Vide P.P.S.i,2 and ii,26 where he specifically addresses this question of language.

[59] P.P.S.iv,6. Newman does not deal directly with the Intermediate State in this sermon. He is at pains to assert that there are only two ultimate states, one of blessedness and one of wrath, which are already operative in their tendencies during our mortal lives.

[60] P.P.S.iv,13.

[61] ibid.

The Consciousness of the Departed

Being assured of the existence of the departed souls, Newman turns to consider the nature of the disembodied state. Scripture describes their state as a state of rest and adds the further note that they are "asleep." We know on the one hand that they are alive, which implies some form of consciousness; but we are also told they are asleep in some coma-like condition, which suggests they are not conscious of their state. What then can one justly infer from what has been revealed?

It would be wrong, Newman surmises, to expect any precise information from Scripture about the disembodied state, for the Bible tells us virtually nothing about the nature of the soul. The difficulty in reconciling these apparent inconsistencies, arises from what philosophy informs us on the nature of the soul and its need to be embodied. Furthermore, there is the logical difficulty that no intermediate stage is possible between being and non-being. A thing either is or it is not; one is either conscious or not conscious. We have however, in the phenomenon of dreaming, an in-between state which can neither be called total consciousness nor total unconsciousness. Perhaps then, an analogy may be found in human experience which might help us to understand a little more about the state of consciousness of the departed. However, just as it would be impossible to describe the state of dreaming to one who has never had a dream, words likewise fail us in describing the condition of the departed to those who have not yet fallen asleep in the Lord.

Newman pursues at some length a dialogue between faith and reason in the hope of ascertaining more about the Intermediate State. Taking the analogy of dreaming he follows a line of reasoning based on antecedent probability, to arrive not at a positive affirmation about the departed soul, but at a negative conclusion. His conclusion is that there is nothing antecedently improbable in the notion implied by Scripture concerning the state of consciousness of the departed. He notes that one cannot argue from the possible to the real - a posse ad esse non valet illatio - hence one cannot conclude from the phenomenon of dreaming that such is the state of the departed. But on the other hand the fact that we do dream and know very little about its true nature, allows us to infer that there is nothing self-contradictory in the notion of a twilight state of consciousness. By describing the state as "sleep," Scripture not only leaves the question open, but actually allows us to draw comfort from the belief that "they are not insensible though they sleep."

228

"...the word "sleep" is the very term applied in Scripture to the state of the saints departed and though we cannot and need not argue from this, that it resembles sleep and dreaming or that from experiencing sleep we can form a notion what it is (for that would be running into the very error I have been exposing, of attempting to judge of things unknown by things known), yet so far may be gathered from the use of the word, that it is an unknown state, neither of perfect consciousness nor of unconsciousness <not like anything on earth, not a state of insensibility but a state of rest>."[62]

Newman has clearly stated that we can draw no firm conclusions, as far as having any positive knowledge about the degree of consciousness of the departed. But there is nothing impossible in the notion that they retain some connection with the past, and some relation with the future, even in their present state of suspension. The argument is based on our own experience of mystical communion with God and of the role which dreams play in putting us in touch with realities, to which we have no tangible access. The departed may in fact be in a much better position than we are, since there are fewer obstacles to communion, such as temptations. This line of thought can be seen in the following passage from Newman:

"...supposing they are left to their own good thoughts and to that secret communion with Christ which they had, in this life, their state in no wise differs in kind from that which good men may in a measure experience in this life <here>, at seasons when temptation has spent its force and rest and peace are given in peculiar abundance to their mind. Nay, we need not disbelieve {i.e.(there is no peculiar improbability in the notion) that as in dreams a mysterious connection is kept up in our minds now with places and times far removed from us, so} in the sleep of the soul visions of the past and of the present, as well as of the future, may be presented to the thoughts - and thus an intercourse kept up with earth even in paradise, and some knowledge of the successive fortunes of those whom they knew and valued in the flesh - and the texts which speak of the disembodied soul's consciousness, certainly connect it with a knowledge too of

---

[62] No. 266 p. 14.

human affairs, <nay, and a power over them>."[63]

The Activities of the Faithful Departed

Another line of consideration which Newman follows is the question of the activities of the faithful departed. Life without action would be meaningless[64]; it therefore follows that the departed are engaged in some form of activity, from the very fact that they are alive. But here again difficulties arise from the apparent inconsistency of Scripture. Being in the state of rest and being active at the same time presents a paradox. Nevertheless, the faithful departed are alive to God and their activity consists essentially in making intercession for us. On the one hand, they have a power of intercession with God, though "this does not imply that they *act*, or that they are *conscious* of their power." But on the other hand, they are "active promoters of the Church's welfare." These apparently contradictory statements may be resolved when we consider that we may know *that* something is true - both statements are true - without necessarily knowing *how* they can be true. Thus Newman concludes that "...it may be no contradiction that the soul of man should sleep in the intermediate state, and yet be awake."[65]

The spirit of inquiry into the condition of the saints departed can also be noted in his sermon on the Church as The Kingdom of the Saints.[66] He introduces the sermon with a remark on the importance of choosing the right perspective to understand any reality. One can choose a vertical or a horizontal viewpoint, or look from above or from below. Some perspectives give us a clearer view than others, or a higher vantage-point from which a fuller picture is seen. As regards the Church, it may be said that the angels have a better understanding of its identity than we have, since they see it from a privileged standpoint. And the souls in the Intermediate State may likewise have a similar advantage and see beneath the surface of things. They may now see more clearly the hand of God in their own personal lives and in the present events in the world. Their position enables them to understand more clearly the

---

[63] ibid p. 16.

[64] This recalls the famous statement in the Grammar that "Life is for action. If we insist on proof for everything, we shall never come to action." G.A.p. 92.

[65] P.P.S.iv,11.

[66] P.P.S.ii,20 .

230

internal life of the Church.

> "And perchance such a contemplation of the providences of
> God, whether in their own personal history, or in the affairs
> of their own country, or of the Church, or of the world at
> large, may be one of the blessed occupations of God's elect
> in the Intermediate State."[67]

Part of the Communion of Saints

The activities and "blessed occupations" of the departed are a
corollary to the fact that they are alive, and form part of the Communion
of Saints. As Newman's understanding of the Church develops there is
a corresponding growth and interest in the state of the souls departed.
In a sermon on the Gift of the Spirit,[68] he notes that Christians live in a
world of spiritual influences, in a network of relationship between parts
of the one body. Hence there is a commerce of grace between the
Church on earth and the Intermediate State. Though the dead are in the
world of spirits, the pilgrim Church is "within reach (as I may say) of
the Saints departed."

The identity of the Church consists in a living communion in
which there is an unbreakable unity among its parts. Not even death can
drive a wedge between the living and the dead, for it is merely "a mark
of distinction, not of division." It is not only powerless in separating us
from Christ, but from one another. With its one unique source of life,
the Mystical Body, though different in its parts, remains the same. On
this basis then, there is no distinction in God's eyes between the living
and the dead.

> "...it is the manner of Scripture to imply that all Saints make
> up but one body, Christ being the Head, and no real
> distinction existing between dead and living; as if the
> Church's territory were a vast field, only with a veil stretched

---

[67] P.P.S.ii,20. The same idea is again proposed in P.P.S. iii,25: "And in some
unknown way, that place of rest has a communication with this world, so that the
disembodied souls know what is going on below."

[68] P.P.S.iii,18.

across it, hiding part from us."[69]

Newman describes the bonds of unity as between "the few who happen still to be on their trial" and "the many who sleep in the Lord." At the beginnings of the Church, the majority of its members were on this side of the grave, save for the just who had died before Christ. But now the order is reversed, since those who have now gone to their reward, vastly outnumber the present visible body. Thus the Church should not only be described as invisible "as regards her vital principle," but even "in respect to her members." In terms of sheer numbers alone, it lies more in the invisible world than in the visible institution of believers.[70] It is a paradox therefore to speak of the Church in such a way as to confine our attention to a visible minority. This tendency is due to an inadequate faith perspective influenced by the world's view that what we see is the centre of all things. By adopting this perspective, we assume that the departed, who are no longer within our sight, have dropped out of the system, and are no longer thought of by us as living members of the Church. Newman points out the deficiency of this view when he says:

"Such is the opinion of the departed; as though *we* were in light and *they* in darkness, - we in power and influence, they in weakness; - we the living, and they the dead; yet with the views opened on us in the gospel, with the knowledge that the One Spirit of Christ ever abides, and that those who are made one with Him are never parted from Him, and those who die in Him are irrevocably knit into Him and one with Him, shall we dare to think slightly of these indefectible members of Christ and vessels of future glory?"[71]

Allied to the question of the Intermediate State, is the practice in the early Church of prayers for the dead and invocation to the Saints. A great deal of controversy surrounded these questions,[72] not so much about the practice itself, which Newman wished to preserve, but about

[69] P.P.S.iii,25.

[70] P.P.S.iv,10.

[71] P.P.S.iv,11.

[72] In the tracts against Romanism Newman published *Archbishop Ussher's Prayers for the Dead*, Tract No. LXXII and *On Purgatory*, Tract No. LXXIX in which the controversy can be followed. The discussion however takes us beyond the scope of the sermons.

its interpretation. His position at the time was that prayers for the dead did not imply a belief in Purgatory, something which the Church of Rome alleged. While accepting the efficacy of such prayers, and the role of intercession of the faithful departed, he sounded a note of caution.[73] He noted the danger of falling into a form of idolatry or saint worship, and insisted that the intercession of the saints is a collective one. Their power of advocacy is as part of the Communion of Saints and not due to their individual merits. Though they are worthy to be remembered, our reverence towards them should be "neither too much nor too little."

> "He has neither told us to neglect the faithful servants of Christ departed, not to pay them undue honour; but to think of them, yet not speak to them; to make much of them, but to trust solely in Him."[74]

The Need for Purification

A factor of far-reaching influence in Newman's theology is the principle of purification. In the light of this, the nature of the Intermediate State is seen by him more and more as a place of cleansing, where the departed soul is fitted for the all-holy presence of God. It is a cast-iron law that the residue of sin must be purged, and unsettled debts accounted for. Moreover, even those who are restored to God's favour by their repentance of sin, may still have a debt to make up. The purpose then of the Intermediate State appears to Newman as a suitable means in God's providence for paying the debt for sins, the consequences of which have not been fully satisfied.

> "As, then, souls may be at present in God's favour, whom He foresees to be His impenitent enemies, and companions of devils for ever, so others also much more may be in His favour, against whom an unsettled reckoning lies, the issue of which is future, who have certain sins as yet unforgiven,

---

[73] Cf. Newman's letter to R.I.Wilberforce. " Henry told me what I was very sorry to hear that you had misunderstood the last sermon in my 3rd volume ...as if I disapproved of prayers of [for] the Dead. It is strange it should have conveyed this impression to you, considering that in this place it was considered to be recommending them..." L.D., Vol. v, p. 260.

[74] P.P.S.iv.11.

and certain consequences of sins as yet unprovided for."[75]

Repentance is a necessary means of obtaining pardon and is required for each and every instance of sin. There is however, an essential difference between the absolute pardon given in baptism, and the pardon for post-baptismal sin. In the latter case there is an absence of information in the New Testament. Once conversion to the gospel has taken place, Scripture does not contemplate any turning back to a life of sin. It therefore does not deal with the question of pardon for sins committed after baptism. Since continual sin was not expected, no mention is made of how pardon may be obtained. We cannot however draw the conclusion that punishment for sin has been abolished, simply on the strength that there is no mention of it in the New Testament. All that we may logically conclude is that pardon for post-baptismal sins "is not explicitly promised in Scripture as a matter of course."[76] But taking the wider framework of the whole of Scripture, we have adequate confirmation of the fundamental law that punishment follows sin. If provision is not made for pardon in the New Testament, this does not mean that the moral law has been abrogated, or that there is no longer need for repentance. It simply means that sin after baptism does not fall within its perspective.

Though the principle of satisfaction for sin is clear, the ways in which it is applied are hidden from us. There is no precise information, except in the case of mortal sin, of how God will exact the penalty for unpaid debts. We believe, nevertheless, that He provides means through which a complete purification is accomplished. Chastisement is part of God's mercy for it is the means by which He prepares us for His presence. Hence Newman suggests that the Intermediate State may be one such way by which we are chastised. He thus surmises that the peace and comfort promised to the departed may be diminished, and in this way the debt may gradually be remitted.

"What its payment consists in, and how it will be exacted, is quite another question, and a hidden one. It may be such, if they die under it, as to diminish their blessedness in heaven...or it may lessen their peace and comfort in the

75 P.P.S.iv,7.
76 ibid.

intermediate state…"[77]

Purification might suggest a purely negative concept of holiness. Newman however points out the positive side of the coin and develops the idea that the Intermediate State is a special opportunity for growth in grace. Unlike the period of probation, no further merit for good works can be acquired, but this does not mean that the process of sanctification has ceased. On the contrary, the circumstances are better suited to allow for the full maturation of grace. Our life on earth was a school of growth through activity ; the Intermediate State is a further period of growth through contemplation. Growth in holiness does not cease at the moment of death but continues right up to the moment when Christ will gather all on the last day.

> "…the time of waiting between death and Christ's coming, may be profitable to those who have been his true servants here, as a time of maturing that fruit of grace, but partly formed in them in this life - a school-time of contemplation, as this world is a discipline of active service. Such, surely is the force of the Apostle's words, that "He that hath begun a good work in us, will perform it *until* the day of Jesus Christ, *until*, not *at*, not stopping it with death, but carrying it on to the Resurrection."[78]

The Roman Doctrine of Purgatory[79]

The only direct reference to Purgatory in the Anglican sermons is found in one preached on All Saints Day in 1835.[80] Given Newman's insistence on the need for purification and his intimations that

---

[77] ibid.

[78] P.P.S.iii,25.

[79] To give an adequate account of Newman's view on Purgatory it would be essential to examine his thorough treatment of it in Tract LXXIX. By that time he had reached a position on the subject similar to his treatment in his Dev. pp. 388-93. His account there is for all but a few omissions taken verbatim from his Tract. In his Catholic period Newman arrived independently at a view on Purgatory which was in substance that of St.Catherine of Genoa.

[80] P.P.S.iii,25 was added to the selection of sermons he made in the autumn of 1835 at Hurrell Froude's home at Dartington. These sermons were published in February 1836 as Volume Three of his Parochial Sermons. Tract LXXIX on Purgatory was written a year later and published on March 25,1837.

satisfaction for the residue of sin has to be made, if not now, at some future time, there is a logical connection which leads him to consider the Roman doctrine of Purgatory. For Newman the most alarming feature of this doctrine is the bleak prospect it holds out to the believer of imprisonment and torment, which is at variance with the comforting picture proposed in Scripture. When one considers our deceased friends and relatives, the idea of Purgatory is repugnant. It is unduly pessimistic to think that, despite all the trials and afflictions of this world, there is nothing better to look forward to in the next. Nevertheless, although the doctrine, which is peculiar to the Roman Church, is not sanctioned by Scripture[81] nor contained in the early teaching of the Church, it is not in itself antecedently improbable. Newman, moreover, does not regard it as a perversion of the truth but as an unwarranted addition to the deposit of faith.[82] When one considers the seriousness of sin and the holiness of God, there may be something to be said in its favour. It is after all "an infinitely less evil to suffer for a time in Purgatory than to be cast into hell for ever."

> "Nay, though the Bible did not positively affirm it, yet if it did not contradict it, and if the opinion itself was very general in the Church (as it is), and primitive too (as it is not), there would be enough in it reasonably to alarm us; for who could tell in such a case, but probably it might be true? This is what might have been; but in fact Christ has mercifully interfered, expressly to assure us that our friends are better provided for than this doctrine would make it appear."[83]

In the above quotation one can see the outline of Newman's method of inquiry into the question. The first line of investigation is to ascertain what is revealed in Scripture, and in such cases where the Bible is silent or ambiguous, then the mind of the Church. This can be known by applying the notes of catholicity and apostolicity to the

---

[81] The Articles of Religion in the Book of Common Prayer describe the doctrine as "a fond thing vainly invented, and grounded upon no warranty of Scripture..." Article xxii.

[82] On his visit to Italy in 1833 he favorably compares the Greek Church to the Roman with respect to the doctrine of Purgatory and the Mass. Neither of these doctrines is taught by the former; they are the "two chief delusions of Romanism". Nevertheless, though they are misconceived "the doctrines of the Mass and Purgatory are not perversions but inventions." L.D., Vol.iii, p. 265.

[83] P.P.S.iii,25.

doctrine. A third step is to examine the truth in the light of reason, not that it must be in conformity with it, but that there is nothing self-contradictory in the proposed truth. In the case of the doctrine of Purgatory there is no express declaration of it in Scripture, though Scripture does not contradict such a belief. Secondly, the doctrine has the strength of wide acceptance within the Catholic Church, but its weakness lies in its uncertain apostolic origins. Finally there are some reasonable grounds for the doctrine if one considers the need for some form of purification and penalty for sin. In spite of this however, the Roman doctrine, by laying stress on the punitive nature of Purgatory, goes beyond the limits of what is revealed in Scripture. The general picture of the Intermediate State which we can discern from revelation offers a more positive view than the notion of Purgatory entails. Though the souls of the departed are in a "sorrowful" condition, they "are ever so secured from actual punishment." They are moreover "sustained under it, soothed, quieted, [and] consoled."

A State of Incomplete Happiness

The text on which Newman preached his sermon on the Intermediate State is taken from the Book of Revelation[84] and refers to the waiting period endured by the martyrs, until the universal victory of the just is complete. In their state of sorrow and expectation "they cry out for some relief" and are each given crowns as a sign of present comfort and the assurance of future bliss. Newman notes that the meaning of the text is difficult since it is couched in the language of prophecy, but also observes that it is intended for our instruction and reverence. It contains a mystery about the world hereafter, a vision granted only to St. John, whose full meaning has not been disclosed to the Church. Taking both the literary genre and the essentially hidden nature of the next world into account, our understanding of the text is extremely limited. However, though written in the language of mystery, it cannot be dismissed as a mere figure of speech, but is meant to lead us into a solemn truth about the nature of the Intermediate State. When combined with other Scripture passages which more clearly refer to a place of rest or paradise, this interpretation is corroborated.

---

[84] Rev.vi,11.

"I see herein a deep mystery, a hidden truth, which I cannot handle or define, shining "as jewels at the bottom of the great deep," darkly and tremulously, yet really there."[85]

Newman's description of the Intermediate State can be summarized under two aspects, one negative and the other positive. In its negative aspect he sees it as essentially a state of suspension and incompleteness, and this in three respects. The first of these is the degree of self-consciousness enjoyed by the departed, which has already been considered in some detail. Their life is impaired by the constraint of living in a twilight existence. They have neither full awareness nor communication with the living on earth or the saints in heaven. They exist in a disembodied state which implies a restriction of their powers, and are in a condition of forced rest. Judged by what is to be their future destiny, their present condition is one of incompletion.

"They are incomplete, as being neither awake nor asleep; I mean they are in a state of rest, not in the full employment of their powers. The Angels are serving God actively; they are ministers between heaven and earth. And the Saints too, one day shall judge the world - they shall judge the fallen Angels; but at present, till the end comes, they are at rest only, which is enough for their peace, enough for our comfort on thinking of them, still, incomplete, compared with what one day shall be."[86]

Secondly, their place of abode is a temporary one and a temporal existence implies incompletion. It is not a lasting place of rest for they have not yet attained their permanent home in heaven. They are confined to "a cleft in the rock," barely touching "the skirts of His glory," and are hidden "under the altar."[87] They live at a distance from heaven, and though they have thrown off "their tabernacle of corruption," they are not yet been fully clothed with the garment of glory. The Intermediate State is therefore blocked off by a cordon sanitaire from the pure air and blessedness of heaven. Thus the departed have no direct access to their future home or to their former dwelling.

Finally the departed are in a state of limited happiness, and the

---

[85] P.P.S.iii,25.

[86] ibid.

[87] ibid.

object of their affections has not yet been fulfilled. The work of sanctification has been left unfinished, and the capacity to enjoy God in His holiness is not yet perfected. Complete happiness will not be possible until the body also shares the glory of resurrection. In the meanwhile, a silent maturation of grace takes place, "an inward development of the good seed sown in the heart," to prepare it for the one and only one object which will fully satisfy it.

Despite these deficiences the general picture of those who have died in Christ is nevertheless one of comfort and hope. They do possess some measure of consciousness and awareness of their role of intercession. They see things from a higher viewpoint and are active in the Church's welfare. They are above the din of the world and can contemplate the mystery of God in a deeper way than while they lived on earth. Moreover, their place of rest is described as "paradise," which suggests a more intimate proximity to the court of heaven than was possible before. Living in the place of spirits they have a greater degree of light and spiritual freedom than they had under the veil of the unseen world. But most of all their trial has ended and their anxiety passed, and they can now devote their entire existence to "growing in holy things." Theirs is a picture of repose and contemplation in the secure knowledge that the crown of victory awaits them. It is on this note that Newman sums up the state of the faithful departed.

> "This then on the whole, we may firmly believe to be the condition of the Saints before the Resurrection, a state of repose, rest, security; but again a state more like paradise than heaven - that is, a state which comes short of the glory which shall be revealed in us after the Resurrection, a state of waiting, meditation, hope in which what has been sown on earth may be matured and completed."[88]

---

[88] ibid..

Part Three
Heaven

"Alas! in any description of the state of those blessed servants and sons of God, we are obliged to make conjectures - for which among us has so risen to the knowledge of it, as to be able to speak fully of it on his own experience? Sure we are at best but labouring to attain it."[89]

"Did any one ask what the blessedness of heaven consisted in, I could but say "I do not know, but I believe..."[90]

In these two quotations Newman dispels any notion of clairvoyance into the mystery of heaven. He does not presume to offer an exposé or explain the secret God has in store for us.[91] But he does not regard instruction on the subject as esoteric. Nothing could be more important or more practical, he believes, than man's ultimate happiness. All that we know however about heaven, is based entirely on the promises revealed, and revelation is itself limited by man's finite capacity to understand.[92] We have no direct knowledge of God or of heaven, and can only derive an understanding of them in faith through the language of revelation. Newman's reflections on heaven are thus strictly based on the content of dogma and contained within its limits. They are characterized by the mark of sobriety which makes them all the more appealing and significant.

Newman shows an intense interest in the subject in his early life when questions of one's salvation were of major concern to him. Later, when we come to his mature writings, his anxiety gives way to a quiet confidence and assurance of the reality of heaven. This may be illustrated by first examining his early sermons and then his later published work. By 1834 he had brought to a close his systematic courses of sermons, and laid a solid groundwork for future

[89] No. 348 p. 13.

[90] No. 385 p. 9.

[91] No. 483 p. 1. Part of this sermon was used for the published version of No. 471 (P.P.S.iv,13) and so only a fragment of it remains extant.

[92] In his sermon *on the doctrine of the Trinity*, Newman refers to the limited human knowledge we can have of God. "God is revealed not as He is in Himself but as He is to us." No. 166 p. 21.

development. The date coincides with the publication of his first volume of Parochial sermons and marks the period of his maturity. By comparing both periods in sequence, one can plot the course of his development on the theme. Each of the following sections therefore begins with the early Newman and then proceeds to his published work.

The Human Desire for Happiness

The starting point for Newman is the paradox that our natural desire for happiness is in radical opposition to our true human fulfilment in union with God.[93] At the very heart of man there is a blindness which prevents him from following the path to true happiness. Due to our corruption we have no natural desire for heaven, but simply for happiness in self-seeking objects of desire. Moreover, despite our constant search for fulfilment, we are plagued by a natural instinctive fear of hell. With heaven cut off from us, and hell the logical outcome of self-gratification, the natural man is in a perilous condition. Heaven can not be attained by our own efforts or desires, for it is a gift of illumination and grace from the Holy Spirit.[94] Hell on the other hand is the just reward for following our corrupt natural inclinations.[95]

The thirst for perfect happiness is as elusive as it is unquenchable, for it is always perceived as something to be obtained beyond the horizon of our present vision. Man has a longing for an eternity of happiness, but the mistaken objects of his affections are those of sense and time. In heaven it shall be otherwise, for the object of desire then is God alone. Hence there must be a transformation of the heart to make the things of God attractive to us now. It is necessary therefore to accustom ourselves to these spiritual realities and to keep the thought of heaven always before us, as our cherished goal. And thus the proper work of man is to regulate the soul, which means detaching oneself from worldly pleasures, so as to acquire the capacity to enjoy happiness in another world.

---

[93] No. 1.This is the theme of his first written sermon, entitled *On the Work of Man*..

[94] No. 12. The necessity for illumination on the true object of happiness is also made in No. 14.

[95] No. 6.

"It is this which renders the thought of heaven infinitely dear to the believer and the pursuits of the vain world inexpressibly trifling - he longs for that hour when his wound shall be completely healed and his triumphant and glorified spirit at length pure, spotless and perfect, shall be united to his God and Saviour for ever and ever."[96]

This radical opposition between God and the world, as the object of our affections, can also be seen in two of his published sermons.[97] The first is an early sermon which was revised in 1831,[98] while the second is a more recent composition first written and preached in 1840.[99] Together they form a diptych in which the contrast between man's natural desire, and the desire of heaven as the object of faith, is clearly illustrated. The continuity with Newman's early ideas is maintained but the opposition has become less strident and severe. It is also interesting to note how the later sermon concentrates more positively on the Christian aspiration for heaven, while still insisting that such a desire is a gift from God, and not something which nature itself suggests.

"If our hearts are by nature set on the world for its own sake and the world is one day to pass away, what are they to be set on, what to delight in then?...what are to be the pleasures of the soul in another life? can they be the same as they are here? They cannot; Scripture tells us they cannot...."[100]

The need for a transformation of the heart is reiterated but the exhortation to acquire holiness is now put in less moralistic tones. Newman had earlier proposed one's own self-interest as a motivation for change[101] but now nothing less than "the love of God can make us believe or obey Him" and "the love of heaven is the only way to

242

heaven."[102] The only way we can learn to appreciate the joys of heaven is by experiencing the gift of the Spirit in a life of holiness here. Heaven is a secret of the heart, and until we have tasted the spiritual delights which religion provides, we cannot form any ideas of what heaven is like. As the pleasures of sin are hidden from the angels, the pleasures of heaven are likewise unknown to the natural man.[103]

Holiness is the Means and Requirement for Heaven

The theme of holiness runs through the whole of Newman's sermons and cannot adequately be treated in the space of a few pages.[104] It is in fact the key to Newman's eschatology[105] for heaven is the end of the process of sanctification; it is the perfection of holiness itself. With respect to the present topic, consideration is confined to one aspect of holiness, namely, the connection between it and the blessedness of heaven.

Newman's very early interest in the relation between heaven and holiness can be found in an unpublished paper dated 1822 or 1823. It is from a concern about salvation that the question assumes fundamental importance for "without holiness, no man can see the Lord." Since heaven is not a natural reward it must be assumed that holiness, which is the means to it, is something greater than morality or religious observance. He argues therefore that its source and summit is found in the eternal world.

> "I shall assume that holiness is something higher and more difficult of attainment then mere morality or mere church-going - that it consists in a certain state of the heart and affections - including indeed good works and religious observances, but only as the external signs and evidences of an inward principle: in a word, that it arises from a practical

---

[102] P.P.S.viii,6.

[103] P.P.S.vii,14.

[104] Cf. P.Boyce, *J.H.Newman: The Birth and Pursuit of an Ideal of Holiness*, Rome, Center of Newman-Friends, 1979.

[105] Cf G.Rowell, *Hell and the Victorians*, Oxford, Clarendon Press, 1974, Ch.5.

conviction of the importance of eternal things."[106]

This "practical conviction" is demonstrated in the sermons by his insistence on its paramount importance from the very outset. Holiness is an inward principle which has been imparted by God, a new heart which we cannot acquire by our own efforts. Heaven and holiness are linked by the fact that neither of them can be merited by us.[107] Natural virtue deserves a natural reward, but holiness, like the blessedness of heaven, is of a different order. Moreover, not even Adam in the state of pure nature, had such a right.[108] Holiness is the wedding garment which is given to us, not acquired by our own effort or desire, and is the means to enable us to enter heaven. It is something we are to wear constantly - it is habitual - and is the only suitable attire for the heavenly banquet.[109] Holiness and heaven are so intrinsically related in Newman's mind that he encapsulates the relation in the axiom "holiness is heaven."[110] Heaven is attained through Christ the Sanctifier, who sets us on the path of holiness which surely and progressively leads to final blessedness.[111] Holiness is the end to which the Gospel is directed and anyone who lives in the hope of heaven must be purified by it.[112] The new world which Christ has brought is new only inasmuch as it is internally transformed; the external visible world has not been changed. He has altered the course of history by founding a spiritual kingdom of grace, whose inheritance will be the glory of heaven.[113]

In Newman's early sermons there is some ambiguity in his understanding of the nature of holiness. On the one hand, it appears as a forensic requirement without any right or reward of heaven, yet simultaneously his repeated emphasis on its inwardness as a heavenly principle, leads to a different conclusion. He believes that the promise of

---

[106] A 91. *Unpublished paper on Holiness* p. 1. dated by Newman as written in 1822 or 1823.

[107] No. 2.

[108] No. 6.

[109] No. 32.

[110] Abstract No. 44. The phrase may simply be a short-hand expression suitable for an abstract. However we find it again in a very late sermon, No. 569 p. 12.

[111] Abstract No. 60.

[112] No. 103. This is the concluding sermon of a course on sins.

[113] No. 114. Newman preached this sermon twelve times which illustrates the importance he attached to it. The sermon is based on Butler's Analogy.

244

heaven is attached to holiness, not by virtue of its nature, but gratuitously because of the promise of Christ. It was a duty commanded of the Jews without any expectation of heaven, for they were simply rewarded by temporal blessings. At the same time he sees an internal connection between the means and the end of sanctification. Holiness provides an internal capacity enabling us to enjoy the bliss of heaven, without in any way establishing a right to it.

> "Obedience does not purchase but prepares for it. The more we strive to obey God, the more is the inward principle of faith and devotion strengthened....that holiness is a condition of salvation, not because of any merit in it but because we could not enjoy salvation without it."[114]

On the other hand, holiness of its very nature prefigures the bliss of heaven, which is the end of the process of sanctification and its perfection.

> "Hence it is that the joys of heaven are represented in Scripture as but the continuation and perfection of present holiness..The grace which is *now* given him shall spread and increase and spring up within him everlastingly - or the eternal bliss of heaven is but a continuation of grace given here."[115]

The spiritual life is a unity connecting this world with the next. The state of grace and the state of glory are substantially the same and differ only in degree; on earth, our communion with God is unseen and lived by faith; in heaven it is face to face in perfect charity. Moreover the life of grace is not something static but is a process of progressive transformation into the likeness of God, which St. Paul describes as passing "from glory to glory."

> "In like manner, the word glory, which at first sight, we are tempted to confine to *future* happiness, is in the epistles not unfrequently applied to the sanctification of the Christian here - evidently showing that sanctification and the bliss of heaven are *in kind* the very same, the one being only the

---

[114] No. 97 p. 11.

[115] ibid.

perfection of the other. Thus St. Paul talks of our being changed into the image of Christ from *glory to glory*, meaning as it appears from one degree of holiness to a still higher - with allusion to progressive sanctification."[116]

From the above quotations it appears that Newman's view of sanctification as an imparted gift, which is of the same nature as the life of glory, was sufficiently developed long before his work on Justification. A Lutheran influence can still be detected, but the general thrust is consistent with his later sermons. His very first published sermon, Holiness necessary for Future Blessedness, may be seen as a statement of first principle in Newman's spiritual teaching.[117] It summarizes his early reflections and explains why holiness is a necessary qualification for heaven. Holiness is necessary not simply because of an external command by God, but "from the very nature of things." "None but the holy can look upon the Holy One; without holiness no man can endure to see the Lord." Even on the hypothesis that an irreligious person were allowed to enter heaven, he could not be happy there. He simply would not have the internal capacity to enjoy the things of heaven. Rather, for such a person it would be equivalent to the experience of hell. Without the principle of holiness, it is metaphysically impossible to remain face to face with God. Hence "heaven would be hell to an irreligious man."

This same idea is even more forcefully stated in a much later sermon on Christmas Day, 1837. Holiness is not a mere ticket to heaven, an admission card which we can throw away once we have gained entrance. Heaven would literally be a place of torment for the sinner, since the sight of a holy God would activate feelings of revulsion. There would be such rebellion inside his soul that he would think he was in hell. Moreover, he would be completely unconscious of the beauty around him and untouched by God's presence, since his character within is one of sin and rejection. Holiness alone gives us an experience of God and a consciousness of heaven.

"We think heaven must be a place of happiness to us, if we

---

[116] ibid p. 12.

[117] No. 153. This is the only sermon to be published from a course of fourteen given in 1829 *On the Letter to the Romans*. It was written in 1826 and then included in the course. Newman was unhappy with the course, possibly because his views on justification were not fully worked out. But he considered this sermon worthy of heading his first volume in 1834, P.P.S.i,1.

246

do but get there; but the great probability is, if we judge by what goes on here below, that a bad man, if brought to heaven, would not know he was in heaven - I do not go to the further question, whether on the contrary, the very fact of his being in heaven with all his unholiness upon him, would not be a literal torment to him and light up the fires of hell within him. This indeed would be a most dreadful way of finding out where he was. But let us suppose the lighter case: let us suppose he could remain in heaven unblasted, yet it would seem that at least he would not know that he was there."[118]

The emphasis on separation from the world and the stress on corrupt human nature, so prominent in his early sermons, might lead one to think that Newman's view of holiness is a distinctly negative one. However, as his interest turns to the mystery of the Incarnation the more positive side of holiness develops.[119] Personal sanctity is that which gives delight to God. He is not a God who merely insists on the duty to attain it, but enjoys the positive beauty He has implanted in His creatures. God's holiness is no longer defined by His distant separation from us in an austere heaven; He shares His holiness with His creation by becoming incarnate.

"There is one and only one state of soul which is pleasing to God - holiness, he takes delight in the holy - and therefore as one would look for in a holy God, He created all His creatures holy. He created those in whom He might take pleasure, those He might love and reward, who might be His servants and sons, not His enemies. This is the acceptable righteousness or justification of all moral beings, holiness."[120]

---

[118] P.P.S.iv,16.

[119] The Incarnation was a cornerstone in the theology of the Tractarians. Having read the Fathers, particularly Athanasius, Newman's theology becomes more incarnational.

[120] No. 441 p. 1.

What does Heaven consist in?

A radical opposition between this world and the next is part of the infrastructure of Newman's early sermons. It is a moral opposition, not a metaphysical one, but the antithesis is so severe as to lead to a virtual dichotomy. The single thread of holiness holds these two worlds together, and forms the basis of continuity between our present life and the next. Apart from holiness there could be nothing but a complete rupture between our present and future happiness.

Newman first of all declares that there can be no direct connection between the spiritual world of heaven and the corrupt material world of earth.[121] Opinions about the nature of heaven are often based on the false assumption that this world and the next admit of a comparison. Such an assumption, he believes, comes from a confusion of two distinct and unconnected categories. For example, people often assume from a naive sentimentalism, that the materially poor will enjoy prosperity in the next world, as a compensation for their sufferings here. However, the truth is that they are not saved because they are poor but because they have the habit of holiness.

> "We here see the origin of the mistake. Men forget or rather do not understand that the joys of heaven are different *in kind* and *nature*, altogether different from those of the world. They look upon heaven as a *place of happiness* - and no more - happiness in their ideas does not depend on any particular state of heart - or arise from some one and only one set of objects....Indeed the joys of heaven arising from holiness of soul are in their nature altogether different from the gratification which results from possessing worldly goods, and cannot be compared with it."[122]

Newman then examines two contemporary views on the nature of heaven, both of which arise from the common fallacy that heaven will resemble worldly pursuits and happiness. It was thought for example, that heaven would disclose all the secrets of the universe and would

---

[121] This principle of an antithesis between the spiritual and the material, the eternal and the temporal is the foundation of Newman's course *On Salvation and Future Promise*. One can also detect the sharp and rigorous logic of the Oriel School in these sermons.

[122] No. 90 pp. 4-5.

248

therefore consist in an infinite knowledge of Nature.[123] Newman dismisses this view by noting that while it may be true that heaven will unfold the secrets of religion, Scripture is almost totally silent on the subject of the natural world. We are commanded to grow in holiness, for that is the means to heaven, but there is no similar command to grow in the knowledge of natural science.

Another popular theory about the nature of heaven springs from the romanticism of the period. It is the picture of the reunion of departed friends.[124] Newman is more sympathetic to this opinion for there is something natural and reasonable in embracing such a hope. Moreover there is nothing repugnant to revelation in such a belief, for Scripture sometimes implies that heaven will be like it. The danger with the view however, is that it leads to sentimental attachments and is in fact an unwarranted assumption, since it clearly has not been promised. In heaven the special bonds of love for our friends and relatives will be absorbed in the love of the elect, who will constitute one great family, each member equally the object of our affection.

An even more serious objection to both of these views is that they place God in a subordinate role to that of the creature. Nature or natural bonds and friendships have become the object of our desires. Since neither view makes any reference to Christ, who is the very centre of heaven, they cannot in any way be considered a Christian vision of the next world.

> "In truth, if we make the promised joys of heaven consist in the acquisitions of science, or merely in the enjoyment of the company of our friends, we run the risk of excluding from heaven the God of heaven. We are indulging prospects of no *Christian* heaven - for Christ is the centre of the Christian heaven - and we may entertain the opinions in question without thinking of Christ."[125]

Both of these views, moreover, can be held by unbelievers and

---

[123] Newman may have in mind the revolutionary ideas on geology which were then current in Oxford. The reference may be to William Buckland who was appointed the first university lecturer in 1819 and his pupil Charles Lyell whose Principles of Geology created quite a stir. Cf. L. E. Elliot-Binns. *Religion in the Victorian Era*, p. 154.

[124] Newman's father had just died within the year and his mother and sisters were part of the congregation as he preached.

[125] No. 102 p. 7.

those who do not live religious lives. They do not require the one and only condition which makes admission to heaven possible, nor do they assume the essential thing in which heaven consists, as being the dwelling place of God and of Christ. Of the two theories the first is the more reprehensible. It so exalts creation as to tend towards a pantheistic conception in which Nature and God are identified. Nature however shares in the sin of the world and like man is in inner conflict with itself. It can only be redeemed by a fresh creation.[126] Thus what has been promised is not the world we see, but a *new* heavens and a *new* earth. Though the world of nature gives us a glimpse of its Maker, it groans, like man himself, under the burden of sin.

Anticipations such as these may however constitute a secondary source of happiness in heaven, but they do not represent what it essentially consists in. By making them the primary object of our desire "we are verging to an idolatrous attachment to things below. We are preferring the creature to the Creator."[127] Heaven is a spiritual kingdom where "there stands but one centre of admiration and love - God and the Lamb - He is the great object of our knowledge, affection and devotion." The only way to attain it is through holiness of life. Though at times our earthly happiness may seem as heaven, such fleeting experiences are merely foretastes and pledges, which in God's mercy are given for our encouragement to strive for a holy life.

Images of Heaven

We have seen how holiness is the slender thread of continuity between this world and the next. But for the most part in Newman's early sermons, discontinuity between the two is underlined. It is easier indeed to say what heaven does not consist in than to positively describe its joys. Our knowledge of it must at best be analogical, and thus we are obliged to have recourse to images to impress upon us the reality of heaven. The most frequent of these images in Newman's sermons is one based on the Communion of Saints.[128] It is the picture of "the whole

---

[126] Newman's view of nature is a deeply ambivalent one. Side by side with an apocalyptic vision of the end in which all creation will be burned up, we have passages of lyrical poetry on the beauty of God's creation. Both views can be seen in P.P.S.iv,13 on *The Invisible World*.

[127] No. 102 p. 10.

[128] The subject of the Communion of Saints has been treated in Chapter Four

250

body of the elect [which] will form one great family and all equally the
objects of our affection and love."[129] Such an image is a family portrait
of Christ who is in the centre surrounded by all His members. In
communion with Him perfect charity reigns; heaven is not a privatized
world of self-contained happiness but a society whose whole activity
consists in love.

> "Consider then it is a place of perfect charity - get ready to
> play your part well in it - there are no jealousies,
> misunderstandings, mutual slights or the memory of insults.
> The whole assembly will be of one heart and one soul for it
> will then be perfectly joined together and completed by that
> which every joint supplieth."[130]

Newman's ecclesiology during his period at St. Clement's was
generally restricted to the view of a spiritual kingdom without much
emphasis on the visible Church. His perspective was then set on the
future hope of glory when we will all dwell in God's House. The
Christian Church "will indeed be in heaven but has not arrived thither
yet."[131] As he gradually adopts the principles of the High Church,[132]
however, his concept of heaven becomes more and more anchored to the
image of the visible Church. A corresponding change takes place which
now shifts his perspective to the present, and his view becomes more
related to a realized experience of worship. Conversely, those who find
no comfort in coming to Church will scarcely find comfort in heaven.

> "Heaven then is not like this world; I will say what it is
> much more like, - a church....And therefore, a church is like
> heaven; viz. because both in the one and the other, there is a
> single sovereign subject - religion - brought before us."[133]

The Church is the temple of Christ and thus the hidden life of

---

under the Church as Eschatological Sign.

[129] No. 102 p. 9.

[130] No. 100 p. 18.

[131] No. 90 p. 13.

[132] Newman writes the following comment on the cover page of No. 157: "This is
one of the first if not the first declaration I made of High Church principles [dated]
Dec.10,1859."

[133] P.P.S.i,1.

heaven is within it. "The titles given it upon earth are a picture of what it will be absolutely in heaven," for heaven is the place where the Church will ultimately be gathered.[134] We need some haven or sanctuary from the distress of the world, and God has provided a sign of ultimate peace and shelter by giving us the Church. It is our temporary home which will one day be made eternal. "No wonder the text actually speaks of the Church as heaven upon earth."[135]

The idea of Christians enjoying the citizenship of heaven is also of frequent occurrence.[136] This idea of citizenship underlines the social nature of heaven - it is belonging to and participating in a society, the communion of saints. Through the Church we gain access to the invisible world and enter into union with Christ in prayer and worship. In this way we experience God's presence and thus form some understanding of heaven. The festivals of the Church are also meant to convey to us a foretaste of heaven. For if we are to enjoy heaven hereafter, we must first learn to rejoice in festivals here below.[137]

Christ is the Centre of Heaven

Newman's early sermons are mainly concerned with salvation, and heaven is understood primarily in soteriological terms, as the goal to which we are destined. The predominant emphasis is on Christ's work of Atonement rather than on His person. Related to this is the work of sanctification and so we find a corresponding emphasis on the Holy Spirit. It is in this context, in two of his early sermons, that we have the first reference to Christ and heaven.[138] The Spirit inspires us with a "heartfelt perception" of Christ who is our peace and our happiness. Through the Spirit, the Christian "sees sights a natural man cannot see - his soul is fixed on Christ." Finally it is the Spirit which brings us from glory to glory until we see "the Captain of our Salvation" face to face.

---

[134] P.P.S.ii,8.

[135] P.P.S.iv,12. This sermon is placed immediately after his sermon *The Communion of Saints* (P.P.S. iv, 11).

[136] Volume iv of Parochial and Plain Sermons contains a cluster of sermons on the Church in which this idea is prominent. P.P.S. iv, 10 - 16.

[137] No. 556 preached on Easter Day 1840.

[138] No. 12 and No. 14.

252

The weaving of holiness, peace and heaven is also found in a
course Newman gave on the 23rd psalm on the sufficiency of Christ for
all our needs.[139] Once again it is the work of Christ and the effects of
His redemption which is the focus of the sermons. Christ is the Giver
of peace,[140] the Sanctifier.[141] He will support us in death[142] and is a
refuge in trouble.[143] Lastly our assurance of final salvation comes from
the sacrifice of Christ who is our hope of glory.[144]

When we come to the published sermons a major change is
Newman's concept of heaven can be noted. His attention is turned
towards the mystery of the Incarnation and his view of heaven develops
along Christological lines. His perspective is influenced less by the
future than by the present realization that we are already in possession
of our inheritance. In the person of Christ heaven is present among us.
Up to then Newman had emphasized the distance between heaven and
our corrupt human condition, but now that our nature is viewed in the
light of the Incarnation, heaven comes closer to us. The thought of
heaven fills us with the thought of Christ's humanity, for our nature,
now renewed, is present there in the person of Christ.

"He came to show us what human nature might become, if
carried on to its perfection. Thus He teaches us to think
highly of our nature as viewed in Him; not (as some do) to
speak evil of our nature and exalt ourselves personally, but
while we acknowledge *our own* distance from heaven, to
view our *nature* as renewed in Him, as glorious and
wonderful beyond our thoughts."[145]

A similar development in Newman's understanding of heaven can
also be seen in his reflections on the mystery of the Ascension. Here
revelation conveys its message to us that the humanity of Christ has
been taken up to the Father. As a consequence of the Ascension, heaven

---

[139] The course consisted of Nos. 56, 58, 60, 62, 64 and 66 but only abstracts of the
sermons are extant.

[140] No. 58.

[141] No. 60.

[142] No. 62.

[143] No. 64.

[144] No. 66.

[145] P.P.S. i.13.

can no longer be thought of merely as a *state* of spiritual blessedness but as a *place* where the glorified body of Christ dwells.

> "First, Christ's Ascension to the right hand of God is marvellous, because it is a sure token that heaven is a certain fixed place, and not a mere state. That bodily presence of the Saviour which the Apostles handled is not here; it is not here; it is elsewhere, - it is in heaven."[146]

By describing heaven as a place, Newman wishes to preserve and protect the primary truth of Christ's bodily resurrection, and our own resurrection on the last day. He is aware that the language of faith differs from that of science and does not attempt to offer a cosmology of heaven. We have no knowledge of the next world which could be described as scientific, for the language of religion is a language of analogy. But neither can all reality by the same token, be comprehended in scientific terms, nor religious truth be regarded as little more than metaphor.[147]

Associated with the question of language is the influence of the romantic literature of the period on Newman's view of heaven. Wordsworth's famous verse that "heaven lies about us in our infancy" finds echoes in Newman's contemplation of childhood as the vestige of our original state of innocence. With the loss of innocence goes our loss of a sense of heaven. Though we have been born through baptism into a state of privilege, sin has dulled our minds to the truth that we are heirs of heaven. This sense of wonder and beauty is restored by the mystery of Christ and His presence among us. We have been called into a spiritual childhood as adopted sons of God and our lives are hidden in Christ. Thus the Christian can secretly live with the thought of heaven before him.

> "to live in heaven in their thoughts, motives, aims, desires, likings, prayers, intercessions, even while they are in the flesh; to look like other men....but the while to have a secret channel of communication with the Most High, a gift the world knows not of; to have their life hid with Christ in

---

[146] P.P.S. ii,18.

[147] J. Coulson in his book, *Newman and the Common Tradition* notes the difference between fiduciary language as in poetry and religious truth, and scientific language.

God."[148]

Being near to Christ becomes synonymous with being near to heaven. Heaven is our birthright[149] and Christ is the shepherd of our souls on our pilgrim journey; we are in search of a better country, in search of Christ.[150] Though our destination is not immediately seen, we have the presence of Christ on the journey and "we see more of the next world than we know we see."[151] We are not to make our own hearts our home, but to call heaven our home, for that is where Christ dwells. At the end of our pilgrimage the full disclosure of His presence will be made, a presence we have had all along the way.

> "The one thing which is all in all to us, is to live in Christ's presence; to hear His voice, to see His countenance."[152]

Christ is the only way to a knowledge of heaven. All other views are the figment of the imagination and wishful thinking. Our concept of heaven is not the product of a happiness we idealize for ourselves, but is grounded on the humanity of Christ. His glorified human nature still bears the marks of the cross, and thus reminds us that suffering is the only way to heaven. Our blessedness depends entirely on how we become like Him, and it is only by our recognition of Him that we form any recognition of heaven.

> "It is we who are not blessed, except as we approach Him, except as we are like Him, except as we love Him. Woe unto us, if in the day in which He comes from Heaven we see nothing desirable or gracious in His wounds; but instead have made for ourselves an ideal blessedness, different from that which will be manifested to us in Him."[153]

---

[148] P.P.S.vi.8.

[149] P.P.S.vi.2.

[150] P.P.S.viii,16.

[151] P.P.S.vi,8.

[152] P.P.S.vi.3.

[153] P.P.S.vii,2. Here we have an allusion to the story told in the life of Martin of Tours about a vision of a heavenly figure like Christ. Suspecting it was a snare of Satan, the saint demands to see the wounds of Calvary as confirmation that it was authentic. Cf. *Church of the Fathers*, 4th ed., London, Burns, Oates and Co., 1868 p. 355-6.

The bliss of heaven is the joy of seeing Christ face to face. Some idea of the effect heaven will have on us is shown in the conversion of St. Paul; an instant transformation took place by the momentary vision he was given. If such a remarkable change can occur by a fleeting glimpse of Christ, what then will be the rapturous joy of heaven when we see Him, not just for an instant but for all eternity? "If such be the effect of a momentary vision of the glorious presence of Christ, what think you, my brethren, will be their bliss, to whom it shall be given, this life ended, to see that Face eternally?"[154]

Peace in the End

The gift of peace is very closely associated with the notion of holiness in the mind of Newman. He first considers it as a natural concomitant of holiness[155] but later realizes that in this world peace and holiness are not always found together. Sometimes a choice must be made to obey the maxim of Scott and choose "holiness rather than peace." Moreover, while it should follow that the holy person enjoys the comfort of peace, God in His providence sends trouble and anxiety lest we should be content with our present condition.[156] He therefore withdraws His peace from time to time to create in us the desire for His future blessing in heaven.

"Lastly, these hidings of God's presence lead us to look forward with ardent expectation to the life to come - had we entire and uninterrupted peace here we might be satisfied to remain as we are - but being subject to vanity we wait for heaven."[157]

Peace is the natural fruit of holiness and when we talk of God withdrawing it from His servants, we are speaking in relative terms. It is intended as a clear mark of discernment of God's presence. Nevertheless since life is a spiritual warfare it would be unreasonable to expect lasting peace in this world. It is only in heaven where perfect

---

154 P.P.S.viii.15.

155 No. 32; No. 33.

156 Nos.47,48,49. This course of sermons was entitled *God's Hiding Himself*.

157 No. 48 p. 20.

peace will be united to perfect holiness. Heaven then is distinguished from the present world by the everlasting peace it brings. And it is to this peace that all God's work and providence tends:

> "All God's providences, all God's dealings with us, all His judgments, mercies, warnings, deliverances tend to peace and repose as their ultimate issue...after all the changes and chances of this troubled unhealthy state, at length comes death, at length the white Throne of God, at length the Beatific Vision...after restlessless comes rest, peace, joy - our eternal portion, if we be worthy - the sight of the Blessed Three, the Holy One."[158]

Christ is the Giver of Peace[159] who has already entered His rest. He is in the place of peace which one day will be ours, for in Him the Sabbath of humanity is begun.

> "Christ is already in that place of peace, which is all in all...He is in the very abyss of peace, where there is no voice or tumult or distress but a deep stillness - stillness, that greatest and most awful of all goods which we can fancy - that most perfect of joys, the utter, profound, ineffable tranquillity of the Divine Essence. He has entered into His rest."[160]

Summary of Chapter Five

Two clear principles were evident in Newman's individual eschatology which bound together the three parts of the chapter. The first principle was the idea of sanctification as an ever-developing process, which began with baptismal incorporation into Christ and came to full maturity in union with God in heaven. This process in Newman's view entailed two stages of spiritual growth, an active stage of good works, and a contemplative stage hereafter when the fruit of grace was matured. Death not only marked the end of the first stage, which was a state of probation, but gave it its particular character as a time of

---

[158] P.P.S.vi.25.

[159] The title of No. 58.

[160] P.P.S.vi.16.

working out one's salvation. It was not the termination of Christian life but the point of transition to an intermediate state. Newman described the latter as an indeterminate period in which the spiritual ore was purified and refined. It was a period of hopeful waiting until the Second Coming of Christ. The final state was heaven, a place of eternal blessedness, where none but the holy could enter.

The second idea which threaded through Newman's eschatology was the doctrine of the Communion of Saints. This linked the subject of the present chapter with the previous one on the Church as eschatological sign. Newman showed that the individual Christian concretely embodied the life of the Church in its journey towards the New Jerusalem. Being part of the pilgrim Church, the individual member was in communion with the faithful departed, and the apparent finality of death did not interrupt the bond of union between members in Christ. Moreover, the faithful at rest enjoyed the special privilege of interceding for those who were left behind. Finally, the individual was destined for a consummated union with Christ, who was the centre of heaven. This union of the Church in glory was described under the image of the Communion of Saints gathered around their Head.

CHAPTER SIX

ESCHATOLOGY AND CHRISTIAN LIFE

In this dissertation I have been engaged up to now in mapping out the content of Newman's eschatology. In so doing, the unfortunate impression may be given that the Anglican sermons were highly theoretical, and scarcely apt to inspire devotion. From the records of those who heard them, however, they were regarded as a tour de force in practical Christianity. Though he offered some very strong meat, his remarkable achievement was to create the perfect marriage between doctrine and life.[1] The themes of eschatology were vividly presented and imbued with a pastoral concern for the spiritual welfare of his flock. Newman believed that knowledge which is not born of lived experience is barren[2] and that doctrine was meant to activate and deepen the spirituality of those under his care. Hence his theology of the last things is clearly intended for its practical import on Christian living, which is thereby shaped and directed towards ultimate fulfilment in Christ.

For Newman, eschatology was understood as a dimension of the spiritual life hidden with Christ in God. This was to be found in the experience of communion with Him, made possible by the gift of the Spirit. This spiritual encounter is with one who has already entered into His glory and is now making intercession for us. Our present life needs therefore to be seen in the light of the next, where Christ waits for us, and where our journey of faith ends.[3] The task then which Newman undertakes is to lead us to a vivid realization of Christ's presence in which the now and the not-yet of eschatology are grasped and acted upon. It is not a theory by which future events are forecast, but a reality

---

[1] Speaking of the spirit of the Oxford Movement, which was so clearly characterized in Newman's sermons, R.C.Church notes the "two distinct though connected lines. It was on the one hand, theological; on the other resolutely practical" Cf. R.C. Church, *The Oxford Movement , Twelve Years 1833-1845*. London, Macmillan and Co., 1892. p. 190.

[2] P.P.S.vi.18.

[3] Newman's eschatology may be thought of as a commentary on the Epistle to the Hebrews to which he frequently refers. Many of the themes we find there are woven into his sermons: e.g. the emphasis on faith in realizing the unseen world, the means of access to God's presence through the liturgy, the Communion of Saints, the power of intercession and the reading of the present life in the light of the next.

accessible by concrete acts of faith. In this way the doctrine of the last things, not in the sense of being last in time but ultimate in meaning, is brought within the lived experience of the Christian.

The present chapter is divided into two parts and aims at showing how Newman integrates belief in the world to come with the practice of Christian living. The first part begins with the realization of the unseen world, in which he invites us to meditate on the end of all things, as something real and palpable. The concrete means to this experience is the act of worship in the Liturgy and in personal prayer, which enables us to live as though the End has come. Such a realization however is partial and provisional, for we have not yet attained the full stature of Christian maturity. This is underlined by the practice of fasting and self-denial which acts as a permanent reminder that salvation is yet to come. Thus the positive act of devotion and the negative denial of self makes "the inward light grow brighter and brighter, and God manifests Himself in us...."[4] It is through these means that we gradually learn how God may become all in all.

Part Two of the chapter is devoted to the significance of the Eucharist as the heavenly banquet. As the highest act of worship it brings us as close as we can get to an anticipation of the next world, while demanding in the same instance a giving over of oneself.

Part One
The Liturgy and the World to Come

Realizing God's Presence

A brief outline has been given in Chapter Three of how Newman described the invisible world known to the believer. The purpose then was to show the basis on which statements about eschatology can be made, keeping in mind that they are totally within the realm of faith. We now pick up this thread of thought to examine further how the unseen world is a reality, not merely to be described, but to be lived, or in Newman's own words, to be "realized."[5]

---

[4] P.P.S.iii,18.

[5] The sermons on "realization" are to be found well into Newman's mature period. They are generally on the subject of internalizing the privileges of Christian life. The

Newman's most damning indictment of anything is summed up in his dismissive remark that it is "unreal." Belief is unreal when we "cultivate the religious affections separate from religious practice"[6]; it is a counterfeit or unauthentic profession. Belief is real, on the other hand, when there is a correspondence between thought and feeling, which moves us to decisive action. "When men realize a truth, it becomes an influential principle within them, and leads to a number of consequences both in opinion and in conduct."[7] True knowledge consists not in theoretical notions, but in the real apprehension of things; it means that we not only grasp what we perceive, but are grasped by it - we become part of that reality, and it in turn becomes part of us. Truth resonates with what is real and has its own distinctive ring. Thus words like "heaven" and "hell" only ring true when they come from a real experience of the unseen world; otherwise they sound as hollow platitudes. It is as if "all these great words, heaven, hell, judgment, mercy, repentance, works, the world that now is, the world to come, [were] little more than lifeless sounds, whether of pipe or harp."[8]

We must aim therefore at things and not at words, at the reality, rather than its representation, and then our words and feelings will find the right expression, in a natural way. We know from experience that things "are but shadows to us and delusions, unless we enter into what they really mean."[9] Likewise, the doctrine of the last things is mere words, if it is not the fruit of a lived experience of God's presence. This is only possible through faith, for faith is "the realizing of things hoped for, the evidence of things unseen." The utmost Christians can do "is to believe, what they cannot see now, what they shall see hereafter; and as believing, to act together with God towards it."[10] However, this experience of God can be more real than if we were to see Him through our senses. "You will perceive that there is a sense, and a true sense, in which the *invisible* presence of God is more awful and overpowering

---

acute awareness of sin, i.e. its realization, was of course already there from the beginning, though not spoken of as "realization."

[6] P.P.S.ii,30; v,3: "the exhibition of thought disjoined from its practice."

[7] P.P.S.vi,18. Newman is not suggesting that all forms of realization are to be commended. It is our duty for example not to actualize temptations, but rather to avoid them.

[8] P.P.S.v,3.

[9] P.P.S.v,3.

[10] P.P.S.iv,17.

than if we saw it."[11] Like Moses, we see the promised land only at a distance; but though we are "as yet not admitted to heavenly glory, yet are given to see much, in preparation for seeing more."[12] The vision of the King in all His glory, which the saints see hereafter, can be applied "in a true and sufficient sense" to our present state.[13] We therefore have all the notes of truth before us, all the means to that truth are given us, if we would but enter and discern His presence.

> "We are no longer in the region of shadows: we have the true Saviour set before us, the true reward, and the true sense of spiritual renewal. We know the true state of the soul by nature and by grace, the evil of sin, the consequences of sinning, the way of pleasing God, and the motives to act upon it."[14]

The difficulty then for Christians is not so much the need of greater evidence for their belief, but their lack of sensibility to the unseen world. It is not so much a question of assent, but of humbly submitting to truth so as to engage the heart. Moreover, assent to a belief is prior to the realization of it. "When we are told a thing, we assent to it, we do not doubt it, but we do not feel it to be true, we do not understand it as a fact which must take up a position or station in our thoughts, and must be acted from, and acted towards, must be dealt with *as* existing; that is we do not realize it."[15] This insensibility, however, is not always morally culpable, but may be due to purely natural reasons. Often great joys and sorrows do not register at first in our minds - we are simply shocked or numbed before coming to a vivid awareness of them; the mere wish, moreover, to understand what has happened is not enough. "It is always very difficult to realize any great joy or sorrow. We cannot realize it by wishing to do so."[16]

Among these factors which block the realization of experience Newman includes "bodily disorder ... anxious self-tormenting dispositions ... depression of spirits .... deadness of the affections."

---

[11] P.P.S.v.2.

[12] ibid.

[13] ibid.

[14] P.P.S.v.3.

[15] P.P.S.vi.8.

[16] ibid.

262

There are, moreover, many upright men "whose religion is of a dry and cold character, with little heart or insight into the next world."[17] But all of these reasons are, in fact, deficiencies, due to human infirmity or, more seriously, to a want of faith. What God intends for us really, is to experience His presence, an experience which, Newman observes, is attended with profound feelings of reverence and joy.

> "They are the class of feelings we *should* have, - yes, have in an intense degree - if we literally had the sight of Almighty God; therefore they are the class of feelings which we shall have, *if* we realize His presence. In proportion as we believe that He is present, we shall have them; and not to have them, is not to realize, not to believe that He is present."[18]

Far from suggesting euphoria or cries of enthusiasm, the feelings Newman speaks of are quiet and often undetected. We should not be discouraged, he says, when we are not bubbling over as we think we should. A subdued response to Easter joy is no reason to doubt the sincerity of our celebration. "We *do* feel joy; we feel more joy than we know we do. We see more of the next world than we know we see."[19] The answer to our difficulty is really a matter of time; we have in fact had the experience of joy but not yet discovered its meaning. And so for all the privileges of the Christian life. It is only by the slow process of "meditation, prayer and work" that "we attain to a real apprehension of what we are" and "approach to the clear view of what God has made us in Christ."[20] This process follows "a remarkable law" which is governed by the power of memory.[21] Though we are brought into the presence of God, His "presence is not discerned at the time when it is upon us, but afterwards when we look back on what is gone and over."[22] It is in the act of re-member-ing, of re-collect-ing or putting together the elements of our experience, that we realize in a vivid way what actually took place. Events act upon us but meaning and recognition come only afterwards – as Newman points out:

---

[17] P.P.S.iv.9.

[18] P.P.S.v.2.

[19] P.P.S.vi.8.

[20] ibid.

[21] Newman's account of how actualization comes from remembrance is reminiscent of Augustine's account of memory in Book x of the Confessions.

[22] P.P.S.iv.17.

"...everyone of us surely must have experienced this general
feeling most strongly, at one time or other, as regards the
Sacraments and Ordinances of the Church. At the time, we
cannot realize, we can but believe that Christ is with us, but
after an interval a sweetness breathes from them, as from His
garments... Services at the time we could not enjoy, from
sickness, from agitation, from restlessness -Services which
at the time, in spite of belief in their blessedness, yet troubled
our wayward hearts...We come like Jacob, in the dark, and
lie down with a stone for our pillow; but when we rise again
and call to mind what has passed ... we are led to cry out
How dreadful is this place! This is *none other* than the
house of God and this is the gate of heaven."[23]

We can now look at the concrete experiences of God's presence,
in public worship and the sacraments, in personal prayer and fasting, to
examine how eschatology can be instanced in the life of the believer.

The Liturgy and Its General Relation to Eschatology

The liturgy is centred around the mystery of Christ in whom the
kingdom of God is fulfilled. It is the way the Church daily relives the
memory of our Saviour and celebrates His victory in heaven. Public
worship proclaims the reign of God in the Church, as both present and
yet to come, a reign which is inseparable from the person and work of
Christ. Hence it is imbued with the spirit of furthering God's kingdom
and its perfection. This characteristic is what may be called the
eschatological dimension of the liturgy, which will now be considered,
first in general terms and then in the act of worship itself.

Newman's close attention to the Prayer-Book in his early sermons
shows an instinctive grasp of the importance of the liturgy in Christian
life. His understanding is as yet, however, inchoate and implicit until he
comes to read the Fathers of the Church. By 1830 a breakthrough
comes in a course of sermons,[24] which, however imperfect he

---

[23] ibid.

[24] Course xxx consists of ten sermons, Nos. 224-233. The course follows
immediately upon his course on *Personal Religion and Private Prayer*, Nos. 220-223.

considered them,[25] are a synthesis of the principles which inform the liturgy. Thereafter, we find a growing confidence in his understanding of worship and a corresponding influence of it in his sermons.[26] When we come to the last years of Newman's Anglican period, the liturgical foundation and framework of his preaching becomes explicit.[27]

He divides the year into two periods with a line marked by the Feast of the Holy Trinity.[28] The first half looks back to the prelude and history of Christ's life, the second looks forward to the end of redemption now carried out by the Spirit. In this division the principle of eschatology is implied. "Hitherto we have celebrated His great works; henceforth we magnify Himself. Now, for twenty-five weeks we represent in figure what is to be hereafter ... for half a year we stand still, as occupied solely in adoring Him."[29] The future of Christ's humanity and our future in Him, is the object of the Church's contemplation, once the Spirit has been given.

> "And thus in commemorating the Spirit's gracious office during the past week [Pentecost], we were brought in our series of representations, to the end of all things; and now what is left but to commemorate what will follow after the end? the return of the everlasting reign of God, the infinite peace and blissful perfection."[30]

---

[25] When requiested by Miss Giberne four years later to have them published, Newman thought them not good enough to do so. L.D., Vol.iv, p. 147. Three of the ten sermons were in fact published viz. P.P.S iii,6 (227); vii,18 (231) and vii,7 (232).

[26] Newman wanted the title of his second volume of sermons to reflect the liturgy of the Saints' Days, but Rivington, his publisher overruled his wish. Because of the popularity of Parochial Sermons the publishing house prevailed upon him to retain the title. Newman finally reached a compromise with Rivington by the Fifth and Sixth volumes, which had the subtitles of the Winter and Spring Quarter of the Liturgical year. His intention to complete the series with a third and fourth volume was overtaken by circumstances.

[27] In the sixth volume of Parochial Sermons we have explicit references to the Christian Life as the reiteration of the life of Christ presented to us in the Liturgy. Cf. P.P.S.vi,11; vi,25.

[28] Within this major division the liturgical year is subdivided by Newman into the Sacramental Season (Lent), The Season of Grace (Epiphany), The Season of Sincerity of Purpose (Christmas) and The Season of Faith (Easter) Cf.P.P.S.vi,11; Advent is "a time of purification...a season for remembering what we are and what we shall be" Cf.P.P.S.v,1.

[29] P.P.S.vi,25.

[30] ibid.

This of course does not mean that it is only after Pentecost when we begin to take note of eschatology in the liturgy. At all times, the Church by her public worship makes an offering to Christ, which denotes her gratitude for the present gift of salvation and her resolve to prepare for the final handing over of her life. This is the only object of the Christian minister - "to offer souls (so to express myself), to bring men near to God, to bind them to God's service and to save them in the end."[31] This service is one of thanksgiving, not of atonement,[32] and in one sense is a future offering, but in another a present one. It is related both to the world to come and to our present stage of growth in the fullness of Christ.

> "This I say is his only object - he is ever preparing that offering when His Master shall take account of His stewardship - That one final offering is his present hope and his joy - In this sense his offering is future, but in another sense, whenever he is enabled to do good, whenever he raises one good thought or desire in another's heart, urges him to one good action he presents a present not a future offering to God and thus he may be said to be ever executing the priest's office about the gospel of God."[33]

A further allusion to eschatology and an indication of how Newman perceived it as a principle imbedded in the liturgy, can be seen in his reflections on the origin and the nature of Christian worship. Here we recall the Communion of Saints and the heavenly Jerusalem. The liturgy is the voice of the Church[34] under the inspiration of the Spirit. Its prayers "have been the sacrifice of faith for many centuries; in the use of them saints of all ages and many countries are bound together in unity."[35] The early Christians who composed them have now passed on to glory, but their bond of communion with the pilgrim Church is unbroken. Their worship continues in the same manner as before, though at an infinitely deeper level. Just as the state of grace and

---

[31] No. 224 p. 4.

[32] The offering which Newman is speaking of is the existential offering of one's own life. In Christ's case it was one of atonement; in the Church's case, it is one of thanksgiving, and both of these are figuratively represented in the liturgy.

[33] ibid. p. 6.

[34] No. 225 p. 23.

[35] No. 226 p. 24.

the state of glory are one and the same, our present liturgy and the worship of heaven are likewise one in substance.

> "And now they are worshipping Him in a place and form far better than any earthly temple supplies - yet their worship is not in substance different from what it was as we know from the Book of Revelation. They use the same words, though doubtless they understand more fully the meaning which these words convey. This thought should teach us reverence. We use high titles in speaking of God which mean much more than we conceive. How much it is to call Him eternal."[36]

The Christian life is represented in its entirety in the Liturgy. It is a synthesis of three fundamental elements:- it consists in knowledge of the faith, in conduct befitting it, and in celebration of the new life in Christ.[37] These elements form the structure of Newman's course which he treats under three aspects or objectives. The Liturgy teaches doctrine, it forms the Christian character, and it expresses the love and communion of the Church in Christ. "In the Prayer Book then we have a system of doctrine, a practical lesson of holiness, and a bond of permanent peace, unity and concord." Each of these objectives has an import for eschatology - "Think of that day which must come, when you will be called to judgment - and what will you say then to excuse your neglect of so great a privilege as the services of the Church."[38]

As regards its teaching function, the liturgy has a "peculiar power...a most winning and impressive way"[39] of presenting the message of Scripture. It is in fact pedagogically more effective than Scripture in conveying the truths of faith, for the Bible is "a large volume - the perfect holy character of it is not traced out on its surface - it is hid deep in the book."[40] Moreover, "in the prayers of the Liturgy

---

36 ibid.

37 The affinity between Newman and Kant has sometimes been drawn particularly in the area of morality. Cf. C.C.J.Webb, *Religious Thought in the Oxford Movement*, London 1928, Ch.3. Though Newman did not come to read Kant until much later in life, Kant's fundamental questions, which have a special relevance for eschatology viz. "What can I know?," "What must I do?" and "What may I hope for?" provide a parallel for faith in the structure of Newman's Liturgy course.

38 No. 225 p. 28.

39 ibid.

40 ibid. p. 19.

we have Scripture digested and commented on by those whose hearts the Holy Ghost has cleansed and made His temple."[41] Thus for example, "in the Burial Service we find especially displayed the consoling doctrine of the resurrection of the body and the life everlasting."[42] But as well as containing the bright promise of eternal life, the Burial Service reminds us of the severe truth of future judgment.

> "Thus the burial service may be profitably meditated on by all of us - each for himself reflecting how awful the contrast his own case will be if, while Christians thank God for him, he then shall be one of those cursed spirits who have made their time of trial a preparation not for heaven but for hell-fire."[43]

The liturgy also teaches us knowledge about one's duty and the orientation of Christian life. The knowledge of faith is always linked in Newman's mind with the doing of faith, or in other words, with obedience. Faith is something practical; it is "the practical perception of the unseen world." Both faith and obedience represent the same state of mind, imply the same spirit of surrender and are oriented to the world to come: "To believe is to look beyond this world to God, and to obey is to look beyond this world to God."[44] But lest we forget our present privileges as Christians and dream away our lives with thoughts of the future, Newman reminds us, in his very next sermon, of the present means of grace and the state of salvation into which we are already called.[45]

---

[41] ibid. p. 22; P.P.S.iii.17; ii.7.

[42] ibid. p. 16.

[43] No. 229 p. 28. In Tract No. III *On Alterations in the Liturgy*, we have an appendage in which the motives for not altering the Liturgy are applied to the Burial Service. Changes had been suggested on the grounds that the service held too high a hope of eternal life for the departed person. Newman will have no diminution of the strong expression of hope contained in the service. "We hear complaints about the Burial Service, as unsuitable for the use for which it was intended. It expresses a hope, that the person departed, over whom it is read, will be saved.....Do you pretend you can discriminate the wheat from the tares? of course not."

[44] P.P.S.iii.6. This is the published version of No. 227 whose original title was *The Liturgy, first, teaches doctrine - viz concerning man's duty*. The published title is *Faith and Obedience*.

[45] No. 228. A reference to the uniqueness of Christian salvation has been made in Chapter Three.

The second use of the Liturgy and its relation to eschatology need not detain us as it has been treated already under the theme of hope,[46] and shall later be considered under self-denial and fasting.[47] Hope and self-denial, however, are designed for one thing only, and that is love, which is the fullest expression of Christian identity. In coming therefore to the third use of the Liturgy, Newman recapitulates what he has said on the formation of Christian character to show how it is linked to its final object. The sermon is related to the Litany of the Saints[48] through which the Church reminds us of our ultimate communion in the New Jerusalem. Newman's last note therefore is on love which gives completeness. It is all that remains when faith and hope have been perfected and when God has become all in all. Quoting the example of St. John, Newman concludes:

> "when he was old and could with difficulty come to Church, and had no strength to preach, had but one word in his mouth - Little children love one another; and when his disciples asked him why he was so frequent in one and the same precept, he said, because it is the Lord's, and because it is all in all."[49]

The Act of Worship and the Sacraments

We now come to examine the act of worship and the sacraments, and how Newman relates them to the world to come. The purpose of coming to church, he tells us, is not to hear the sermon, but to offer the active worship of united prayer and praise. "God's grace is promised not through preaching, but through the sacraments and through whatever has a sacramental character, and public prayer is of this kind."[50] These are the means by which we prepare for the next world.

---

[46] No. 230. *The Liturgy, second, forms the character viz. to hope.* Cf. also No. 233 pp. 5-6. This has been treated under Chapter Three.

[47] No. 232 in its published version is P.P.S.vii,7. This is treated in another section of this chapter. The sermon has reference to the Commination and Lent Services.

[48] No. 233 is entitled *The Liturgy forming the character viz. to charity - The Litany.*

[49] No. 233 p. 10. This is a later redaction for St.John's Day in 1838.

[50] No. 290 .

Hence the "most momentous reason for religious worship... [is]...to prepare us for this future glorious and wonderful destiny, the sight of God - a destiny which, if not most glorious, will be most terrible."[51] In the services of worship we have the "anticipations and first-fruits of that sight of Him, which one day must be."[52] It is with this view in mind, with the view to our future full encounter with God, that we come to church. In so doing we are granted "a glimpse of a Form which we shall see hereafter face to face" and are allowed to enter heaven though we do not see it.

> "I come then to Church, because I am an heir of heaven. It is my desire and hope one day to take possession of my inheritance: and I come to make myself ready for it, and I would not see heaven yet, for I could not bear to see it. I am allowed to be in it without seeing it, that I may learn to see it. And by psalm and sacred song, by confession and praise, I learn my part."[53]

The act of worship is the entrance into the presence of God. It is the connecting link between our present and future life. This link however, may be regarded in one of two ways; it may be thought of as a series of stepping stones set across a perilous river, or as a secure bridge spanning both banks. The degree of continuity is estimated differently, depending on the perspective of eschatology. In Newman's earlier view, we have an emphasis on the chasm which exists between the present life and the life to come. This world has nothing of the face of heaven on it; it is noisy and troublesome and full of constant interruption. How unlike it is to the future presence of God "which may best be described as an endless and uninterrupted worship of the Eternal Father, Son and Spirit"! Hence "we are distinctly told, that the future life will be spent in God's *presence*, in a sense which does not apply to our present life."[54] Nevertheless, he still recognizes the power of worship to ford the stream between time and eternity, though it is at best tenuous and uncertain.

Newman's estimation, however, of how close we are to God grows

---

[51] P.P.S.v,1.

[52] ibid.

[53] ibid..

[54] P.P.S.i,1.

270

as the sacramental principle develops, and a more confident conviction in the power of worship may be seen. "I referred just now to our Sacred Services; these again, may be made to furnish a support to our faith and hope. He who comes to church to worship God, be he high or low, enters into that heavenly world of Saints of which I have been speaking. For in the services of worship we elicit and realize the invisible."[55] The connection between the two worlds is now more securely fastened. Though a veil hangs between them, it is not so opaque or unmoveable as to prevent a continuous and sure sight of God. Though our encounter is not face to face, we truly enjoy an experience of Christ's presence, as Newman explains:

> "That veil is so far removed in the Gospel, that we are in a state of preparation for its being altogether removed. We are with Moses in the Mount so far, that we have a sight of God; we are with the people beneath it so far that Christ does not visibly show Himself. He has put a veil on, and He sits among us silently and secretly. When we approach Him, we know it is only by faith; and when He manifests Himself to us, it is without our being able to realize to ourselves that manifestation."[56]

As Newman's eschatology becomes more and more realized, God, who is the sole object of worship, appears more and more in human form. The incarnation is the cornerstone, and the sacraments the vehicle, which transport us into the presence of Christ. "The sacraments are the instruments the Holy Ghost uses"[57] of "those heavenly glories which are concentrated in Him."[58] With the sacraments we have the certainty of God's present favour, and the assurance, if we are faithful, of His future gift of eternal life. They are the "keys which open the treasure-house of mercy - ordinances in which we not only ask, but receive, and know we receive...the certainty of God's present favour...[and that He] will so supply our need, that henceforth we shall lack nothing for the completion and overflowing sanctification of our defective and sinful nature."[59] With Christ and in Him, heaven and earth meet; though He

---

[55] P.P.S.iii,17.

[56] P.P.S.v,1.

[57] P.P.S.iii,16.

[58] P.P.S.iii,20.

[59] ibid.

has gone to the Father, He has left us signs of His presence and power, in which He is all but visibly revealed.

> "To view Christ as all but visibly revealed -to look upon His ordinances, not in themselves, but as signs of His presence and power, as the accents of His love, the very form and countenance of Him who ever beholds us, ever cherishes us - to see Him thus revealed in glory day by day ...in which by faith, we see Him manifested day by day, and through which we hope to receive the imputation of those merits, once for all wrought out on the cross, and our effectual help in the day of account."[60]

The sacraments are neither empty rituals nor dead forms of worship, for there is nothing dead and earthly under the Gospel.[61] To abandon them in the name of a supposedly higher goal of spiritual religion is, in Newman's view, to espouse a false anthropology. "We may as well expect that the spirits of men might be seen by us without the intervention of their bodies, as suppose that the Object of faith can be realized in a world of sense and excitement without the instrumentality of an outward form..."[62] Since there is "no such thing as abstract religion...the forms of devotion are part of devotion."[63] They are "the slender threads on which precious pearls are strung," and hence we must beware of those "who hope, by inducing us to lay aside our forms, at length to make us lay aside our Christian hope altogether."[64] Since they are impregnated with the spirit of Christ, it is Him and Him alone whom we touch through the medium of an external form.

> "Which of our ordinances is not expressly adapted to bring Christ before us?... Surely all our rites are full of Him and full of Him alone...These are His breath, His word, His touch, the hem of His garment - they are left us as

---

[60] P.P.S.iii,19.

[61] P.P.S.iii,19; vii,16.

[62] P.P.S.ii,7. Newman here shows the complementary nature of Scripture and the Liturgy of the Church similar to what we have seen in the Liturgy course: "Scripture gives the *spirit* and the Church the *body*, to our worship."

[63] ibid.

[64] ibid.

memorials of Him full of virtue."[65]

The presence of Christ elicited in the sacraments endows the act of worship with an experience of the ever present. For worship is the highest form of transcendence in which we lose ourselves fully in the object of love. "The mind is not detained for a moment from Him ..."[66] With our minds and hearts transfixed on Christ, we experience a new order of being, in which the things of time and place are suspended,[67] but which for all that, is not illusory. "Time and space have no portion in the spiritual Kingdom which He has founded; and the rites of His Church are as mysterious spells by which He annuls them both."[68] Though we are bodily anchored in this world, we are lifted spiritually, to become "as it were, sensible of the contact of something more than earthly. We know not where we are."[69] Time flows into eternity and place is transformed into presence. The "endless and uninterrupted worship" which defined the future life, is brought to us in the liturgical rite, which thus provides a present anticipation of the world to come. This is the true significance of the Gospel privileges - to enable the Christian to live God's own mode of being, the life of eternity as the ever present.[70]

The effects of the fruitful participation in the liturgy are to be seen in the lives of Christians. They have witnessed the New Jerusalem and have drunk deep of the waters of the risen life. They have received a power which sets them above all earthly things, and can speak like prophets whose strength comes solely from God. They have tasted "the

---

[65] No. 381 pp. 16-17.

[66] P.P.S.iii,19.

[67] The distinction between time as measurable duration (philosophic time) and time as lived experience (durée réelle), is pertinent to the question of worship Cf. E.Brunner, *Eternal Hope, pp.* 42-58; J.L.Ruiz de la Peña, *La otra Dimensión, pp.* 18-23. Newman's view of time owes much to Augustine. Though it still exposes its roots in Plato, it approximates the later clarifications of Bergson in its search for the actualization of experience.

[68] ibid.

[69] P.P.S.v,1.

[70] Cf. E.Brunner, *Eternal Hope,* Philadelphia, Westminster Press, 1954, p. 50: "The present of God does not crumble away like the temporal present, it alone does not hover between being and non-being. We share in this plenitude of the divine present by the gift of the Holy Ghost, through whom Christ is present with us. The life of the Christian, in its difference from that of everyman, is life in the Holy Ghost, life in the radiant present of God. It is - if only in a borrowed and provisional form - in very truth eternal life. The life of the believer is in fact eschatological, a manner of life according to ultimate reality."

powers of the world to come" and now appear as risen from the dead. They have lived in the Communion of Saints and have a realized experience of the unseen world. Describing these effects, Newman tells us that the Christian believer

> "... will have a natural power over the world, and will seem to speak, not as an individual, but as if in him was concentrated all the virtue and the grace of those many Saints who have been his life-long companions. He has lived with those who are dead, and he will seem to the world as one coming from the dead, speaking in the name of the dead, using the language of souls dead to things that are seen, revealing the mysteries of the heavenly world, and awing and controlling those who are wedded to this."[71]

The Place of Worship

In several of Newman's Anglican sermons[72] we find a reference to church architecture and decoration which reflects his interest in the contemporary liturgical renewal along those lines.[73] He believed that the church building should in itself be a support and expression of the services of worship, by reminding us of their significance. Places always carried special associations for Newman[74] and had a power of evoking precious memories. They fixed the attention and stimulated the mind to relive events, which were often more intense in their remembrance, than at their first occurrence. Places thus have an important role in recalling what has now past, and in helping us to realize the invisible.

---

[71] P.P.S.iii,17.

[72] e.g. in the published sermons P.P.S.vi,19-20-21 and in the unpublished No. 317; No. 388; No. 427.

[73] The Camden Society founded in Cambridge in 1839 was mainly concerned with practical matters of church liturgy, while the Oxford Movement developed the principles on which a renewal of worship should proceed. The Tractarians quickly espoused the renewal in Church architecture though Newman later fell out of sympathy with it when it degenerated into a ritualistic concern with externals.

[74] L.D. Vol.ii, p. 69 where the countryside around Oxford recalled memories of Mary: "Dear Mary seems embodied in every tree and hid behind every hill." A visit to Alton evokes memories of his father, Cf.Vol.v, pp. 331-2.

"If you want to realize to yourself the thought of God, what will you do?...It is not good enough to say that He is everywhere - you must fix your attention on some particular place, event or circumstance...It is by repeating this act of the mind, by again and again singling out spots and thinking of Him who is there because He is everywhere, that you will best come to have a notice of His invisible presence...Now this is just the service which a place dedicated to God does to the Christian."[75]

The support to faith which the place of worship gives, adds an earnestness to our prayers and hence "the stronger and more encouraging will be our hope of heaven."[76] This among other reasons is the purpose for which churches are built. Moreover if we had not the visible symbol of a church, much would be lost of the simple but fundamental truth about the transient nature of life, and of eternity before us. Thus we see the need for such a place, "bidding us as in a type consider the eternity of God and our perishable state on earth." It is there that the Sacraments are administered, which "are calculated (what else we should forget) [sic] the reality of religious obligation and the powers of the world to come."[77]

Signs and symbols speak more effectively than loud and wordy declarations. "We teach by signs and symbols, as well as by word of mouth. We make the building itself, its doors and windows, silently teach. Again we teach by our postures and attitudes which are silent, yet impressive."[78] The church building is therefore an expression of the faith of believers gathered by a common salvation into the Communion of Saints. It is to "profess and confess Christ their Saviour"[79] and is thus constructed in the form of a cross. Each of its various parts is designed so as to be a silent sermon on the Christian mysteries. The baptistry is located in the West which is the chief entrance, and the altar of communion in the East. The Christian life is a journey from west to east, from a new birth to final resurrection.

---

[75] No. 388 p. 12.

[76] ibid.

[77] No. 317 p. 4 The sermon was given for the Society for the Propagation of the Gospel, which was founded 130 years before, and whose work was the building of churches in the colonies.

[78] No. 427 p. 12.

[79] P.P.S.vi,21.

The East has a special significance in illustrating and reminding us of the last things. Not only is the church itself laid out facing East, directing our minds to the New Jerusalem, but even our bodies are laid in the ground east and west. The early Christians prayed towards the East from where their hopes arose. While many reasons may be given for the Christian custom of looking to the East, all have a bearing on eschatology and final salvation in Christ.

> "Some persons suppose that when our Lord comes again to judge the world, He will appear in the East, upon the Mount of Olives - therefore when we pray we look towards the East, as watching for and expecting His coming. Others suppose that this usage is in memory of the garden of Eden, which was planted in the East - and to which we look, as if waiting for the time when God will take us to Himself and restore us to it. Others consider that the East is the place from where the Gospel was published, to look at it as if in thankful acknowledgment of the gift; thus Daniel when in captivity looked towards Jerusalem. And others consider that since the sun rises in the East, the East represents to us the break of spiritual day and the Coming of the Sun of righteousness."[80]

Personal Prayer and Eschatology

The role of prayer in the spiritual life and its relation to eschatology is a theme frequently found in the Anglican sermons. Newman regards prayer, first of all, as a necessary means of access to the unseen world, in which one may anticipate the reality of the last things. This experience in prayer takes two different forms, depending on the eschatological perspective one assumes. When the far horizon of salvation and final judgment is considered, prayer takes the form of hope and a plea of deliverance from evil. But as the present privileges of the Christian come more into view, it becomes the prayer of intercession.[81] As hope and aspiration are the prayer of the "not yet," intercession is the characteristic of a realized eschatology. From these

---

[80] No. 427 p. 16.

[81] The two forms of prayer are contrasted in Newman's poem entitled *The Power of Prayer*, VV.cx.

two standpoints one can assess the respective roles of prayer and service to the world, in which the Christian duty of giving glory to God is fulfilled.

Newman first deals with the necessity of prayer in a life destined for eternity. "Prayer may be called the *breath* of spiritual life. Unless we breathe, we die" and without this life-support "all heavenly affections will languish, droop and at length perish."[82] Moreover it not only sustains life but is "a *test* by which we may try ourselves whether we are in the path of life or of death." Hence "it may [also] be considered as the *pulse* of spiritual life."[83] By its very nature then, prayer is not just one of the duties of religion "but more properly it is *the* duty, nay our *whole* duty to God."[84] It is to be understood not in the formalized sense of saying prayers, but in its inner significance of communion with God. "It is to realize things unseen, to see with the eye of faith those holy truths which the Bible teaches, to speak as before the throne of God...in a word to be *one* with Him."[85] Thus prayer is the means of seeing through the deception of the outside world and the instrument of perceiving the world to come. In a spirit of simple trust and innocent dependence on God, we may attain a real communication with the next world.

> "Thus the true Christian pierces through the veil of this world and sees the next. He holds intercourse with it; He addresses God as a child might address His parent, with as clear a view of Him and with as unmixed a confidence in Him; with deep reverence indeed and godly fear and awe, but still with certainty and exactness."[86]

Newman is not content with simply stating the necessity of prayer but offers practical advice on how to pray. The essential thing is to build a habit of prayer which takes time and effort. "You cannot see the

---

[82] This is the opening sentence of Newman's first sermon *On Prayer*, No. 5 p. 1.

[83] ibid. p.8. Both these expressions may be found again in a later sermon, first preached in 1829 and later published in 1843. P.P.S.vii,15: "Prayer is to spiritual life what the beating of the pulse and the drawing of the breath are to the life of the body." The metaphor of the pulse comes from Thomas Scott. Cf. No. 5 p. 8 [*this* I find in Scott], of whom Newman said "to whom (humanly speaking) I almost owe my soul." Apo. p. 5.

[84] No. 152 p. 2.

[85] ibid.

[86] P.P.S.vii,15.

unseen world at once. They who ever speak with God in their hearts, are in turn taught by Him in all knowledge."[87] This can best be acquired by prayers at fixed times, which "put us in that posture...in which we ever ought to be; they urge us forward in a heavenly direction, and then the stream carries us on."[88] By such regular recourse to prayer "the act of faith is likely to be stronger and more earnest; and then we realize more perfectly the presence of that God whom we do not see."[89] Similarly, prescribed forms of prayer are helpful to maintain a spirit of attentiveness, as we cannot "trust the matters of the next world to the chance thoughts of our own minds, which come this moment and go the next..."[90] They enable us to put "this world more out of sight ...[which] doubtless will engross us, unless we also give Form to the spiritual objects towards which we labour and pray." If time and reflection are necessary even in the mundane decisions of life, how much more so "in that one really needful occupation, the care of our eternal interests?"[91] Moreover, "conscientious men require continual aids to be reminded of the next world."[92] The aim therefore of fixed times and forms of prayer, is to acquire "an abiding motive to seek the world to come, an abiding persuasion[93]... a believing spirit and a praying and devotional heart."[94]

Newman's early view on prayer is largely the product of an unrealized eschatology. It is shaped by the future which holds the promise of salvation and is marked by the hope of the reward to come. Seen in this light, "prayer,... implies *four* things - *indigence, desire, dependence,* and *expectation.*"[95] A recognition of our need, a longing to

---

[87] ibid.

[88] P.P.S.i,19.

[89] ibid.

[90] P.P.S.i,20. Course xxix(a) *On Personal Religion and Private Prayer* consists of Nos. 220,221,222 and 223 and was immediately followed by the Liturgy course. Nos. 222 and 223 are not extant and No. 221 was published in two parts, P.P.S.i,19-20. No. 220 was also published as P.P.S.vii,15 entitled Mental Prayer. When the course was repeated in 1832, Newman added four more sermons: No. 340 (P.P.S.i,3); No. 224; No. 342 (P.P.S.i,7) and No. 343.

[91] P.P.S.i,19.

[92] P.P.S.i,20.

[93] ibid.

[94] No. 152 p. 14.

[95] No. 5 p. 2. Newman acknowledges that his sermon is based on Scott's Essays, No. xxiii.

have it fulfilled, an acknowledgment of God's power to supply it and His willingness to do so, all point to the future blessing. Hence "prayer implies hope - as the Apostle tells us if we *hope*, then do we with patience *wait* for it."[96] It also entails a poverty of spirit, "a deep consciousness of our original corruption and actual transgression and a firm reliance on God's mercy in Christ Jesus."[97] Despite our sinful condition, we have an anchor, the symbol of hope, which steadies us in the storm, while our hearts are fixed upon a future heaven.

> "But the spirit of prayer removes this deceiving veil - it gives us an anchor of the soul, sure and steadfast, it brings us tidings of a far country, it fixes our affections on heavenly things."[98]

Within this framework, prayer is generally a form of petition, especially for one's own personal needs. But these needs, Newman stresses, are spiritual and future. Of the six petitions in the Lord's Prayer,[99] only one concerns our material well-being and is to be sought for in the spirit of what is sufficient for the day. "Let us learn from this not to be anxious for the things of earth - or to pray too earnestly for present happiness - our happiness is *future*, our place of rest is *unseen*, our inheritance is *spiritual*."[100] Consistent with this view is Newman's observation on the promise of long life attached to the Fifth Commandment. This was given to the Jews, who knew little about a future life, but is "clearly not belonging to us Christians - for Christ's kingdom and promises are not of this world but spiritual...we have better promises. Christ promises us not long life but eternal life hereafter."[101]

---

[96] ibid p. 5.

[97] ibid p. 7.

[98] No. 5, p. 12.

[99] The Lord's Prayer is "to be the pattern for our devotion, a kind of example brought into a little compass of the Christian spirit, a kind of abridgment of a Christian life" No. 152 p. 15. The structure we later find in the Liturgy course is already present in this sermon. Later still, he says that the Lord's Prayer is "given as a model for our worship...upon this model our own Liturgy is strictly formed" P.P.S.i.14. This summary of the Christian life is referred to frequently in the sermons e.g. P.P.S.i.3; i.14; i.19; i.20; ii.19; iii.21; S.D. xix.

[100] No. 152 p. 8.

[101] No. 154 p. 3. *The Lord's Prayer* (No. 152), *The Ten Commandments* (No. 154), *The Creed* (No. 155) and *The Sacraments* (No. 156) are constituent parts of the Catechism in the Book of Common Prayer. In this course at Ulcombe, Newman has

Running parallel with these aspirations of hope in future happiness, is an undercurrent of fear in the power of evil and the threat of God's consuming wrath. Once again prayer is invoked, this time as a defence against an evil world and the remedy for overcoming its enormous power. The enemy of the soul knows only too well the efficacy of prayer and hence "wishes to frighten thee from approaching God.... Prayer is the most formidable weapon thou can use against him - it must eventually prevail."[102] "Be sure" he reminds his congregation, "whoever of you is persuaded to disuse his morning and evening prayers, is giving up the armour which is to secure him against the wiles of the Devil."[103] The kingdom of Satan is widespread and entrenched, while Christ's church is but a little flock permanently under the threat of persecution. It is at just such times of trial that the spirit of prayer must be intensified. Such was the example of the early Christians who gathered to watch and pray, when and where they could. Hence "the more troubled and perplexed the affairs of this world become" the greater becomes the need for prayer; "... these gathering tokens of God's wrath are but calls upon us for greater perseverance in united prayer."[104]

So far we have seen the character of prayer which corresponds to a view of salvation which lies in the future. When however, Newman shifts the focus to the present state of salvation, there is a notable change of emphasis. The form of prayer which was once shaped by one's individual hopes and fears, is passed over in favour of the prayer of intercession for others.[105] The key to this understanding is his realized eschatology which puts the powers of the world to come at the present disposal of Christians. Now it is no longer a plea for personal deliverance but a recognition that salvation is already here. Christians are God's priestly people and the office of priesthood is one of intercession.[106] Hence intercession becomes the peculiar stamp of

---

changed the order by placing the sermon on the Lord's Prayer at the head, thus giving it a pre-eminence and influence over the rest. It may be noted that the important sermon, *Holiness necessary for Future Blessedness*, is No. 153.

[102] No. 5 p. 13-14; No. 152 p. 4: "While our souls are lifted up in prayer to God our enemy the devil is defeated."

[103] P.P.S.i,19.

[104] P.P.S.iii,21.

[105] The note of intercession for others can be found as early as No. 152 p. 10 but is only later developed. Similarly, prayer to withold God's wrath is found in the mature Newman e.g. No. 343 p. 14 but no longer predominates.

[106] P.P.S.ii,25: ."..the office of intercession, which though not a peculiarity, is

Christian prayer and exceeds all others. It signifies the Christian privilege of sharing in the priesthood of the glorified Christ, whose distinctive role now in heaven is to make intercession with the Father. While Christ intercedes for us above, the members of His Body intercede for the world below.

"Such an one, I repeat it, is plainly in his fitting place when he intercedes. He is made after the pattern and in the fullness of Christ - he is what Christ is. Christ intercedes above, and he intercedes below...[he] is already in a capacity for higher things. His prayer henceforth takes a higher range."[107]

A similar change can be seen in Newman's ecclesiology with the move from an individual piety to a communitarian one giving prominence to the Communion of Saints. "Intercession becomes a token of the existence of a Church Catholic."[108] It is "the characteristic of Christian worship, the privilege of the heavenly adoption" and the acknowledgment that victory has already come. "Let no one say that our reward is altogether future. Our great reward doubtless is in the next world, but the true Christian has his present powers and privileges, seeing it, I may say, the visible exercise and fruits of them."[109] Hence the prayer of the just man takes on a special efficacy, in being the instrument of the power of Christ.

"The most exalted men of this world, all human wisdom, and human resources, are as nothing before the strength of those who are in the confidence of Almighty God...For the confirmed Christian may, in fact, do all things by the force of his prayers...His privilege is unlimited, both as regards its exercise and its effect."[110]

However, lest one should presume to be in such a state of

---

ever characteristic of the Priestly Order."

[107] P.P.S.iii,24.

[108] ibid.

[109] No. 343 p. 16.

[110] ibid p. 18. Newman's firm belief in the efficacy of prayer can be seen in a letter to his aunt Elizabeth: "I am quite sure it is by prayers such as yours, of those whom the whole world knows nothing of, that the Church is saved." L.D., Vol.v, 120; Cf. also Vol.vi, p. 56 on the encouragement he receives from knowing that others are praying for him.

worthiness before God, Newman adds a word of caution; he reminds us that "our first prayers must ever be for ourselves. Our own salvation is our personal concern."[111] Nevertheless, the privilege of intercession "is a trust committed to all Christians who have a clear conscience and are in full communion with the Church."[112] It is not something to be locked away, but to be used in the service of others. This extraordinary power "is the kind of prayer distinguishing a Christian from such as are not Christian."[113] What St. Paul says about the primacy of love, Newman applies to the role of intercession. "Let him pray; especially let him intercede. Doubt not the power of faith and prayer to effect all things with God...Did you give your body to be burned, and all your goods to feed the poor, you could not do so much as by continual intercession."[114]

The theme of intercession raises the question of the relation between the life of prayer and service to the world, a relation which is ultimately governed by one's eschatology. Where the opposition between this world and the next is emphasized,- and this is a feature of an unrealized eschatology - there is an inherent tendency towards a rejection of the present order, and a self-regarding concern for one's own salvation. But when one underlines the present blessing of the new creation, a more sympathetic and secure relationship of service is enjoined. In the first case, prayer may unwittingly become an escape mechanism from the world of obligation, whereas in the latter, it may fruitfully assume the role of intercession for the world. The debit side however of such intercession is the refusal of the world to recognize the prayer of faith as a valid and relevant service.

The tension between these two perspectives in Newman's eschatology has been noted throughout the course of this study. What has not yet been considered is how they affect the relationship between the active and contemplative life. Surprisingly, Newman's position regarding prayer and service to the world shows a marked consistency, which transcends the division between his early and later eschatology. The source of this consistency is the vertically fixed attitude of doing all for God's glory, at the same time allowing the horizontal view of the world to rise or fall. Thus, when we might expect outright rejection as a

[111] P.P.S.iii,24.

[112] ibid.

[113] ibid/

[114] P.P.S.iii,23.

282

result of his early pessimism, we find a commitment to the world, albeit narrow and limited.[115] Moreover, he commends the habit of morning and evening prayer on the principle of active engagement in the world and personal accountability -"in the morning because we are about to enter into the affairs of life...in the evening because that is a fit time to review our conduct during the day."[116] In the same breath he notes that several of the petitions in the Lord's prayer "are not about ourselves, but relate to *the glory of God*" and that we are "to think affectionately of all men and to pray for their spiritual good."[117] So that while the early Newman shows a tendency of withdrawal from the world and fixes a concentrated eye on the next life, he never loses sight of doing one's duty in the present circumstances.

In his later sermons this call to obedience and active pursuit of God's glory becomes all the more insistent. He condemns the barren formalism of prayer which fails to respond to one's duty in life: "a person may bow and kneel, and look religious, but he is not all the nearer heaven, unless he tries to obey God in all things, and to do his duty."[118]Likewise, he notes that prayer may degenerate into a too earnest fixation on the next world, which immobilises us from acting in this. "When [Christians] feel that the next life is all in all, and that eternity is the only subject that really can claim or fill their thoughts, then they are apt to undervalue this life altogether, and to forget its real importance."[119] Contemplative prayer need not interfere with the duty of actively seeking God in our everyday duties. While it may be difficult to realize both, the end and the means to that end are intrinsically connected. The attitude of the Christian must be "steadily to contemplate the life to come, yet act in this." It is a misconception to think that one precludes the other, or that a life of prayer and relevant service to the world are in any way opposed.

---

[115] No. 5 p. 12: "By prayer we benefit our families, friends and country;- we procure peace and prosperity to the Church - the conversion of sinners, the extension of Christ's kingdom - yea, all good things, more than we can think of, even more than we *can* pray for."

[116] No. 152 p. 6.

[117] ibid. pp. 9,12.

[118] P.P.S.viii,1. This sermon, No. 429, should be read in conjunction with P.P.S.viii,11, No. 430. They were preached on the same day, 30th Oct.1836 and are complementary to each other. Newman connects the two sides of the question under the titles of *Reverence in Worship* and *Doing Glory to God in the Pursuits of the World*.

[119] P.P.S.viii,11.

"In various ways does the thought of the next world lead men to neglect their duty in this; and whenever it does so we may be sure that there is something wrong and unchristian, not in their thinking of the next world, but in their manner of thinking of it."[120]

Though Newman is unequivocal in the need for an active ministry to the world, he is still more conscious of the danger of being absorbed by its demands, which results in the neglect of prayer. "I am almost afraid to speak of the duty of being active in our worldly business, lest I should seem to give countenance to that miserable devotion to things of time and sense...."[121] Christ's words on the two ways of serving Him - "by active business, and by quiet adoration" - did not mean that "Christians were called to nothing but religious worship, or to nothing but active employment." What is at issue however is "not to labour less, but to labour more directly for the Lord" as is shown in the better part chosen by Mary, the sister of Martha.[122] It is far more likely, in a secular age, for people to disparage the devotional life of prayer than to undervalue the importance of Christian involvement. This can be seen "when our defenders recommend the Church on the mere plea of its activity, its popularity, and its visible usefulness."[123]

The growth of the Kingdom, in Newman's view, lies in its vertical relationship with Christ rather than along the horizontal axis of service to the world. This direct link can best be secured by the spirit of watching and waiting on the Lord, which is a characteristic feature of the view of salvation as yet to come. Hence, though we have seen an evolution of Newman's ideas towards a realized eschatology, the prayer of dependence and expectation is never diminished. To release the tension between the now and the not-yet inevitably leads to a separation of perspectives with serious consequences to both. It means, in practice, a flight into otherworldliness, by the denial of the "now," or a secularized salvation by the denial of the "not-yet." It is prayer which is the lynch-pin to bind the two together.

---

[120] ibid.

[121] ibid.

[122] P.P.S.iii,24. This sermon is one of a cluster of related sermons on worship and prayer P.P.S.iii,21-24.

[123] ibid.

The Shadow Side of Eschatology - Fasting and Self-Denial

One of the characteristics of Newman's spirituality is its realism. "We become real in our view of what is spiritual by the contact of things temporal and earthly."[124] If we are to rise then to a vivid apprehension of the unseen world, we cannot short-circuit the mundane and concrete world we live in. This visible world appears on the surface to be made for man, to enjoy all it can offer and to find within it whatever happiness and meaning is humanly possible. It prevails upon us to think of it as an end in itself, to consider the natural world all that there is to know, and thus to deny the existence of the next world.[125] Newman's realism is shown by how seriously he takes this challenge of the secular in obscuring the objects of faith. Its power of fascination plays upon our weak human nature which responds blindly and "blunts our perception of that world we do not see...it weighs on us and pulls us down when we would lift up our hearts, lift them unto the Lord."[126]

The very notion of religion, not to mention love, implies the practice of self-denial.[127] The pattern is set by God Himself whose own condescension involved the giving up of His visible glory. "It was this spontaneous and exuberant self-denial which brought Him down."[128] In our upward movement towards Him, we too must deny ourselves even in legitimate matters, such as our own comforts. "Nothing is so likely to corrupt our hearts, and to seduce us from God as to surround ourselves with comforts."[129] It is the height of folly not to see that "they become practically a substitute in our hearts for that One Object to which our supreme devotion is due."[130] From experience we learn that every advance entails the sacrifice of cherished ways, and that growth in all its forms inevitably involves a weaning process. And just as "children are weaned from their first nourishment, so must our souls put away childish things, and be turned from the pleasures of earth to

---

[124] P.P.S.v.3.

[125] S.D. vii, pp.82-89; cf also S.D.viii and P.P.S.vii,3.

[126] P.P.S.vi,8.

[127] P.P.S.vii,7. Newman holds this practice in the highest regard as "the essence of religious obedience." ibid.

[128] ibid.

[129] P.P.S.vii,7.

[130] P.P.S.ii,28.

choose those of heaven."[131] We are engaged in a war against our spiritual enemies and must therefore act like "soldiers of Christ who are making their way towards the world to come."[132]

> "Till we in a certain sense, detach ourselves from our bodies, our minds will not be in a state to receive divine impressions, and to exert heavenly aspirations. A smooth and easy life...full meals, soft raiment...these and the like if we are not careful, choke up the avenues of the soul, through which the light and breath of heaven might come to us."[133]

Just as in the case of prayer, self-denial and fasting play a parallel role as the breath and pulse of spiritual life. Self-denial is the breath, for without it one could scarcely speak of a Christian life at all; it is the means by which we "instance and realize [our] faith." But even more so than prayer, it is the pulse of the spiritual life as being a clearer test of the genuineness of our faith. Here we have a reality principle as devoid of self-delusion as is possible in matters of human discernment. "We cannot indeed make ourselves as sure of our being in the number of God's true servants as the early Christians were, yet we may possess our degree of certainty, and by the same kind of evidence, the evidence of self-denial."[134] Fasting, in particular brings home the sincerity of our commitment.

> "This is the one great end of fasting...to bring home to your mind that in fact you do love your Saviour, that you do hate sin, that you do hate your sinful nature, that you have put aside the present world. Thus you will have an evidence (to a certain point) that you are not using mere words."[135]

The foundation on which self-denial and fasting is laid is the ground of unrealized eschatology. It is the recognition of the "not yet," of the fact that the work of salvation is still in process and will not be complete until the Last Day. In this in-between time we must face the

[131] P.P.S.vii.7.
[132] ibid.
[133] P.P.S.v,23.
[134] P.P.S.i,5.
[135] ibid.

continued opposition from the world, even if the final victory is assured. We are reminded by it that our condition is "a painful toil, of working out our salvation with fear and trembling, of preparing to meet our God, and waiting for the judgment."[136] This shadow side of eschatology is most clearly seen in the case of fasting and the apostles. While they enjoyed the presence of the Bridegroom, the apostles, under Christ's direction, saw no point in calling a fast, but rather a feast. But when possession was taken away, and He was no longer in their sight, they then resumed their fasting. They were now to live by faith, to look out for His Return, and fasting was the sign of their absent Lord. It was not only the sign of His physical absence, however, but also the instrument of eliciting His spiritual presence. Fasting therefore is basically associated with the absence of Christ, and, paradoxically, with the desire to narrow the distance between Him and His disciples by sharpening the awareness of His abiding presence.

> "The one thing, which is all in all to us, is to live in Christ's presence; to hear His voice, to see His countenance.... They were to follow Him through the veil, and to break the barrier of flesh after His pattern. They must as far as they could weaken and attenuate what stood between them and Him; they must anticipate that world where flesh and blood are not; they must discern truths which have a life, not of sense but of spirit; they must practice those mortifications which former religions had enjoined, which the Pharisees and John's disciples observed, with better fruit, for a higher end, in a more heavenly way, in order to see Him who is invisible."[137]

Newman chooses the theme of fasting to highlight the Christological significance of all spiritual exercises. Fasting was that practice which was most likely to be misunderstood as something less than Christian, as a relic of Judaism or of the need for appeasing God's wrath, as in natural religion.[138] In fact this is how it was perceived by the "two-bottled" clergymen in Oxford, who saw it as symptomatic of

---

[136] P.P.S.vii,7.

[137] P.P.S.vi,3.

[138] Newman's earlier view of fasting (in 1833), was scarcely different. In a remark on the practice of the Greek Church he says: "fasting of the Greek Church [are] as Masses are of the Latin; and they both answer the same purpose and are a substitute apparently for moral obedience and an opiate to the conscience." Cf. L.D., Vol.iii, p. 239.

the extravagant nature of the Movement. Though there were indeed excesses among the Tractarians, Newman consistently advocated moderation, while following a strict regime of fasting for himself.[139] It was therefore in this context that he underlined the habit of fasting as having no other purpose than communion with Christ. It is out of love of Him, and not in any Manichean spirit, that Christians fast, "for it is only acceptable when done for His sake."[140] The only purpose of weaning ourselves from the things of sense is to enhance our awareness of the presence of Christ. The aim and object therefore of all spiritual exercises, of prayer, the sacraments, fasting and self-denial is the apprehension and possession of Christ.

> "To be possessed by His presence as our life, our strength, our merit, our hope, our crown; to become in a wonderful way His members, the instruments and visible form, or sacramental sign, of the one Invisible Ever-present Son of God, mystically reiterating in each of us all the acts of His earthly life, His birth, consecration, fasting, temptation, conflicts, victories, agony, passion, death, resurrection and ascension; His being all in all."[141]

While fasting has a supremely positive purpose, its power resides in the negative side of life. Newman's view of fasting is remarkably similar to what psychologists since Jung have described as the shadow side of the personality. Here a great reservoir of energy is stored which can be released either to destruction or to a creative end. It is the energy of inner conflict which may result in self-defeat or be harnessed to a victory over self. Making friends with the shadow is to respect its power and to integrate it into the full development of the personality. This can only be done with patience and moderation. And so it is with fasting which is the valve which opens the flood-gates of conflict and the powers of the world to come. Though "it *is* always, under God's grace, a spiritual benefit to our hearts eventually," it invites a trial and temptation which may in many cases lead to one's fall. "In all cases it is therefore

---

[139] In the Letters and Diaries we find Newman using a short-hand notation for his record of regular fasting. The entries begin on Jan.27 1837 Cf. Vol.vi,p.17. On the question of excesses in fasting Pusey took things to extremes often imposing the practice on his family. Newman's plea for moderation is clearly seen in his sermon on *Apostolic Abstinence A Pattern for Christians*, P.P.S.vi,3.

[140] P.P.S.vi,1.

[141] ibid.

to be viewed, chiefly as an *approach to God* -an approach to the powers of heaven - yes, and to the powers of hell. And in this point of view there is something very awful in it."[142]

Turning the negative into a positive, and absence into presence, Newman attempts to resolve the tension between an unfulfilled and a realized eschatology. This is the special value he attaches to the Christian practice of fasting. When we know what we are really about, "such exercises give the soul power over the unseen world ...and prayer and fasting, do in fact, declare the conflict and promise this victory over the evil one." This was the case of the prophets, especially of Daniel, whose two recorded fasts bore the fruit of intercession and prophecy. His second fast "seems to have had an influence (if I may use such a word) on the unseen world, from the time he began it."[143] It is the inner meaning of Christ's fasting in the wilderness, which began with conflict and ended with victory, shown by the angels ministering to Him. This is the pattern for all Christians who struggle in the desert but are empowered with the victory of Christ over evil.

A special instance of the promised victory after conflict is seen in the practice of the Eucharistic fast. Here we see a clear connection between mortification and the promise of bodily resurrection. This dying to the flesh is "a needful medicine to bring his sinful nature into subjection" and "a healthful exercise for such as were redeemed and sanctified by the name of Jesus Christ."[144] But it also has a special significance in preparing our bodies for the glorified life hereafter. It is "an effectual monitor,"[145] a concrete reminder that redemption is whole and entire and extends to our very bodies.

> "That body, which through the grace of Christ shall rise again at the last day and live for ever in God's presence, required to die as it was sanctified fully, needed to die daily for its own good, needed ever to be resisted and subdued lest it should be the instrument of Satan's temptation instead of a

---

[142] P.P.S.vi.1.

[143] ibid. Cf. Newman's Tract *On Mortification of the Flesh*, No. XXI, in which he makes a similar reference to the fasting of the prophets. Their fasting was "a preparation for His presence," "an intimation serviceable for Christian practice" which demonstrates "a more excellent way of obedience." The tract was written as an appendage to Pusey's Tract *On Fasting*, No. XVIII.

[144] No. 351 p. 11.

[145] No. 459 p. 14.

temple of the Holy Ghost. Then only was it duly prepared to
be mystically nourished by the Body and Blood of our
Saviour Christ and so gradually be changed into His servant
from being instead His foe, when it was subjected to this
godly discipline. What a view is here presented to us of the
sinfulness of our nature and the necessity of a newness of
life such as to extend even to our very bodies in order that
they may be fit dwellings of the Holy Ghost."[146]

It is to the Eucharist and its promise of resurrection that we must
now turn in the second part of this chapter.

Part Two
The Eschatological Banquet

Among the theological achievements of the Oxford Movement, a
renewed understanding of the Eucharist was perhaps the most
distinctive. It was the crystallization of a theology centred on the
Incarnation and the Church.[147] The inexhaustible nature of the
sacrament left room for several avenues of approach and Newman had
his own particular perspective on the subject.[148] His long-standing
interest in soteriology led him to stress the effects of the Eucharist in
the work of salvation.[149] From this viewpoint the eschatological
significance of the Eucharist emerges in Newman's sermons and may
be described under four general headings.

The Eucharist is first of all the pledge and the portion of eternal
life; it is both the promise of future blessedness and the present earnest
of the life of heaven. Second, Newman conceives the sacrament as the

---

[146] No. 351 pp. 4-5.

[147] cf The best study on the question is by A.Härdelin, *The Tractarian
Understanding of the Eucharist*, Uppsala, 1965. Härdelin however barely touches on
the eschatological significance of the Eucharist which I am here concerned with, and to
which my attention is confined.

[148] Froude, Keble, Palmer and R.I.Wilberforce were the chief exponents of
eucharistic theology together with Newman. Wilberforce's synthesis in three volumes viz
The Doctrine of the Incarnation (1848), *The Doctrine of Holy Baptism* (1849) and *The
Doctrine of the Holy Eucharist* (1853) marks the high point of incarnational
ecclesiology. cf. D.Newsome, *The Parting of Friends*, London, John Murray, 1966, pp.
371-383.

[149] cf. Härdelin, op.cit.p.155: ."..Newman primarily emphasized the link between
soteriology and sacramental theology..."

link between the First and the Second Coming of Christ; it is the legacy left to the Church on His departure, which proclaims His presence among us until He comes again. A third aspect of the Eucharist is found in its relation to the Last Judgment. It is the unique means of preparation for the Day of Account and the preservation of the Church from the power of evil. Finally, as the food of immortality, the participation of Christ's Body and Blood is the present assurance of belief in the resurrection of the body.

The Pledge and Portion of Eternal Life

Newman's first sermon on the Eucharist is on the parable of the Great Supper to be held at the end of time. Like many of the other parables in this series, it is treated in an eschatological key.[150] The Lord's Supper is an image of "our chief good" and is one of "the foretastes and earnests of the heavenly glory." In attending it Christians keep alive the heart's desire for ultimate fulfilment and are made conscious that "eternity is not less certain of coming because it is as yet future and the next <unseen> world is as much a matter of fact as this is."[151]

The first note therefore which Newman strikes is one which underlines the future prospect of the gift, symbolized by the bread and wine. It is quite a hollow note however, for it is merely the emblem of a spiritual good rather than the effectual instrument of it. In a rapid series of steps, Newman however quickly moves beyond this purely figurative meaning, common to evangelicals, to a fuller notion of it as a sacrament. Little more than a year later we find him distinguishing the sacrament of the Lord's Supper from the empty ceremony of Jewish rites; it is "a powerful and effectual sacrament - a means of grace - a pledge and seal of forgiveness... a covenant founded on better promises and more spiritual conditions than that of Moses."[152] When he comes to his first course on the sacraments, he has all but completed the journey from a

---

[150] No. 24, *The Lord's Supper*. In a similar fashion the parables of *The Sower* (No. 18), *The Talents* (No. 22), *The Prodigal Son* (No. 26), *The Fig-Tree* (No. 28) and *The Wheat and Tares* (No. 30) are interpreted with reference to the End. Though Newman did not list this series of sermons on the parables as a course, it is numbered as Course x by Pett, cf.Pett, op.cit. p. 81.

[151] No. 24.

[152] No. 138, 19th Feb.1826. No. 24 was preached on 3rd Oct.1824.

receptionist theology of the Eucharist, to one which stresses its instrumental efficacy - the sacrament not only "promises grace" but "conveys it."[153] Nevertheless the traces of his earlier view still linger on in his retaining the nebulous notion of "spiritual influences," which may or may not be imparted by the sacrament.[154] Moreover, he sees it more as a help to final salvation than a present realization of it. Though the Lord's Supper is a means of grace, Newman's emphasis is more on its being a pledge of something yet to come.

> "That it is a pledge is shown in several ways -it is a pledge of God's mercy to us for the very reason because Christ told us to celebrate it - for why should He tell men to commemorate an event in which they were not interested and in the advantages of which they did not partake? - Again it is certainly a pledge from the very form of the outward rite. We eat bread and drink wine. But why partake in the Church of an outward blessing except as an earnest of something beyond?"[155]

Though Newman here speaks of the Lord's Supper as an "earnest" of eternal life, the term at this stage of his development is, as yet, interchangeable with the idea of a "pledge," though somewhat more emphatic. It is only later in his published sermons where we find a clear distinction between them, in which he illustrates the difference between what is purely future and what is partially anticipated. He thereby gives a more exact meaning to the word "earnest," and reserves it for the notion of realized eschatology; it "is rather more than a pledge, for an earnest is not a mere token which will be taken from us when it is fulfilled, as a pledge might be, but a something in advance of what is one day to be given in full."[156] This development takes place in conjunction with a shift of focus from the Atonement to the mystery of the Incarnation. In a marked development of the sacramental principle, the Eucharist is enveloped in the mystery of Christ's birth and

---

153 No. 172. This is the last of six sermons in 1828 in preparation for Confirmation.

154 ."..not that at the very time in which it is received, divine aid is necessarily given...[but] we on the whole receive spiritual influences which we should otherwise not receive." No. 172 p. 9.

155 ibid p. 5.

156 P.P.S.ii,19.

resurrection.[157] The sacrament of Christ's Body and Blood is "the effectual type of that gracious Economy [for] no one realizes the Mystery of the Incarnation but must feel disposed towards that of Holy Communion."[158] Moreover, as Newman's understanding of the Real Presence[159] grows, he sees the Eucharist not simply as a pledge of future blessedness and present mercy, but as a true portion and earnest of eternal life.

Newman avoids doctrinal elucidations on the mystery of the Eucharist and generally confines his remarks to emphasizing the effect of the sacrament on those who receive it. At the same time however, his thought goes deeper than the virtualist understanding he once ascribed to it. Soteriology continues to play a major role, but is no longer considered purely in terms of future salvation. No longer are "our blessings all future and distant"[160] but we already have "a real communication of Himself...a Holy Mystery, in which we receive (we know not how) the virtue of that Heavenly Body, which is the life of all who believe."[161] It is not merely a spiritual influence but "a receiving of the gift of eternal life in the form of bread and wine, [and] this refreshment is nothing short of life, eternal life."[162] Nor is it merely a promise of God's favour, or the symbol of our personal covenant with Christ. "Persons there are who explain our eating Christ's flesh and blood, as merely meaning our receiving a *pledge* of the *effects* of the *passion* of His Body and Blood; that is in other words, of the *favour* of

---

[157] In Newman's first course of *Easter sermons* and in his course on *Salvation and the Future Promise*, there is a notable absence of any mention of the Eucharist. In his published sermons, however, the theme of the Eucharist is invariably linked with the Easter season.

[158] P.P.S.vi,11.

[159] A discussion on Newman's belief in the Real Presence would carry us beyond the scope of the present topic. It is however the true basis for attributing to the Eucharist its significance as a portion, and not just as a pledge of eternal life. Newman did in fact believe in the Real Presence "indeed *spiritually, sacramentally, in a heavenly way*" (P.P.S.i,21) but eschewed the tendency towards a materialist conception of the Eucharist, or attempts of a rationalistic and "explanatory" character, of which he thought transubstantiation was an instance.(cf.P.P.S.vi,11). For an account of the matter cf. Härdelin, op.cit.p.134ff. On Froude's influence in leading Newman to an understanding of the Real Presence cf. Apo. pp. 24-25, but see also L.D., Vol.v,pp.225-6 on Newman's non-acceptance of the Roman doctrine: "Transubstantiation as held by Rome, involves in matter of fact, profane ideas."

[160] P.P.S.vii,12.

[161] P.P.S.ii,13.

[162] P.P.S.vii,11.

Almighty God."[163] Such descriptions are inadequate to express exactly what the Eucharist is, which is none other than the gift of the glorified Body of Christ. It is as real a blessing spiritually, as the manna in the desert was real materially, and as such is a present concrete participation in the life to come.

> "The manna in the wilderness was a real gift, taken and eaten; so is the manna in the Church. It is not God's mercy, or favour, or imputation; it is not a state of grace, or the promise of eternal life, or the privileges of the gospel, or faith in that doctrine; but it is what our Lord says it is, the gift of His own precious Body and Blood, really given, taken, and eaten as the manna might be (though in a way unknown), at a particular time, and a certain particular spot; namely, as I have already made it evident, at the time and spot when and where Holy Communion is celebrated."[164]

In this brief outline, the horizon of Newman's thought has been shown to change considerably from the distant future to the here and now. Nevertheless, he does not lose touch with his original perspective or discard his former insights. This is but an example of a pattern of true development in which early elements, which are as yet inadequately formed, are recovered and fleshed out in a wider framework of interpretation. In one of his late sermons, Newman combines the two poles of significance of the Eucharist, and illustrates the eschatological tension of the "not yet" and the "already." This is a composite sermon on the Gospel Feast, which may suggest that originally the two distinct aspects were treated separately.[165] Here we find an echo of two early sermons on the parables of the Great Supper and the Ten Virgins. "What is that Heavenly Feast which we are now vouchsafed, but in its turn the earnest and pledge of that future feast in the Father's Kingdom, when the marriage of the Lamb shall come and His wife shall make herself ready...?." But though it is still another type of a future gift, the Eucharist is also the fulfilment of prophecy and the realization of that salvation which has already come. The Old Testament descriptions of

---

[163] P.P.S.vi,11.

[164] ibid.

[165] P.P.S.vii,12 entitled *The Gospel Feast* is combined from Nos. 506 and 508 which were delivered on consecutive Sundays during the Easter period of 1838. The original manuscripts however are not extant. Other combined sermons on the Eucharist are P.P.S.vii,11 (Nos. 287 & 289) and P.P.S.vi,9 (Nos. 483 & 485).

294

the heavenly banquet are "intimations and promises there given of that sacred Feast of Christ's Body and Blood which it is our privilege now to enjoy till the end come." Though we still live in faith and hope of the future feast of heaven, Newman reminds us that we enjoy the present possession of eternal life.

> "But let us come in faith and hope, and let us say to ourselves. May this be the beginning of us of everlasting bliss! May these be the first fruits of that banquet which is to last for ever and ever; ever new, ever transporting, inexhaustible in the city of our God."[166]

The Sacrament of the End-Time

In comparing the two sacraments of the gospel, Newman notes that "the Lord's Supper is more complex in its meaning and objects than the Sacrament of Baptism."[167] While baptism "looks principally to the blessings themselves" the Eucharist is more wide-ranging in its significance. In being a feast, it "implies having received certain advantages," and hence it is a celebration of a present good. Moreover, as the commemoration of Christ's death, it "looks more to the past than to the future." But the Lord's Supper is something more than a "thankful memorial" of the past, for it contains the "token of a promise from Him." It thus points to the future and inspires hope, and hence we are commanded to proclaim the Lord's death until He comes. Combining these three dimensions, the past, the present and the future, the Eucharist gathers up all seasons of time, and is the sign of Him who is "the same yesterday, today and the same forever."[168]

The Eucharist is also comprehensive in the objects it embraces. As the sacrament of Christ's Body and Blood, its origin and foundation is the mystery of the Incarnation. Secondly, the virtue and power of the sacrament comes from the Passion of Christ, since the Eucharist "especially draws our attention to that great atonement itself."[169]

---

166 P.P.S.vii,12.
167 No. 172 p. 2.
168 Heb.13,8.
169 No. 172 p. 2.

Finally, the sign of the Eucharist is the same in nature as the sign of the Lord's Resurrection.[170] Hence all the essential mysteries of Christ's life are enveloped sacramentally within it. With regard to revelation then, and its two-fold dimension: i.e. in its transcendental aspect as mystery, and in its categorial or historical aspect, the Eucharist encapsulates the nucleus of Christian faith.[171]

Far more complex still is the nature of Christ's presence in the Eucharist. However, prescinding from the inner mystery of Christ's Body and Blood, and considering it simply as an act of faith and hope, the Eucharist typifies the nature of Christian life. It shows it to be essentially a life of prayerful waiting for Christ. It is the way of living in the in-between time, between His departure and His future Coming. In a world that is passing away, the Christian stance is "an attitude of one who waits for Christ, who trusts for salvation in Christ."[172] By leaving us a sign which is to remain until He comes, "the Sacrament of the Holy Communion is the connecting link between His going and His returning: it is the memorial of His death, it is the pledge of His final triumph."[173]

> "In His coming at the end of the world, all our wishes and prayers rest and are accomplished; and in the present communion we have a stay and consolation meanwhile, joining together the past and the future, reminding us that He has come once, and promising us that He will come again."[174]

Newman pays a good deal of attention to the significance of the Eucharist as the sign of transition and passage. It marks the separation from the old world and the taking up of a new way of life. It is the critical moment of farewell to things familiar, for the acquisition of the blessings of the unseen world. The feast of Cana "was the last scene of

---

[170] P.P.S.vi,9. In this sermon on *The Gospel Sign addressed to Faith*, Newman draws a close parallel between the sign of Christ's Resurrection and the abiding sign of the Eucharist. ."..whatever be the manifestation promised to Christians by our Lord, it is not likely to be more sensible and more intelligible than the great sign of His own Resurrection."

[171] K.Rahner treats revelation under the two aspects of mystery and event in *Sacramentum Mundi*, Vol.V, pp. 348-353.

[172] No. 449 p. 1.

[173] ibid.

[174] P.P.S.vii,11.

the old life" and the beginning of Christ's manifesting His glory. It was there that He "bade farewell to His earthly home" and later declared that He had "no mother or brethren after the flesh." From that moment until the end of His public ministry, the gospel is silent about His mother Mary. But as He comes to the end, there is a reunion with her, when "His love revived as His Father's work was ending." Once again a farewell feast is celebrated to signify the final stage of Christ's earthly life. But while Cana and the Last Supper are moments of departure, the separation is but for a while, and the promise of His return is given.

> "It will be observed, then, that though He was bidding farewell to His earthly home in the one, and His disciples in the other, yet in neither case was He leaving them for good, but for a season. His mother He acknowledged again when He was expiring; His disciples on His resurrection. And He gave both the one and the other intimations, not only that He was then separating Himself from them, but also that it was not a separation for ever."[175]

The nuanced description of Our Lord's Last Supper and His First, leads to two lessons which may be drawn on the meaning of the Eucharist. The sacrament first underlines the spirit of detachment from the world. It signifies our saying farewell to the things of sense, since we have "been called to quit things visible and temporal for the contemplation and the hope of God's future promises."[176] It means a new order of recognition by faith, for "we have lost the sensible and conscious perception of Him."[177] As the Last Supper was the signal of Christ's death and resurrection, the Eucharist means our parting from the sensible consolation of sight, to an awareness of the spiritual presence of the Risen Lord. "His coming up from the earth was a sign for faith, not for sight; and such is His coming down from heaven as Bread."[178]

Vastly more important however, is the second level of significance. The Eucharist is above all the sign of eschatological hope and present rejoicing. In his sermon on "Feasting in Captivity," Newman notes the

---

[175] S.D.iii, p. 34.

[176] ibid. p. 38. The quotation directly refers to the season of Lent but the context underlines the aspect of the Eucharist as a moment of separation from earthly things.

[177] P.P.S.vi.10.

[178] P.P.S.vi.9.

paradox that in the age of the Church "her times of humiliation should be times of rejoicing."[179] The sacrament is not just a privilege, to be availed of when success calls for celebration; it is also a duty, in which we must "look to the future and rejoice." The Eucharist never loses its character of being a feast, something which becomes all the more necessary in times of distress or when hopes are low. "There is an ordinance we are bound to observe always till the Lord come: is it an ordinance of humiliation and self-abasement, or is it a feast? The Holy Eucharist is a Feast; we cannot help feasting, we cannot elude our destiny of joy and thanksgiving, if we would be Christians."[180] Though all things may appear dark and gloomy, the flame of hope is kept alive by the Eucharist. "Nature fails, the sun shines not, and the moon is dim, the stars fall from heaven, and the foundations of the round world shake; but the altar's light burns ever brighter."[181] To neglect this sacrament therefore, is to deny ourselves the source of our very hope.

> "...and if they feel their affections are not with Christ let them ask themselves whether they lift up their hearts in the Lord in that ordinance in which they are enabled to lift them up effectually. That Sacrament is the Sacrament of hope. It is meant as a stay till the Lord come. It is an earnest given to those who say "how long?" that they may last yet for a little season - it reminds, and comforts, and prepares for what one day shall be..."[182]

Preservation from Evil and the Day of Judgment

The idea of moral accountability and the Day of Judgment was never far from Newman's thoughts. It was his parting shot in many of his early sermons, often leaving a sombre note in the air. Few of these sermons end with any mention of the Eucharist, but in his later preaching, it was frequently referred to in his concluding words.[183]

---

[179] S.D. xxv, p. 385.

[180] ibid. p. 389.

[181] P.P.S.vii,11.

[182] No. 266 p. 20. This is a redaction, probably in 1839, of Newman's sermon on the *Intermediate State* first preached on All Saints Day in 1830. The sermon was preached four times in all on the feast day.

[183] Härdelin, op.cit. p. 272 correctly states that "In Newman's earliest sermons we

Without minimizing the momentous nature of the Last Day, Newman later combined the thought of judgment with the sacrament of the Eucharist, as a preparation and anticipation of it. In this way he softened the severity of his early admonitions, and, more importantly, offered positive instruction on the meaning of the Sacrament. Instead of fear at the thought of judgment, words of encouragement to attend the Communion service became the dominant note.

Newman's insistence on frequent attendance[184] at the Lord's Supper is a practical conclusion to his dogmatic development. As his understanding of the divine presence in the Eucharist deepened, the loss incurred by a neglect of the Sacrament seemed to him incalculable.[185] By not coming to Holy Communion, Christians not only deprived themselves of an ineffable mystery, but missed a unique means of protection against evil. By habitually refusing the Gift, they emphatically showed their "indifference to the salvation He has prepared," and this amounted to "a rejection from the Lord and from the glory of His power."[186] The fear of unworthily receiving the Lord's Body was the standard excuse for staying away, based on St. Paul's warning about "discerning the Lord's Body." Responding to this fear, Newman explains that these words must be taken in their proper context, which was one of gross profanation at Corinth, - an incident not likely to occur now. Such "misconceptions" and "superstitious dread" perverted the meaning of the sacrament, which "instead of being a means of grace, was in its direct tendency a means of damnation."[187] Continual neglect of the Eucharist was "a perilous and desperate omission"[188]; by so doing "we are fearfully bearing witness against

---

still do not hear any demands for a more frequent use of the sacrament."

[184] Cf. Härdelin, op.cit. on The Increasing Frequency of Celebrations pp. 271-278 and on The Question of Manducatio Indignorum, pp. 168-176.

[185] On the loss suffered cf No. 459 pp. 5-7. Despite the necessity of receiving the Sacrament, salvation is not absolutely dependent on it: "God *can* sustain us, not by bread alone, but this is His *ordinary* means, which His will has made such. He can sustain our immortality without the Christian Sacraments, as He sustained Abraham and the other saints of old time; but under the Gospel these are His *means*, which He appointed at His will." P.P.S.i,21.

[186] No. 120 p. 22-23. This was first preached in 1825 but the rewritten manuscript we have is dated August 23, 1827.

[187] No. 172 p. 17. On the opposite page he adds the following later redaction: "The Father of our Lord Jesus Christ is not a God of terror...and the rite commemorating that love must be one of comfort, joy and cheerful hope."

[188] ibid. p. 21.

ourselves, a witness which will rise up against us at the last day."[189]

Despite these initial references to the need for regular reception of the Eucharist, it is surprising that a considerable interval passed before Newman changed the existing practice from a monthly Communion Service to a weekly one.[190] The fear of innovation and the need to proceed cautiously held him back.[191] However by 1837 he felt bold enough to institute the desired change which he announced from the pulpit. In this and in a subsequent sermon[192] he gives his reasons for the change, and tries to quell objections to the new practice. Among other things, he notes the role of the Eucharist as a bulwark against evil, and emphasizes the moral declension which results from its neglect. Giving a brief history of the early church, he shows how abuses and corruptions subsequently crept in when the practice of frequent Communion was abandoned. Closer to home, he records the state of church services in London 120 years prior, which compares more favorably with ancient custom than with 19th century practice.[193] This, Newman remarks, is not a plea born of nostalgia for the past, but a recognition of how the Church of England has fallen "in faith and principle" because of a neglect of the eucharistic liturgy.

> "Now, I ask, how do we know, but that these corruptions were suffered to come in, in consequence of this great neglect of a plain and solemn duty? Is it not likely? It was believed in primitive times to be a preservation against sin to all true Christians. When they neglected it, they let go that divine gift, by which the devil was kept out of the Church."[194]

---

[189] No. 213 p. 23. This is an introductory sermon to Course xxviii, *On The Church and Public Worship*, Nos. 213-218.

[190] He announced his plan at the conclusion to No. 449 given on 19th March 1837. The daily Service was revived some years earlier in 1834, cf. L.D., Vol.ii,pp.50-54; P.P.S.iii,21.

[191] Cf. L.D., Vol.iv, p. 275. In his letter of June 1834 to Froude he confesses that "it is now a year since I have been anxious to begin a weekly celebration of the Lord's Supper -but as yet I have not moved a step - there are many difficulties. I think I shall begin with Saints Days first."

[192] Nos. 449 and 459.

[193] ibid; P.P.S.ii,32: "I say this neglect of religious Ordinances is an especial fault of these latter ages."

[194] No. 449 p. 6. Out of a similar concern, Newman had earlier introduced a daily service in the Church. P.P.S.iii,21: "It was, that the state of public affairs was so

In his promotion of frequent attendance at Communion, Newman does not discount or overlook the danger of irreverence and profanation. "We are told that the peril of disease and death attends the unworthy partaking of the Lord's Supper. Is this wonderful, considering the strange sin of receiving it into a body disgraced by wilful disobedience?"[195] An even stronger statement on the enormity of the sin is made in a sermon before the university, in which he decries the custom of compulsory attendance by students. The guilt involved is "the crime of crucifying Him anew, as not discerning what lies hid in the rite."[196] It is indeed true that "there is a peril attached to the unworthy reception," and those who make the excuse "would rather give up the promise than implicate themselves in the threats that surround it."[197] Newman therefore grants some substance to the plea of not sharing in the Sacrament because of unworthiness. He points out nevertheless, that the remedy lies not in omitting it, but in preparing more earnestly for it. "It is our duty to be watchful, not to omit attendance."[198] By taking the necessary safeguards and following the exhortations of the Prayer Book, we can, at Newman's urging, confront the danger of incurring God's wrath.

"Doubtless in calling you, my brethren, to frequent communion, I call you to a danger. Doubtless and so I should if I called you to the front ranks in a battle, where weapons of death were flying about. But as on earth the way to gain mortal glory is to front danger, so it is in heavenly things...We labour for an immortal crown - we must disdain all petty, cowardly courses - we must not attempt to creep on heavenwards by a merely safe course."[199]

The encounter with Christ in the Eucharist is an anticipation of His Coming in judgment at the end of time. Christ meets us first under the

threatening that I could not bear to wait longer; for there seemed quite a call upon all Christians to be earnest in prayer, so much the more, as they thought they saw the Day of vengeance approaching."

[195] P.P.S.i,21.

[196] U.S.viii, p. 152. From this statement and from a similar passage in the sermon, Härdelin argues to Newman's belief in the Real Presence, cf. Härdelin, op.cit.p.170.

[197] P.P.S.vii,11.

[198] P.P.S.iv,5.

[199] No. 459, pp. 14-15.

veil of a sacrament, so as to prepare us for our final meeting face to face. "He who is at the right hand of God manifests Himself in that Holy Sacrament as really and as fully as if He were visibly there";[200]in the Eucharist "He all but reveals to us His heavenly countenance."[201] In the Sacrament He manifests His mercy, so that we may later bear the manifestation of His justice. Hence, if a Christian "is unprepared to meet Christ in His Sacrament, he is unfit to meet Him in judgment; if he is not in a state to bear His presence in mercy, much less could he bear His presence in glory."[202]

The characteristic feelings of fear and hope, which the Second Coming of Christ inspires, accurately describes the temper of Christians as they approach the Eucharist. It offers a sign of hope, but reminds us first of our need of deliverance from sin. "How are we to get rid of this chain of sin dragging us down to hell? We cannot of ourselves...Why, the only way is to come to God's ordinance and sacrament for deliverance."[203] Preparing for it is preparing for the final judgment and by partaking of it "we lay up in our hearts the seed of eternal life against the day of His Coming...that we may have confidence and not be ashamed..."[204]

"I have spoken of coming to God in prayer generally; but if this is awful, much more is coming to Him in the Sacrament of Holy Communion; for this is in very form an anticipation of His Coming, a near presence of Him in earnest of it. And a number of men feel it to be so; for, for one reason or another, they never come before Him in that most Holy Ordinance, and so deprive themselves of the highest of blessings here below."[205]

---

[200] P.P.S.iv,9.

[201] P.P.S.vi,9.

[202] No. 459 p. 11.

[203] No. 479 p. 13.

[204] P.P.S.iv,9; No. 402 p. 16.

[205] P.P.S.v,4.

The Food of Immortality: [206]

From what we have just seen, Newman considered the Eucharist as the mirror in which the Second Coming of Christ is reflected. Our Judge and Saviour comes to us under a sign, which enables us to anticipate that final meeting with Him on the Last Day. Christ will come however, not only to judge the world, but to gather His faithful into the glory of the resurrection. This final act of the drama, unlike the actual judgment itself, is beyond our powers of anticipation. It is impossible to register, in our earthly bodies, feelings which may correspond to a future glorified state. Nonetheless, a process of transformation, invisible to the senses, is already begun through participation in the Eucharist. The life of the Spirit is received in the body as well as in the soul. Though we do not see its effect, our bodies are being prepared for the state of glorification, which will be manifested in the next world.

> "*Doth any man doubt* that even *from the flesh of of* [sic] Christ our *very bodies* do receive that life which shall make them glorious at the latter day; and for which they are already accounted parts of His glorious body?"[207]

Participation in the Eucharist is a sharing in the Risen Body of Christ. If the state of future blessedness is a mystery impossible to describe, "there is a higher mystery still, in the state of those who sup with Christ."[208] The Communion in His Body and Blood is truly the beginning of heaven, and is "the process of renewal of our corrupt human nature." This renewal affects both body and soul, through the application of the power of Christ's resurrection. "Christ who died and rose again for us, is in it spiritually present, in the fullness of His death and of His resurrection."[209]

"The streams of life flow to us from Him through His holy

---

[206] The theme of immortality has already been treated in Chapter Three. The Eucharist is here considered in its significance as a support to Christian faith in the resurrection of the body.

[207] No. 348 p. 15. Newman is quoting Hooker, Vol.ii,p.229ff but the underlining is his own. This is an Advent Sermon of 1833 in which the resurrection of the body is related to the Eucharist. Later, in 1836 in P.P.S.v,4, which is also an Advent sermon, he connects the Eucharist and the final judgment.

[208] ibid. p.13.

[209] P.P.S.vi,11.

body and blood sacrificed and risen again...there He is present, not in His divine essence only but in His manhood and applies through His flesh and His blood to our souls that eternal life, that principle of sanctity, immortality and glory...as a first fruits of grace and truth for the leavening elect people redeemed out of this corrupt and sinful world."[210]

Since our destiny is intrinsically linked with Christ, our resurrection from the dead is the fruit of His Paschal Mystery. That future event of bodily resurrection is made proleptically present in the Eucharist, whose effect is known only to faith. By means of this Sacrament, Christ nourishes the members of His glorified Body with the food of immortality. "While He feeds you prepare for the heavenly feast...Lay up year by year this seed of life within you, believing it will one day bear fruit."[211] Newman thus finds a mutual correlation between the mystery of the Eucharist and the resurrection of the flesh. Both are in the same order of faith, and are so far above reason that it is impossible to speculate or argue upon them. We cannot understand *how* Christ is present in the Sacrament, just as we cannot conceive *how* we will rise again. All we can do, is to believe in the effect which the Sacrament contains.[212] But just as it is the sign to the Church of Christ's resurrection, it is likewise the pledge of our own glorified nature hereafter.

The Sacrament of the Eucharist has a special heuristic role in fostering assent to the Christian belief in the resurrection of the body. Referring to the difficulty of accepting this extraordinary doctrine, Newman points to the Lord's Supper as a means of instruction in faith. The unitary nature of man and the nature of redemption as whole and entire, are implied in the total self-giving of Christ in the sacrament. "You will see this more clearly by considering what our Saviour says about the Blessed Sacrament of His Supper."[213] Here there are no distinctions of body and soul, in us who receive, or in Christ who gives Himself. It is Christ in the fullness of His humanity, who fills the whole person with His risen life. Just as food is necessary for the preservation

---

[210] No. 405 p. 15.

[211] P.P.S.i.21.

[212] ibid. "All that we are concerned to know is, *the effect* upon us of partaking of this blessed food."

[213] P.P.S.i.21.

of the whole man, body and soul, so the spiritual food of the Eucharist is the means of eternal life, which comes to its perfection in the resurrection of the body.

> "Now there is no distinction made here between soul and body. Christ's blessed Supper is food to us altogether, *whatever* we are, soul, body, and all. It is the seed of eternal life within us, the food of immortality, to preserve our body and soul unto everlasting life...Bread sustains us in this *temporal* life; the consecrated bread is the means of *eternal* strength for soul and body. Who could live this visible life without earthly food? And in the same general way the Supper of the Lord is the *means* of our living for ever."[214]

Summary of Chapter Six

Chapter Six examined the ways in which Newman's spirituality was shaped by his eschatology, and how the present life must be read in the light of the next. In this respect, the Liturgy of the Church held for him the supreme importance of enabling us to live as in the presence of the end of all things. Along with public prayer, the sacraments of the Church provided a provisional anticipation of the life of heaven. Private or personal prayer drew back the veil of the world of sense and gave access to the unseen world of faith. In the prayer of hope and deliverance, Christians experienced the "not-yet" of salvation, while the prayer of intercession underscored the reality that salvation had already come. Both forms of prayer, however, were not opposed to a life of service to the world. By the prayer of intercession, our minds were turned from otherworldly dreams to the needs of others, and by recognizing our own dependence on God we averted the danger of falling into a secularized salvation.

Newman also saw the Liturgy as forming the Christian character and this entailed the need for self-denial and fasting. By weaning us from the world of creature comforts, self-denial and fasting were a reminder that salvation was a task of fear and trembling. Though self-mortification was negative in itself, it was intended for the positive end of uniting us to Christ, for whose sake alone it was acceptable. Fasting

---

[214] ibid.

was a declaration of war on evil and not to be undertaken lightly. When exercised with discretion and moderation, it offered, with God's grace, a pledge of victory over sin. Hence the Eucharistic fast prepared us to subdue our sinful nature and receive the assurance of the resurrection of the body.

Part Two of the chapter treated Newman's appreciation of the eschatological significance of the Eucharist. As the highest act of worship, the sacrament of the Lord's Supper brought us as close as we can get to an anticipation of the next world. It contained the promise of future blessedness and was a present earnest of heaven. As the symbol of hope and present rejoicing, the Eucharist was the sacrament of the End-Time, linking Christ's First Coming with His Return in glory. It was the medicine of the soul which preserved the Church from evil and prepared us for the Judgment to come. Finally, the Eucharist was intended as an assurance to our faith of the fulness of redemption in the resurrection of the body.

CHAPTER SEVEN

SUMMARY AND CONCLUSIONS

The aim of the preceding chapters was to present the eschatology of Newman by a detailed study of his Anglican sermons. My main concern was to allow Newman to speak for himself and to minimize as far as possible any personal intrusions on my part. The object of this final chapter, however, is quite different; it is to offer an evaluation of his eschatology and formally state my conclusions. Before doing so however, it may be helpful to review first the main points of his argument.

Summary of Newman's Eschatology

The opening theme of the dissertation was the Coming of Christ, which was treated under four different aspects in the Advent sermons. Newman's attention was first directed to the Second Coming as the moment of God's sudden judgment on a wicked generation. He then drew a parallel between the apocalyptic signs of Scripture and the situation of his own day, which he viewed with great alarm. Though he did not identify the signs of the times with the advent of the Antichrist, he considered them tokens and anticipations of the last day. The Second Coming was a call to moral conversion and a reminder of God's consuming wrath.

The Advent sermons of 1824 and 1830 on unfulfilled prophecy contained scarcely any reference to the First Coming of Christ. When Christ's future coming was seen however, through the prism of the Incarnation, the prospect changed dramatically. Within this new framework, fear gave way to hope, and anxiety to a spirit of equanimity. The birth of Christ brought us salvation and provided all the means of moral and sacramental preparation for the fullness of eternal life. Thus we were enabled to encounter Him first in mercy, that we might bear the dreadful nature of His judgment at the Second Coming. Our present duty was to wait for His return as we would for a long-departed friend: not just for Him, but with Him, with hearts filled with expectation and joy.

A third aspect of these sermons concerned the delay of the Parousia which made a spirit of readiness for the Coming of Christ difficult to sustain. Reason provides no grounds of probability for His imminent Return, and history has shown the credulous and superstitious nature of such belief. To this Newman replied that Christians may have been wrong in particulars but not in the expectation itself. The climax of history has been reached in Christ's First Coming and subsequent events simply mark time with the mystery of His presence among us. Thus we can live as though the End has come and join sacramentally in the fullness of salvation. Though we cannot calculate the hour of His arrival, we can live with an intense awareness of His Coming.

In its original meaning parousia signifies the presence of someone as well as one's arrival. Newman used the former sense of the word in his special set of Advent sermons, which sought to determine the signs of Christ's presence in the Church. Though its external notes were faded, the Anglican Communion still revealed by its inner life the precious tokens of Christ. With renewed confidence he remained attached to the Church of his birth in the poignant hope that Christ's voice, which was now faint, would one day be heard aloud at His Second Coming.

The second chapter continued the theme of Christ's Coming under its foremost aspect of judgment. In line with Newman's general view of religious experience, the encounter with Christ will be "fearful before it is ecstatic". The roots of this fear was the axiomatic belief in the corruption of our human nature which was the ground and soil on which our salvation was laid.

The certainty and universality of the Last Judgment underlined the notion of moral accountability which would ultimately be weighed in an eternal balance. Judgment was the prerogative of God alone and the time of judgment was the Day of the Lord. Though His sentence was deferred to the end of time, it was operative throughout history in a hidden manner. However, this did not permit us to determine the actual instances of God's present justice. But in our own case, we could interpret present affliction as both a penalty for sin and a token of mercy. God's justice was not absorbed by His mercy and the higher order of His love did not abrogate the more fundamental law of justice. All that we know was revealed in Christ the merciful judge, who was no stranger to our infirmity.

A separate but related issue was the real possibility of eternal punishment, a doctrine Newman defended on the plain word of Scripture. Attempts to explain it away were founded on errors, all of which boiled down to a defective notion of sin. Though the belief was not central to the gospel message, it was an integral part of it; to reject it would dismantle the whole system of Christian doctrine. Though it was a source of perplexity, we must be content to gain religious light at the cost of intellectual darkness. The only proper response was to hold an attitude of reserve as we do for all the Christian mysteries.

The shadow side of Newman's eschatology was so deep and pervasive that only the most intense light could rescue it from total darkness. By His resurrection however, Christ won our justification by making a new creation, which effectively overpowers our original corruption. This revolution of a new heavens and a new earth contains the promise and possession of eternal life. Under the ministration of the Spirit, however, it is invisible to the naked eye and can only be discerned by the light of faith. But though we see things only in a mirror darkly, the state of grace in which we live, and the state of glory to which we are destined, are really one and the same. This is the core of Christian eschatology, which formed the theme of Chapter Three, and which reveals our human condition as fundamentally one of hope and joy.

We have seen that Newman's theology of hope did not appear on the surface of his sermons, but was hidden deep within them. He did not confuse it with shallow optimism or identify it with natural blessing. Hope was a grace whose warrant and foundation was the sacrifice of Christ, which did not deceive. Though it included desire, it was more a virtue to be exercised, than a dream to be gratified. With its origin and object in God alone, hope reached its goal in the Coming of Christ. This must be understood, not as the private fulfilment of the individual, but as the salvation of all. While hope was distinct from faith, it has been united to it since the time the gospel promises were proclaimed. Thus the past becomes the pledge of the future and faith formed in love is the assurance of our hope.

Hope implied the absence of a good while joy was the fruit of its possession. While hope looked to the future, where the fullness of salvation lay, joy celebrated its presence in the gift of Christ Himself. Thus the paradox of Christ's absence was the condition of His more intimate presence and marked the Christian life as a mixed economy of hope and joy.

Newman's treatment of life after death began with the intimations of reason about the immortality of the soul. He then outlined the progressive disclosure of the hereafter in the Old Testament. A quantum leap took place with the Christian revelation in the resurrection of the body. Christ was the origin and ground of our immortality and His Spirit was the instrument which transformed our bodies into living temples of God. Such a startling truth was beyond the power of reason but clearly affirmed that our salvation was whole and entire, of body and soul.

Up to Chapter Three the dissertation was concerned with the inner dynamic of eschatology which Newman derived from the Christ-Event. Now in Chapter Four we were to see its application and significance for the community and the individual. The Church was the historical fruit of Christ's resurrection and the vehicle by which the mystery of salvation was made present. In being the fulfilment of prophecy, it represented the end-time and signs of its future glory were revealed within it. "Viewed as God's design, viewed in its essence, viewed in its tendency and in its ultimate blessedness", the pilgrim Church was a sign of its absolute perfection in heaven.

Secondly, the Church is the Body of the Elect, which is God's "peculiar people" delivered out of an evil world. Its members are chosen in order to salvation and shall be the actual resulting fruit of their election on the last day. It is the little flock, the holy remnant which is sustained by the grace of Christ against the powers of the world. Moreover, persecution is the permanent badge of its holy vocation and the confirmation of its identity. It is meant not for this world but for the world to come.

The eschatological sign of the Church was also seen in its sharing in the Communion of Saints. Being ontologically grafted onto Christ, it became the Sacrament of risen life, in which the powers of the next world were realized. In contrast to the Body of the Elect which hoped for salvation, the Communion of Saints is a privilege we now enjoy. Its present notes will be brought to perfection in the heavenly Jerusalem. As the indefectible body of Christ, it will last to the end of time and when it ends with the Coming of Christ, the world will end with it.

The presentation next showed in Chapter Five how Newman saw the journey of the Church towards perfection was concretely enacted in the life of the individual Christian. Each member of the body passed through stages of probation and purification towards the heavenly city. Death marked the point of transition to an intermediate state, during which the fruit of grace was matured before entering into full communion with Christ. It was a momentous event of universal significance, but was transformed in Christian faith from being the termination of all things, to being but a moment of change. It was a gracious deliverance from a sinful world rather than an absolute victory of evil over our mortal bodies. Thus life and death in Christ are really a mark of distinction rather than division, for in death our union with Him remains unbroken. But the true goal of Christians was not the moment of death, but the Coming of Christ in whom salvation is achieved.

Death was the passage to an intermediate state of purification, between our earthly life and the resurrection of the body. This purification included the payment of the debt of sin, but consisted primarily in a school of contemplation. The intermediate state was by its nature incomplete: it was a twilight state of consciousness, a temporary abode, and one in which the object of our affections was as yet unfulfilled. It was nevertheless a state of comfort and of hope. Though they were at rest, the souls of the departed were alive to God and active in their intercession. Their trial had ended, their anxiety had passed and they waited with full assurance for the crown of victory.

The experience of isolation in death and the solitude of incompleteness in the intermediate state gives way to the fulness of Christ in heaven, in whom the individual and the community are united. Heaven was described as a place of holiness where none but the holy might enter. It consisted essentially in one unique object of admiration and love - God and the Lamb. Christ is the centre of heaven as He is the centre of the Church. And thus the Church mirrors the hidden life of heaven. In the experience of worship we have the foretaste of the joy to come. Heaven was not a chilly state of disembodied life but a warm dwelling place where everlasting peace pervades. Heaven was the fulfilment of our quest for happiness and the Sabbath Day of our humanity.

Newman's treatment of the last things was all to one purpose - to show how the world to come was within the lived experience of the Christian. Eschatology was not a theory on which future events were forecast, but a dimension of the Christian life whose reality was accessible by concrete acts of faith. It was by prayer and the sacraments, by fasting and self-denial that we grasped the meaning of the last things in our daily life. The principal means to this end was the liturgy in which a provisional and sacramental anticipation of the life of heaven was attained. Personal prayer enabled us to penetrate the veil of this world and hold communion with the next. It was of two kinds, the prayer of hope and deliverance and the prayer of intercession, each in turn representing one or other aspect of eschatology. Prayer was not opposed to a life of service but was the safeguard of promoting the growth of God's Kingdom. It was not an escape from duty but the means of labouring more directly for the Lord. By the prayer of intercession the danger of otherworldliness was averted, and by the prayer of dependence the fall into a secularized salvation.

Self-denial and fasting provided spirituality with the hallmark of realism. They were the means of weaning us from the world of sense and taught us to seek our salvation in fear and trembling. They had the positive end of uniting us to Christ, for whose sake alone they were acceptable. Fasting declared a conflict with evil, which under God's grace would be overcome. Hence the Eucharistic fast was a preparation to subdue our sinful nature and receive the promise of victory in the resurrection of the body.

The presentation ended with the significance for Newman of the Eucharist as a promise of future blessedness and a present earnest of heaven. It was for him the link between Christ's First Coming and His Second and the symbol of hope and present rejoicing. The Eucharist was also an encounter with Christ in mercy before meeting Him later in judgment. Finally, it was an aid to our belief in the resurrection of the body and a present assurance of the fulness of redemption.

Final Comments and Conclusions

In evaluating the eschatology of Newman I have borne in mind two things. The first is that there are two distinct stages of his work, a formative phase[1] (1824-1831) and a period of maturity (1834-1843), and that a fair evaluation should respect this distinction. The second observation is a familiar one which daunts every student of Newman. One is slow to pronounce a verdict on a mind so rich and creative as Newman's; he is full of surprises, and conclusions about his work are often premature and relative. However, Newman himself offers encouragement to all who would care to comment. In a disarming way

---

[1] In December 1831 Newman brought his list of sermon courses to an end. Until that year he had never repeated a series of sermons in the same pulpit. There are no newly written courses in 1832 or 1833, part of which year he was in Italy. The following year, 1834, saw the publication of his first volume of Parochial Sermons. It is on the basis of this information that one can distinguish between a formative and a mature period in Newman's sermons. Cf. Pett p. 91ff.

he reminds us that "No man will be a martyr for a conclusion. A conclusion is but an opinion." Thus the conclusions I have derived from this study are in the nature of personal opinions, and should neither enhance nor hurt the substantial contribution of Newman himself.

1. Newman's Eschatology and the Principle of Dogma

Newman's eschatology is founded on solid ground. It is firmly based on revelation, and the principle of dogma is its guiding spirit. Holy Scripture and Tradition (seen in the witness of the Fathers) and the doctrines of the Church, form one intimate bond in Newman's theology of the last things. His eschatology never goes beyond the limits of the revealed message and is free of all speculation on the hereafter.

Christ is the origin and centre of Newman's eschatology and a Christological perspective is maintained throughout all his sermons. It is a Christology seen under the aspect of the future of all things in Christ. It holds in view our ultimate communion with Christ, on the strength of our present communion with Him in the Spirit. Allied therefore to his Christology is Newman's rich theology of the indwelling of the Holy Spirit. On these two great pillars - Christology and Pneumatology - Newman builds a solid house in which the doctrine of the last things is secure.

Newman's adherence to revealed truth is second only to his ability to communicate it to others. His eschatology vibrates with life so that we no longer think of the last things in an unrelated future, but as existentially present in the experience of faith. By describing so vividly the unseen world we come to realize the meaning and direction of our relationship with Christ as it tends to its fulfilment.

One of the most positive features is Newman's constant stress on the hiddenness of eternal life. It is the mystery hidden with Christ in God which is the kernel of his eschatology. He goes to considerable depth in interpreting the mystery as known by faith and hope, without ever trespassing on its essentially hidden nature. In doing so, he fully respects the revealed truth itself and man's capacity and reception of it in faith. He thereby fulfils the criteria for the hermeneutics of eschatological assertions.

2. The Creative Tension of Eschatology

The internal tension between the "now" and the "not-yet" of salvation is of the very essence of eschatology. Since this tension is itself the result of two moments within the Christ-Event, - the First and Second Coming - eschatology, as we have noted, is intrinsically dependent on Christology. This polar relationship in the mystery of Christ sets up a magnetic field of grace which draws all things to itself. Salvation is thus a dynamic process of sanctification which finally ends in the fullness of Christ. Newman's sermons capture in a remarkable way the dynamic nature of salvation. He makes the Coming of Christ the governing principle of his eschatology and the centre around which all the moving parts revolve.

3. The Atonement-Incarnation Relation:

The above tension is further transposed onto the two central mysteries of Christ's life, the incarnation and the redemption. It is the atonement for sin which dominates Newman's early sermons. With it are associated all the elements of a consequent or unrealized eschatology. The Atonement signifies God's judgment on the world and the cross of Christ is the permanent reminder of the just deserts of sin. Though Christ has paid the debt of future punishment, His death sets in relief the thought of final judgment at the Second Coming. Thus the severe side of Newman's eschatology has its foundation in the mystery of the Atonement. The themes of guilt, judgment, punishment, hope, persecution, separation from the world, the body of the elect, the prayer of deliverance and fasting all cluster round a Christus Redemptor theology, which underpins a salvation of the "not-yet". When however Newman directs his attention to the Incarnation, we see the emergence of a realized eschatology. The First Coming was a Coming in mercy and the memory of this past event removes the anxiety of the future. The powers of the world to come are already imparted by virtue of the renewal of our nature in Christ. The incarnation is the basis of the sacramental principle through which salvation is realized in the eschatological present. This is concretely illustrated in the joy of Christ's spiritual presence, the Communion of Saints, the Liturgy of the Church especially in Baptism and the Eucharist, and the prayer of intercession. In these we have a Christus Consummator theology underpinning a realized eschatology.

The relation between these mysteries and the effect on Newman's eschatology is not one of perfect balance. There is a tendency to overstress one or the other at different times. In his formative period, his focus on the Atonement tends to be too absorbing; in his later sermons he tends to overstate the derived truths implied in the Incarnation. This I shall presently consider, but for the moment I wish only to draw attention to the major role both mysteries play in his eschatology.

4. The Influence of Calvinism

One of the defects of Newman's atonement theology can be seen in his early view on the nature and extent of human corruption. Even were one to grant him a wide margin of rhetorical licence, it would still appear that Newman attributed an exaggerated power to evil. To have the mind fixed on evil and sin is not to overcome it, but paradoxically to promote and encourage its growth. Here we find the source of Newman's pessimism in his early period. It is the result of an exclusive attention to the infinite gap between God's sovereignty and the guilt and nothingness of man. Though I have shown that his early sermons are free from any ultimate metaphysical dualism, and that he did not employ terror as a motive for moral conversion, there is still enough cause for alarm.

I tend to differ with Newman's own evaluation that his early sermons were only "mildly evangelical". I also believe that the "moderate" Calvinism usually ascribed to him, understates the case. This is not a value judgment on evangelical or Calvinist theology but a judgment on the fact and degree of their influence on Newman. From a study of the Anglican sermons, I conclude that this influence was deeper than Newman himself realized and that it extended far beyond his formative period and into his mature years.

Two examples may serve to illustrate the case and to show how it affects his eschatology. Both are related to final salvation, the first on the question of election, the second on the reality of eternal punishment. Newman firmly believed that the number of the elect will be small (see pp. 185-189). Apart altogether from his questionable exegesis of "many are called but few are chosen", is the influence of a Calvinist conception of the elect. When one, for example, compares Newman's sermon (P.P.S.v,18) with that of Bishop Beveridge's (Private Thoughts), whose Calvinist credentials are acknowledged, Newman is in fact more severe.

Though he does not limit God's salvific will antecedently to the predestined nor subscribe to dual predestination, his view of election has the serious de facto result of limiting God's grace. "So certain, so uniform is the fact, that it [the salvation of the few] is almost stated as a doctrine." One may also observe in passing the presence of another factor, which is a cultural rather than a theological one, in the emphasis he places on excellence and the near rejection of the mediocre.

Part of Newman's defence of the doctrine of eternal punishment was to safeguard the Atonement from being undermined, and in consequence the whole system of Christian belief from collapsing (see p. 94). This argument would stand if the Atonement was to be understood primarily in juridical and satisfactional terms. However, if Christ's redemptive sacrifice is seen, not as the just retribution for sin to an offended God, but the work of love, the argument for eternal punishment does not have to follow necessarily. Moreover, the Atonement can continue to hold its central place in the system of doctrine, without needing the prop and deterrent of eternal punishment. The latter doctrine, which is as incomprehensible to us as is the enormity of sin, also remains an integral part of what has been revealed. But there is nothing, to use Newman's own words, "peculiarly Christian" in it, both by reason of the fact that other religions have the same belief, and because it is not central to the gospel. What can be seen is not so much Newman's retention of the doctrine on the plain word of Scripture - with which I am in agreement - but the intensity of feeling with which he holds it. An intensity, I suspect, which he retained from the Calvinist evangelical days.

5. The Principle of Hope

The pessimism which is the by-product of Newman's conviction about the corrupt state of human nature is paradoxically the ground for his finely wrought principle of hope (see pp. 129-134). It is from the ashes of despondency that our nature rises in a phoenix-like manner through hope in Christ. The dark background against which Newman sketches his theology of hope gives the clearest definition to the unique source of light in Christ's new creation. He highlights the theological nature of hope - God alone is its source and object. He further distinguishes it from the moral virtue of fortitude and radically contrasts it with all forms of optimism that depend in the last analysis on human effort. The gratuitous nature of hope is thereby clearly underlined in

Newman's theology.

Having emphasized the character of hope as a supernatural grace rather than a natural blessing, Newman further stresses its role as a virtue to be exercised rather than a sentiment to be nursed. In this way he shows the complementary nature of salvation as a gift from God freely and fruitfully joined to the human task of responding to grace. The pilgrim's progress passes through the martyrdom of gnawing doubts to emerge finally with the steadfast companion of hope en route to the heavenly city. Newman thus draws on his deep personal trials to offer an appealing message of hope to the perplexed world of today. He exhibits an open sympathy with the vulnerable and the failed to rescue them from despair by a hope which bears the hallmark of authenticity.

Despite therefore - or rather due in great measure to - his early Calvinism, Newman's eschatology rises from a de profundis to a sursum corda. The most clear expression of this development is the melodic counterpoint between hope and joy. The theme of hope is composed in the minor key appropriately reminding us of the shadow from which it emanates. But his modulation to the major is reserved for his ode to joy, which becomes the dominant tone of his sermons. Thus the gloom of sin and atonement which formed the backdrop to the search for hope is dispelled by the realization of joy in Christ's incarnate presence.

6. The Dangers of a High Viewpoint

The excess of the early sermons with regard to the Atonement, shows a similar pattern in his later preaching with respect to the Incarnation. Each mystery was regarded by him, at different periods, as the cornerstone of Christianity. Having seen something of the effect of the Atonement on his eschatology, we can now look at the implications of the Incarnation. Here we see the dangers of a high Christology and a parallel high ecclesiology on Newman's theology of the last things.

The first point concerns the relation between the mystery of Christ's Resurrection and the Incarnation. Newman's view of the resurrection, unlike his view of Christ's death of atonement, changed very little throughout his sermons. But as his emphasis on the incarnation grows, there is a tendency to absorb the paschal event into the all-embracing truth of the Word made flesh. Though we have in the incarnation the substance of all revelation, each of the mysteries of

Christ's life has its own particular role in the total sum of revealed truth. The resurrection therefore is not simply a logical consequence of the Incarnation, or an extrapolation on the basis of Christ's incorrupt human nature, as Newman seems to imply (see pp. 150-154), but a unique act of God in raising mortal man from the dead. The resurrection of Christ is *the* eschatological event, and not the Incarnation. To it alone is due the fact that we can speak at all of a Christian eschatology. Newman's emphasis on the Incarnation tends to place in the background, without ever denying of course, the significance of the resurrection for Christian eschatology.

The influence of Alexandrian Christology can be seen also in the docetic tendency to pass over the sharp finality of death, and to spiritualize its real impact. This applies both to Christ's death and to our own. Death is not the death of a body but of a person. It was Christ who died, not just His body or His human nature, and His death radically meant the end of all our hopes. By blurring, in his later sermons, the radical nature of death as an abyss, Newman undervalues the significance of the fact that it was the action of God, and not the inherent power of Christ, which raised Him from the dead. Likewise in our own case, death is not merely, to use Newman's words, "a mark of distinction", but a rupture, which is not healed by Platonic assurances, but by naked trust in God's power.

Another example of Newman's excessive stress on the implications of the Incarnation, relates to the Church as the eschatological sign, and is of a more serious nature. This is the tendency in his later sermons to see the Church as an extension of the incarnation and to identify it with the Kingdom of God. On the positive side, Newman conceives the Church as a real symbol of the Kingdom of God *(Realsymbol)*, and not merely a representative one *(Vertretungssymbol)*. It is the historical embodiment of the Reign of Christ, in which the eschaton is present. From His presence within the Church, the visible institution takes its sign-value as the repository of realized salvation. In the context of enthusiasm and millenarianism it was necessary to insist on such a truth. But it is one thing to declare that the Kingdom is present in the Church and another to identify it with the Church, and thereby declare that the Church is the Kingdom of God on earth (see pp. 165-168).

Newman's ecclesiology is a good illustration of how the central motifs of Atonement and Incarnation shape his eschatology. In his atonement theology, the Church was seen as "remedial, temporal and relative", a mediatorial kingdom of a functional nature. It was a kingdom within the absolute Kingdom of God. Only in the next world would it be fused with God's eternal reign. In this picture we see the Church as the sign of the "not-yet" of salvation. The deficiency of this view was noted by Newman in the implications it had for Christology. Thereafter, in his sacramental theology, he describes the Church not in functional terms, but as a mystery within the mystery of the Incarnation. The Church then became the sacramental presence of Christ in the world and the sign of the "already" of realized salvation. But as we have an excessive dependence on the Atonement in his earlier view, we likewise have an excessive stress on the Incarnation in his later sermons. The balance then between the "now" and the "not-yet" is not quite perfectly struck.

7. A pre-critical interpretation of Prophecy

Though the stirrings of modern Biblical criticism were faintly heard during Newman's Oxford days, the movement did not gather strength in England until some twenty years after the last of the sermons we have considered. We are thus in the pre-critical period of biblical scholarship. Newman's knowledge of Scripture is nothing short of extraordinary, but there is a naivety of interpretation which is particularly evident in his understanding and use of prophecy. Prophecy was the Achilles heel of the traditional defence of the Word of God against rationalist doubts. However, when compared with many contemporary views, Newman's use of prophecy is marked by sobriety and caution. He understood the prophecies as something more than detailed prediction, but as types and paradigms which could be used to interpret the present age, and from which he could draw conclusions for our moral life. This typological reading, which is a limited understanding, was compounded by a more serious failure - though an unavoidable one - to distinguish between the apocalyptic and the prophetic genre in Scripture.

Naivety however does not entail the falsification of the Scripture message. Typology may be a simplified understanding of matters in themselves complex; it may be the misuse rather than the abuse of prophecy, but it is not wrong in itself. However the danger of a simplified picture is the promise of security it seems to offer, a security which often dissolves when a more critical and accurate view is taken. Newman's intense interest in prophecy seems to arise from this need, though his use of it can not be faulted, granted the limited understanding of the day.

The same may also be said of Newman's penchant for the apocalyptic passages of Scripture which was not confined to his early period, when insecurity and anxiety were much in evidence. On the one hand, he recognized the primary meaning of apocalyptic as signifying God's transcendence and sovereignty over history. It contained a message of consolation in times of distress. He also noted that the language in which it spoke of future events was figurative. But the severity with which he read them tended towards a literalist interpretation of the events at the end of time. His mistake lay as much in his own temperament and need for certitude, as it did in the inadequate tools he had for interpreting Scripture.

8. A Tendency towards Fideism

At the root of Newman's strict attention to prophecy lies a tendency towards fideism. This tendency is more overt in his Scott and Newton days, but can also be seen in his later sermons, though in a more concealed way. In the first case it manifests itself in expressions of bitter intolerance with values and ideas which threaten the religious and political status quo. His sermons on unfulfilled prophecy (see pp. 17-35) reverberate with alarm at the spectre of liberal ideas of democracy and freedom, which he considered the prelude to unbelief. Newman's rejection of these ideas is almost total and reactionary, and an undisguised need for religious security lies behind it.

In his later sermons, a similar tendency can be seen in the brake he puts on intellectual inquiry. His advice that it is best not to inquire "into over-subtle questions of the exact limits and character of our natural corruption" (see p. 68), carries a hint of anti-intellectualism in one for whom the belief in man's corruption was axiomatic. Similarly, his sacrosanct attitude to eternal punishment breathes too demanding a spirit of sacrificium intellectus for the sake of religious light. Again, the principle of reserve, which caused misunderstanding among many of his contemporaries, though in itself sound, appears at times over protective. Newman's protectionism is seen also in the parable of the prodigal son (see p. 87), which he interprets in a regressive manner to illustrate God's justice rather than His mercy - all to the purpose of defending the basis of greater certainty over the notion of favour, to which we can have no right or assurance.

Finally, we have Newman's tacit support for superstition as preferable to skepticism in matters of belief. While there is a strong positive side to his position, there are times when the balance is tipped too heavily against reason. This is particularly noticeable in his willingness to be party to misjudgments concerning the imminence of the Second Coming. Though he distances himself from the adventist alarms of the day, he has considerable sympathy with those who held credulous expectations of the signs (see pp. 48-49, 51-55). The law of probability, which was his staff of certitude, is quietly put aside when reason and history offer no affordable grounds for looking out for Christ's Coming. He does not acknowledge different degrees of assent in faith, but draws too sharp a division between it and reason, in their respective claims of evidence.

9. Newman's Eschatology and History

The lack of modern literary criticism of the Bible is relatively easy to point out in Newman's sermons, though this does not invalidate his use of Scripture. What is more difficult to estimate is the degree to which its twin companion of acceptable historical canons is employed. Newman's Anglican period marked the threshold of modern scientific history and there was a fervid interest in the subject at the time. Moreover, few have shown such a respect for the facts of history as Newman has, and so it is all too facile to mark him down as unhistorical. What is more to the point is to appreciate his philosophy of history and draw some value from it, at the same time recognizing some of its defects.

Newman's conception of history is basically a romantic one with a predilection for an age of purity and innocence. However, it is not a mere nostalgia, but combines, in Dawson's words, "a universalism with a sense of the uniqueness and irreversibility of the historic process". There is in Newman a sense of wonder at the kaleidoscope of events and a desire to find order and symmetry in their inner significance. The facts themselves are not self-interpreting but display the presence of a personal agency, either human or divine, by whose will they come into existence. For Newman, however, the sacred is the key to the profane history of the world. His romantic vision subtends a sacramental view in which historical events are signs and symbols of a deeper inward movement and agency.

In a way similar to his view of prophecy, Newman uses typology to understand the inner meaning of historical events. "In truth every event of this world is a type of those that follow, history proceeding forward as a circle ever enlarging". The idea of a type allows for the phenomenon of change, for a type is not identical with earlier or later manifestations. Moreover history is a forward movement which suggests the notion of freedom and non-determinacy. It is not a cyclic but a radial conception of history. But the idea of a circle establishes an order whose centre is God, who in His providence keeps matters under His care and prevents seemingly random events from ending in chaos. Newman's configuration of the problem is an attempt to reconcile the workings of divine providence and prophecy with the freedom of the human agent, in which history consists. To what degree the autonomy of the latter is upheld and how it affects his eschatology is the question that must be asked.

Newman's early view of providence comes from his evangelical background, which emphasized God's personal involvement in our daily life. This evangelical view may be seen as a response to the deism of the 18th century and its emphasis on the impersonal laws of Nature. It is related to the need of assurance that God is not irrelevant or inactive in our world. The greater Newman's assurance grows in a power working below the surface of things, the less he is disposed to call upon special providence for every detail. "His voice is so low...and His signs are so covert ... that it is difficult to determine when He addresses us." Moreover, he challenges the predestinarian position, itself caught in the contradiction of "working anxiously, because in reality, you have no work to do", with his own clear statement that the two doctrines of God's sovereignty and man's freedom "need not at all interfere with each other. They lie in different provinces, and are (as it were) incommensurables." Newman therefore upholds the autonomy of history which is the very foundation of human responsibility. The events of history are neither neutral nor accidental, but are the means to fulfilment in heaven or to destruction in hell.

What is lacking however in Newman's sermons is a sufficient regard and value for the idea of human progress. In an age which has been described as a time of anxious optimism, Newman shared all its anxiety with little of its optimism. Social and political developments towards a more just and prosperous society were not seen as contributory to the growth of God's kingdom. He looked with a jaundiced eye on schemes of social amelioration on the grounds that they were "especially dangerous for fixing as they do, our exertions on this world as an end, [and] go far to persuade us they have no other end." Here we must distinguish between his personal attitude to the poor, which was one of generosity and care, especially in his later days, and his ideological conservatism which resisted change in the structures of social deprivation.

The cause of this blind spot may be traced to two factors. The first is the pessimistic view of human nature he acquired from early Calvinism, and the second is the inflated role he gives to the Church. Both are restrictive of the freedom of history, the first by its low estimate of the value of human endeavour, the second by identifying the building up of the kingdom solely with the growth of the Church. The result is that the secular sphere has no role, which is proper to it, in furthering the kingdom; it acquires legitimation only in the name of the Church, and projects of human development are to be undertaken for conscious religious ends. In this way a dichotomy appears in Newman's eschatology between the fulfilment of the reign of God and history. His distinction between God's kingdom and human progress all but becomes a division, which leaves little room for man's contribution to the making of a new heavens and a new earth.

There is one aspect however where Newman sadly overvalues man's role in bringing the kingdom to its fullness. This is the power of man to promote the accumulation of evil, which eventually provokes God's final intervention on the last day. Newman's vision of the End relies on the apocalyptic passages of Scripture which underline God's transcendence, and is accompanied by a view of history in which the past is the mirror of the future. The partial fulfilment of Daniel's prophecies marked a victory of God's word over the evil history of man. The preservation of the faith by the fourth century Fathers likewise witnessed the triumph of religious truth. On both scores Newman saw the supremacy of God's word and the dogma of the Church over the challenges of history. The continuous conflict between the kingdom of evil, of man's own making, and the kingdom of God will end in a cataclysm in which God's word will conquer. History began with Adam's Fall; it suffered a fatal defeat with the Coming of the Second Adam, but its final overthrow awaits the Incarnate Word when He comes in all His glory.

I have described the relation between truth and history as an oppositional one in which truth eventually claims the victory. This I said was due to Newman's limited understanding of the role of history and the restrictions he put on it. After twelve years of considering the problem, Newman preached, in his last university sermon in 1843, on the development of doctrine. He distinguished between the dogmatic principle which remains unchanged and the dogma or doctrine which is subject to historical development. In doing so, history was no longer seen as a threat to the immutability of truth, but the very condition for its life and continuity. Thus it is towards the end of his Anglican sermons that we reach the highest point of Newman's regard for history and the autonomy which it has in the development of truth.

10. Newman's Eschatology and Worship

Though Newman's philosophy of history, useful in its own right, shows him to be a man of his time, his grasp of the relation between worship and eschatology has a lasting value. It is in the realm of worship that the life and language of the unseen world assume their proper significance. Liturgy is the locus classicus of eschatology; the adage lex orandi, lex credendi, is nowhere more pertinent than in the question and meaning of the last things. When the Church ceases to pray, she ceases to believe in the reality of the world to come. Newman's theology of the last things is the fruit of a lived experience of prayer. It is here that we find in him a master communicating the treasures of the spiritual life. Combining the intellectual and the devotional, he forms a synthesis of what we are to believe, how we are to live and what we have to hope for, based on the liturgical life of the Church. This is perhaps his greatest achievement and one which sets his eschatology apart.

11. Newman's Eschatology and Creation

The distinction between the early and the later Newman is nowhere more ad rem than when one comes to consider his view of creation. Here again we are brought back to the dialectic between the Atonement and the Incarnation. The early pessimism of "the world lieth in wickedness" is replaced by the later lyrical appreciation that "this earth, which now buds forth in leaves and blossoms, will one day burst forth into a new world of light and glory." Newman however, as far as one can discover from the sermons, does not allow the romanticism he shared with the nature poets, to affect his theological view of the material world. There is in fact little one can find to constitute a theology of creation, and what we have is a rather negative appraisal. Newman's eschatology is personal but anthropocentric. Though he acknowledges a new dynamism in the world of nature as a result of Christ's resurrection, his incarnational theology in the Anglican sermons is not extended in a developed way to material creation, with regard to its final end. Creation began with God's fiat, and as it began, so will it end, with God's direct intervention. The original chaos which God turned into cosmos, reasserts itself at the end of the world. An apocalyptic shroud hangs over creation, which will be destroyed - "even the very work of His hands", in the making of a new heavens and a new earth.

12. Postscript

As I come to the end of this study I am conscious that the work by which Newman's theology of the last things is most popularly known, has received no mention. Here I refer to the *Dream of Gerontius* which is the most celebrated exposition of Newman's theology of death and purgatory. Written in 1865, the poem takes us well into his Catholic period and thus beyond the area of research set by the dissertation. It may be helpful, however, to give some brief indication of Newman's eschatology since 1845 when he became a Roman Catholic. While this account can be nothing more than a bare outline, it is justified on the score that it is wrong to leave the impression that Newman's reflections on eschatology ceased when he delivered his last Anglican sermon. Moreover, to put his Catholic period into cold storage would misrepresent Newman, whose life displayed such a singular unity and development. It has also an adverse effect on the Anglican sermons themselves, by implicitly suggesting that this chapter of his life had no bearing on his later work, and may thus be regarded as a closed book. To forestall such an idea and to round off this thesis, I shall sketch some of the changes in Newman's theology of the last things during his Catholic days.

The elements I have selected for this purpose have reference to three areas which would, however, require a detailed study. First, we have three volumes of Catholic sermons, namely, his *Sermons on Various Occasions* (O.S.,1870), *Discourses Addressed to Mixed Congregations* (Mix.,1871), and the *Catholic Sermons of Cardinal Newman* (Cath.S), edited posthumously in 1957. A large volume of

Newman's *Sermon Notes* (S.N.), covering the period 1849-1878, was also published afer his death, in 1913. Second, in Newman's *Philosophical Notebook* there are several entries which are relevant to eschatology, such as his reflections in 1875 on the Intermediate State, his belief in the reality of the Unseen World (1876) and his pondering over the meaning of eternity (1880). Third, the *Dream of Gerontius* must be regarded as of special importance in the development of Newman's individual eschatology. In addition to these, the *Letters and Diaries* of the Catholic period, comprising twenty-two volumes, would seem to offer abundant material similar to the themes discovered during his Anglican period. Many of Newman's late letters demonstrate the constancy of his belief in Eternal Punishment and his *Letter on Matter and Spirit* (Appendix to The Philosophical Notebook pp. 199-216) marks an advance in his epistemology which has implications for his view of creation. The mention of these alone gives sufficient indication that Newman's eschatology was not confined to his Anglican period.

Keeping the above references in mind, we recognize that the outline which follows cannot be more than a naked signpost indicating the direction of Newman's Catholic eschatology. Of necessity it must be limited to the most tentative and general of observations which will be listed rather than argued with any assurance.

1) With regard to Newman's preaching as a Catholic, the form and style of his sermons changed considerably and this had its effect on their content. In deference to Catholic practice he preached rather than read his sermon, and adapted his thought, as always, to his new congregation which was much less educated than the fellows and undergraduates of Oxford. His Catholic parochial sermons are thus less refined and less theological than those delivered in St Mary's. There is, moreover, another equally important reason for this change. In coming to Catholicism, Newman came, as he remarked, into a state of repose, which did not require the finely measured argument he used to persuade his Anglican parishioners. Having arrived at what he considered the refuge and the home of truth, he no longer felt the need, so evident in his Anglican sermons, to make a case for Catholic doctrine. After the theological battles of the past, now was the time for devotion, a feature of Christian life which the Roman Catholic ethos fostered.

2) There is no break in continuity with the eschatological themes of the Anglican sermons. One can find abundant references in Newman's Catholic preaching as a counterpart to the themes of each chapter of this thesis. The advent theme of eschatological waiting for the

Coming of Christ is found in many of his sermons with titles such as *Waiting for Christ* (O.S.iii), *The Last Times of the World* (S.N. Dec.16,1849) , *Advent of Christ Foretold* (S.N. Dec.25,1870), *The Second Coming* (S.N. April 21 1872), *First and Second Advents* (S.N. Nov.19 1876), *The Second Advent* (S.N. Dec.3,1876), *Signs of the Second Advent* (S.N. Dec.17,1876), *First Advent* (S.N. Dec.24, 1876) and *Infidelity of the Future* (Cath.S.ix). Moreover the apocalyptic seasoning of Newman's futurist eschatology is preserved.

On the theme of Judgment and the severe side of eschatology, a similar continuity of theme with his Anglican eschatology can be found. We have sermons such as *Preparation for the Judgment* (Cath.S.ii), *The Call of Grace* (Cath.S.iii) and *The World and Sin* (Cath.S.vi). Likewise, in his Sermon Notes, there are many titles related to the theme: e.g. *Suffering* (S.N. Feast of Holy Innocents, 1856), *The State of Original Sin* (S.N. Mar.3, 1861), *The Divine Judgments* (Aug.6,13,20,27; Sept.17, 1871), *Hell* (Mar.12, 1876), and *Punishment of Sin* (Mar.19, 1876). The intensity of Newman's conviction of the enormity of sin, and the firm belief expressed in his Anglican sermon on *Justice, as a Principle of Divine Governance,* are retained.

The theme of the New Creation and Eternal Life is also abundantly treated in Newman's Catholic period. He deals with the present state of grace and salvation in three of his *Discourses Addressed to Mixed Congregations* (Mix.,vii,viii,ix) and his Sermon Notes are replete with references to the theme of Chapter Three of the dissertation, e.g. his sermons on *Grace the Principle of Eternal Life* (S.N. Feb.24, 1850), *The State of Innocence* (S.N. Feb.24, 1861), *Victory of Good over Evil* (S.N. Easter Day, 1872), *The Riches of His Glory* (S.N. Sept.8, 1872), *The Seen and Unseen Worlds* (S.N. Mar.28, 1875), *Gifts of the Resurrection* (S.N. Easter Day, 1876), *Coming of the Holy Ghost* (S.N. Pentecost 1878), and *On the New Creation* (S.N. July 21, 1978).

Sermons related to the Church as Eschatological Sign are surprisingly few in Newman's Catholic preaching. In his Sermon Notes, however, there is an occasional reference to the theme, such as his sermon on *The Visible Temple* (S.N. July 2,1871), *Manifestation of the Kingdom of Christ* (S.N. Jan.12, 1873) and *Faith Failing* (S.N. April 14, 1872). A possible explanation will be offered when we look at some of the ways in which Newman's eschatology changed during his Catholic period.

In contrast to the diminished treatment on the Church there is an increased interest in individual eschatology. We have two sermons which were preached at the funeral Mass of close friends (O.S.xiii, xiv) and in the Sermon Notes there are many dealing with the theme of death and the necessity to use the present time of preparation: e.g. *On Death* (S.N. Dec.1, 1850), *On the Death of the Sinner* (S.N. Aug.10, 1851), *Life a Pilgrimage* (S.N. Jan.9, 1876), *Final Perseverance* (S.N. Oct.20, 1872), *The End of Man* (Aug.25, 1877). Sermons on the Intermediate State and Heaven as the end of human fulfilment, are also prominent in his Catholic preaching, e.g. his sermons on *Purgatory* (S.N. Nov.11, 1849) and *The Past not Dead* (S.N. Dec.31, 1876), while on Heaven we have *God the Stay of Eternity* (Aug.19, 1860), *God our Stay in Eternity* (Aug.28, 1870; Mar.2, 1873). The necessity of holiness as a requirement for heaven may be seen in his sermon *Saintliness, the Standard of Christian Principle* (Mix. v).

Finally, the continuity with the Anglican sermons on Eschatology and Christian Life is also evident in his Catholic sermon notes on the Eucharist and the need for self-denial. There is an undated sermon entitled *Self-Denial in Comforts* and two on the sacrament, viz. *Devotion to the Holy Eucharist* (May 25, 1856) and *The Holy Eucharist* (April 25, 1858).

Continuity with the Anglican sermons can also be seen in Newman's customary practice of writing a course or a series of sermons on a particular topic. This began with his goal of providing a comprehensive form of instruction at St. Clements; though the writing of courses was later shelved as being too confining, it was never totally abandoned as can be seen from his Advent and Lent series during his mature Anglican period. A vestige of the same practice can be found in his Catholic period in his Advent series of sermons in 1876, a series on the theme of Judgment in 1871, a course of sermons on the Angels in 1860 and a Lent series for 1876. We also have a counterpart to his Anglican preparation for Confirmation in his catechetical instruction of 1849 with their Latin titles, cf. Sermon Notes, pp. 289-333.

3) If continuity rather than change is the more notable feature of Newman's Catholic sermons when compared with those of his Anglican period, there are also important differences. In all his preaching at Oxford, no mention was found for the belief in the particular judgment which takes place immediately upon the death of the individual. "A Protestant," he remarks, "really has no notion of it" (S.N. p. 40). As we saw from the dissertation, Newman radically subordinated his theology of death to the goal of Christ's Second Coming and the General Judgment. Though the latter did not mean an impersonal and

undifferentiated sentence, but involved the taking of evidence in each particular case, the universal judgment would be deferred until the Last Day. In his Catholic sermons, however, Newman makes room for the notion of a particular judgment, without impairing his view of the primacy of the General Judgment, (cf. his *Preparation for the Judgment*, Cath.S.ii, p. 35 and his sermon *On the Particular Judgment*, S.N. July 14, 1850).

With his acceptance of Catholic teaching, Newman no longer refers in his sermons to the period between death and the resurrection of the body as the Intermediate State, but quite simply as Purgatory. Though this alteration is more than a cosmetic change of name, he continues to emphasize the more benign view he held in his Anglican days, rather than the fearful description common among Catholics, of Purgatory as a chamber of extreme torment. Newman in fact did much to promote the positive side of the doctrine and purify Catholic misconceptions of exaggerated notions of the pain of sense. By illustrating from Catholic authors themselves, such as St. Francis de Sales and St. Catherine of Genoa, he showed how his own more wholesome view of Purgatory was within accepted Catholic teaching.

There is a general tendency in Newman's Catholic sermons towards further development of an individual perspective of the last things and a diminution of the collective eschatology of the Church. This is perhaps the single most important difference between his Anglican sermons and those of his Catholic period. The influence of Catholic treatises on de novissimis can be seen in his refering to the "four last things" (Cath.S.iii, p. 46), a terminology never employed in the Anglican sermons. This tendency is more evident in the period immediately following his reception into the Catholic Church, but can also be seen in his much later preaching. A possible explanation of why he has less to say about the eschatological nature of the Church, may be found in the fact that there is less need to emphasize such a view, since he has now found a haven of assurance. Moreover, the role of Our Lady as the virginal image of the heavenly Jerusalem, assumes an added significance. Her faith and sanctity become the model for the Church's devotion, and an expression of its sign as a Body destined for the next world. Thus we find the frequent occurrence of the theme of Our Lady as representative of what the Church should be, e.g. *Our Lady in the Gospel* (Cath.S.viii), *Glories of Mary for the Sake of her Son* (Mix.,xvii) - which is reminiscent of P.P.S.iv,10 *The Visible Church for the Sake of the Elect*, - and its companion sermon *On the Fitness of the Glories of Mary*, (Mix.,xviii). In Newman's Sermon Notes there are two other sermons on our Lady which have a distinctive bearing on Catholic eschatology, viz. *On Our Lady as in the Body* (S.N. Aug.15, 1852), where the tendency to docetism found in the Anglican Sermons can likewise be detected, and on *The Immaculate Conception* (S.N. Dec.10, 1876).

In his later life, thoughts on the meaning of eternity begin to preoccupy him. Eternity is not, he believes, the prolongation of time without end, but the absence of change - "as soon as there is no change in it (time), it is eternity" (S.N. *Eternity*, Jan.1, 1865). Though there are many sermons during the Anglican period on the passage of time, it is only here that we find him directly grappling with the idea. The sermon was written just prior to the Dream of Gerontius and adds confirmation to the events surrounding the poem that he indeed felt near to death.

It must naturally have seemed to Newman that death was ever closer when, in 1880, he ponders over the meaning of eternity (The Philosophical Notebook, Sept.12, 1880, p. 190). "Eternity, as such," he writes there, "is not an object of desire, rather the contrary...". It is a purely negative concept and only has meaning in terms of its opposite, which is not time, but life itself. But since there is no object, "such as a quality" attached to the notion of eternity, it simply refers to "the new and alternative state which is unknown."

What is known, but unseen, is the invisible world whose reality Newman argues can be proved from personal experience. "The fact that there is a world unseen but real is not based <merely> upon tradition, an authoritative dictum, imagination, hope or wish, but <is based> on our experience of each other..." (The Philosophical Notebook, Sept.10, 1876, p. 188). It is this firm conviction in the reality of God and a world of spirits that makes the thought of eternity free of anxiety and filled with hope.

A rich part of human experience lies within the twilight world of dreams. In the Anglican sermons, "dream" was generally used pejoratively to denote a fantasy or to describe something as unreal. We have seen, however, the positive use Newman made of the phenomenon of dreaming to support the belief that the semi-consciousness of the Intermediate State involves no self-contradiction. Nonetheless, he was extremely cautious not to rest his argument on purely subjective grounds, or make positive declarations about the condition of the departed. Psychologist that he was, dreams held a fascination for him. In his Catholic period Newman showed a greater freedom, which he would not have allowed himself during his earlier days, to accept that

330

truth may be conveyed by dreams. One such instance was an old lady's dream about the Intermediate State just before she died (The Philosophical Notebook, Aug.29, 1875, pp. 181-187). On this dream, told to him by the woman's daughter, Newman remarks: "I am more struck with the dream, because I have either long or <at least> held about the Intermediate State all the six points I have enumerated". These six tenets of belief were contained in the story of this "very remarkable dream, as being very unlike what would occur to a Protestant, as the Lady was, nay to most Catholics."

It is however in *The Dream of Gerontius*, that we find Newman's most eloquent meditation on Christian death and Purgatory. The poem is set in the liturgical framework of the Roman Ritual. Guided by the prayer of the Church, Newman explores the unseen world of faith and "dreams that are true, yet enigmatical." Time and eternity, sense and symbol, dream and reality are woven into a unity of faith in which the night is the herald of a new dawn.

As a final comment it must be said that Newman's work on the last things stands as a considerable contribution to theology and bears favourable comparison to his other achievements by which he is better known. In presenting his eschatology in the Anglican sermons, it is my hope that this dissertation may in a small way encourage interest in it. As for myself, it only remains to express my gratitude and affection to Newman, for rekindling the hope that is within.

BIBLIOGRAPHY

A. Primary Sources

1. The Anglican Sermons:

a. The Published Sermons

Newman, J.H. *Parochial and Plain Sermons,* 8 Vols., London, Longmans, Green and Co., 1868.

———————— *Sermons preached before the University of Oxford,* London, Longmans, Green and Co., 1872.

———————— *Sermons bearing on Subjects of the Day,* London, Longmans, Green and Co., 1869.

———————— *Tract LXXXIII, Advent Sermons on Antichrist,* (1838), later republished as 'The Patristic Idea of the Antichrist' in *Discussions and Arguments,* London, Longmans, Green and Co., 1872, pp.44-108.

Sermons given in Adam de Brome chapel at St. Mary the Virgin, Oxford, were designated as lectures but were numbered by Newman in one series with the Anglican sermons. The following published volumes had their origin in Newman's preaching and may properly be considered as belonging to the sermon genre:

Newman, J.H. *Lectures on the Doctrine of Justification,* London, Longmans, Green and Co., 1874.

———————— *Lectures on the Prophetical Office of the Church,* (1837), later republished as *The Via Media,* Vol.1, London, Longmans, Green and Co., 1877.

———————— Tract LXXXV: *On the Scripture Proofs of the Doctrine of the Church,* (1838), later republished as 'Holy Scripture in its Relation to the Catholic Creed', in *Discussions and Arguments,* London, Longmans, Green and Co., 1872, pp.109-253.

b. The Unpublished Sermons

At the Birmingham Oratory the manuscripts of Newman's Anglican sermons are found in labelled boxes. The following is a chronological list of these unpublished sermons, giving the number assigned by Newman, the archival reference, the date of first preaching and the title where Newman gave one.

List of Unpublished Sermons

Number	Reference	Year	Date		Title
2	A.17.1	1824	23	June	waiting on God
1	A.17.1		27	June	the work of man
6	A.17.1		18	July	self-righteousness
4	A.17.1		25	July	The wounded spirit
5	A.17.1		1	Aug	prayer
8	B.3.4		1	Aug	parable of ten virgins
10	B.3.4		8	Aug	the man of God from Judah (and old prophet)
12	B.3.4		15	Aug	religion, alone sufficient for man
13	A.17		22	Aug	parable of the vineyard
14	A.17.1		22	Aug	illumination
15	A.17.1		29	Aug	parable of the Pharisee and publican
18	A.17.1		5	Sept	parable of the sower
17	B.3.6		12	Sept	character of God and His holy law
20	A.17.1		12	Sept	parable of the good Samaritan
19	A.50.6		19	Sept	corruption of human nature
22	B.3.4		19	Sept	parable of the talents
24	B.3.4		3	Oct	parable of the great supper
26	A.17.1		10	Oct	parable of the prodigal son
28	A.17.1		17	Oct	parable of the barren fig tree
27	A.17.1		24	Oct	The atonement of Christ
29	B.3.4		31	Oct	the effects on the mind of the doctrine of the cross
16	A.17.1		7	Nov	parable of the labourers in the vineyard

36	A.17.1		21	Nov	God's word a refuge in trouble
40	B.3.4		5	Dec	on reading Scripture (2nd Advent)
42	A.50.2		12	Dec	on attending the ordinances of grace (3rd Advent)
45	B.3.6		25	Dec	Christ, the Comforter of the mourner
46	A.17.1		26	Dec	Christ's divine and mediatorial kingdoms
50	A.17.i	1825	2	Jan	preparation for death
			15		April 1832
51	B.3.4		2	Jan	nature and history of the
			cf. 25		Dec. 1826, Mediatorial kingdom
			15		April 1827
47	B.3.4		16	Jan	different cases of God's hiding Himself from us (cf 1 Jan 1832)
48	B.3.4		23	Jan	different cases of God's hiding Himself from us (2)
49	B.3.4		30	Jan	different cases of God's hiding Himself from us (3)
54	B.3.4		30	Jan	blessedness of affliction
57	A.17.1		20	Feb	nature and object of faith
61	A.17.1		6	Mar	justification through faith only
67	A.17.1		27	Mar	faith connected with, and confirmed by the inward witness
74	A.17.1		1	April	review of Christ's sufferings and death
69	B.3.6		3	April	consolatory truths implied in resurrection
70	B.3.6		10	April	personal interest in Christ
78	B.3.4		1	May	evidences of the resurrection
73	A.17.1		8	May	on faith, hope, and charity
79	B.3.6		8	May	John and Christ's baptisms compared
81	A.50.1		29	May	on the Trinity
84	B.3.4		19	June	pride (towards man)
85	B.3.4		19	June	conscience, its use etc.
86	B.3.4		3	July	against sins of the tongue

87	A.50.6	3	July	difference between grace and blessing
89	A.17.1	10	July	against worldliness
90	B.3.4	17	July	poverty will not *save* a man
92	B.3.4	24	July	God does not govern us by judgements
93	B.3.4	31	July	exceptions to the foregoing
95	B.3.4	31	July	on the sin of presumption
96	B.3.6	7	Aug	uncharitableness
97	B.3.4	7	Aug	future reward not merited by us
99	B.3.4	14	Aug	the Chritsian promise not temporal
100	B.3.4	21	Aug	on defects in meekness, long suffering etc.etc.
101	B.3.4	28	Aug	on sins against conscience
103	A.17.1	4	Sept	holiness the end of the Gospel
102	B.3.4	4	Sept	on the *nature* of the future promise
104	B.3.4	11	Sept	probable reasons for the partial extension of Christianity
106	A.17.1	18	Sept	state of the heathen world an evidence of the need of a revelation
108	A.17.1	25	Sept	on the *principles* common to all revelation (1)
109	B.3.6	25	Sept	the blessedness of obedience
110	A.17.1	16	Oct	on the *feelings* produced in common by all revelation (2)
111	A.17.1	23	Oct	on the compatibility of spiritual feelings with scanty knowledge in ancient believers
112	B.3.4	30	Oct	on the knowledge of the gospel in the *antediluvian* age
114	B.3.4	(1825) (6	Nov)	The world a discipline of moral character
115	B.3.4	1825	6 Nov	on the knowledge of the gospel in the *patriarchal* age
117	B.3.4	13	Nov	on the knowledge of the gospel *under the Mosaic dispensation*
116	B.3.6	13	Nov	the Holy Spirit, the agent in forming habits

118	B.3.4		20	Nov	our admittance into the church our title to the Holy Spirit
120	A.50.2˙		27	Nov	on the communion of saints
119	B.3.4		4	Dec	on natural religion
121	A.50.2		4	Dec	on the use of the visible church
122	A.50.2		11	Dec	instruction, a duty of the members of the church
123	B.3.4		11	Dec	on the internal evidence of the evangelical doctrine
128	B.3.4	1826	8	Jan	on some popular mistakes as to the object of education
130	A.50.1		15	Jan	on the differences of religious opinions in the world
133	A.17.1		29	Jan	the Jewish law useful in checking idolatry
134	A.50.4		29	Jan	on St Luke and his Gospel
135	B.3.4		12	Feb	on the means adopted in separating the Jews from the world
137	P.C.84		19	Feb	the faith of Mary
138	B.3.4		19	Feb	on the Jewish rites as directed against idolatry
139	B.3.4		26	Feb	on the Jewish Theocracy
142	B.3.4		5	Mar	on the laws protecting the Theocracy
143	B.3.4		12	Mar	on the temporal sanctions of the Jewish law
144	A.50.3		12	Mar	on infant baptism
145	B.3.4		19	Mar	on the sabbath, as a sign of the creation to the heathen
146	B.3.4		24	Mar	on the penitent thief
149	B.3.4		16	April	on the faithfulness etc of God as shown to the heathen in His dealings with Israel
150	A.17.1		23	April	general observations on the whole subject. conclusion
152	A.17.i		30	July	on the Lord's Prayer
154	A.17.1	1826	13	Aug	On the ten commandments
155	A.50.1		27	Aug	On the Creed

156	A.50.3		10	Sept	On the Sacraments etc.
157	A.50.2		19	Nov	On the One Catholic and Apostolic Church
158	B.3.4		25	Dec	On the Mediatorial Kingdom of Christ
159	B.3.4	1827	21	Jan	Almsgiving on Christian principles
160	A.8.1		15	April	On the Mediatorial Kingdom of Christ
162	B.3.4		19	Aug	On general education as connected with the Church and religion
161	A.50.1		2	Sept	On the Christian law of liberty
[?]	B.3.6		9	Sept	
163	A.50.5	1828	2	April	On the death of a very dear Friend
164	B.3.4		4	May	on the ultimate extension of Chritianity over the whole world
166	A.50.1		1	June	On the doctrine of the Trinity
169	A.50.3		22	June	On Infant Baptism - part ii
170	B.3.6		29	June	Infant baptism, the doctrine of the *Church.* part iii.
171	A.17.1		6	July	on Confirmation
172	A.50.3		13	July	on the Lord's Supper
175	B.3.4	1828	7	Sept	On the mediatorial Kingdom of Christ (generally)
176	B.3.4		14	Sept	On the Christian scheme of mediation *as connected* with the natural and Jewish systems
177	B.3.4		21	Sept	On the divine nature of our Mediator
178	B.3.4		12	Oct	On the atonement (considered generally)
180	B.3.4		26	Oct	On the atonement
188	A.50.6	1829	18	Jan	On Justification by faith only
182	B.3.6		25	Jan	Lectures on Romans. Introduction
185	A.50.6		8	Feb	Faith the one condition of acceptance under every dispensation since the fall
184	B.3.6		15	Feb	
186	A.50.6	1829	22	Feb	Imputed rightteousness
187	A.17.1		1	Mar	justification through the Law, and

					the connexion of the Law and the Gospel
191	A.50.5		22	Mar	Sermon on the intercourse between parish Priest and his charge - anniversary sermon of my entering into St Mary's
192	A.50.6		29	Mar	The flesh
193	B.3.6		17	April	The sufferings of Christ
194	B.3.6		10	May	Gratitude to Christ
197	B.3.6		31	May	Spiritual freedom which the Jews had not
198	A.50.5		7	June	Christian's spiritual obedience; - the Holy Spirit author of it
200	A.50.6		21	June	The Christian election, and how the Apostles treated it
201	B.3.6		28	June	The rejection of the Jews
202	B.3.4		12	July	Introductory. - character of Abraham
205	B.3.6		2	Aug	Abraham's history in connexion with Isaac
206	B.3.4		9	Aug	History and character of Esau
208	B.3.6		23	Aug	Jacob and Joseph
209	B.3.4		30	Aug	remarks on the history and character of Jacob
210	B.3.4		6	Sept	Early history and character of Moses
213	A.17.1		25	Oct	On the duty of Public Worship
214	B.3.6		1	Nov	On preaching
216	A.50.2		15	Nov	On Church - union, and the sin of schism
224	A.50.3 4	1830	31	Jan	The Liturgy the service of the Christian Priest
225	A.50.3		7	Feb	The Liturgy public - its three peculiar uses
226	B.3.6		14	Feb	The Liturgy, *first*, teaches doctrine - viz concerning God
227	*P.S.* III,6		21	Feb	Faith and Obedience.
	A.6.14				The Liturgy, *first*, teaches doctrine - viz concerning man's duty

228	B.3.6	28 Feb	The Liturgy, *first*, teaches doctrine - viz concerning means of grace
229	B.3.6	7 Mar	The Liturgy, *second*, forms the character - viz to faith
230	B.3.6	14 Mar	The Liturgy, *second*, forms the character - viz to hope
232	*P.S.* VII,7	28 Mar	The Duty of Self-denial
	B.3.6		The Liturgy forming the character - viz to self denial - the Commination and Lent Services
233	B.3.6	4 April	The Liturgy forming the character - viz to charity. - The Litany
235	A.17.1	25 April	Sermon on St Mark's day - his history and character
236	B.3.4	2 May	History contained in the book of judges
241	B.3.6	11 June	St Barnabas, - his history and character, - on brotherly kindness and fellow-feeling
242	B.3.4	13 June	History and character of David illustrated in his care of the ark and preparations for the temple
243	B.3.4	20 June	Reflections on the providential arrangement of the foregoing history - and account of the event in which it terminated - the building of the temple
244	B.3.6	24 June	St John Baptist - his history and character - we must do our duty in our station even against hope
245	B.3.4	27 June	The history and character of Solomon
246	A.50.4	29 June	St Peter's authority - and thence on Church authority etc
247	A.50.2	18 July	Sermon on the death of King George IV, - containing remarks on the Kingly Power in England and the subject's duties
248	A.50.4	22 July	St Mary Magdalene's example, as teaching us love is more than gifts and station

249	A.17.1		25	July	The life of St James the Greater - his request to Christ and its answer as teaching use narrowness of the way of life
251	B.3.6		6	Aug	Transfiguration - The nature and circumstances of future happiness
252	B.3.4		8	Aug	The history of Israel and Judah from their separation to the alliance of Ahab and Jehoshaphat
253	B.3.4	1830	15	Aug	The mission of the Prophets, especially in the Kingdom of Israel - and its effects
261 [b]	B.3.6		[?]	Aug	
255	A.50.4		24	Aug	St Bartholomew a pattern of guilelessness - addresst to persons about to be confirmed
256	B.3.4		29	Aug	Hezekiah and other strengtheners of Judah down to Christ's coming
259	B.3.6		21	Sept	St Matthew - wealth is of little value except for God's service
260	A.50.4		29	Sept	St Michael and the angels - their guardianship and care of the saints
261	A.17.1		18	Oct	St Luke, and thence on the variety of fortune and character found in the first followers of Christ
266	B.3.6		1	Nov	All saints - on the intermediate state
267	A.50.2		7	Nov	The responsibility of Christian Missions - as resulting from the *object* proposed in them - and as determining the *spirit* in which they are to be undertaken
269	A.50.2		21	Nov	Doubts in religion do not interfere with practical obedience
270	A.50.2		28	Nov	The Church a guide and refuge to those who are perplexed with doubt
273	B.3.4		12	Dec	Christ will come in a wicked age - with a reference to these times
274	B.3.4		19	Dec	Christ will come suddenly - with a reference to these times
276	A.50.1		25	Dec	Commune for Christmas tide, or

					Advent, or Purification
278	B.3.6		27	Dec	St John the Evangelist - union of love and strictness high excellence understood only by practice
279	A.50.4		28	Dec	The Holy Innocents - connexion of virtue with suffering in this life
281	B.3.6	1831	6	Jan	Epiphany - why Christ's appearance not fully realized since His coming
285	B.3.6	(1831)(20		Feb)	the doctrine of the Atonement, and some of its practical uses
286	A.50.4	1831	24	Feb	St Matthias. The peculiar qualification of an Apostle
290	A.50.5		20	Mar	On the object and effects of preaching
291	A.50.4		25	Mar	The Annunciation of the Blessed Virgin Mary - on the honor due to her
174	A.50.4		10	April	Commune for end of the year
302	A.17.1		11	June	St Barnabas's day - On spending money
309	B.3.6	1831(?)21		Sept (?)	St Matthew - on almsgiving
317	A.50.2		13	Nov	In behalf of the Society for the Propagation of the Gospel. (in consequence of the King's letter)
319	B.3.4		27	Nov	Mere works fall short of the religious service necessary for salvation (6)
323	A.50.2		18	Dec	On the Ministerial Order, as an existing divine institution. Ordination Sermon
325	A.50.1		26	Dec	St Stephen's day - on his speech before his martyrdom
328	A.50.1	1832	6	Jan	On the Epiphany, as the commemoration of our baptism
332	B.3.4		21	Mar	On our national sins - for the Fast day
333	P.S. II, 12/C.5.12		25	Mar	The Reverence due to the Blessed Virgin Mary The Annunciation - On the Virgin Mary as the Mother of our Lord

337	A.50.1		1	May	Revelation of God in the New Testament
339	A.17.1		10	June	On the Holy Spirit - His nature and office
343	B.3.4		21	Oct	The efficacy of the prayer of the righteous
347	B.3.4	1833	14	April	
348	A.50.3		8	Dec	
351	B.3.4	1834	16	Mar	On mortification of the flesh
352	B.3.4		28	Mar	The atonement, and its connexion with Christ's divinity
354	A.50.1		28	June	The Form of sound words, a trust committed to the Christian minister
360	A.17.1		16	Nov	Regeneration
381	A.50.3		23	Nov	Christian Sacraments contrasted to Jewish Rites
376	A.50.2	1835	30	Jan	King Charles the Martyr
385	B.3.6		19	April	
388	A.50.2		31	May	on the sanctity of Churches
389	A.50.2		7	June	On the Kingdom of heaven or the Church as mysterious
398	B.3.4		27	Dec	Slavery allowed not encouraged under the Gospel
400	A.50.4	1836	13	Mar	
402[a]	B.3.6		27	Mar	
404	B.3.6		17	April	
405 [a]	B.3.6		24	April	
406	B.3.6		1	May	
407	B.3.6		8	May	
408	B.3.6		16	May	
425	A.50.2		22	Sept	
426	A/50.2		16	Oct	
427	A.50.2		23	Oct	
435	A.50.4		27	Nov	
441	B.3.4	1837	5	Feb	

449	A.50.5		19	Mar	
459	A.50.3		23	April	
462	A.50.4		4	May	
474	A.50.1		30	July	
478	A.17.1		17	Sept	
479	A.17.1		22	Sept	
482	A.50.2		5	Nov	
483	B.3.6		12	Nov	
	cf. *P.S.* IV, 13				
485	B.3.6		26	Nov	
494	*P.S.* V, 14 / B.3.6		25	Mar	Transgressions and
				cf. 3	Dec. 1837 Infirmities
511	A.17.1	1838	27	June	
517	A..50.4		29	Sept	
518	B.3.6		28	Oct	
533	B.3.4	1839	24	Mar	
540	A.50.1		29	Sept	
543	B.3.4		10	Nov	
550	B.3.6	1840	8	Mar	1st Sunday in Lent
552	B.3.4		22	Mar	
554	A.50.1		5	April	After catechising on Baptism
556	B.3.6		19	April	
562	B.3.4		17	May	
563	B.3.4		24	May	
565	A.17.1		31	May	
568	A.11.12		18	Oct	
569	B.3.6		1	Nov	
576	A.50.1	1841	31	Jan	
577	B.3.4		14	Feb	
603	A.50.1	1843	11	June	
101					
348	A.50.4		2	July	
434					

Newman kept a Book of Abstracts of his early sermons, labelled A.7.1. at the Birmingham Oratory. It was made up to sermon no.135 but nos.69-85 are missing, though the Scriptural texts for the missing abstracts are given. (See also Pett, D.E. *The Published and Unpublished Anglican Sermons of John Henry Newman/ Prolegomena to an Edition*, Diss. Ph.D., University of Sussex, 1974).

2. Tracts for the Times

The *Tracts for the Times* were published by Rivingtons of London between 1833 and 1841 and are listed in an appendix to the third volume of H.P.Liddon's *Life of Pusey* (see below). Of the ninety tracts, twenty nine are attributed to Newman. For the purpose of this dissertation the following tracts, all by Newman except where otherwise indicated, were studied:

Tract III	*Thoughts on Alterations in the Liturgy - The Burial Service*, 9/9/1833.
Tract VIII	*The Gospel a Law of Liberty*, 31/10/1833.
Tract X	*Heads of a Week-day Lecture*, 4/11/1833.
Tract XI	*The Visible Church, Letters I and II*, 11/11/1833.
Tract XVIII	*Thoughts on the Benefits of the System of Fasting enjoined by our Church*, E.B.Pusey, 21/12/1833.
Tract XX	*The Visible Church, Letter III*, 24/12/1833.
Tract XXI	*Mortification of the Flesh a Scripture Duty*, 1/1/1834.
Tract XXVII	*The History of Popish Transubstantiation*, (John Cosin, Bishop of Durham), 24/2/1834.
Tract XXXIV	*Rites and Customs of the Church*, 1/5/1834.
Tract LVIII	*On the Church as Viewed by Faith and by the World*, By a Layman (J.W.Bowden), 19/4/1835.
Tract LXXII	*Archbishop Ussher on Prayers for the Dead*, 6/1/1836.
Tract LXXIII	*The Introduction of Rationalistic Principles into Revealed Religion*, 2/2/1836,(later published in *Essays Critical and Historical*, Vol.I, pp.30-101).
Tract LXXV	*On the Roman Breviary as embodying the Substance of the Devotional Services of the Church Catholic*, 24/6/1836.

Tract LXXIX	*On Purgatory*, 25/3/1837.
Tract LXXX	*On Reserve in Communicating Religious Knowledge*, Parts i-iii, I.Williams, undated.
Tract LXXXVII	*On Reserve in Communicating Religious Knowledge*, (conclusion), I.Williams, 2/2/1840.
Tract XC	*Remarks on Certain Passages in the Thirty-Nine Articles*, 25/1/1841.

3. Autobiographical Materials

Birmingham Oratory ed. *Correspondence of John Henry Newman with John Keble and Others, 1839-1845*, Birmingham, Birmingham Oratory, 1917.

Dessain, C.S. et alii eds. *The Letters and Diaries of John Henry Newman*, Vols.1-6;11-31, Oxford, Clarendon Press, 1961-1977.

Mozley, A.   *Letters and Correspondence of John Henry Newman during his Life in the English Church, with a brief Autobiography*, 2 Vols., London, Longmans, Green and Co., 1891.

Newman, J.H.   *Apologia pro Vita Sua*, London, Longmans, Green and Co., 1873.

4. Other Works by Newman during his Anglican Period

Newman, J.H.   *The Arians of the Fourth Century*, London, Basil Montague Pickering, 1876.

_____ *Essays Critical and Historical*, 2 Vols., London, Longmans, Green and Co., 1888.

_____ *Two Essays on Biblical and on Ecclesiastical Miracles*, Westminster Md., Christian Classics Inc., 1969.

_____ *Select Treatises of St.Athanasius*, 2 Vols., London, Longmans, Green and Co., 1920.

_____ *Verses on Various Occasions*, contained in *Prayers, Verses and Devotions*, San Francisco, Ignatius Press, 1989.

An Essay on the Development of Christian Doctrine,
Westminster Md., Christian Classics Inc., 1968.

A. 91. _Unpublished Paper on the Nature of Holiness_,
Birmingham Oratory Archives, dated by the author as
written in 1822 or 1823.

The Church of the Fathers, London, Burns, Oates and
Co., 1868.

Discussions and Arguments on Various Subjects,
(fifth edit.), London, Longmans, Green and Co., 1888.

'Cooper's Crisis', _Quarterly Review,_ June 1825, pp.
33-44.

B. Secondary Sources

1. The Historical and Theological Background

Balleine, G.   _A History of the Evangelical Party in the Church of England_, Longmans, Green and Co., London, 1908.

Bebbington, D.W. _Evangelicalism in Modern Britain, A History from the 1730s to the 1980s_, London, Unwin Hyman, 1989.

Beresford-Hope, A.J.B. _Worship in the Church of England_, London, John Murray, 1875.

Best, G.F.A.   'The Evangelicals and the Established Church in the early Nineteenth Century', _Journal of Theological Studies_, Vol.10, 1959, pp.63-78.

Bicknell, E.J.   _The Thirty-Nine Articles of the Church of England_, (revised by H.J.Carpenter), London, Longmans, Green and Co., 1955.

Carpenter, S.C.   _Church and People, 1789-1889_, London, S.P.C.K., 1933.

Chadwick, O.   _The Victorian Church, Part I, 1829-1859_, (3rd edit.), Cambridge, Cambridge University Press, 1971.

Cragg, G.   _From Puritanism to the Age of Reason_, Cambridge, Cambridge University Press, 1950.

——————— *The Church and the Age of Reason*, London, Collins, 1960.

Cross, F.L. & Livingstone, E.A. *The Oxford Dictionary of the Christian Church*, (2nd edit.), Oxford, Oxford University Press, 1984.

Daly, G.   *Transcendence and Immanence*, Oxford, Oxford University Press, 1980.

Davies, H.   *Worship and Theology in England, from Newman to Martineau*, Princeton, Princeton University Press, 1962.

Drummond, A.L. *Edward Irving and His Circle*, London, J.Clarke and Co., 1938.

Elliot-Binns, L.E. *Religion in the Victorian Era*, (2nd edit.), London, Lutterworth Press, 1946.

——————— *The Evangelical Movement in the English Church*, London, Methuen and Co., 1928.

Harrison, J.F.C.   *Early Victorian Britain, 1832-51*, London, Fontana Press, 1979.

——————— *The Second Coming: Popular Millenarianism, 1780-1850*, London, Collins, 1979.

Hempton, D.N.,   'Evangelicalism and Eschatology', *The Journal of Ecclesiastical History,* Vol. 31, 1980, pp. 179-194.

Hennell, M.   *Sons of the Prophets*, London, S.P.C.K., 1979.

——————— *John Venn and the Clapham Sect*, London, S.P.C.K., 1958.

James, W.   *The Varieties of Religious Experience*, London, Penguin Books, 1982.

Jay, E.   *The Religion of the Heart, Evangelicalism and the Nineteenth Century Novel*, Oxford, Clarendon Press, 1979.

Knox, R.A.   *Enthusiasm: A Chapter in the History of Religion*, Oxford, Oxford University Press, 1950.

Leavis, F.R.   *Mill on Bentham and Coleridge*, Cambridge, Cambridge University Press, 1978.

McAdoo, H.   *The Spirit of Anglicanism*, London, A.C. Black, 1965.

Neill, S.   *Anglicanism*, London, Penguin Books, 1960.

Newsome, D.   *The Parting of Friends, A Study of the Wilberforces and Henry Manning*, London, John Murray, 1966.

—————   'Justification and Sanctification: Newman and the Evangelicals', *Journal of Theological Studies*, Vol.15, 1964, pp.32-53.

—————   *Two Classes of Men, Platonism and English Romantic Thought*, London, John Murray, 1974.

Oliver, W.H.   *Prophets and Millenialists, the uses of Biblical Prophecy in England from the 1790s to the 1840s*, Auckland, Auckland University Press, 1978.

Orchard, S.C.   *English Evangelical Eschatology, 1790-1850*, Diss. Ph.D., Cambridge University, 1968.

Prickett, S.   *Romanticism and Religion: The Tradition of Coleridge and Wordsworth in the Victorian Church*, Cambridge, Cambridge University Press, 1976.

—————   *Words and "the Word"*, Cambridge, Cambridge University Press, 1986.

Reardon, B.M.G.   *Religious Thought in the Nineteenth Century*, Cambridge, Cambridge University Press, 1966.

—————   *From Coleridge to Gore*, London, Longmans, 1971.

Rowell, G.   *Hell and the Victorians*, Oxford, Clarendon Press, 1974.

—————   *The Vision Glorious, Themes and Personalities of the Catholic Revival in Anglicanism*, Oxford, Clarendon Press, 1983.

Russell, G.W.E.   *A Short History of the Evangelical Church*, London, Mowbray, 1915.

Storr, V.F.   *The Development of English Theology in the Nineteenth Century*, London, Longmans, Green and Co., 1913.

Strachey, L.   *Eminent Victorians*, London, Penguin Books, 1948.

Toon, P.   *Evangelical Theology, A Response to Tractarianism 1833-1856*, London, Marshall Morgan & Scott, 1979.

Tulloch, J.   *Movements of Religious Thought in Britain during the Nineteenth Century*, Leicester, Leicester University Press, 1971.

Vidler, A.R.   *F.D.Maurice and Company*, London, S.C.M. Press, 1966.

Warnock, M.   *Imagination*, London, Faber Paperbacks, 1976.

Woodward, E.L.   *The Age of Reform 1815-1870*, Oxford, Oxford University Press, 1962.

2. Studies on Newman

a. Bibliographies and Indexes

Artz, J.   *Newman-Lexikon*, Mainz, Matthias-Grünewald-Verlag, 1975.

Blehl, V.F.   *John Henry Newman: A Bibliographical Catalogue of his Writings*, Charlottesville, University Press of Virginia, 1978.

Earnest, J.D. - Tracey, G.   *John Henry Newman: An Annotated Bibliography of his Tract & Pamphlet Collection*, New York, Garland Publications, 1984.

Griffin, J.R.   *Newman: A Bibliography of Secondary Studies*, Front Royal, Christendom College Press, 1980.

Rickaby, J.   *Index to the Works of John Henry Newman*, London, Longmans, Green and Co., 1914.

Svaglic, M.J. & Dessain, C.S. 'John Henry Newman' in D. J. de Laura ed., *Victorian Prose - A Guide to Research*, New York, Modern Language Association of America, 1973, pp.115-184.

b. Collections and Commemorative Papers

The following are listed in their order of appearance.

Ward, W.   *Last Lectures*, London, Longmans, Green and Co., 1918.

Corniche, F.   *Newman and Littlemore*, Oxford, The Salesian Fathers, 1945.

Tierney, M. ed.   *A Tribute to Newman*, Dublin, Browne & Nolan, 1945.

Tristram, H. ed.   *John Henry Newman: Centenary Essays*, London, Burns, Oates and Washbourne, 1945.

Ryan, J.-Benard, E. ed. *American Essays for the Newman Centennial*, Washington D.C., Catholic University Press, 1947.

Coulson, J.-Allchin, T. *Newman: A Portrait Restored*, London, Sheed and Ward, 1965.

——————— *The Rediscovery of Newman: An Oxford Symposium*, London, Sheed and Ward, 1967.

Houppert, J. ed. *John Henry Newman*, St.Louis, Herder, 1968.

Anon. *The Newman Conference, 1976*, Hawkesyard Priory, Spode House Review No.3, 1976.

Strolz. M.K. ed. *John Henry Newman: Commemorative Essays on the occasion of his Cardinalate, 1879 - May - 1979*, Rome, The Centre of Newman- Friends, 1979.

Rowell, G. ed. *Tradition Renewed: The Oxford Movement Conference Papers*, London, Darton, Longman and Todd, 1986.

Jaki, S.L. *Newman Today, Proceedings of the Wetherfield Institute*, San Francisco, Ignatius Press, 1988.

Brown, D. ed. *Newman: A Man for Our Time*, London, S.P.C.K., 1990.

Fries H.- Becker W. *Newman Studien*, 14 Vols., Nürnberg, Glock und Lutz, 1948-1990.

Ker,I-Hill,A.G. ed. *Newman after a Hundred Years*, Oxford, Clarendon Press, 1990.

Merrigan, T. ed. *John Henry Cardinal Newman, A Special Issue of Louvain Studies*, Vol.15, 1990, pp.100-350.

c. Biographical Studies

Gilley, S. *Newman and His Age*, London, Darton, Longman and Todd, 1990.

Ker, I. *John Henry Newman, A Biography*, Oxford, Oxford University Press, 1988.

Mozley, T. *Reminiscences chiefly of Oriel College and the Oxford Movement*, 2 Vols., London, Longmans, Green and Co., 1882.

O'Faolain, S. *Newman's Way: The Odyssey of John Henry*

	Newman, New York, Longmans, Green and Co., 1952.
Trevor, M.	*Newman, the Pillar and the Cloud*, New York, Doubleday, 1962.
_____	*Newman, Light in Winter*, New York, Doubleday, 1963.
Ward, M.	*Young Mr.Newman*, London, Sheed and Ward, 1948.
Ward, W.	*The Life of John Henry Newman based on His Private Journals and Correspondence*, 2 vols., London, Longmans, Green and Co., 1912.

d. Studies on Newman's Work

Artz, J.	'Newmans Vier Maximen', *Catholica*, Vol.2, 1979, pp.134-152.
_____	'Newman im Gespräch mit Kant', *Philosophische Jarhbuch*, Vol.76, 1969, pp.197-203.
Bacchus,J.-Tristram,H.	'Newman', *Dictionnaire de theologie catholique*, Vol. 11, Paris, Librairie Letouzey et Ané, 1931, pp.327-398.
Bacchus, F.	'Newman's Oxford University Sermons', *The Month*, July 1922, pp.1-12.
Becker, W.	'Realisierung und Realizing bei John Henry Newman', *Theologische Jahrbuch*, Vol.4, 1961, pp.177-190.
Biemer, G.	*Newman on Tradition*, Freiburg, Herder, 1966.
Blehl, V.F.	'Newman, The Fathers and Education', *Thought*, Vol.45, 1970, pp.196-212.
_____	*The Essential Newman*, New York, New American Library, 1963.
_____	'The Patristic Humanism of John Henry Newman', *Thought*, Vol.50, 1975, pp.266-274.
Boekraad, A.	*The Personal Conquest of Truth According to John Henry Newman*, Louvain, Nauwelaerts, 1955.
Bokenkotter, T.S.	*Cardinal Newman as an Historian*, Louvain, Publications universitaires de Louvain, 1959.
Bouyer. L.	*Newman: Sa Vie et Sa Spiritualité*, Paris, Les éditions du Cerf, 1952.

————————— 'Newman and English Platonism', *Monastic Studies*, I, 1963, pp.285-305.

————————— *Newman's Vision of Faith*, San Francisco, Ignatius Press, 1987.

————————— *Life and Liturgy*, London, Sheed and Ward, 1956.

Boyce, P. *J.H.Newman: The Birth and Pursuit of an Ideal of Holiness*, Rome, Centre of Newman-Friends, 1979.

————————— 'Christian Perfection in the Writings of John Henry Newman', *Etudes Carmelitaines*, Vol.24, 1973, pp.215-290.

Bremond, H. 'Les Sermons de Newman', *Etudes Jeux*, Vol.72, 1897, pp.343-368.

Brilioth, Y. *The Anglican Revival*, London, Longmans, Green and Co., 1933.

Burtchaell, J.T. *Catholic Theories of Biblical Inspiration since 1810*, Cambridge, Cambridge University Press, 1969.

Butler, F. *John Henry Newman's Parochial and Plain Sermons Viewed as a Critique of Religious Evangelicalism*, Diss. S.T.D., Catholic University of America, 1972.

Cameron, J.M. *The Night Battle*, London, Burns and Oates, 1962.

Chadwick, O. *From Bossuet To Newman: The Idea of Doctrinal Development*, (2nd edit.), Cambridge, Cambridge University Press, 1987.

————————— *Newman*, Oxford, Oxford University Press, 1983.

————————— ed. *The Mind of the Oxford Movement*, London, Adam and Charles Black, 1960.

Chester, V. *The Rhetorician as Theologian: A Study of the Sermons of John Henry Newman*, Diss. Ph.D., Marquette University, 1971.

Chitarin, L. 'Annotazioni Newmaniane sulla Predicazione Universitaria', *Studia Patavina Rivista di Scienze religiose*, Vol.35, 1988, pp.133-138.

Church, R.C. *The Oxford Movement, Twelve Years 1833-1845*, (3rd edit.), London, Macmillan, 1892.

Connolly, F.X. *A Newman Reader*, New York, Image Books, 1964.

Coulson, J. *Newman and the Common Tradition: A Study of the*

352

Church and Society, Oxford, Clarendon Press, 1970.

'Belief and Imagination', *Downside Review*, Vol.90, 1972, p.1-14.

Culler, A.   *The Imperial Intellect: A Study of Newman's Educational Ideal*, New Haven, Yale University Press, 1955.

Dawson, C.   *The Spirit of the Oxford Movement*, London, Sheed and Ward, 1933.

Dessain, C.S.   'Cardinal Newman and Eternal Punishment', *The Ampleforth Journal*, Vol.76, 1971, pp.66-69.

"Newman's First Conversion", *Studies*, Vol.13, 1957, pp.44-59.

'Cardinal Newman and the Doctrine of Uncreated Grace", *Clergy Review*, Vol.47, 1962, pp.207-225.

John Henry Newman, London, Nelson, 1966.

'Newman's Spirituality and its Value Today', *Clergy Review*, Vol.45, 1960, pp.257-282.

Faber, G.S.   *Oxford Apostles: A Character Study of the Oxford Movement*, London, Penguin Books, 1954.

Ferreira, J.M.   'Newman and William James on Religious Experience: the Theory and the Concrete', *The Heythrop Journal*, Vol.29, 1988, pp.44-57.

Ffinch, M.   *Cardinal Newman: the Second Spring*, London, Weidenfeld and Nicholson, 1991.

Fisichella, R.   'Newman John Henry', in *Dizionario di Teologia Fondamentale*, eds. R.Latourelle - R.Fisichella, Assisi, Cittadella Editrice, 1990, pp.823-828.

Fries, H.   'Theologische Methode bei John Henry Newman und Karl Rahner', *Newman Studien*, Vol.11, 1980 pp.191-209.

'Newmans Bedeutung für die Theologie', *Theologische Quartalschrift*, Vol.3/4, 1946, pp.329-356.

Forrester, D.W.F.   *The Intellectual Development of E.B.Pusey 1800-1850*, Diss. D.Phil, Oxford University, 1967.

Gilley, S.   'Newman and prophecy, Evangelical and Catholic', *Journal of the United Reformed Church History*

Govaert, L.

Society, Vol.3, 1985, pp.160-188.

Kardinal Newmans Mariologie und sein persönlicher Werdegang, Salzburg-München, Universitätsverlag, Pustet, 1975.

Graef, H.

God and Myself: The Spirituality of John Henry Newman, London, The Catholic Book Club, 1967.

Hammond, T.

'Imagination and Hermeneutical Theology: Newman's Contribution to Theological Method', *Downside Review*, Vol.106, 1988, pp.17-34.

Härdelin, A.

The Tractarian Understanding of the Eucharist, Uppsala, Almquist and Wiksells, 1965.

Harrold, C.F.

'Newman and the Alexandrian Platonists', *Modern Philology*, Vol. 37, 1940, pp. 279-291.

Hefling, C.

'On Apprehension, Notional and Real', Unpublished Paper at *Lonergan Workshop*, Boston, 1988.

Henkel, W.

'Der Traum des Gerontius von J.H.Newman', in *Der Tod in Dictung, Philosophie und Kunst*, H.H.Jansen ed., Darmstadt, Steinkopff Verlag, 1989, pp.399-408.

Hermes, G.

'Ist Die Hölle leer? Kardinal Newman antwortet Hans Urs von Balthasar', *Der Fels*, Vol.9, 1984, pp.250-256.

Hole, H.

A New Look at Newman's "The Dream of Gerontius", Diss. Ph.D., University of Indiana, 1970.

Hollis, C

Newman and the Modern World, London, Hollis & Carter, 1967.

Holmes, J.D., de Archaval, H.M et alii eds., *The Theological Papers of John Henry Newman*, Oxford, Clarendon Press, 1976.

Holmes, D.

'Cardinal Newman and the Study of History', *Dublin Review*, Vol.239, 1965, pp.17-31.

—————

'Newman, History and Theology', *Irish Theological Quarterly*, Vol.36, 1969, pp.63-86.

Kenny, T

The Political Thought of John Henry Newman, London, Longmans, Green and Co., 1957.

Ker. I.

The Achievement of John Henry Newman, London, Collins, 1990.

—————

Newman on Being a Christian, South Bend Indiana,

354

University of Notre Dame, 1990.

Komonchak, J.

John Henry Newman's Discovery of the Visible Church 1826-1828, Diss., Th.D. Union Theological Seminary, 1976.

Lamm, W.R.

The Spiritual Legacy of Newman, Milwaukee, The Bruce Publishing Company, 1948.

Liddon, H.P.

Life of E.B.Pusey, 4 vols., London, Longmans, Green and Co., 1893-7.

Linnane, J.E.

The Evangelical Background of John Henry Newman 1816-1826, Diss.S.T.D., University of Louvain, 1965.

_____

'The Search for Absolute Holiness: A Study of Newman's Evangelical Period', *The Ampleforth Journal*, Vol.73, 1968, pp.161-174.

Louth, A.

Discerning the Mystery, Oxford, Clarendon Press, 1983.

MacDougall, H.

The Acton-Newman Relations: The Dilemma of Christian Liberalism, New York, Sheed and Ward, 1962.

McGrath, F.

The Consecration of Learning: Lectures on Newman's Idea of a University, Dublin, Gill and Son, 1962.

Meyer, N.

Motives for a Christian Life in the Sermons of Cardinal Newman, Teutopolis Ill., Worman Co., 1960.

Misner, P.

'Newman and the Tradition Concerning the Papal Antichrist', *Church History*, Vol.42, 1973, pp.377-395.

_____

Papacy and Development: Newman and the Primacy of the Pope, Leiden, E.J.Brill, 1976.

Murphy, M.

'Unity of the Visible Church: Six Anglican Sermons of Cardinal Newman', *Faith*, Vol 6, 1974, pp.16-20.

Murray, P.

Newman the Oratorian: His unpublished Oratory Papers, Dublin, Gill and Macmillan, 1969.

_____ ed.

John Henry Newman: Sermons 1824-1843, Vol.1, Oxford, Clarendon Press, 1991.

Norris, T.

Newman and his Theological Method, Leiden, E.J.Brill, 1977.

	'Did Newman preach a Gospel of Gloom?', *Irish Theological Quarterly*, Vol.50, 1983, pp.198-211.
Oakley, F.	*Historical Notes on the Tractarian Movement*, London, Longmans, Green and Co., 1865.
Oxenham, H.N.	*Catholic Eschatology and Universalism*, London, W. H. Allen and Co., 1876.
Pailin, D.	*The Way to Faith: An Evaluation of the Contribution of Newman's Grammar of Assent as a Response to the Search for Certainty in Faith*, London, Epworth Press, 1969.
Palmer, W.	'Newman's Sermons on Subjects of the Day", *Ecclesiastical Review*, Vol.1, 1944, pp.305-346.
Payer, A.	'Die Bezeugnung der Heiligkeit Gottes nach John Henry Newman', *Der Grosse Entscluss*, Vol. 24, Nov.1968, pp.62-66.
Rowell, G.	'The Dream of Gerontius', *The Ampleforth Journal*, Vol.73, 1968, pp.184-192.
Selby, R.C.	*The Principle of Reserve in the Writings of John Henry Cardinal Newman*, Oxford, Oxford University Press, 1975.
Seynaeve, J.	*Cardinal Newman's Doctrine of Holy Scripture*, Tielt, Publications universitaires de Louvain, 1953.
Sillem, E. ed.	*The Philosophical Notebook of John Henry Newman*, 2 Vols., The Birmingham Oratory, Nauwelaerts, 1969-70.
Sharkey, M.	*The Sacramental Principle in the Thought of John Henry Cardinal Newman*, Diss. S.T.D., Gregorian University Rome, 1976.
Sheehan, B.	*Worship and Christian Life in the Anglican Sermons of John Henry Newman*, Diss. S.T.D., University of Louvain, 1974.
Sheridan, T.	*Newman on Justification, A Theological Biography*, New York, Alba House, 1967.
Stern, J.	*Bible et Tradition chez Newman*, Paris, Aubier, 1948.
Stockley, W.F.P.	*The Dream of Gerontius, Introduction and Notes*, London, Heath-Cranton, London, 1922.

Strange, R.	*The Gospel Message of Christ*, Oxford, Oxford University Press, 1981.
Strolz, W.	'Newman als Prediger', *Anzeiger für die Katholische Geistlichkeit*, Vol.70, 1961, pp.410-418.
Stunt, T.C.G.	'John Henry Newman and the Evangelicals', *Journal of Ecclesiastical History*, Vol.21, 1970, pp.65-74.
Thomas, S.	*Newman and Heresy, the Anglican Years*, Cambridge, Cambridge University Press, 1991.
Tolhurst, J.	*The Church...a Communion - in the preaching and thought of John Henry Newman*, Southampton, Camelot Press, 1988.
Tristram, H.	'Cardinal Newman and Baron von Hügel', *Dublin Review*, 1966, pp.295-302.
Udini, P.	*Il Messaggio di J.H.Newman nei Sermoni Parrocchiali*, Vicenza, Edizioni L.I.E.F., 1981.
Vargish, T.	*Newman and the Contemplation of Mind*, Oxford, Clarendon Press, 1970.
Velocci, G.	*Newman Mistico*, Roma, Libreria Editrice della Pontificia Università Lateranense, 1964.
_____	'Newman, Pensieri sulla Speranza', *Ecclesia Mater*, Vol.4, 1973, pp.217-221.
Walgrave, J.	*Newman the Theologian*, London, Geoffrey Chapman, 1960.
Wamsley, G.	'Newman's Dream of Gerontius', *Downside Review*, Vol.91, 1973, pp.167-185.
Webb, C.C.J.	*Religious Thought in the Oxford Movement*, London, S.P.C.K., 1928.
White, W.D.	*The Preaching of John Henry Newman*, Philadelphia, Fortress Press, 1969.
Willam, M.	'Gott - Alles in Allem', *Christliche Innerlichkeit*, Mai 1979, pp.172-178.
_____	'John Henry Newman, der grosse Kerygmatiker', *Theologie und Glaube*, Vol.5, 1957, pp.363-374.
Yearly, L.	*The Ideas of Newman: Christianity and Human Religiosity*, Philadelphia, Penn State University Press, 1978.

Zeno, J.   *John Henry Newman: His Inner Life*, San Francisco, Ignatius Press, 1987.

3. Modern Studies on Eschatology

Alfaro, J.   *Christian Hope and the Liberation of Man*, Rome & Sydney, E.J.Dwyer, 1978.

Alves, R.A.   *A Theology of Human Hope*, Indiana, Abbey Press, 1975.

Aries, P.   *A History of Death*, London, Pelican, 1988.

————   *Western Attitudes toward Death from the Middle Ages to the Present*, London, Marion Boyars, 1976.

Balthasar von, H.U. *I Novissimi nella Teologia Contemporanea*, Brescia, Queriniana, 1967.

————   'Eschatology', in J. Feiner et al., eds., *Theology Today*, Milwaukee, Bruce Publishing Co., 1965.

————   *Engagement with God*, London, S.P.C.K., 1975.

————   *Man in History, a Theological Study*, London, Sheed and Ward, London, 1968.

————   *Dare we Hope "that all men may be saved"?* San Francisco, Ignatius Press, 1988.

————   *A Theology of History*, London, Sheed & Ward, 1963.

————   *Theodramatik IV: Das Endspiel*, Einsieldeln, Johannes, 1983.

Bauckham, R.   *Moltmann, Messianic Theology in the Making*, Basingstoke, Marshall Pickering, 1987.

Becker, E.   *The Denial of Death*, New York, The Free Press, 1973.

Benoit, P.   'Resurrection: at the End of Time or immediately after Death?', *Concilium*, Vol.8, No.6, 1970, pp.103-114.

Berdyaev, N.   *Freedom and the Spirit*, London, Centenary Press, 1935.

————   *The Meaning of History*, London, Centenary Press, 1936.

358

_____   *The Destiny of Man*, London, Centenary Press, 1937.

_____   *The Beginning and the End*, New York, Harper and Brothers, 1952.

Berkhof, H.   *Well-Founded Hope*, Richmond Virginia, John Knox Press, 1969.

Blenkinsopp, J.   'Theological Synthesis and Hermeneutical Conclusions', *Concilium*, Vol.8, No.6, 1970, pp.115-126.

Boice, J.M.   *God and History*, Downers Grove, Intervarsity Press, 1981.

Boros, L.   *The Moment of Truth, Mysterium Mortis*, London, Search Press, 1965.

_____   *We are Future*, New York, Herder, 1970.

Braaten, C.E.   *Eschatology and Ethics: Essays on the Theology and Ethics of the Kingdom of God*, Minneapolis, Augsburg Press, 1984.

_____   *Christ and Counter-Christ: Apocalyptic Themes in Theology and Culture*, Philadelphia, Fortress Press, 1972.

_____   *The Future of God: The Revolutionary Dynamics of Hope*, New York, Harper and Row, 1969.

Brunner, E.   *Eternal Hope*, Philadelphia, Westminster Press, 1954.

Bultmann, R.   *History and Eschatology*, Edinburgh, Edinburgh University Press, 1957.

Caird, G.B.   'Les Eschatologies du Nouveau Testament', *Revue d'histoire et de philosophie religieuses*, Vol.49, 1969, pp.217-27.

_____   'On Deciphering the Book of Revelation', *The Expository Times*, Vol.74, 1962-3, pp.13-15; 51-53; 82-84; 103-105.

Carmignac, J.   'Les Dangers de L'Eschatologie', *New Testament Studies*, Vol.17, 1971, pp.365-390.

Carrez, M.   'With what Body do the Dead Rise again?', *Concilium*, Vol.8, No.6, 1970, pp.92-102,

Collingwood, R.G.   *The Idea of History*, Oxford, Oxford University Press, 1961.

	The Idea of Nature, Oxford, Oxford University Press, 1960.
Cox, H.	'Evolutionary Progress and Christian Promise', *Concilium*, Vol.6, No.3, 1967, pp.35-47.
Croce, V.	*Quando Dio Sarà Tutto in Tutti,* Casale Monferrato, Edizioni Piemme, 1987.
Cullmann, O.	*Immortalità dell'Anima o Risurrezione dei Morti?*, Brescia, Paideia Editrice, 1986.
	Christ and Time, London, S.C.M. Press, 1951.
Daley, B.E.	*The Hope of the Early Church: A Handbook of Patristic Eschatology,* Cambridge, Cambridge University Press, 1991.
Eliade, M.	*Cosmos and History,* New York, Harper Torchbooks, 1963.
Ellul, J.	*Apocalypse: The Book of Revelation,* New York, Seabury Press, 1977.
Fuellenbach, J.	*The Kingdom of God,* Manila, Divine Word Publications, 1989.
George, A.	'The Judgment of God', *Concilium*, Vol.1, No.5, 1969, pp.6-12.
Greshake, G.	*Breve Trattato sui Novissimi,* Brescia, Queriniana, 1978.
	Gottes Heil - Glück des Menschen, Freiburg, Herder, 1983.
Hanson P.D.	*The Dawn of Apocalyptic,* Philadelphia, Fortress Press, 1975.
Hayes, Z.	*Visions of a Future: A Study of Christian Eschatology,* Wilmington, Glazier, 1989.
Hick, J.	*Death and Eternal Life,* London, Macmillan, 1985.
Kehl, M.	*Eschatologie,* Würzberg, Echter Verlag, 1986.
Kirkby, G.	'Kingdom Come: the Catholic Faith and Millenial Hopes' in Leech and Williams, eds., *Essays Critical and Radical,* 1983, London, Bowerdean Press, pp.52-69.
Koch, K.	*The Rediscovery of Apocalyptic,* London, S.C.M. Press, 1967.

360

Küng, H.   *Eternal Life?*, London, Collins Fount Paperbacks, 1985.

Ladaria, L.F.   *Antropologia Teologica*, Roma, Università Gregoriana Editrice, Edizioni Piemme, 1986.

_____ 'Escatologia' in *Dizionario di Teologia Fondamentale*, eds. R.Latourelle - R.Fisichella, Assisi, Cittadella Editrice, 1990, pp.392-395.

McDannell,C.-Lang,B. *Heaven, A History*, New Haven, Yale University Press, 1990.

McIntire, C.T. ed. *God, History and Historians*, New York, Oxford University Press, 1977.

Moltmann, J.   *A Theology of Hope*, London, S.C.M. Press, 1967.

_____ *The Future of Creation*, London, S.C.M. Press, 1979.

_____ *Theology and Joy*, London, S.C.M. Press, 1973.

Moody, R.A.   *Life after Life*, Covington Georgia, Bantam Books, 1975.

Moule, C.F.D.   'The Influence of Circumstances on the use of Eschatological Terms', *Journal of Theological Studies*, Vol.15, 1964, pp.1-15.

Müller-Goldkuhle, P. 'Post-Biblical Developments in Eschatological Thought', *Concilium*, Vol.1, No.5, 1969, pp.13-21.

Nicholls, D.   'Stepping out of Babylon: Sin, Salvation and Social Transformation in Christian Tradition', in Leech and Williams, eds., *Essays Critical and Radical*, London, Bowerdean Press, 1983, pp.38-51.

Nocke, F.J.   *Eschatologia*, Brescia, Queriniana, 1984.

Pannenberg, W.   *Theology and the Kingdom of God*, Philadelphia, Westminster Press, 1969.

Peña de la, J.L.   *La otra Dimensión*, (3rd.edit.), Santander, Sal Terrae, 1986.

Perrin, N.   *The Kingdom of God in the Teaching of Jesus*, London, S.C.M. Press, 1963.

Pettinger, N.   *After Death: Life in God*, New York, Seabury Press, 1980.

Pozo, C.   *Teologia dell'Aldilà*, (4th edit.), Torino, Edizioni Paoline, 1986.

Rahner, K.   'The Resurrection of the Body', *Theological Investigations*, Vol.2, London, Darton, Longman and Todd, 1963, pp.203-216.

_____   'The Hermeneutics of Eschatological Assertions', *Theological Investigations*, Vol.4, London, Darton, Longman and Todd, 1966, pp.323-346.

_____   'The Life of the Dead', *Theological Investigations*, Vol.4, London, Darton, Longman and Todd, 1966, pp.347-354.

_____   'The Church and the Parousia of Christ', *Theological Investigations*, Vol.6, London, Darton, Longman and Todd, 1969, pp.295-312.

_____   'He will come again', *Theological Investigations*, Vol.7, London, Darton, Longman and Todd, 1971, pp.177-80.

_____   'On Christian Dying', *Theological Investigations*, Vol.7, London, Darton, Longman and Todd, 1971, pp.285-293.

_____   'Eternity from Time', *Theological Investigations*, Vol.19, London, Darton, Longman and Todd, 1983, pp.169-179.

_____   'Purgatory', *Theological Investigations*, Vol.19, London, Darton, Longman and Todd, 1983, pp.181-193.

Ratzinger, J.   *Eschatology, Death and Eternal Life*, Washington D.C., Catholic University of America Press, 1988.

Russell, D.S.   *The Method and Message of Jewish Apocalyptic, 200 BC-AD 100,* London, S.C.M. Press and Westminster Press, 1964.

_____   *From Early Judaism to Early Church*, London, S.C.M. Press, London, 1986.

Ryan, F.   *The Body as Symbol*, Washington D.C., Corpus Books, 1970.

Sachs J.H.   'Current Eschatology: Universal Salvation and the Problem of Hell', *Theological Studies*, Vol.52, 1991, pp.227-254.

Sac. Cong. Pro Doctrina Fidei *Epistula ad Venerabiles Praesules Conferentiarum Episcopalium de quibusdam*

362

quaestionibus ad Eschatologiam spectantibus, Acta Apostolicae Sedis, Vol.71, 1979, pp.939-943.

Schillebeeckx, E.   'Some Thoughts on the Interpretation of Eschatology', *Concilium*, Vol.1, No.5, 1969, pp.22-29.

Schnackenburg, R.   *Christ - Present and Coming*, Philadelphia, Fortress Press, 1978.

Schoonenberg, P.   'I believe in Eternal Life', *Concilium*, Vol.1, No.5, 1969, pp.50-57.

Schwartz, H.   *On the Way to the Future: A Christian View of current Trends in Religion, Philosophy and Science*, Minneapolis, Augsburg Publishing House, 1972.

_____   'The End of the Beginning: Millenarian Studies 1969-1975', *Religious Studies Review*, Vol.2, 1976, pp.1-14.

Sider, R.   'The Pauline Conception of the Resurrection Body in 1Cor.xv,35-54', *New Testament Studies*, No.21, 1975, pp.428-439.

Sharkey, M. ed.   'Select Themes of Ecclesiology on the Occasion of the Eighth Anniversary of the Closing of the Second Vatican Council' in *International Theological Commission - Texts and Documents 1969-1985*, San Francisco, Ignatius Press, 1989.

Varii Auctores   *Credere Oggi: La Sopravvivenza e L'aldilà*, Vol.45, Padova, Edizioni Messaggero Padova, 1988.

Wainwright, G   *Eucharist and Eschatology*, New York, Oxford University Press, 1981

Wall, R.W.   'The Eschatologies of the Peace Movement', *Biblical Theology Bulletin*, Vol.15, 1985, pp.3- 11.

Whitney, B.L.   *What are they saying about God and evil?*, New York, Paulist Press, 1989.

NAME INDEX

Abel, 148
Abraham, 139-140, 148-149, 155, 187, 298 n185
Adam, 68-69, 82, 152-153, 243
Alton, 273 n74
Annunciation, Feast of, 153, 177
Antiochus, 29
Aristotle, 155f
Arnold, M., 208 n7
Arnold, T., 168 n30
Athanasius, 5, 246 n119

Baptist, John the, 60, 286
Bebbington, D.W., 2 n1,
Bentham, J.,93
Bergson, H., 272 n67
Best, G.F.A., 194 n147
Beveridge, Bishop 314
Birmingham Oratory, 2, 9, 212 n24
Blehl, V.F., 5 n9
Bouyer, L., 165 n21
Bowden, J.W. 196 n155
Boyce, P., 242 n104
Bremond, Henri, 87 n126
Brighton, 67 n28
Brunner, E., 272 n67, n70
Buckland, William, 248 n123
Bush, George, 1
Butler, J., 140 n139, 195, 243 n113

Camden Society, 273 n73
Cana, 195
Carmignac, J., 5 n10, 6,
Carpenter, S.C., 22 n26, 108 n213
Christ Church, 181
Church, R.C., 258 n1

Cicero (Tusculanae Questiones) 148 n173
Clarke, S., 4 n6
Clement of Alexandria, 5
Constantine, 33
Cooper E., 28 n49
Copeland, W.J., 47 n98, 57 n120, 69 n37
Corinth, 298
Coulson, J., 251 n147
Cullmann, O., 147 n166

Daley B.E., 4 n7
Daniel, 34, 150, 161f, 275, 288
Darby, J.N., 48 n100
Dartington, 234 n80
David, 150; house of, 178
Davidson, John, 3
de la Peña, J.L., 6 n13, 272 n67
De Laura, D.J., 10 n16
de Lubac, H., 183 n94
Dessain, C.S., 10, 17 n9, 110 n222, 111 n229
Doddridge, P., 4 n6
Drummond, A.L., 52

Ealing, 1, 209
Eden, 275
Egypt, plagues of, 74
Elgar, Edward, 208 n1
Elijah, 60-61, 200 n166
Elisha, 199, 200 n166
Elliot-Binns, L.E., 93 n147, 248 n123
Enoch, 148
Esau, 80

Foudrinier, J., 1
Froude, Archdeacon, 1

364

SUBJECT INDEX

activism, 2

Adam, 68, 152, 243: A's race,
153 n197; burdened by
A.'s fallen nature, 69

Advent, analysis of A.
sermons, 15-61; apoca-
lyptic texts of, 59; titles of
A. sermons which
indicate a futuristic
perspective, 18, 25;
summary of A. sermons
11-12, 306-307; season of
A. 59, 208 n8, 210, 264
n28; A. connecting
Eucharist and final
judgment 302 n207; A.
courses, 15; time of
personal meditation on
last things, 35

Adventism, 10, 320

Affliction, significance of, 12,
78-85; and fallen state, 70
n44, 82; distinguished
from judgment, 75-76;
transformed by hope,
135-136; as merciful
chastisement, 78-84, 233-
234; as punishment for
sin, 79f; its redemptive
value, 82-83, 254

alarmists, discredited by
history, 48

Alexandrian Fathers, 5 n9

Alexandrian theology,
influence of, 153 n196;
school of ... held a
principal attraction for
N, 5

angels, their announcement
of Christ's birth, 143;
company of angels, 197-

200; fallen a.,100; life of
a., 98, 242; their ministry,
237, 288; their privileged
standpoint, 229

Anglican Church, 56f;
community 59; member-
ship of, 56 n118;
questioning its claims to
be the true Church, 57,
162 n6; real reason for
remaining in it, 59;
Anglican orders, 209 n9;
Anglican period, 9, 130
n76, 20; the liturgical
foundation and frame-
work of his preaching
becomes explicit in his
last years of, 264

Antichrist, 12, 306, passim,
27-35, mark of, 29;
primary characteristic of,
30; prophecies concern-
ing the, 32; strategy of,
30; The City of the
Antichrist, 32f; The
Persecution of the Anti-
christ, 33-35; The
Religion of the Anti-
christ, 30-32; The Time
of the Antichrist, 28-30

Anticipation, anticipated
encounter with Christ,
12; of the Church's
perfection, 13, 201; of
final judgment, 19-20, 35;
of the second coming
through prayer and
worship, 37-40, 269, 272,
275, 291; by means of
watchfulness, 43; fore-
bear anticipating the next

Catholic University of Ireland, 2

chastisement, see affliction

Christ, 32, 51, absence of Christ, 47; merely an advocate, 89; alone is the Immortal One, 150; attitude of, 89; being near to Christ becomes synonymous with being near to heaven, 254; came in the Person of His Spirit, 194; Christ and the Ministration of the Spirit, 123-125; Christology/Pneumatology, twin pillars on which the doctrine of the last things is secure, 312; Foundation in Christ and the Spirit, 190-194; Christ's death, his atonement for sin, 69, 82, 114, 123, 152; Christ's Death transforms the Meaning of Death, 216-218 − this fundamental union with Christ in his death and resurrection changes our whole conception of death, 217; Christ's incorruptible nature is the source of our immortality, 152; Christ's presence, 56, 59, 124, 313 − hiddenness of his presence, 57, 125 − N.'s own search for C.'s presence in the church, 57f − C. present by virtue of the Incarnation, the Paschal Mystery and the Law of the Spirit, 142f − realization of joy in Christ's incarnate presence, 316; Christ's reign, 161 − his spiritual kingdom, 32; Christ's Resurrection, 114, 123, 308 − a new objective reality has been brought into being by, 191 − a spiritual regeneration of our nature, 152 − source of eternal life is the mystery of, 114 − dissertation critique of Incarnation-Resurrection relationship 316-317; Christ is our Almighty Stay, 132-134; Christ is the Giver of Peace, 256; Christ is the Origin of our Immortality, 154; His future arrival, 56; His death and Resurrection, 150-154; integral parts of the drama of redemption, 114 − his death sets in relief the thought of the final judgment, 313; humanity of, 91; innocence of, 82; C. is the only way to a knowledge of heaven, 254; is the origin and centre of N's eschatology, 8, 312; is the Second Adam, 152; life-giving grace of Christ, 126; Christ the Merciful Judge, 89-92, 307; Love for Christ, 83 − turns suffering into a redemptive experience, 83; mediation of, 82; mystery of Christ, 50; mystery of redemption in, 84, 151; our only hope

from a Sinful World, 214ff; Death is a Point of Transition, 218-221; The Implications of the Christian View of Death, 221; Preparation for Death, 222f

dependency on God, 23, 277f

detachment, feeling of, exercised major influence on N.'s concept of Church, 174; single-minded spirit of, 44

dissertation, development of, 11-14; scope of 8f; two-fold definition of eschatology proposed by Carmignac used in this d., 6

dissertation points of critique:

1. Newman's Eschatology and the Principle of Dogma, 312

2. The Creative Tension of Eschatology, 313

3. The Atonement-Incarnation Relation, 313f

4. The Influence of Calvinism, 314f

5. The Principle of Hope, 315f

6. The Dangers of a High Viewpoint, 316-318

7. A pre-critical interpretation of Prophecy, 318f

8. A Tendency towards Fideism, 319f

9. Newman's Eschatology and History, 320-323

10. Newman's Eschatology and Worship, 323

11. Newman's Eschatology and Creation, 323f

12. Postscript, summary of eschatology during N's Catholic period, 324-330

doctrine, on the development of, 323; doctrines may change as revelation progresses, 85-86, 187 n111; with prophecy and precept one of the three dimensions of Scripture, 18; d. of future life progressively revealed, 147-150; d. of apostolical succession, 195 n149; d. of eternal punishment a matter for personal conversion, 111, 195 n149

dogma, 102, 118; dogmatic principle, 102-110, 115-118, 239, 259, 312

Dream of Gerontius, 10, 324, 330 − a vivid picture of Christian death, 208; phenomenon of dreaming, 227-228

early Christians, coming round again to time of, 23; misunderstanding of ... concerning time of parousia, 47; infancy of church, 165, 169; joy of, 146; frame of mind of early Christians under persecution 181, 285; ... and bond with pilgrim Church unbroken, 265; endured their trial for Love of Christ, 83, 179; prayed towards the East, 275

disposition of, 83; f. provides its own evidence, 54; reality and knowledge of, 115; realm of faith, 40; reason as a marriage partner to, 156; receiving the faith promotes a life of holiness, 107; skepticism in matters of, 55; spirit of, 54; the desire of heaven as the object of, 241; the realizing of things hoped for, 260; The Relationship of Faith and Hope, 137-141; Justifying Faith and the Principle of New Life, 125-129

Fall, 62, 120, 132, 153

fallen nature of man, doctrine of, 68

false otherworldliness, 48, 176

false interpretation of times, 49

Fasting and Self-denial, 14, 313; f. ... brings home the sincerity of our commitment, 285; f. done out of love and not in Manichean spirit, 287; f. ... is the valve which opens the flood-gates of conflict and powers of the world to come, 84, 287; f. associated with absence of Christ, 286; f. done in secret, 118 n15; reminder that salvation is yet to come, 259, 304; an exercise of faith, 136-137; full implications of f., 84; N chooses theme of f. to highlight the Christo-

logical significance of all spiritual exercises, 286; shadow side ... clearly seen in f. of apostles, 286; Fasting and Self-Denial, 284-289, 310; − provide spirituality with the hallmark of realism, 284, 311; self-denial is the pulse of the spiritual life, 285

Fate of the Damned, 99-101; misery of damned arises from within themselves, 101

Fathers, 28, 128, 246 n119, 263; influence of F. on N's theology, 2, 4-5, 92, 128, 153 n196; authority of, 28; authentic witnesses of Catholic faith, 28; Church of the Fathers, 254 n153; interpretations of the F., 31

final perseverance, no assurance of, 141; N abandons belief in, 173; gift of, 183-185

forgetfulness of God, 23

French Revolution, 22, 29f

futuristic perspective, under which N considered the Coming of Christ, 18, 25

futurity of the present, as it grows out of man's reception of Christ's message, 8

GOD, beauty of God's creation, 249 n126; benevolence of, 94 − God's unmixed benevolence, 77; glory of, 170; is infinite justice and

ing Christ face to face, 255; Christ is the Centre of Heaven, 251-255; Christians enjoying citizenship of, 199, 251; N's early understanding of H. is primarily based on soteriology, 251; due to our corruption we have no desire for, 240; influence of romantic literature on N's view of, 253; H. is a spiritual kingdom ... attained by holiness, 249; Images of Heaven, 249-251; church as heaven upon earth, 171, 176; Christians as heirs of heaven, 269; "a new heavens and a new earth", 119-123, 164, 249; literally a place of torment for the sinner, 245; promise of H. is attached to holiness ... because of promise of Christ, 244; with the published sermons a major change in N's concept of H. ... develops along Christological lines, 252; The Human Desire for Happiness, 240-242; What does Heaven consist in? 247-249

Hell, 99; believes H. is not empty, 100; damnation is entirely due to human freedom, 100; characteristic of hell is total absence of human affection, 101; the creation of an evil self-will 101, 113;

danger of hell, 78; powers of hell, 84; inward fire of, 95; heaven and hell at war, 110; Purgatory infinitely less evil than h., 235; just reward for following our corrupt natural inclinations, 240; dragged down to hell by chain of sin, 301; heaven would be hell to an irreligious man, 245-246; lifeless sounds, 260

History, 16, 18, 20, 29, 31, 33; began with Adam's Fall, 322; Christian meaning of, 49-51; final overthrow awaits the Incarnate Word, 322; N's attempts to construct a theory of development based on the history of salvation, 85 n117; N's concept of history is romantic, 320; N upholds the autonomy of h. which is the very foundation of human responsibility 321; N's limited understanding of the role of h. and the restrictions he put on it, 323; N uses typology to understand the inner meaning of historical events, 321; h. of our world, 6; reached its climax in Christ, 49; suffered a fatal defeat with the Coming of the Second Adam, 322; true meaning of, 31

Holiness, 241f; an inward principle imparted by

147; The Relationship of Faith and Hope, 137-141.

human corruption, doctrine of, 67f

human existence, living both in a world of sense and a world of spirit, 117

human freedom, 62; capacity to frustrate God's plans, 63; false idea of, 86; so totally perverted by sin, 100; principle of holiness subject to h. f., 162;

idolatry, 30, 174, 232; destruction of idols, 30; false reverence to saints, 198 n161, 232

illative sense, 116

imagination, role of the imagination, 53; danger of deception by i., 43, 51; eternal punishment too severe to the i., 99, 104, 112; truth and religious i. 116-117

Immortality, 13, 308f; Christ is the Origin of our Immortality, 150-154; Cicero's proof for, 148 n173; communicated by virtue both of the Paschal mystery and of the Incarnation, 151; conceived as immersion into Christ, 151; Development of the Idea of Immortality, 150; history of our, 152; in the new horizon of i. the moral for Christians is to consider the present time a period of probation, 209; Immortality and Resurrection of the

Dead, 147-160; The Food of Immortality, 302-305 — participating in the Eucharist is a sharing in the Risen Body of Christ, 302 — bodily resurrection proleptically present in the Eucharist, 303; The Body, The Soul and The Self, 154-156

in-between time, the time of the Church, 160, 295

INCARNATION, 25, 102, 105, 142, 151-154, 157, 162 n8, 172, 218, 246, 252, 292ff, cornerstone in the theology of Tractarians, 246 n119; denial of I., 30; relationship between mystery of Resurrection and I., 316-317; emergence of a realized eschatology, 313; Judg-ment must be seen in the new light of, 90; mystery of I. dispels complexity of theoretical debate on divine mercy and justice, 89; tendency to see Church as extension of the incarnation and to identify it with the Kingdom of God, 317; The Atonement-Incarnation Relation: 313-314 — dialectic between, 323; the basis on which the resurrection of the body can be affirmed, 152

intellectual darkness, 102, 105

intercession, role of Christ's priesthood, 50, 162, 258;

everyday life, 77; an encounter with God in human form, 90; becomes the Day of the Lord, 91, 307; certainty of, 36, 307; Day of, 25, 36f, 90; human j. a child of ignorance and prejudice, 74-75; J. of God, 21, 26, 75, – can only depend on, 75; J. to come is an untrue belief if it is not linked to the sacrifice of Christ, 92; particularly severe on Christians, 73; Joy and Fear at the Day of Judgment, 36f; Judgment on a Wicked Generation, 19-21; Preservation from Evil and the Day of Judgment, 297-301; role of Christ in, 89; The Certainty of a Universal Judgment, 71-74; The Last Judgment, 71-92, 307

Justice, fundamental law of, 87; Jewish Law, a system of temporal rewards and punishments based on the rule of justice, 86; principle of, 85; without j., moral order would collapse, 87; The Relation between God's Justice and Mercy, 85-88

justification, doctrine of, 92, 125-129, 245

KINGDOM OF GOD, 6, 57; attains its full stature at the Day of Judgment, 161; fulfilment of Daniel's prophecy, 162, 165, 322; growth of K. lies in vertical relationship with Christ, 283; in substance identical with the Church, 167; N overvalues man's role in bringing the kingdom to its fullness, 322; two kingdoms, 170-171; unlike kingdoms of world, 57, 167; The Kingdom of Heaven, 161-173; The Mediatorial Kingdom, 161-165

laissez-faire, philosophy of, 86

Last Day, 14, 21, 39f, 285; climax of a process, 77; definitive separation on, 77; drama of, 35; not message of doom and gloom, 37; Person who will be our judge at, 90

Last Judgment, 12, 63, certainty of, 71-74; time of, 74-78; Eucharist and the Last Judgment, 297-301

Liberalism, 22, 24, 181; consequences of, 24; liberal cries for Church reform, 86; parent of unbelief, 22; liberal attack, 94, 102 n188, 181; liberal mind, 108, 145 n158

liberty, 30,

life after death, see **Immortality**

LITURGY, 11, 107, 210f; L. and the Lord's Prayer, 278 n99; centered around the mystery of Christ, 263; Christian life is

Peace, at the core of Christian living is an experience of, 46; clear mark of discernment of God's presence, 58, 255; p. of mind, 45; natural fruit of holiness, 255; Peace in the End, 255-256; Christ the giver of p., 252; diminishment of peace in intermediate state, 233; intermediate state enough for their peace, 237

Penance, voluntary, 84; the sign of persecution kept alive in the internal life of penance, 180

Pentecost, 192f, 265

perplexity, 102, 131; comes from nature of revelation itself, 105; component of Christian hope, 129-130; obedience is the remedy for all perplexity, 103

persecution, A Persecuted Church, 165, 174, 179-182, 190, 279; arises also from frailty of Church, 182; times of trial warn us of the final p., 34-35; mark of p. test of genuineness of faith, 83 n109; mirror of first beginnings of church, 34; permanent historical feature, 180; reminder to church of incomplete victory over evil, 35; sign of Antichrist, 180; sign of end, 34; teaching of Fathers on p., 34; death likened to deliverance from persecution, 214-215

personal history, 6, 221

pilgrim, mind of pilgrim, 45; pilgrim church, 190 n120, 201, 206, 257, 265; pilgrim journey of Christian, 195, 204, 207, 254

Platonism, 156; Platonic doctrine, mutual exclusivity with primitive Christian belief, 147 n166

PRAY/PRAYER: 37ff, 275-283; 311, anticipating our encounter with Christ, 39; essential to build a habit of, 276; generally a form of petition, 278; implies hope, 278; intercession peculiar stamp of Christian p., 279f; p. of intercession ... to be used in the service of others, 281; is invoked against an evil world, 279; language of prayer, 38; means of access to the unseen world, 275; necessary means to maintain an eschatological perspective in daily Christian living, 38; necessity of p. in a life destined for eternity, 276; N's early view of p. a product of unrealized eschatology, 277; prayer of deliverance, 275, 313; relation of life of p. and service to the world ... ultimately governed by one's eschatology, 281; Personal Prayer and Eschatology,

275-283 signifies ... sharing in the priesthood of the glorified Christ, 280 – tension between two perspectives of p. affects the relationship between the active and the contemplative life, 281f – two forms of p. – plea of deliverance and of intercession 275, 279, 313; when Church ceases to pray she ceases to believe in the reality of the world to come, 323

predestination, N eschewes doctrine of dual p., 99; Fate of the Damned, 99-101; misery of damned arises from within themselves, 101; background to Church of the Elect, 160, 182-184, 182 n89, 186-187

Prepare the Way of the Lord, 35-46

pride, 21, 23; fruit of, 23

principle of antecedent probability, no grounds of p. for belief in imminence of parousia, 53-54; re. eternal punishment, 96; law of probability a guide to certitude, 129 n75, 140 n139, 320; applied to consciousness of the departed, 227-228; re. belief in life after death, 147-148; applied to doctrine of Purgatory, 235

principle of reserve, 102, 110-113, 133 n102; a principle ... of sensitivity in communicating Christian mysteries, 110; need for reserve, 110; seen in severity of Christ to disciples, 111; never expose the Christian mysteries to argument or debate, 111

principle of satisfaction for sin, 75, 89-90, 233, 315

progress, 23, 30, 56; lacking in N's sermons a sufficient value of human progress, 321; new age of, 23; value of work, 56

Prophecy, 16, 17-35 passim; Achilles heel of traditional defence of the Word of God against rationalist doubts, 318; N's naivety in interpretation ... especially his understanding and use of, 318; fulfillment of p., 49; N's strict attention to p. had its roots in a tendency to fideism ... more overt in his Scott and Newton days, 319; of the Second Coming, 25; prophecies of destruction, 20; p. regarding Church, 160-173; should be given a literal interpretation, 166; sermons on unfulfilled p., 17-35 passim; Practical End of Prophecy, 23

prophets, 197; false prophets, 52; p. of the Old Testament, 25, 79f;

Protestantism, 32; extreme, 32; popular, 33; evangelicalism a popular Protestant movement, 2

Christian belief of, 303; final r., 13, 115; new order of, 119; of the body, 13, 309; Christ's r. origin of our immortality, 150-154; quantum leap in the Christian revelation of bodily r., 309; The Resurrection of the Body, 156-159; the mystery of r. and not the incarnation the eschatological event, 317

Revelation, 64; criterion for belief in human immortality, 147; conveys a message in a human way, 116; decisive criterion for belief in human immortality, 147; fullness of revelation, 50; intellectual difficulties as a necessary consequence of the nature of, 106; perplexity comes from nature of, 105

romanticism, N's romantic view of church, 169 n34; state of original innocence, 143, 153, 253; r. of the age, 248-249; N's romantic view of history, 320; nostalgia, 299, 320; does not affect N's theological view of material world, 323

Rome, 2, 32f; pagan spirit of Rome in the Church, 32

Sabbath, in Christ the S. of humanity is begun, 256; lasting sign of creation, 174; Lord's Day, sign of Christian redemption, 174

Sacraments, 17, 39ff, 52, 58, 168; attendance at the Church's s. safeguard against adventist appeals, 52; neither empty rituals nor dead forms of worship, 271; Sacrament of Christ, 190; sacramental principle, 195 n148, 291; significance of, 39; to abandon them is to espouse a false anthropology, 271; vehicle which transports us into the presence of Christ, 270

salvation, 7, 24, 41; essentially a hidden reality, 114f; never have certainty of, 41, 129f; The State of Salvation, 115-129 – A New Heavens and a New Earth, 119-121

Satan, 66, 71, 82, 103, 105, 107, 254 n153, 288, 299; god of this world, 82; kingdom of, 279

school of contemplation, Intermediate State as, 14, 207, 234

scientific knowledge, supreme reliance on, 23

Scott and Newton Days, 3, 64, 319

Scripture, 17, 24, 26, 48, 52, 55, 66, 72, 94, 163, 177, 225, 227, 233, 235f, 308, 318, 322; almost totally silent on subject of natural world, 248; N's fidelity to, 156; comple-

mentary nature of S. and
the Liturgy, 271 n62;
informs us of the nature
of God's design, 183;
revealed word of, 52,
164; three dimensions of,
18; voice of, 109
self-deception, 43, 53, 220,
222; a mind ever alert to
dangers of, 96, 129, 260;
deception of world, 276;
self-denial devoid of, 285
signs, 13, 51-53; two sets of,
external and internal, 57-
58; notes of the church,
200-204; Eucharist as
sign of transition and
passage, 295f
signs of the times, 20-23, 28-
31, 34-35, 48-49; N does
not identify the signs of
the times with the advent
of the Antichrist, 22, 306
sin, 20, 63f, 66; a deeply
seated principle within
us, 125; N's Anglican
view of original sin, 69;
awareness of our sinful-
ness, 39; Christ died for
s., 69; death is the
culminating debt for,
216; God's temporal
punishment for, 76; how
sinful s. is must be a
matter of revelation, 95;
human misery due to, 70;
nature of, 67 – of
original s., 63-64, 67 n28,
69 n37, 125f, 152-153;
penalty for s. is second
death, 95; personal s. an
inward fire, 101;
principle of s. cause of

eternal death, 127; social
sin, 73 n66
skepticism, 54-55, 134 n110;
skeptical world, 48; open
door of s., 103; skeptical
attitude, 116, 139;
struggle between faith
and s., 130, 118
**Society for the Propagation
of the Gospel,** 274 n77
soul, immortality of, 148
n173, 149; body-soul
relation, 154-157;
departed souls, 225-229;
pleasures of the soul
hereafter, 241; true
nature of soul, 261
**SPIRIT: Holy Ghost: Holy
Spirit:** 17, 45, 92, 158,
267; brought under the
ministration of the, 12;
gift of, 120; indwelling of
... as the formal cause of
our justification, 127;
Law of the ... a spirit of
joy, 142; life-giving
principle of, 125 n53;
new life of, 114; power
of, 157; primarily given
for the building up of the
general body, 193;
presence of, 123; neither
an alternative nor a
supplement to the
presence of Christ, 124;
Regeneration in the, 172
spirit of optimism, ... and
ambition augured a
forgetfulness of God, 23;
shallow o., 71; false o. of
age, 77, 321; optimism
not to be confused with
hope, 129, 315

God's w. by unworthy
reception of Holy
Communion, 300; state
of nature is a state of w.,
125; Christ suffered the
real agony of God's
wrath, 217; appeasing
God's wrath, 286

DDP